ROBERT HOLCOT

GREAT MEDIEVAL THINKERS

Series Editor
Brian Davies
Fordham University

DUNS SCOTUS
Richard Cross

BERNARD OF CLAIRVAUX
Gillian R. Evans

JOHN SCOTTUS ERIUGENA
Deirdre Carabine

ROBERT GROSSETESTE
James McEvoy

BOETHIUS
John Marenbon

PETER LOMBARD
Philipp W. Rosemann

ABELARD AND HELOISE
Constant J. Mews

BONAVENTURE
Christopher M. Cullen

AL-KINDĪ
Peter Adamson

ANSELM
Sandra Visser and Thomas Williams

HUGH OF SAINT VICTOR
Paul Rorem

JOHN WYCLIF
Stephen E. Lahey

JOHN BURIDAN
Gyula Klima

AVICENNA
Jon McGinnis

ROBERT HOLCOT
John T. Slotemaker and Jeffrey C. Witt

Robert Holcot

John T. Slotemaker and Jeffrey C. Witt

OXFORD
UNIVERSITY PRESS

Oxford University Press is a department of the University of Oxford. It furthers the University's objective of excellence in research, scholarship, and education by publishing worldwide. Oxford is a registered trade mark of Oxford University Press in the UK and certain other countries.

Published in the United States of America by Oxford University Press
198 Madison Avenue, New York, NY 10016, United States of America.

Oxford University Press 2016

All rights reserved. No part of this publication may be reproduced, stored in a retrieval system, or transmitted, in any form or by any means, without the prior permission in writing of Oxford University Press, or as expressly permitted by law, by license, or under terms agreed with the appropriate reproduction rights organization. Inquiries concerning reproduction outside the scope of the above should be sent to the Rights Department, Oxford University Press, at the address above.

You must not circulate this work in any other form
and you must impose this same condition on any acquirer.

CIP data is on file at the Library of Congress
ISBN 978–0–19–939124–0 (hbk.); 978–0–19–939125–7 (pbk.)

1 3 5 7 9 8 6 4 2
Paperback printed by Webcom, Inc., Canada
Hardback printed by Bridgeport National Bindery, Inc., United States of America

*For
Becky,
Sophia, and Susanna*

CONTENTS

Series Foreword xi
Acknowledgments xv
Abbreviations, Symbols, and Conventions xvii

Introduction: The Life and Works of Robert Holcot 1
    The Life of Robert Holcot 1
    The Writings of Robert Holcot 4
    A Life in Three Stages: A Friar's Life 12
    The Structure and Argument of the Book 13

1. Covenantal Theology 17
    Introduction 17
    God's Covenant and the Ages of History 18
    Holcot's Obligational Theology and
        the *Ars Obligatoria* 26
    The Divine Covenant 30
    The Two Powers 32
    Conclusion 37

2. On Faith 40
    Introduction 40
    Merit and Divine *Acceptatio* 42
    Faith and Cognitive Assent 47
    Conclusion 62

3. Human Knowledge and the Divine Nature   64
    Introduction   64
    Human Reason and the Existence of God   66
    The Triune God   73
    Conclusion   84

4. God, Creation, and the Future   87
    Introduction   87
    Future Contingents and Divine Foreknowledge   87
    Revelation and Divine Deception   94
    Conclusion   99

5. The Sacraments: Baptism, Confession, and the Eucharist   101
    Introduction   101
    Baptism   103
    Confession and Penance   111
    Eucharist   118
    Conclusion   123

6. The Biblical Commentary Tradition   125
    Introduction   125
    The Biblical Commentaries   126
    The Historical Context and Holcot's Sources   129
    Conclusion   138

7. The Twelve Prophets   141
    Introduction   141
    Holcot's Exegesis   143
    The Pictures in Holcot's Commentary on Nahum   144
    The Development of the Picture Technique   156
    Conclusion   160

8. The Book of Wisdom   162
    Introduction   162
    The Nature and Style of Holcot's Commentary on the Book of Wisdom   163
    The Prologue   168
    Holcot's Book of Wisdom in Outline   171
    Conclusion   186

9. Holcot's Political Philosophy   189
    Introduction   189
    The Goal of Life   189
    The State of Innocence and the State of Nature   192
    Laws   195
    Justice and Equity   200
    Authority   205
    Family   208
    Conclusion   213

10. Late Medieval Preaching   215
    Introduction   215
    The Late Medieval Sermon   217
    The *Artes Praedicandi*: Preaching Manuals   228
    Conclusion   231

11. The *Moralitates*   233
    Introduction   233
    Contextualizing the *Moralitates*   234
    The Text of the *Moralitates*   236
    Reading the *Moralitates*   239
    Conclusion   249

12. Holcot as Preacher   250
    Introduction   250
    Peterhouse 210: A Systematic Overview   251
    Holcot the Homilist   253
    Conclusion   259

Appendices   261
    Appendix A: Holcot's Commentary on the *Sentences*   261
    Appendix B: The Quodlibetal Questions   267
    Appendix C: The Wisdom Commentary: *Dubitationes*   275
Notes   281
Bibliography   331
    Primary Sources   331
    Secondary Sources   337
Index   353

SERIES FOREWORD

Many people would be surprised to be told that there *were* any great medieval thinkers. If a *great* thinker is one from whom we can learn today, and if *medieval* serves as an adjective for describing anything that existed from (roughly) the years 600 to 1500 AD then, so it is often supposed, medieval thinkers cannot be called "great."

Why not? One answer often given appeals to ways in which medieval authors with a taste for argument and speculation tend to invoke "authorities," especially religious ones. Such subservience to authority is not the stuff of which great thought is made—so it is often said. It is also frequently said that greatness is not to be found in the thinking of those who lived before the rise of modern science, not to mention that of modern philosophy and theology. Students of science are nowadays hardly ever referred to literature earlier than the seventeenth century. Students of philosophy are often taught nothing about the history of ideas between Aristotle (384–322 BCE) and Descartes (1596–1650). Contemporary students of theology are often encouraged to believe that significant theological thinking is largely a product of the nineteenth century.

Yet the origins of modern science lie in the conviction that the world is open to rational investigation and is orderly rather than chaotic—a conviction that came fully to birth and was systematically explored and developed during the Middle Ages. And it is in medieval authors that we find some of the most sophisticated and rigorous discussions ever offered in the areas of philosophy and theology—not surprisingly, perhaps, if we note that medieval philosophers and theologians, like their contemporary counterparts, were often university teachers (or something like that) who participated in an ongoing worldwide debate and were not (like many seventeenth-, eighteenth-, and even nineteenth-century philosophers and theologians), working in relative isolation from a large community of teachers and students with whom they were regularly involved. As for the question of appeal to authority: it is certainly true that many medieval thinkers believed in authority (especially religious authority) as a serious court of appeal. But as contemporary philosophers increasingly remind us, authority is as much an ingredient in our thinking as it was for medieval authors. For most of what we take ourselves to know derives from the trust we have reposed in our various teachers, colleagues, friends, and acquaintances. When it comes to reliance on authority, the main difference between us and medieval thinkers lies in the fact that their reliance on authority (insofar as they display it) was often more focused and explicitly acknowledged than it is by us. It does not lie in the fact that it was uncritical and naive in a way that our reliance on authority is not.

In recent years, such truths have come to be recognized at what we might call the "academic" level. No longer disposed to think of the Middle Ages as "dark" (meaning "lacking in intellectual richness"), many university departments (and many publishers of books and journals) now devote a lot of energy to the study of medieval authors. And they do so not simply on the assumption that medieval writers are historically significant but also in the light of the increasingly developing insight that they have things to say from which we might learn. Following a long period in which medieval thinking was thought to be of only antiquarian interest, we are now witnessing its revival as a contemporary voice—one with which to converse.

The *Great Medieval Thinkers* series reflects and is part of this exciting revival. Written by a distinguished team of experts, it aims to provide substantial introductions to a range of medieval authors. And it does so on the assumption that they are as worth reading today as they were when they wrote. Students of medieval "literature" (e.g., the writings of Chaucer) are currently well supplied (if not oversupplied) with secondary works to aid them when reading the objects of their concern. But those with an interest in medieval philosophy and theology are by no means so fortunate when it comes to reliable and accessible volumes. The *Great Medieval Thinkers* series aspires to remedy that deficiency by concentrating on medieval philosophers and theologians and by offering solid overviews of their lives and thought coupled with contemporary reflection on what they had to say. Taken individually, volumes in the series provide valuable treatments of single thinkers, many of whom are not currently covered by any comparable volumes. Taken together, they constitute a rich and distinguished history and discussion of medieval philosophy and theology considered as a whole. With an eye on college and university students, as well as the general reader, authors of volumes in the series strive to write in a clear and accessible manner so that those who have no knowledge of these thinkers can learn about them. But each contributor to the series also intends to inform, engage, and generally entertain even those with specialist knowledge in the area of medieval thinking. So, as well as surveying and introducing, volumes in the series seek to advance the state of medieval studies both at the historical and the speculative level.

The subject of this book is less well known than some of the figures to which previous books in the series have been devoted. Yet, as John Slotemaker and Jeffrey Witt admirably and engagingly demonstrate, Robert Holcot (d. 1349) was one of the great and original thinkers of his time.

An Englishman, who became a Dominican friar and priest, Holcot (likely born around 1290) taught in Oxford, possibly Cambridge, and Northampton. He also worked in London under the patronage of Richard de Bury (1287–1345), then Bishop of Durham. Holcot died of the plague in 1349 while reputedly ministering to the sick in Northampton.

He wrote a variety of works. Some deal with theological and philosophical questions. Some are commentaries on the Bible. Some are designed explicitly to aid Christian preachers working in pastoral contexts. Holcot also left behind a number of sermon texts. His literary remains, therefore, allow us to acquire serious insight into his person and thought, written, as they are, in different genres and covering a wide range of topics. As Slotemaker and Witt note, this makes Holcot unique among early-fourteenth-century authors.

While drawing attention to all that can be known of Holcot's life and intellectual achievements, this book provides a scholarly overview of Holcot while seeking to understand him accurately and to engage with him critically. In doing so it contributes valuably to medieval scholarship and should become the standard reference work on Holcot for some time to come.

Brian Davies
Series Editor

ACKNOWLEDGMENTS

Our understanding of Holcot has benefited greatly from conversations and correspondence with Jack Bell, Stephen F. Brown, William J. Courtenay, Hester G. Gelber, Susan L'Engle, R. James Long, Penn R. Szittya, and Ueli Zahnd. There are several scholars working in late medieval sermons, preaching resources, and biblical commentaries who assisted us in learning new fields. We are grateful to Marjorie Burghart, Holly Johnson, and Kimberly A. Rivers for answering questions and providing secondary and primary sources. Kimberly kindly made available a copy of her thesis (MSL) from the University of Toronto that contained a transcription of Holcot's commentary on Nahum. Siegfried Wenzel has been a constant source of encouragement and critique. He was our first introduction to late medieval preaching and has contributed greatly to our understanding of Holcot's sermon collection.

We are grateful to Anna Sander, the archivist and curator of manuscripts at Balliol College, for providing digital access to several of the manuscripts and for allowing us to examine them *in situ*. Thanks are also due to the Basel Universitätsbibliothek (Basel), Balliol Library (Oxford), the British Library (London), Cambridge University Library (Cambridge), The

National Library of Scotland (Edinburgh), and the Vatican Film Library (St. Louis) for permitting access to their manuscript and film repositories. We are also grateful to Brian Davies for including this volume in his series and to the two anonymous reviewers who offered helpful suggestions and criticism. Finally, we thank the respective publishers and copyright holders for the permission to use material published in Slotemaker (2014) and Slotemaker-Witt (in press).

ABBREVIATIONS, SYMBOLS, AND CONVENTIONS

Primary Sources

Adam Wodeham
- *Lect.*   *Lectura secunda*
- *Ord.*   *Ordinatio Oxoniensis*

Aristotle
- *Post. An.*   *Posterior Analytics*
- *Metaph.*   *Metaphysics*
- *NE*   *Nicomachean Ethics*

Augustine
- *De Trin.*   *De Trinitate*

Boethius
- *De Trin.*   *De Trinitate*

Cornelius de Lapide
- *Sap.*   *Commentarius in librum Sapientiae*

Duns Scotus
- *Lect.*   *Lectura*
- *Ord.*   *Ordinatio*

Quodl.	*Quodlibeta*
Rep.	*Reportatio Parisiensis*

Guido of Monte Rochen
HFC	*Handbook for Curates*

Humbert of Romans
OFP	*On the Formation of Preachers*

Jean de Lorin
Sap.	*Commentarius in librum Sapientiae*

John Mair
Sent. I	*Joannes Major in primum Sententiarum*
Sent. IV	*Quartus Sententiarum Johannis Majoris*

Peter Lombard
Sent.	*Sententiae in quatuor libris distinctae*

Peter Plaoul
Comm.	*Commentarius in libros Sententiarum*

Robert Holcot
Quodl.	*Quodlibeta*
Sap.	*Super libros Sapientiae*
Sent.	*In quatuor libros Sententiarum quaestiones*
Sex art.	*Sex articuli*
Serm.	*Sermones*
Sup. XII	*Super XII Prophetas*
Sup. Eccle.	*Super librum Ecclesiastes*
Sup. Eccli.	*Super librum Ecclesiasticum*

Thomas Aquinas
Scriptum	*Scriptum super libros Sententiarum*
SCG	*Summa contra gentiles*
ST	*Summa theologiae*

Thomas Waleys
DMCS	*De modo componendi sermones*

Walter Chatton
Lect.	*Lectura super Sententias*

Rep.   *Reportatio super Sententias*

William Crathorn
Sent.   *Quaestiones super librum Sententiarum*

William of Ockham
SL   *Summa logicae*
Quodl.   *Quodlibeta septem*
Ord.   *Ordinatio*
OT   *Opera Theologica*
OP   *Opera Philosophica*

Editions and Translations
ACW   *Ancient Christian Writers*
ANF   *Ante-Nicene Fathers*
Dec. Greg. *Decretales Gregorii P. IX*
WSA   *The Works of Saint Augustine: A Translation for the 21st Century*

Series and Reference Works
BGPTM   *Beiträge zur Geschichte der Philosophie und Theologie des Mittelalters*
CCCM   *Corpus Christianorum Continuatio Mediaevalis*
CCSL   *Corpus Christianorum Series Latina*
DThC   *Dictionnaire de théologie catholique*
PL   *Patrologia Latina*
SEP   *Stanford Encyclopedia of Philosophy*

Manuscript, Incunabula, and Early Modern Edition *Sigla*

The *sigla* are alphabetized by individual *siglum* and not place or library information. See the bibliography for a complete list of manuscripts alphabetized by place.

A   Padua, Biblioteca Antoniana 515
A1   London, British Museum, Add. 21,429
B   Oxford, Balliol College Library 246
B1   *In librum Sapientiae regis Salomonis praelectiones.* Basel, 1586
B2   Oxford, Balliol College Library 27
B3   Oxford, Balliol College Library 26
B4   Oxford, Balliol College Library 71
B5   Oxford, Bodleian Library 216

ABBREVIATIONS, SYMBOLS, AND CONVENTIONS

BA	Basel, Universitätsbibliothek A.II.26
BA1	Basel, Universitätsbibliothek A.V.33
BA2	Basel, Universitätsbibliothek A.XI.36
BA3	Basel, Universitätsbibliothek B.V.11
BA4	Basel, Universitätsbibliothek B.VIII.10
BC	Rome, Biblioteca Casanatense, cod. Basil A.V.23
BN	Paris, Bibliothèque Nationale, lat. 590
BN1	Paris, Bibliothèque Nationale, lat. 15853
BR	Braunschweig, Stadtbibliothek 136
CC	Oxford, Corpus Christi 138
D	Düsseldorf, Universitäts-und Landesbibliothek F.5
GI	London, Gray's Inn 2
H	Heidelberg, Universitätsbibliothek, Cod. Sal. VII, 104
L	*In quatuor libros Sententiarum quaestiones*. Lyon, 1518
L1	*Super quatuor libros Sententiarum quaestiones*. Lyon, 1497
LA	London, Lambeth Palace 221
LM	Oxford, Bodleian Library, Laud Misc. 160
LP	Leipzig, Universitätsbibliothek 344
M	Paris, Bibliothèque Mazarine 905
MD	Madrid, Biblioteca nacional 507
O	Oxford, Oriel College 15
ON	Oxford, New College 53
P	Cambridge, Pembroke College Library 236
P1	Cambridge, Peterhouse 210
R	London, British Library, Royal 10.C.VI
R1	London, British Library, Royal 2.D.IV
R2	London, British Library, Royal 2.F.VII
R3	Oxford, Bodleian Library, Rawlinson C 427
R4	Reims, Bibliothèque Municipale 506
S	Paris, Bibliothèque de la Sorbonne 193
S1	London, British Museum, Sloane 1616
SA	Halle, Universitäts-und Landesbibliothek Sachsen-Anhalt Yc 2° 1
SC	Oxford, Bodleian Library, SC 2648 (Bodl. 722)
ST	Strasbourg, Bibliothèque nationale et universitaire 0.074
T	Troyes, Médiathèques de l'agglomération troyenne 634
T1	Troyes, Médiathèques de l'agglomération troyenne 907
T2	Toulouse, Bibliothèque Municipale 342
V	Valencia, Cathedral 191

ABBREVIATIONS, SYMBOLS, AND CONVENTIONS xxi

V1	*Super librum Ecclesiastici.* Venice, 1509
VD	Vienna, Dominikanerbibliothek 14/14
VC	Vatican, Biblioteca Apostolica Vaticana, Chigiani A.IV.84
VO	Vatican, Biblioteca Apostolica Vaticana, Ottoboniani Latini 215
VO1	Vienna, Österreichische Nationalbibliothek 4149
VP	Vatican, Biblioteca Apostolica Vaticana, Palatini Latini 118
W	Worcester, Cathedral Library F.126

Sigla Miscellanea

a./aa.	articulus(i)
dub.	dubium(a)
c./cc.	caput (heading/chapter)
ca.	causa
cap.	caput
cn.	canon
co.	corpus (the body of a scholastic distinction/article)
col./cols.	column(s)
d./dd.	distinctio(nes)
n	footnote(s)
f./ff.	folio(s)
ms./mss.	manuscript(s)
lec./lecs.	lectio(nes)
lib.	liber
ob.	objectio(nes)
p.	pars
prin.	principium
q./qq.	quaestio(nes)
qu.	quodlibet
resp.	respondeo
tit.	titulus
tr.	tractatus
un.	unica(us)
vol./vols.	volume(s)
[...]	words added by the authors for sense or clarity
...	lectio incerta

Conventions

Robert Holcot's commentary on the *Sentences* is referenced as Holcot, *Sent.* I, q.3 (L d.2$^{\text{rb-va}}$; O 132rb). The edition (L) is referenced in parentheses by quire (d), folio (2), and recto/verbo and column in superscript. We have also provided manuscript information, citing the manuscripts by their *sigla* and the appropriate foliation. Citations of the commentary on Wisdom and other works follow a similar practice: for example, Holcot, *Sap.* lec.1 (B1 4; B2 3^{r}). Holcot's quodlibetal questions have been cited as Holcot, *Quodl.* 85 (P 197vb) with the quodlibetal question number following the designation in Appendix B. For edited texts we cite the editor, page, and (if given) the line numbers in superscript.

We have given abbreviated references to secondary scholarship that are keyed to the bibliography and cited by name/date: for example, Courtenay (1990) or (for multiple works by the same author) Wenzel (1998 and 2005a). For primary texts we have given abbreviated references throughout (see Abbreviations), with full bibliographic information appearing in the bibliography of primary texts. We have only been able to provide the Latin (where necessary) for unedited or untranslated works. Longer citations (block quotes) of Robert Holcot's works are preserved in an endnote, while for the numerous shorter quotations we have preserved only the *incipit* (first few words) of the Latin text. This *incipit* method will assist the reader in locating the quoted material in manuscripts, incunabula, or early-modern editions. For all biblical citations we follow the Douay-Rheims translation of the Latin Vulgate modifying archaic verbs and pronouns.

ROBERT HOLCOT

INTRODUCTION

The Life and Works of Robert Holcot

The Life of Robert Holcot

Robert Holcot was the born in the village of Holcot, located in Northamptonshire in the east Midlands of Great Britain. The date of his birth is unknown, although it is probable that he was born around 1290. The village of Holcot is approximately 40 miles west of Cambridge and 45 miles northeast of Oxford, and Holcot would spend most of his life in the roughly rectangular area between Holcot, Cambridge, Oxford, and London. Holcot probably entered the Dominican priory at nearby Northampton, where he received his initial training in the liberal arts.[1]

Having been instructed in the liberal arts within the Dominican schools, he began his studies at Oxford University in 1326. The members of the religious and monastic orders were not permitted to take the arts degree and become a Master of Arts (*magister artium*). These students would be trained at a local priory or *studium* and as a consequence would embark on a longer period of theological study at the University. Holcot, therefore, probably studied the Bible and the *Sentences* of Peter Lombard for six years. Following this period of introductory study, Holcot would have been admitted to three more years of preparatory studies in which he could participate in formal debates, first as an opponent for two years and for a final year as a respondent. Following the prescribed nine years of academic study, Holcot was permitted to lecture on the *Sentences* between 1331 and 1333.[2] Holcot began his lectures on book 1 of the *Sentences* in the fall of 1331, continuing his lectures on book 2 of the *Sentences* sometime in 1332.[3] Between his lectures on books 2 and 3—perhaps during the summer interim, and as a result of the criticism he received from contemporaries William Chitterne (fl. c. 1330) and William Crathorn (fl. c. 1330)—Holcot composed the *Six Articles* (*Sex articuli*).[4] Holcot lectured on book 2 in the spring of 1332. He probably lectured on book 4 prior to book 3, beginning his lecture on book 4 in the fall of 1332 followed by book 3 in the spring of 1333.[5]

After completing his lectures on Lombard in 1333, Holcot began his lectures on Scripture on February 10, 1334.[6] During this period Holcot also began his commentary on Matthew.[7] Based on this timeline, the earliest Holcot could have completed his studies was in 1335. Having completed the course of studies, Holcot became licensed to teach as a regent master (*magister regens*) within the faculty of theology. The regent masters were those who had completed the course of studies and were permitted to teach as a master within their respective faculty. Holcot probably served as regent master in theology at Oxford between 1336 and 1338.[8] While serving as regent master, Holcot was increasingly busy working on several scholastic works. First, it is probable that during this period he reworked his commentary on the *Sentences* of Peter Lombard with the intention of publishing the work in an *Ordinatio* (an ordered or authorized edition).[9] Holcot also lectured again on the Scriptures, and his commentary on the Twelve Prophets probably dates to this period during his regency.[10] It was during his regency at Oxford that Holcot also completed his extant *Quodlibetal Questions*, the *De imputabilitate peccati*, and *De stellis*.[11]

Around the time that Holcot completed his regency at Oxford (c. 1338), he became increasingly connected with the house of Richard de Bury.[12] Bury was the Bishop of Durham and a noted scholar in his own right. Holcot's association with the house of Bury lasted until sometime around 1340 when Bury left London for northern England.[13] This relationship with the house and patronage of Bury was important for Holcot's continued intellectual development. This is understandable, as Bury was a noted bibliophile who probably introduced Holcot to sources and texts that were unknown to him.[14]

The association with the house of Bury is significant in several ways. First, as a result of his prolonged engagement with Bury, Holcot continued to read, study, and incorporate classical sources into his writings. Richard de Bury was profoundly interested in books and the academic culture of his time. He is suspected to be the patron, if not the author, of the *Philobiblon* (*On the Love of Books*), a work focused on the acquisition and preservation of books. While Holcot had access to classical sources before his patronage by Richard de Bury (see the discussion on the commentary on the Twelve Prophets in chapter 7), the noted bibliophile likely introduced Holcot to a greater diversity of sources. Second, because of Holcot's association with Bury he was more closely linked with London than he probably would have been if he had remained in Oxford. On the basis of textual evidence, William Courtenay has noted that Holcot was revising his commentary while in residence in London and therefore would have been working on it while under the patronage of Bury well into the late 1330s.[15] Finally, Holcot worked in a community of scholars while in the household of Bury. Conor Martin notes that between 1334 and 1345 the group included four Mertonians (i.e., the Oxford "Calculators"),[16] Thomas Bradwardine (†1349), Walter Burley (†1344), Richard Kilvington (†1361), and John Maudith (†c. 1343), the theologian Richard FitzRalph (†1360), two civil servants, Richard Bentworth, and Walter Segrave, as well as the canonist John Acton (†1343).[17] While Courtenay is quick to remind us that it is improbable that all of these scholars inhabited the house simultaneously or worked as a small coterie, Martin disagrees, writing that "they were at dinner daily with [Bury], and after dinner there was learned discussion. Bury's library, one must conjecture, was at their disposal."[18] Whatever the truth of this arrangement, it is probable that Holcot benefited from the association with Bury and his household.

There is a strong tradition that Holcot served a second period as regent master in theology at the University of Cambridge. According to this tradition, Holcot's most famous work—the commentary on the book of Wisdom—was delivered as a set of lectures at Cambridge. While it is possible that Holcot never served as regent master at Cambridge, Beryl Smalley and, more recently, Hester Gelber entertain this hypothesis. However, there is not enough evidence presently to either reject or endorse this claim as it rests on the fact that a few manuscripts describe Holcot as being "from Cambridge."[19] Indeed, Holcot's commentary on Wisdom covers a two-year lecture cycle and clearly originated within a university setting. If Holcot served as regent master at Cambridge, it was likely after Richard de Bury left for the north in 1340 and before Holcot returned to Northampton early in 1343. The period of Holcot's life between 1338 and 1342 remains somewhat unclear, but sometime during this period Holcot probably wrote the *Convertimini* (literally, *Be Converted*) and the *Moralitates* (*The Moralizations*).[20]

Following his possible regency at Cambridge, there are few events that stand out in Holcot's biography. In 1343 he returned to the priory at Northampton where he was initially educated. Between 1343 and 1348, Holcot received a steady stream of licenses to hear confession.[21] There is a fragment of a commentary on Ecclesiastes that Holcot probably wrote at Northampton, and at the time of his death he was giving a series of lectures on the book of Ecclesiasticus.[22] Robert Holcot, like so many of his generation, succumbed to the plague in 1349.[23] According to tradition, Holcot abandoned his lectures on Ecclesiasticus to serve a suffering community. While he probably had the opportunity or means to flee the plague, he remained in service to a people who struggled to understand a truly apocalyptic event alongside the providential goodness of God. The lectures break off after chapter 7, and it may well have been the last few verses of Ecclesiasticus 7 that sustained Holcot in his final work:

> Be not wanting in comforting them that weep, and walking with them that mourn. Be not slow to visit the sick: for by these things you will be confirmed in love. In all your works remember your last end, and you shall never sin.[24]

The Writings of Robert Holcot

The writings of Robert Holcot can be divided into scholastic works, biblical commentaries, and sermons. Here we briefly discuss the works that contribute to these three categories, keeping in mind that the categorical divisions between these texts are somewhat artificial and the unity of Holcot's thought can only be understood by considering the entire body of his work.

Scholastic Works

By "scholastic works" we designate those texts that Holcot produced within the university setting, with the exception of his biblical commentaries. Holcot's scholastic treatises include (a) his commentary on the *Sentences* of Peter Lombard, (b) a collection of ordinary and quodlibetal debates (quodlibetal debates examine questions on "any topic whatsoever"), and (c) the *Six Articles* (*Sex articuli*) treating questions of epistemology.

As a requirement for his degree in theology, Robert Holcot lectured on the *Sentences* of Peter Lombard.[25] Peter Lombard wrote the book known as the *Sentences* during the mid-twelfth century, and it was adopted as the standard medieval textbook for teaching theology at the Universities of Paris and Oxford by the thirteenth century. The *Sentences* consist of four books treating (1) the triune God, (2) creation, (3) the incarnation of Christ, and (4) the sacraments of the Church and last things. In the period following Lombard, the four books were divided into almost 200 distinctions to facilitate their effectiveness within the medieval classroom.[26] In the thirteenth century, the commentaries on the *Sentences* followed the structure established by Lombard and tended to treat each distinction with some thoroughness. For example, the commentaries of Alexander of Hales (†1245), Richard Fishacre (†1248), Bonaventure (†1274), and Thomas Aquinas (†1274) are comprehensive in treating all four books of the *Sentences* and all of the corresponding distinctions. However, over time—and as the *Sentences* were increasingly established as the place for concentrated theological and philosophical speculation[27]—medieval theologians began selectively omitting certain distinctions or even whole books. This initial development can be observed in the commentaries of John Duns Scotus (†1308) and William of Ockham (†1347), who often condensed or collapsed various distinctions together. That said, the commentaries of Scotus and Ockham retain the order of questions established by Lombard and still treat the majority of the distinctions. However, despite the fact that Holcot lectured on the *Sentences* within two decades of William of Ockham, his commentary is remarkably different from the type of commentary written by Scotus or Ockham.

During the third and fourth decades of the fourteenth century, English theologians began exercising a remarkable freedom in their treatment of the *Sentences*. Holcot's near contemporaries, Arnold of Strelley (†c. 1350), Richard FitzRalph, and William Crathorn abandoned the traditional distinctions and favored questions instead; rejecting the almost 200 distinctions, Strelley's commentary contains 21 questions, FitzRalph's 25, and William Crathorn's 20.[28] This dramatic reorganizing of the *Sentences* is also evident in Adam Wodeham's *Lectura secunda* and *Ordinatio Oxoniensis*. The former, composed at Norwich sometime in the late 1320s, resembles in its organization and structure the commentary of William of Ockham, while his *Ordinatio Oxoniensis*, delivered at Oxford between 1332 and 1334, is remarkably unique in its structure and in many ways is a hybrid between the distinction-based commentaries and the question-based commentaries.[29] The English Franciscan Roger Rosetus lectured on the *Sentences* at Oxford in the mid-1330s and pushed the boundaries of the genre to the breaking point.[30] In such selective commentaries, theologians abandoned the traditional distinctions altogether, opting instead for a series of questions treating each book. It is within this context that Holcot lectured on Lombard's *Sentences*, developing his own distinctive approach to the genre in his lectures.

Holcot's commentary, unlike that of many of his contemporaries, comments on all four books of the *Sentences*. That said, Holcot was highly selective regarding which topics he treated. This is evident when one considers the table of questions comprising Holcot's commentary.[31] Instead of detailing the numerous distinctions of the four books of the *Sentences*, Holcot limits his commentary to 19 questions. These lectures are one of Holcot's first scholastic works and form the starting point for any significant analysis of his thought.

Holcot composed the *Six Articles* (*Sex articuli*) between his first and second year of lecturing on the *Sentences*.[32] Throughout this short work, Holcot was strongly influenced by the philosophical views of William of Ockham and was responding to the criticism of his fellow Dominican William Crathorn and the Franciscan William Chitterne.[33]

While serving as regent master in theology at Oxford, Holcot composed a series of three quodlibetal debates. Holcot's quodlibetal questions have received much more attention from modern scholars than his commentary on the *Sentences*, and several of them have been edited in modern editions. In the case of Holcot, his quodlibetal questions often treat more fully select theological topics that Holcot either omitted from his commentary on the *Sentences* or treated with some brevity.

Quodlibetal questions developed at the University of Paris sometime around 1230.[34] At that time the academic calendar was divided into two periods by the Church calendar, with a significant holiday recess at Christmas and Easter. During the period leading up to the two recesses, the university suspended classes and held questions *de quodlibet*—or, concerning anything (i.e., quodlibetal questions). Interestingly, while the masters of theology presided over the debates, the audience asked the questions. This presented an interesting challenge for the theologians, as the questions could treat any topic that was of interest to someone in the audience. The informal style of the quodlibetal questions means that they are often a source of diverse material. The quodlibetal debates became increasingly popular at Paris and were subsequently introduced to Oxford. Somewhat inexplicably, the tradition of editing quodlibetal questions for publication ended around the 1330s, first at Paris and then at Oxford.[35] The quodlibetal questions of Robert Holcot, therefore, are some of the final quodlibetal questions prepared for publication in the fourteenth century.

As is the case with his commentary on the *Sentences*, the quodlibetal questions of Holcot present various problems with respect to dating and the manuscript tradition. First, it has proved difficult to date Holcot's quodlibetal questions. Based on the dating of Holcot's commentary on the *Sentences*,[36] his quodlibetal questions are dated by Heinrich Schepers, William Courtenay, and Katherine Tachau to the years 1333–1334.[37] More recently, Hester Gelber has argued that his *Quodlibets* most likely occurred during his period of regency at Oxford between 1336 and 1338.[38] In a subsequent article, Rondo Keele correctly pointed out that, at present, the date of the *Quodlibets* cannot be determined with any finality and that it is best to state that they probably date from between 1333 and 1338.[39] Second, while the dating of Holcot's *Quodlibets* is difficult enough to determine, establishing the list of questions debated (and their proper order) is much more complex.[40] The reason for this is that Holcot's *Quodlibets* include over 100 individual questions preserved in three distinct traditions.[41] The majority of the quodlibets are rather short, with the typical question ranging from a single column of text up to a folio. Only a few of the questions extend to more than two folios in length.

Holcot's numerous quodlibetal questions can be divided thematically into three broad categories: (a) the doctrine of God and the Holy Trinity,

(b) Christ and human salvation, and (c) human nature and questions of morality and sin. While several of the questions do not fit easily within these three categories, the majority do. Here it is useful to consider a couple of questions from each subdivision. Concerning God and the Trinity the following are representative:

> Q.87: Whether this is conceded: "God is Father, and Son, and Holy Spirit."
> Q.90: Whether within the unity of the divine essence there persists a plurality of persons.
> Q.91: Whether God is able to make anything whatsoever from anything else (*quodlibet de quolibet*).

The questions on God and the Trinity form the shortest list of questions among the three groups, while greater attention is paid to the questions within the second and third groups. Within the second group of questions, the following questions are representative:

> Q.4: Whether the history of Christ's conception [in the Gospels] is completely true.
> Q.8: Whether divinity is part of Christ.
> Q.10: Whether the human will in Christ was conformed to the divine will.

Finally, within the third group treating questions of human nature, morality, and sin, Holcot treats numerous questions. The following give the reader a sense of the questions treated:

> Q.25: Whether human beings are able to sin.
> Q.28: Whether God can be the cause of sin.
> Q.58: Whether God can make a sinless rational creature.
> Q.83: Whether sinning deserves to be punished.
> Q.98: Whether the charity of the blessed in heaven can be corrupted.

As is evident, the quodlibetal questions of Robert Holcot cover a vast range of topics. However, while Holcot's questioners were able to inquire *de quodlibet*—or, regarding anything they wanted to inquire about—the central focus of these questions is the nature of human salvation as offered by Jesus Christ and mediated through the Church and the seven sacraments. This focus is one that Holcot clearly shared with his interlocutors.

Closely related to Holcot's quodlibetal questions are the *Determinations* (*Determinationes*): the collection of 15 *Determinations* are included within the early modern editions of Holcot's commentary on the *Sentences* and demonstrate a close relationship to Holcot's *Quodlibets*.[42] As numerous scholars have demonstrated, the *Determinations* recorded in the early printed editions have a textual basis in the extant manuscripts of the *Quodlibets*.[43] Thus it is best to understand the *Determinations* as expanded versions—at times treating more than one quodlibetal question in a single *Determinatio*—of Holcot's *Quodlibets*.

Biblical Commentaries

Robert Holcot's most famous works in the fourteenth and fifteenth centuries were his commentaries on Scripture. These were written with an eye to instructing young friars in the arts of preaching (*artes praedicandi*). This emphasis on preaching is evident throughout his biblical commentaries.[44] Holcot's central exegetical works (works of biblical interpretation) include the commentary on Wisdom, the commentary on the Twelve Prophets, the lectures on Ecclesiasticus, the incomplete commentary on Ecclesiastes, and probably a commentary on the Apocalypse. For purposes of introducing this genre, we focus on the commentary on Wisdom and the Twelve Prophets, the two commentaries we consider at length in later chapters.[45]

Robert Holcot's commentary on the book of Wisdom was a medieval bestseller; as Beryl Smalley notes, almost every well-stocked fifteenth-century European library owned a copy.[46] The choice to lecture on the book of Wisdom was unusual given that there were few commentaries on this biblical book in the patristic and medieval periods.[47] This is perhaps because Jerome (†420)—the early Church Father and translator of the Vulgate—argued that the book was falsely attributed to Solomon and written by the great Jewish scholar Philo of Alexandria (†50).[48] This tradition was followed by authors such as Cassiodorus (†585),[49] and by the fourteenth century it was commonly held that the author of the work was Philo. As a result of this previous patristic and medieval tradition, there are few commentaries on Wisdom written in the Middle Ages. The earliest extant commentary is by Rabanus Maurus (†856).[50] Closer to the time of Holcot, there are also commentaries by Bonaventure (†1274), Meister Eckhart (†1328), and Nicholas of Lyra (†1349).[51]

Holcot's commentary on Wisdom is a massive work. Recent estimates state that it is preserved in at least 175 fourteenth- and fifteenth-century manuscripts as well as a dozen incunabula and early modern printings.[52] It was written, it seems, to serve as both a commentary on Holy Scripture as well as a preaching and study aid for the friars. Thus the work contains material that is useful for understanding the biblical text as well as guides for helping the friars develop sermons. While scholars have long admitted the significance of the work for late medieval preaching and theology, it has been studied only sporadically since the pioneering work of Beryl Smalley.

Holcot's commentary on the Twelve Prophets is dated to the period of his regency at Oxford. As regent master, Holcot was expected to lecture simultaneously on one book of the Old Testament and one book of the New Testament, and his other extant works on the Old Testament were clearly written at a later date. Thus besides the now-lost commentary on Matthew that is extant only in fragments, the commentary on the Twelve Prophets is Holcot's earliest biblical commentary.[53] The commentary is extant in four manuscripts and has the benefit of being studied in some depth by Kimberly Rivers.[54] One striking feature of the commentary on the Twelve Prophets is the extensive use of classical sources that Holcot employs. While it is often implied that Holcot was introduced to classical sources through the patronage of Richard de Bury, it is clear that as early as his regency at Oxford he made extensive use of classical sources. The commentary on the Twelve Prophets has one further claim to fame: it is in this biblical commentary that Holcot, for the first time, began using his method of "verbal pictures." This technique, which probably developed as a mnemonic device for preachers, indicates that in his earliest biblical commentaries Holcot was focused on educating future preachers.[55]

Sermons and Preaching Aids

Closely related to Robert Holcot's biblical commentaries are his two works written for the instruction of preachers (the *Moralitates* and *Convertimini*) and his collection of sermons. The *Moralitates* is a somewhat unique work, in that it consists of stories from antiquity that are the subject of analysis and explication. The stories are mostly taken from Ovid, Pliny, Seneca, or Valerius Maximus. Following a given story, Holcot presents a moral exposition (*expositio moralis*) or a tropological interpretation (*expositio tropologica*) of the passage. The work is intended for preachers and presents various moralizations for the edification of the clergy.[56] The *Convertimini*, like the *Moralitates*, is a work for the instruction of preachers. The authorship of the work is somewhat dubious, although it has often been attributed to Robert Holcot.

Robert Holcot's collection of sermons is found in a single Cambridge manuscript.[57] This collection of sermons has not been the subject of extensive study and, given Holcot's numerous other works related to preaching (e.g., his biblical commentaries and preaching aids), this remains a serious lacuna within the field.[58] Holcot, unlike other authors, left a considerable amount of scholastic literature and biblical commentaries that would warrant serious comparative work between the various genres. This is precisely what is unique about Holcot among the authors of the early fourteenth century. Unlike many of his predecessors and contemporaries—for example, John Duns Scotus, William of Ockham, Walter Chatton, or Adam Wodeham—Robert Holcot left a remarkable variety of writings.

When contrasted with their twelfth- and thirteenth-century predecessors, the fourteenth-century friars and theologians are often known exclusively through their scholastic treatises. Thinkers such as Hugh of St. Victor, Bonaventure, or Thomas Aquinas left a broad range of writings. Each of these authors wrote biblical commentaries, sermons, and scholastic treatises that are all available for study; the result, in short, is that it is possible for modern scholars to paint a remarkably broad portrait of their thought. This is not true, by contrast, for William of Ockham. As a mendicant friar, Ockham wrote biblical commentaries and gave sermons, but those works have not been preserved. The result is that modern scholars cannot present the full breadth of his thought; unfortunately, the evidence is lacking. Thus when compared with other fourteenth-century thinkers,

Robert Holcot is unique because the writings described here represent a broad variety of genres that span the length of his adult life. This book, therefore, is able to paint a much broader picture of Robert Holcot than would be possible for almost any of his Oxford contemporaries.

A Life in Three Stages: A Friar's Life

The life and works of Robert Holcot are easily divided into three distinct periods and corresponding bodies of literature. During his time at Oxford and perhaps Cambridge, Holcot engaged in a purely scholastic period during which he wrote his commentary on the *Sentences* and other scholastic works. Toward the end of this time—perhaps during his regency at Cambridge—he began writing significant scriptural commentaries. This second period overlaps with Holcot's purely scholastic period (e.g., the commentary on the Twelve Prophets was begun during his regency at Oxford) but extends into a period in his life when he was affiliated with the house of Richard de Bury. Thus this second period can be considered the time during which Holcot developed the approach of the "Classicizing Friars," to use the phrase of Beryl Smalley. Finally, with the return to Northampton in 1342–1343, Holcot entered the final period of his life. His focus was no longer on purely scholastic works, and his attention turned to his Ecclesiasticus commentary and the local community of friars. It was during this period, one can conjecture, that he implemented the preaching strategies developed in his biblical commentaries and became a full-time preacher of the Gospel.

The three stages of Holcot's career correspond somewhat loosely to the *Three Holcots* known to scholars and described in Beryl Smalley's groundbreaking article titled simply "Robert Holcot." Smalley's description of the *Three Holcots* is important to consider in some detail because it forms both the impetus and the structure of the present work. Smalley writes:

> Holcot has attracted the attention of medievalists from three points of view. Historians of scholasticism know him as an intellectual sceptic who rejected the traditional and Thomistic proofs for the existence of God, and who was one of the principal "Pelagians" attacked by Bradwardine in his defense of predestination. Students of medieval learning and early

humanism know him as an assistant of the great book collector and book lover, Richard de Bury, bishop of Durham, a correspondent of Petrarch and author of the *Philobiblon*. De Ghellinck pointed out the extravagant richness and variety of quotation in Holcot's Wisdom-commentary in his study of Richard de Bury. Lastly, Holcot has a place in the history of preaching in England. Dr. G. R. Owst stresses the artificial, over-ingenious and pagan element in Holcot's *Moralitates*. The abbé J. Th. Welter gives him an important role in the evolution of the *exemplum*.[59]

The *Three Holcots* described by Smalley can be divided roughly into (a) the scholastic master who is identified—we argue problematically—as an intellectual skeptic; (b) the biblical commentator who was interested in classical sources and their implementation within Christian interpretations of the biblical text; and (c) the preacher who, again following classical pagan sources, was influential in late medieval preaching through his commentaries and preaching handbooks. As the previous historical overview indicates, these three aspects of Holcot's corpus roughly correlate to the historical progression of Holcot's life. Thus this book follows a broadly chronological order, focusing on the *Three Holcots* known to scholars.

Interestingly, while Smalley's comment that there are *Three Holcots* known to scholars of late medieval England was made over half a century ago, there has been no attempt to either present a historical overview of Holcot's life and works or to interpret the *Three Holcots* as a coherent and cohesive whole. The *Three Holcots* are, after all, the accidental result of the division of labor among historians of philosophy, theology, late medieval preaching, and various other fields. This accidental division of labor among specialists is unfortunate. There is, in the end, only one Holcot, and this book focuses on understanding the breadth and diversity of his literary work within its intellectual and historical context.

The Structure and Argument of the Book

Marie-Dominique Chenu wrote that "The evangelical vocation of Friar Thomas Aquinas is the source of his theology"; this statement, made in reference to the relationship between Aquinas' vocation as a Dominican friar and his theology, is no truer for the Angelic Doctor than it is for

Robert Holcot.[60] Holcot, first and foremost, was a Dominican friar. This simple historical fact is the most reliable hermeneutical key to interpreting his thought. Holcot was educated in a Dominican *studium* and spent his entire life within the ecclesial and academic world of the friars. As such, Holcot's life was occupied with studying Scripture and attempting to communicate the truths of the Word through both academic and nonacademic works. The unity of Holcot's thought, therefore, is found in the relationship between the various types of writings that he produced and his life as a Dominican: his life as a friar, as with Thomas, is the foundation of his thought and our best key to interpreting it.

This work presents a reading of Holcot that is consistent with the diversity of his extant writings and is structured around the three stages of Holcot's academic and ecclesial career. This structure allows the work to be both chronologically and thematically organized, as Holcot's career and extant writings move from the university classroom to the pulpit. Of course this is not to deny that Holcot was preaching much earlier than 1335, or that his scholastic works did not influence his preaching in the late 1340s. But, for ease of presentation, this work moves thematically and chronologically through the *Three Holcots* known to scholars: Holcot the scholastic, Holcot the biblical commentator, and Holcot the preacher.

Part I of the book considers in detail Holcot's approach to questions of philosophy and theology as developed in his purely scholastic writings. The first chapter provides an overview of Holcot's larger philosophical and theological worldview and how this affects his method of investigation. The second chapter treats questions of merit and faith, looking specifically at the role of reason in the life of faith. Chapter 3 provides an overview of Holcot's account of the divine nature and the Trinity—topics that are often pointed to as evidence of Holcot's skeptical inclination. Here we continue a revaluation of this assessment begun in chapter 2 that is carried forward in the rest of the book. The fourth chapter turns to Holcot's discussion of the nature of creation and the relation of creation to its creator. Special focus is given to the question of future contingency, the possibility of divine deception, and what this means for the life of the faithful. Finally, chapter 5 examines Holcot's discussion of key sacraments and their place in the life of faith and Church polity. These first five chapters generally focus on Holcot's commentary on the *Sentences*, supplemented by important discussions in his quodlibetal questions. Thus, taken together, they offer an overview of Holcot's early ideas as they were developed and presented at Oxford during his time as bachelor and regent master.

The second part of the book turns to Holcot's scriptural commentaries. As discussed earlier, following his years as regent master of Oxford and possibly Cambridge, Holcot was increasingly associated with the house of Richard de Bury. Holcot's biblical commentaries overlap with his scholastic writings but also mark a unique development in his academic career. Chapter 6 offers an introduction to medieval biblical commentaries and Holcot's general approach. Chapter 7 then introduces Holcot's commentary on the Twelve Prophets and explains his unique methodology of creating verbal pictures for his readers. The focus of chapters 8 and 9 is Holcot's massive commentary on Wisdom. Chapter 8 provides an introduction to the commentary and an analysis of Holcot's understanding of the purpose, message, and structure of the work. Because, as we will see in chapter 8, the work is both intended for political rulers—and thus replete with political ideas—and fairly unsystematic in its presentation of philosophical material, chapter 9 attempts to construct a systematic overview of Holcot's political philosophy gleaned from his Wisdom commentary.

Part III turns to Holcot the preacher. Holcot's extant literary production includes both manuals for preachers and sermons. This part begins with a general introduction to fourteenth-century preaching, setting the stage for the following two chapters. Thus chapter 10 treats, in a general way, late medieval preaching and the preaching manuals of the fourteenth century. Chapter 11 considers Holcot's *Moralitates* and his methodological approach to the art of preaching (*ars praedicandi*). Finally, chapter 12 concludes with an analysis of a particularly important and representative sermon from Holcot's corpus.

Medieval theologians such as Thomas Aquinas, John Duns Scotus, William of Ockham, and Robert Holcot are often thought of as system builders—architects, that is, of systematic presentations of Christian theology. Referencing these systematic treatises, the great historian of Christian thought, Jaroslav Pelikan, wrote:

> For not only has the historical scholarship of the past century underemphasized the exegetical basis of dogma, it has also tended to minimize the role that exegesis has played in the creative and systematic thought

of the makers of Christian theology. As a consequence, these systems have been fearfully oversimplified in modern handbooks ... Once the importance of exegesis in the theological systems of the past centuries has been recovered, it may prove more difficult to interpret these systems ... if this word is still applicable at all.[61]

The three parts of this book attest to the complexity suggested by Pelikan. In the same passage, Pelikan argues that when such an approach is adopted, the "propositional clarity and simplicity of dogmatics" is replaced by the "fecundity and complexity of exegesis."[62] Parts II and III leave the world of propositional clarity and enter into the complexity of late medieval exegesis and preaching. The thesis of this work is that it is only by examining the fecundity and complexity of Holcot's exegetical and homiletical works that the reader can achieve a historically accurate portrait of Holcot the great medieval thinker.

A central implication of this recovery of Holcot's entire corpus is the argument, developed throughout this work, that Holcot demonstrates a profound pastoral concern for the human pilgrim. There is no denying the fact that Holcot's work is preoccupied with issues of merit and salvation. He takes every opportunity to encourage his reader to put purity of heart and the desire to follow God's commands above all else. His message to other pastors is that God is beholden to no master and therefore God may accept whom he pleases. His message to every seeker is to replace the fear of failing to believe or worship correctly with an honest and genuine search for God.

I

COVENANTAL THEOLOGY

Introduction

Central to Robert Holcot's thought is the belief that the God of the Christian Scriptures has entered into a relationship with humanity. This relationship—as witnessed to in the Old and New Testaments—is grounded in God's desire to be in a covenant with his people: a covenant according to which God promised to be the God of his people and in return the people promised to follow him. The first evidence of this relationship is found in God's covenants with Noah (Genesis 9:9–12) and Abraham (Genesis 17) and extends throughout the rest of the Christian Scriptures. However, as Holcot and the previous Christian tradition realized, God's covenantal history narrated in the Old and New Testaments is remarkably complex and bears witness to numerous permutations and alterations. For example, in Genesis 17:14, God told Abraham that circumcision is required of all male members of the covenant, while at the Jerusalem Council the Apostle Peter argued that circumcision is not required of followers of Jesus who are in covenant with God (Acts 15 and Galatians 5). The Old and New Testaments, therefore, bear witness to seemingly contradictory claims about the requirements of God's covenantal relationship with humanity.

Early Christians analyzed the changes in God's covenant (or covenants) with his people, and Robert Holcot inherited this theological tradition.[1]

We examine this topic at the outset because in the process of explicating how the God of Abraham, Isaac, and Jacob enters into relationship with humanity Holcot elaborates several of the central features of his thought. This discussion is followed by an analysis of Holcot's obligational theology: a theological method that adopts the obligational arts as a complex analogy in order to introduce us to God's unique relationship with humanity. This analogy is the foundation of Holcot's covenantal theology, which we will see at work throughout this book. The covenant, or pact (*pactum*), is Holcot's way of articulating that God and humanity enter into a relationship by means of an act of free will rather than necessity. It is only within the context of the divine covenant that we can understand God's relationship with humanity and his power over creation.

God's Covenant and the Ages of History

Christian theologians of the patristic and early medieval periods understood world history as divided into three distinct ages: (a) a time before the Mosaic law (*ante legem*), (b) a time under the Mosaic law (*sub lege*), (c) and a time under grace or after the law (*sub gratia, post legem*). According to this scheme, each age was distinct with respect to God's relationship to humanity: there was the time before the Mosaic law when the world was ruled by the law of nature; there was the time under the law that extended from the time of Moses until Christ; and there was the time after the law, extending from Christ up through the present. This understanding of the three ages can be found in Augustine,[2] Isidore of Seville (†636), and twelfth- and thirteenth-century writers such as Rupert of Deutz (†c. 1130), Hugh of St. Victor (†1141), Anselm of Havelberg (†1158), and Robert Grosseteste (†1253).[3] This is a heritage that was passed down to the scholastics of the thirteenth and fourteenth centuries.[4]

As we will see in the following chapters, Holcot employs this schema of the three ages throughout his writings. In the *Moralitates*, for example, Holcot moralizes various pre-Christian texts by interpreting them alongside the Christian schema of the three ages.[5] However, within the context of Holcot's obligational theology and his understanding of the covenant, these three ages take on particular importance. For Holcot, as for other medieval thinkers, the challenge was how to interpret these three ages and God's ongoing work of salvation.

Isidore of Seville, the Three Ages, and Augustinian Theology

Medieval theologians regarded the *Etymologies* of the early seventh-century Archbishop Isidore of Seville as an authoritative guide to both biblical and extra-biblical history. According to Isidore, the first age is referred to as the time before the law and includes the biblical history from Adam up through Moses (i.e., the Pentateuch). While it is true that God's first covenant with the people of Israel would be established through the person of Abraham (Genesis 15), it was not until the giving of the law on Mount Sinai (Exodus 20) that the people entered into a new age. Thus medieval authors often refer to individuals living in this early period as those living before the law. This category is somewhat complicated by the fact that while the age *ante legem* referred to the time before Moses, it is also used to describe more broadly the state of Gentiles (after the law was given on Sinai) who live in ignorance of the law.

The second age is the age under the law and refers to the period from Moses until Christ. Isidore lists Moses as being born in the 3,728th year since the creation of the world and as the receiver of the law from God.[6] The time of the law is dominated by the covenant between God and his people; a covenant that remains intact throughout this historical period, so long as the Jewish people follow the law given by God on Mount Sinai. The Old Testament books of Exodus, Leviticus, Numbers, and Deuteronomy establish the law as given by God.

The third age is characterized by grace (*sub gratia*) and is known as the period after the law (*post legem*); this period, from the medieval Christian perspective, extends from the time of Jesus Christ up until the present day. Quintessential to this era is the fact that God has offered humanity grace and salvation through the death and resurrection of Jesus Christ. As a result, the law is traditionally understood to be replaced or superseded by the Gospel of Jesus Christ such that salvation is offered to humanity not by means of the observance of the law but on account of the death of Christ. Isidore helpfully summarizes the relation between the three orders: "for the first age is before the Mosaic law, the second under the law, and the third under grace; where the sacrament is now manifest, earlier it was hidden in prophetic enigma."[7]

Medieval theologians realized that the first period, before the law, raised various theological questions. For example, righteous Gentiles—that is, those who lived in a way pleasing to God before and after the giving of the law—presented a challenge for Christian theologians. The Old Testament figures of Melchizedek, Noah, Job, and Ruth are examples of those who had a special relationship with God but did not live under the Mosaic law or the Gospel of Christ. In his *Etymologies*, Isidore of Seville is ambiguous about who wrote the book of Job; however, Isidore is convinced that Job was a contemporary of Moses.[8] He argues that Moses' son Shem had five sons who "brought forth individual nations:" Elam, Asshur, Arpachshad, Lud, and Aram. The fifth son, Aram, had five sons of his own, one of whom was Uz, whose descendent was Job (Job 1:1). The Hebrew people, by contrast, come from the lineage of Arpachshad, whose grandson was Heber, the father of the Hebrews.[9] Thus, according to Isidore, Job was a Gentile who lived during the time of Moses. As such, Job did not have the benefit of the law and did not live under it (*sub legem*). But how could Job be saved, if he lived neither under the Mosaic law nor under the grace of Christ?

To answer such problems, medieval theologians turned to Augustine. In *The City of God* and *The Trinity*, Augustine of Hippo employed the division of the three ages described previously.[10] Alongside this interpretive framework—for example, in his work *Adversos Iudaeos*—Augustine presents a theological reading of the distinction between the time under the law and the time under grace. He develops a hermeneutical approach that distinguishes between a carnal and a spiritual understanding of Scripture: (a) a carnal or literal reading that was an appropriate interpretation of the text before the coming of Christ, and (b) a spiritual reading that was/is an appropriate interpretation of the text after the coming of Christ and in light of his revelation. Further, Augustine emphasizes the superiority of the spiritual reading and on the basis of Galatians 3:3 criticizes the carnal reading ("Christ has redeemed us from the curse of the law"). For example, in his early comments on Romans 5:20, Augustine writes:

> Paul sufficiently indicated the Jews did not understand why the law had been given. It was not to bring life, for grace does this through faith. But

the law was given to show what great and tight bonds of sin bound those who presumed to attain righteousness by their own strength.[11]

In this sense, Augustine understood the law to function as a teacher instructing humanity in the will of God.

The instructional aspect of the Jewish law is central to Augustine's "Christological interpretation of the law."[12] But, what does a Christological interpretation of the law mean? For Augustine, the law as teacher points to Christ, and Christ, through his incarnation, death, and resurrection, is the fulfillment of the law. As Augustine writes in *Against Faustus*: "the same law that was given to Moses *became* grace and truth in Jesus Christ."[13] This, of course, has implications for how Augustine thinks about the keeping of the law for the Old Testament patriarchs. Paula Fredriksen is correct to note that for Augustine "[a] special group within Israel—patriarchs, prophets, holy women and men—enlightened by divine revelation, had understood the ultimate Christological significance of the law."[14] The keeping of the law, therefore, was efficacious for such persons precisely because it was interpreted as anticipating Christ.

One implication of Augustine's theology is that the law is not understood as providing grace per se. In *On the Spirit and the Letter* Augustine observes that "the law written on tablets could not bring about for the Jews this writing of the law upon their hearts, which is justification, but could only bring about transgression."[15] The carnal (i.e., nonspiritual) reading of the law did not and could not point to Christ, and because the majority of the Jews interpreted the law literally, they failed to understand the spiritual meaning imbedded within it (i.e., that it pointed to Christ).[16] A particularly striking explication of this theology in the twelfth century can be found in Hugh of St. Victor's *The Mystic Ark*. This treatise, known to Holcot,[17] presents a complex analogy of the three ages according to which "the people of the natural law are openly bad, while the people of the written law are fictitiously good, and the people of grace are truly good."[18] Working out the implications of the Augustinian heritage, Hugh argues that while there are examples of each type of person in each period, an instance of a person who lived according to grace in either the era of the written law or natural law is only possible on account of a special grace given by the Holy Spirit.[19] As Paul Rorem summarizes Hugh, the practices of the old law "are not themselves signs of invisible grace but rather the signs of the later visible sacramental signs; they were not necessary for salvation in the later sense; they were not efficacious until the Incarnation itself opened heaven."[20]

Augustine's theology of the old law culminates in *The City of God* and *Against Faustus* with the argument that the Old Testament is a hidden form of the New Testament.[21] This implies, for Augustine, a profound continuity of Scripture. Therefore, while there may appear to be contradictions between the Old and New Testaments (and their theologies of salvation), he argues that the two testaments do not fundamentally contradict.[22]

Holcot, Jewish Law, and the Three Ages

Holcot's understanding of the three ages can be found in a quodlibetal question addressing whether the observance of the Mosaic law by the Jews merited them eternal life.[23] What is striking about Holcot's interpretation of this question is how he confronts, head on, the contradictions between the Old Testament and the New Testament. While Augustine argued that when one finds an alleged contradiction one must conclude that "either the manuscript is defective, or the translator made a mistake, or you do not understand [the text],"[24] Holcot accepted that there are substantive theological disagreements between the Old and New Testaments. For example, in this quodlibetal question he points to the following contradictions: (a) baptism by water is not necessary for salvation (according to the Old Testament) and (a¹) baptism by water is necessary for salvation (according to the New Testament); or (b) animal sacrifice bestows the remission of sins (according to the Old Testament) and (b¹) animal sacrifice does not bestow the remission of sins (according to the New Testament).[25]

In the same question, Holcot presents and critiques a rather standard and straightforward interpretation (grounded in Augustine) of the relationship between the old law and the new law. He begins with a quotation from Acts 15:10 in which Peter argues that the old law placed a yoke upon humanity that "neither our fathers nor we have been able to bear."[26] This passage, he complains, is used by medieval theologians, following Augustine, to support an interpretation according to which the new law confers grace (*conferunt gratiam*) and the old law merely signifies (*significant*) grace. On this reading of Acts, the old law did not confer the grace necessary for following God's commands, while the new law can be borne precisely because it confers grace.[27] Here Holcot probably has in mind Peter Lombard, who argued that "those things which were instituted only for the sake of signifying are merely signs, and not sacraments; such were the carnal sacrifices and the ceremonial observances of the old law, which could never justify those who offered them."[28] As Marcia Colish has argued, Lombard "views these Old Testament ceremonies as significant, but not as a means for the transmission of divine grace."[29] Following the predominant Augustinian tradition, Peter Lombard held that the old law merely signifies the grace of God but does not sanctify the individual.

Holcot rejects this understanding of the distinction between the old law and the new law and argues explicitly that the old law can confer grace. For example, he argues "every just person before God is worthy of eternal life, and every observer of the Mosaic law is justified before God."[30] This is clear in Scripture because people such as Moses, Joshua, Samuel, David, Ezekiel, Josiah, Judas Maccabee, and many others (*multis aliis*) merited eternal life.[31] However, Holcot is not satisfied with a general account and provides explicit examples observing that "circumcision conferred grace, just as now baptism confers grace."[32] Holcot strengthens his position by arguing that in Leviticus 4 and 6 an animal sacrifice was offered for the sin of the people (*pro peccato populi*) and that this sacrifice conferred the forgiveness of sin. Holcot is clear that "those sacrifices bestowed the remission of sins" and, as such, bestowed grace (for to give grace and to remit sins is identical).[33] In his gloss on Romans 1:7, Holcot unambiguously states that "Grace is the remission of sins (*gratia est remissio peccatorum*)." Thus he concludes, "if some sacrament (*sacramenta*) of the old law conferred the remission of sins, it conferred grace."[34]

Holcot argues that, under the old law, grace is conferred through the sacrament of circumcision and broadens his understanding of baptism to include acts of regeneration that extend beyond baptism by water. This question is somewhat complicated, however, as Holcot defends the claim that both baptism and grace are necessary for salvation. On scriptural grounds this can hardly be disputed, given that Jesus (John 3:5) said explicitly, "unless a person is born again of water and the Holy Spirit (*ex aqua et Spiritu*), he cannot enter the kingdom of heaven."[35] However, Holcot defends a broad definition of baptism to include the repentance of the faithful, martyrdom, and baptism by water. As we shall see, such acts of regeneration necessarily include the conferral of grace and are interpreted, broadly speaking, as modes of baptism. Thus Holcot argues affirmatively that Jews under the law are given grace by God.

Given that Holcot thinks the old law confers grace, what does he think about those who live before either the old law or the dispensation of grace? Holcot's presentation of Job is of particular importance here because the commandment concerning circumcision was not given to all but only to the Jews. Therefore, if Gentiles like Job were saved (as the Scriptures imply), they were saved without circumcision (*salvatus sine circumcisione*). This example had been introduced into the discussion by the *socius* (i.e., Holcot's antagonist in this debate), and Holcot responds to the arguments of the *socius* by claiming that Job is not saved under the old law (as he was a Gentile).[36] However, Holcot insists that one cannot say that Job was saved without grace, for God clearly gave grace to his servant Job. Holcot asks the following question: Is it possible for someone who is brought up from infancy (*ab infantia*) outside the context of God's law to be saved?[37] Holcot responds that if such a person chooses the better sect (*sectam meliorem*) among the available options, and genuinely wills to follow it, she can be conferred grace.[38] If she does not present an obstacle to God's grace, then God will confer a baptism of the Spirit (*baptismum flaminis*).[39]

What is striking about this quodlibetal question is that Holcot rejects the Augustinian and Lombardian solution and argues that God could provide grace—through circumcision and the remission of sins through sacrifice—to Jews living under the Mosaic law. Further, God can also provide grace and the remission of sins to those living before the Mosaic law and according to the law of reason or nature (so long as they do their best to seek God).

In sum, Holcot argues that there are three ages representing a time before the Jewish law, a time under the Jewish law, and a time under grace. God's grace is given presently through the Church and the salvific work of Christ. However, as noted, Holcot's understanding of the first two ages (i.e., the time before the law and under the law) is somewhat distinct from the antecedent Augustinian tradition. As Holcot makes clear in this quodlibetal question, God granted the remission of sins, and therefore grace, to those living under the law. God also granted grace to those who lived prior to the law and Gentiles, such as Job, who lived during the time of the law but in ignorance of it. Indeed, Holcot maintains that God can grant salvation to those ignorant of the articles of faith if their ignorance arises from no fault of their own.⁴⁰ Holcot writes that many of the philosophers and wise men—Job, Socrates, Plato, Aristotle, and most of the Stoics—lived in a divine cult according to some rite (*ritus*) and profession (*protestationes*) and were saved (*salvati sunt*).⁴¹ This sensitivity to the genuine seeker and God's promise to respond is considered again in the following chapter and, as we will see, emerges as a dominant theme throughout Holcot's work.⁴²

The Critique of Walter Hilton

The theology of Robert Holcot did not remain unchallenged in the fourteenth century. Walter Hilton's (†1396) *Scale of Perfection* offers one such challenge.⁴³ Hilton belonged to the order of Augustinian Hermits and flourished during the second half of the fourteenth century. In book 2 of his Middle English *Scale of Perfection*, Hilton critiques a particular modern view that sounds astonishingly like Holcot. Hilton argues in a discussion of the Jews that salvation offered to the patriarchs of the Old Testament was through Christ. He writes:

> all chosen souls that were before the incarnation under the Old Testament had faith in Christ—that he should come and reform man's soul—either openly, as the patriarchs and prophets and other holy men had, or else secretly and generally.⁴⁴

This is the position of Augustine, Peter Lombard, and Thomas Aquinas, according to which all salvation is through Christ: that is, the Old Testament patriarchs were saved because of their faith in the coming Savior. This view, Hilton argues, is to be contrasted with those who argue that Jews

> can be saved by keeping their own law (*Bi kepynge of hire owen lawe*), although they do not believe in Jesus Christ as the holy church believes, inasmuch as they think their own faith is good and sure, sufficient for their salvation, and in that faith they do, as it seems, many good works of righteousness.⁴⁵

This last phrase, Alastair Minnis observes, sounds intriguingly like Holcot's injunction to "do what lies within you" (*facere quod in se est*).⁴⁶ While there is little direct evidence that Hilton knew Holcot's writings, the point here is that the theological position defended by Holcot was being discussed in the fourteenth century and, in particular, was described by Hilton and rejected as heterodox. This short discussion of Hilton's critique of Holcot is instructive in directing our attention to the aspects of Holcot's thought that are somewhat extraordinary given the Augustinian and Lombardian heritage. What Holcot argues—and what Hilton objects to—is that the law of the Jews in the time "before the grace of Christ (*ante gratiam Christi*)" was in fact not a time before grace at all. Grace was given through the old law. Further, Holcot does not argue, as Augustine and Lombard did, that the old law saves because it points to Christ or because those who followed the law followed it in anticipation of Christ. Rather, those living in the two earliest dispensations were saved according to the covenant governing the established dispensation.

Holcot's Obligational Theology and the *Ars Obligatoria*

God's interaction with human beings in the three dispensations is understood by Holcot to be analogous to medieval disputations referred to as the *ars obligatoria* (obligational art).[47] Fritz Hoffmann first argued that disputations *de obligationibus* are central to Robert Holcot's theological method, and the recent work of Hester Gelber has confirmed and expanded this insight.[48] It is important, therefore, to consider the nature of the obligational arts and Holcot's use of them as a complex analogy for God's relationship with humanity. This analogy helps clarify Holcot's understanding of the distinct covenantal dispensations discussed earlier.

The *obligationes* (lit. obligations) were a method of academic disputation that developed in the Arts Faculty of the University of Paris in the thirteenth century.[49] The debate took place between two scholars, an opponent (*opponens*) and a respondent (*repondens*). The debate begins when the opponent states a proposition (of the form, "I posit that A," with A being called the *positum*) and the respondent either concedes (*concedo*), denies (*nego*), or is doubtful about (*dubito*) the proposition. If the respondent accepts the proposition by obliging himself to it (*se obligat*), the debate begins. In the debate, the *positum* functions as the basis for the subsequent exchange (with the respondent agreeing to accept the proposition as true for the remainder of the debate). Having posited the first proposition, the opponent continues by suggesting further propositions that either follow from, contradict, or are irrelevant to the first proposition. The respondent continues the debate by either accepting, rejecting, or denying the relevance of subsequent propositions. The respondent is to accept nothing contradictory to the first proposition and is required to accept propositions that necessarily follow from it. The opponent stops the debate by stating "time is up."

This description of the obligational arts is characteristic of the type of debate referred to as the *positio* (the position), which is perhaps the most common form. Stephen Read recently observed four variants of the obligations in Thomas Bradwardine's *Insolubilia*: the *positio*, noted earlier, but also the *institutio* (in which the original proposition is given an unusual signification), the *depositio* (in which the original proposition must be denied) and the *dubitatio* (in which the original proposition must be doubted).[50] In the writings of Walter Burley and William of Ockham, one finds two other variants: the *rei veritas/sit verum* (the truth of the matter) and the *petitio* (petition).[51] Thus in the early fourteenth century there were six kinds of obligations (a number reduced to three or four by the early fifteenth century; e.g., Paul of Venice). This diversity is important to recognize,[52] for, as will become clear, Holcot has a somewhat unique position regarding the relationship between the *positio* and the *depositio*.

Many scholars have debated the purpose of the obligational arts within medieval universities. The questions arise because the obligations are not formal debates (with two opposing positions). Further, it is unclear how such "debates" instructed students in the rules of dialectic. One hypothesis is that they functioned as exercises in counterfactual reasoning or thought experiments.[53] As argued by Fritz Hoffmann and Hester Gelber, these debates function in Holcot's theology as a complex analogy for the divine-human interaction. This interpretation of Holcot is grounded in several passages, but central to Gelber's argument is a passage from his *Sentences* commentary:

> It seems to me for now that one should speak to this according to the obligatory art. For that God reveals proposition *a* [i.e., "Only those who are numbered among tomorrow's mortal sinners will be saved"] to Socrates and that Socrates believes this proposition, God teaching it to him, and that so it will be as [that revelation] denotes, is the same as if [God] were to say to him: "I pose *a* to you (*pono tibi* a), such that

afterwards you should concede and deny [as in an *obligatio*]." And having made such a revelation, the revealed proposition ought to be conceded as often as it is proposed, and every formal consequence following simply [from that] ought to be conceded. To everything, however, that does not follow from that, one should respond as to an irrelevant proposition.[54]

In this analogy God is the opponent (*opponens*) and Socrates is the respondent (*repondens*), and God reveals (*revelo*) a proposition to Socrates. What is central to the analogy is that God both *reveals* and *teaches* the proposition to Socrates in such a way that Socrates believes the proposition. Thus Socrates has no excuse; that is, he is not ignorant of the proposition, as God has communicated it to him. Holcot continues by arguing that Socrates is not only bound to this individual proposition but is bound to all formal consequences following from it. However, with respect to propositions that do not follow directly from the *positum*, the respondent (i.e., Socrates) is to treat them as irrelevant propositions. This analogy, Holcot argues, is similar to God's revelation to humanity. God has revealed and taught humanity the original *positum,* and humanity is obligated to follow it. The picture, though, is somewhat more complicated than this, for Holcot also argues that following the model of the obligational arts, God has a right to change or modify the *positum* (i.e., his revelation to humanity).

Holcot's analogy is further clarified in the following passage in which he provides four rules that govern the obligational arts.[55]

Rule 1: When an opponent poses a case (*casum*) and the respondent admits it, the respondent is obligated to respond according to the case. Therefore, whenever it is said by the opponent: "Let it be posited that it is so" (or the equivalent), he makes a *positio* to the respondent that is a kind of obligation if the respondent admits it.

Rule 2: That everything following formally from what is posed ought to be conceded, and that everything repugnant to what is posed ought to be denied, and for what is irrelevant, the respondent should respond as it is evident to him from how things are.

Rule 3: Every *positio* is equivalent to a *depositio*, because [*positio* and *depositio*] are equivalent for the respondent ... therefore, someone who poses one of two contradictories, deposes the other.

Rule 4: Having posed a false contingent, it is not inconvenient to concede the impossible *per accidens*.

The first rule establishes the basic structure of the interaction: when the opponent poses a case (or proposition) and the respondent admits it, the opponent has established a *positio* that (if accepted) forms an obligation for the respondent. This is somewhat standard for the obligational arts. However, Holcot builds on this basic structure by arguing that in Rule 3, when the opponent poses the initial *positio*, he is also implicitly deposing (or rejecting) the contradictory. The implication is that by admitting the contradictory of the initial *positio* into the debate, the debate in essence begins again with a new *positio* contrary to the first. To give an example: if the opponent states in the original proposition that "there is a God," he is also implicitly rejecting the contradictory "there is not a God." But to begin the debate again with the contradictory proposition is to oblige the respondent to a new proposition that is in fact contradictory with the first. With these rules firmly in place, Holcot's understanding of the analogy comes into full view.

Holcot argues that it is entirely possible that God's interactions with humanity are analogous to the rules of the obligational arts. God establishes a given order and is free to choose between logically consistent possibilities. God is like an opponent in a debate who is free to choose between contradictory propositions (e.g., God is free to say: "let it be posited that a" or "let it be posited that not a"). Humanity is like the respondent who is obliged to work within the logical constraints of the given order. With respect to the respondent, it makes little difference what God chose as the original proposition (note Holcot's language in Rule 3 that "every *positio* is equivalent to a *depositio*, because [they] are equivalent for the respondent"). As argued, Holcot understood these debates in a particular way, such that for every proposition the contradictory of that proposition was also admitted into the debate as a new proposition. Applying this to the analogy, Holcot argues that God's relationship with humanity is similar in that God is free to establish a given order and to abolish that order and establish a new order at any time (even one that contradicts the first).

While it is clear that as an analogy for the divine-human relationship this model ascribes to God the freedom to do as he wills, it is also a useful model for articulating how the old dispensation and new dispensation can contain contradictory propositions while both being ordained by God. To return to the discussion of the three ages and the possibility of contradictory theological propositions, we recall that the proposition "animal sacrifice is required for the forgiveness of sins" was true for those living under the old dispensation, although the same proposition was false for those living under the new dispensation. According to Holcot, the *ars obligatoria* analogy provides a precise explanation for how God is free to ordain distinct orders or dispensations as he wills. Further, the analogy also explains how the Bible contains seemingly contradictory claims regarding human salvation and morals (e.g., consider the truth of the proposition "it is licit for a man to have more than one wife" under the old and new dispensations). Holcot disagrees with Augustine and argues that the Scriptures do contain logically contradictory propositions.

While it may seem that in this system God is radically free and can arbitrarily change the rules of the game at will, Holcot insists God never acts inordinately within a given order. That is, while God can alter the parameters of his relationship with humanity from one dispensation to the next throughout the course of human history, he does not do so capriciously within a given order. Theologically Holcot grounds his obligational theology in a robust notion of covenant.

The Divine Covenant

Holcot's discussion of the contingency of God's created order has led scholars, such as Gordon Leff, to argue that he developed an "extreme scepticism, which allows anything to be possible."[56] And while such readings are understandable, it is important to examine how Holcot guards against a theology of radical contingency in which God could be understood as an arbitrary and, indeed, inordinate Creator.[57]

Holcot defines God's covenant as his promise to humanity. In his commentary on Wisdom he writes that God's covenant can be described as an unfailing necessity appropriate to God "because of his promise, that is, his covenant, or established law" (*in Deo ex promisso suo et pacto, sive lege statuta*).[58] Here Holcot links the covenant with the idea not only of a promise but of the notion of an established law. This is important because for Holcot the notion of the covenant is grounded in his discussion of the three ages and the idea that God has established a distinct law governing each dispensation.

Heiko Oberman emphasized the covenantal theme in Holcot's thought.[59] In the *Forerunners of the Reformation*, Oberman examined the covenantal theme, writing that

> Holcot saw man as the partner of God, in a covenantal relationship to which God had freely committed himself. Within this covenantal relationship, immutable because of God's fidelity and inner consistency, man had to determine the course of his own life and shoulder the responsibility for his eternal lot; God would support his serious effort ... God's mercy underlies the making of the Covenant; God's justice obliges man to live according to the laws of the Covenant.[60]

While Oberman is correct that the covenant between God and humanity is what grounds Holcot's understanding of God and guards against a purely capricious understanding of the divine, he has, generally speaking, oversimplified the situation by not attending to the nature of Holcot's obligational theology. The problem is that Oberman's reading does not fully acknowledge God's freedom to ordain a new covenant. Oberman states that the covenantal system is "immutable because of God's fidelity and inner consistency," which is accurate as a description of an individual ordained order but fails to capture the contingent nature of the existing order.

As a corrective, we begin with Oberman's claim that the covenantal relationship is "immutable because of God's fidelity and inner consistency." The first thing to note is that Holcot's understanding of the covenant could be interpreted as immutable, only in the sense that Holcot insists that God will not act inordinately with respect to an established covenant. While the term "immutable" could be interpreted in this sense, Oberman imports a much stronger interpretation of the covenant than Holcot intends. For Holcot, God is always free to ordain his creation as he sees fit; the covenant is God's promise that he will not act inordinately. However, as noted, a given covenant is neither necessary nor immutable.[61] Second, Oberman claims that the reason for the immutability of the covenant is a result of God's fidelity and inner consistency. Again, the choice of words is stronger than is warranted; while Holcot does argue that God will not act inordinately with respect to an established covenant, it is odd to label this as being grounded in God's fidelity, given that Holcot thinks God can ordain a completely new order at any moment (and, in fact, has done so historically).[62] Thus while it is true that God will act consistently within a given order and one can have faith in God's fidelity to that order, it is misleading to state that God's covenant itself is grounded in God's fidelity. Indeed, Holcot argues the opposite; God is bound to no "higher order"—or ethical system—that commands his fidelity. Finally, turning to Oberman's claim of "inner consistency," it must be insisted that *inner consistency* applies to a given ordained system but in fact is not true when one compares two distinct ordained systems. As noted earlier, a given proposition *a* (it is licit for a man to have more than one wife) is true in one dispensation, while proposition *not-a* (it is not licit for a man to have more than one wife) is true in the subsequent dispensation. The notion of *inner consistency*, therefore, can only apply within a given order, such that Holcot argues that *a* and *not-a* cannot be true for a given individual at the same time.[63]

In support of his analysis, Oberman considered Holcot's discussion of the divine–human relationship as allegorized in Romans 9 through the analogy of God as the potter and humanity as the clay. Here Holcot argues that when comparing God to his creatures, the analogy found in Romans cannot be applied to all aspects of the divine-human relationship. First, Holcot argues that the analogy breaks down because there is no covenant (*pactum*) between a potter and his clay as there is between God and humanity. Further, Holcot argues that if we imagine such a covenant between a potter and his clay, the potter could break the covenant and the covenant would remain. By contrast, he argues, if God breaks the covenant with humanity, then the covenant no longer remains.[64] While this appears, at first, to support the claim of Oberman that God is eternally faithful to the covenant, all that Holcot is arguing is that the analogy does not hold. If God were to act contrary to a given order, he would be nullifying that order and reasserting a new order. Thus, what one is left with is the reassertion that God does not act outside of an ordained order, except when he intends to ordain a new dispensation or covenant.[65]

The Two Powers

Holcot's theology of the three ages, obligational theology, and covenantal theology constitute the interpretive framework within which one can understand the nature of God's power over creation: specifically the distinction between God's ordained power and absolute power.[66] Holcot's analysis of divine power is heavily influenced by the obligational theology described here and embedded within a discussion of God's covenant(s) with humanity.

The Origin of the Distinction

The distinction between God's ordained power and absolute power has its origins in the eleventh century and emerged in full form during the twelfth and thirteenth centuries through the analysis of the divine attributes. During the twelfth century the discussion centered on how God's power relates to his will, reason, and goodness.[67] For example, many twelfth-century theologians focused on the relationship between God's omnipotence and his will: can God, for instance, will to do other than what he has in fact already willed to do? What is the relationship between God's power and his will?

The specific theological question motivating the discussion of the two powers was the claim that God is omnipotent and immutable. This is discussed in distinction 42 of book 1 of Peter Lombard's *Sentences*, where he defines God's omnipotence as the ability to do all things that do not contradict God's nature (e.g., God cannot lie or sin).[68] Theologians in the thirteenth and fourteenth centuries interpreted this to mean that God can do all things that do not involve a logical contradiction. Thus God could have created any number of possible scenarios (or possible words) but in fact ordained one set of compatible possible scenarios that constitute the actual world.

The historiography of the two powers has been extensively and highly disputed.[69] William Courtenay argues that between 1930 and 1960 the distinction between the two powers was primarily negative in the literature, such that (a) "*de potentia* arguments assumed that God might in fact change the present order or intervene in ways that contradicted that order" and (b) "the Nominalist or Ockhamist use of the distinction led to skepticism, fideism, and the destruction of metaphysics and natural theology."[70] This characterization can be referred to as a *voluntarist* interpretation of the two powers because it interprets theologians such as William of Ockham as arguing that God could change the currently established moral order when employing his absolute power (*de potentia absoluta*).

This understanding of the two powers was challenged by Paul Vignaux, who defined the late medieval distinction between God's ordained and absolute powers by distinguishing between the order established by God and the order determined by logic.[71] Heiko Oberman defended Vignaux's basic approach and continued to refine the discussion by insisting that, for thinkers such as William of Ockham, Robert Holcot, and Gabriel Biel

> the distinction should be understood to mean that God can—and, in fact, has chosen—to do certain things according to the laws which he freely established, that is, *de potentia ordinata*. On the other hand, God can do everything that does not imply contradiction, whether God has decided to do these things [*de potentia ordinata*] or not, as there are many things God can do which he does not want to do. The latter is called God's power *de potentia absoluta*.[72]

As Oberman observes, the distinction between the two powers is primarily a logical distinction clarifying different aspects of God's power from two different vantage points. It is not, therefore, about dual modes of divine action within creation history. This fact can be easily observed in the writings of both Ockham and Holcot.

William of Ockham and Robert Holcot

The fact that there has been so much ink spilled on analyzing this basic scholastic distinction is somewhat astonishing, particularly given that thinkers such as William of Ockham are clear and unambiguous in defining the terms. Ockham writes:

> God is able to do certain things by his ordained power (*potentia ordinata*) and certain things by his absolute power (*potentia absoluta*). This distinction should not be understood to mean that in God there are really two powers, one of which is ordained and the other of which is absolute. For with respect to things outside himself there is in God a single power, which in every way is God himself. Nor should the distinction be understood to mean that God is able to do things ordinately (*ordinate*) and certain things absolutely and not ordinately (*non ordinate*). For God cannot do anything inordinately (*Deus nihil potest facere inordinate*). Instead the distinction should be understood to mean that "power to do something" is sometimes taken as "power to do something in accordance with the

laws that have been ordained and instituted by God," and God is said to be able to do these things by his ordained power. In an alternative sense, "power" is taken as "power to do anything such that its being done does not involve a contradiction" . . . for there are many things God is able to do that he does not will to do.[73]

This definition of Ockham is consistent with the theologies of other late-thirteenth- and early-fourteenth-century theologians, including both Thomas Aquinas and Robert Holcot.[74]

Ockham begins by clarifying what the distinction does not mean. First, Ockham argues that within God there are not two powers but one power. That is, within God there is just one power and that one power is God himself (*est ipse Deus*). This claim has its roots in Jewish reflections on God (see the *Shema*, Deuteronomy 6:4) and is grounded in the notion of divine simplicity developed by early Christian theologians and endorsed by all medieval Christians. Second, Ockham argues that God does not act inordinately within the established or ordained order. The distinction does not mean, Ockham insists, that God acts *ordinately* by means of his ordained power and *inordinately* by means of his absolute power; God never acts inordinately. Positively, Ockham argues that the distinction is a way of interpreting the phrase "the power to do something (*posse aliquid*)" as used with respect to God. Thus if one says that God has the "power to do something in accordance with his established law," one can state that God is said to be able to do such things by means of his ordained power. Conversely, if one says that God has "the power to do anything that does not involve a logical contradiction," one can state that God is said to be able to do such things by means of his absolute power. For, as Ockham insists, there are "many things God is able to do that he does not will to do."

In book 2 of his commentary on the *Sentences* Robert Holcot defines the two powers according to either consistent or contradictory propositions. Holcot argues that if one considers all possible propositions, God "cannot do what would entail contradictory [propositions] being true simultaneously." However, God "can do all the things that . . . entail no contradictory [propositions] being true simultaneously."[75] Thus, as noted earlier, God can establish two or more dispensations or ordained orders that do not entail two contradictory propositions being true at the same time (although, as was also argued, the various dispensations can contain contradictory propositions that are true at different times). Following this logic, when human beings speak of God acting according to his ordained power, they mean that God can do *a* and that God doing *a* is consistent or compatible with the given ordained dispensation. Further, when they speak of God acting according to his absolute power, they mean that God can do an act *b* (i.e., *b* is logically possible) and that God doing *b* is not compatible with the ordained dispensation.

In addition to this passage, Holcot's clearest articulation of the two powers is found in a quodlibetal question.[76] Following Ockham, Holcot begins his definition by arguing that in God there are not two powers (*non quod in Deo sit duplex potentia*), nor does God have a twofold power (*duplex potentia*). Instead, Holcot argues the phrases *de potentia absoluta* and *de potentia ordinata* should be understood as modifiers for a proposition such as "God can produce *a*." This is not unlike Ockham, who argues that these phrases modify the expression "the power to do something (*posse aliquid*)." For example, if the phrase *de potentia ordinata* modifies the phrase "God can produce *a*," it means that God has the power to constitute *a* in being such that the proposition "God can produce *a*" is true and does not violate any law within God's ordained order. Thus God can produce *a* while preserving every law ordained or established by him (*omnem legem ordinatam ab eo vel statuam*). Further, if the phrase *de potentia absoluta* modifies the phrase "God can produce *a*," it means that God is a certain power (*Deus est quaedam potentia*) that can produce *a* in being without any other cause being added to it. However, God cannot constitute *a* in being while preserving every law of the ordained order because constituting *a* in being contradicts a law of the ordained order.

> Therefore, because that *a* be constituted in being by God and some other proposition included in some law ordained by God [taken together] imply that contradictories are true at the same time, God cannot constitute *a* in being and preserve that ordained law. Yet he has the power through which he can constitute *a* in being if he wishes to change the ordained law.[77]

Thus Holcot concludes by arguing that for God to exercise his absolute power would be for God to abolish or change the ordained law.

In sum, Ockham and Holcot agree that (a) in God there is only one power, which is identical to God himself, and (b) God does not act inordinately.[78] Thus one must always keep in mind that when speaking about God's absolute power, one is speaking about logical possibilities that do not (and will not) obtain *within* a given ordained dispensation because God is faithful to the statutes governing a particular ordained order.[79] Yet, as we saw for Holcot, it always remains within God's power to change from one ordained system to another.

Conclusion

Medieval theologians were well aware that the God revealed in the Old and New Testaments established different laws of salvation according to three distinct ages or dispensations. Within this basic framework, however, God seemingly required different things of different people in the various dispensations. For example, according to the old law, God required circumcision as revealed in the book of Genesis, while according to the new law, revealed in the Gospels, God no longer requires circumcision. Further, as argued earlier, Augustine provided the generally accepted theological framework for responding to this exegetical tension. What emerges in the theology of William of Ockham and, more centrally, Robert Holcot is a willingness to reevaluate this theological framework. Holcot, in particular, rethinks God's revelation in Scripture alongside other theological categories such as the three ages, the obligational arts, God's covenant with humanity, and the two powers. One final example will demonstrate just how intertwined these theological categories are with Ockham's and Holcot's interpretations of Scripture.

Both Ockham and Holcot conclude their definition of the two powers with a discussion of the relationship between the old law and the new law. Ockham writes:

> the Savior says in *John* 3: "Unless one is born again by water and the Holy Spirit, he cannot enter the kingdom of God." For since God is just as powerful now as he was before, and at one time there were some who entered the kingdom of God without any kind of baptism (as is clear in the case of children who, having been circumcised during the time of the law, died before they attained the use of reason), this is possible even now. Nonetheless, what was at that time possible in accordance with the

laws then instituted is not now possible in accordance with the law that has been instituted since that time, even though it is possible in an absolute sense.[80]

This passage demonstrates that Ockham understood the distinction between the two powers to be intimately related to the discussion of the two dispensations and ultimately Scripture.

Following Ockham, Holcot concludes his definition of the distinction between the two powers with a similar passage:

> From which it seems to follow that God cannot do something from his ordained power at one time that he can do at another time, and conversely; just as at one time he could not save a Jew without circumcision and yet in another way he could; and at one time he could have saved a man having the wherewithal and the opportunity for baptism, without baptism, and yet in another way from his ordained power now he cannot. Yet he can absolutely, because he can change and dispense with the enacted laws.[81]

Here Holcot argues that God ordained both dispensations, first ordaining the old law and subsequently ordaining the new law. Thus while the shift from one dispensation to another provided Holcot with a coherent explanation of how God's interaction with humanity changed over time, theologians such as Ockham and Holcot denied that God could act inordinately within either dispensation.

Holcot's distinction between God's absolute and ordained power is fundamentally a theological distinction.[82] Robert Holcot's theology is an attempt to take seriously the biblical witness to three distinct ages or covenants established by God. Holcot recognized that Scripture bears witness to numerous persons living in earlier ages and following diverse laws established by God (e.g., the natural law, the Mosaic law, the Gospel of Christ); the Scriptures also bear witness to the fact that God grants grace and saves many of these people (e.g., Adam, Abraham, Moses, Job). Interestingly, Holcot was unflinching in his acceptance of the fact that such persons are saved not according to their faith in the future death and resurrection of Jesus Christ but on account of their faithfulness to the law (or ordained system) established by God. The theological tools Holcot employs as a way of explicating this theology—that is, his obligational theology, covenantal theology, and distinction between God's absolute and ordained power—must be understood in the context of this particular theological vision. Restated, one could say that Holcot develops his obligational theology, covenantal theology, and the distinction between the two powers as a way of faithfully articulating the witness of Scripture.

2

ON FAITH

Introduction

Who by faith conquered kingdoms, wrought justice, obtained promises, stopped the mouths of lions, quenched the violence of fire, escaped the edge of the sword, recovered strength from weakness, became valiant in battle, put to flight the armies of foreigners.

(Hebrews 11:33–34).

Robert Holcot opens his academic career by challenging the traditional interpretation of Hebrews 11:33–34. Holcot identifies these verses as one of many biblical passages that support the commonplace and seemingly innocuous position that it is by faith that we are saved.[1] He begins his commentary on the *Sentences* with the question of whether or not a pilgrim existing in the state of grace can merit eternal life by assenting to the articles of faith.[2] Here he is asking about something more than merely acquiring God's favor or assistance. His concern is with the ultimate and final grace of divine acceptance (*acceptatio*), recognized as God's acceptance of a worthy (*dignus*) human being into the divine beatific life.[3] Likewise, his question shows that, by faith, he means a cognitive assent (yes or no) to a specific set of explicitly defined propositions. In other words, Holcot wants to know whether the writer of Hebrews really meant to say that it is through our cognitive assent to explicitly defined articles of faith that eternal life is earned, that is, that *kingdoms are conquered, justice is wrought, and promises are fulfilled*.

Holcot's choice to wrestle with this passage from Scripture can be traced to an impulse that defines his intellectual and pastoral career. In one of the opening arguments against the claim that one does indeed merit eternal life through assent to the articles of faith, Holcot asks us to consider the *vetula*. The *vetula*, or the illiterate but pious old woman, was a common medieval trope for identifying a sincere believer, who nevertheless cannot read the Bible or understand the complexities of subtle academic theology. If, Holcot reasons, we are obliged to believe the articles of faith in exchange for eternal life, then the *vetula* must either know all the articles of faith and therefore all of Scripture or at the very least be aware of all heresies so as to avoid them. In either case, the argument suggests that such a requirement is unreasonable and ultimately cruel.[4] Holcot extends the example by noting the unforgiving consequence that would follow for the *vetula*, who despite trying her very best (*facit quod in se est*), nevertheless errs due to an invincible ignorance. He then considers whether it would be sufficient to leave off the requirement that the *vetula* must know all of Scripture or all potential heresies and simply accept that it is enough for the *vetula* to believe what her parish priest teaches. But even here we can imagine a situation in which the parish priest teaches something false and the pious *vetula*, unaware of the error, is willing to die to uphold it. In such a case, Holcot wonders if God must still deny merit to the *vetula*, who with ardent zeal sacrifices her life for a falsehood.[5] His deeper concern is about the burden that such a direct and linear connection between belief and salvation places on the shoulders of human beings.

Holcot's focus on the pilgrim's best efforts (*facit quod in se est*) and the problem of an invincible ignorance (*ignorantia invincibilis*) are common themes in his work.[6] They are representative of a lifelong pastoral concern for the simple believer within the economy of salvation culminating in his own parish work in the final years of his life.[7] For the present, it is enough to point out that the debate over human agency and divine freedom in procuring salvation can be seen from two vantage points. The attempt to sever any absolute connection between human effort and merit (and divine *acceptatio*) can be seen negatively as a theological point of view that depicts God as capricious, untrustworthy, and a being for whom—in the words of Gordon Leff—"nothing is guaranteed."[8] However, it can alternatively be seen in a more positive light as a viewpoint that attempts to ensure God's capacity to relieve fallible humans of the burden of measuring up to a preestablished and seemingly inflexible order. Holcot frequently invokes God's freedom regarding the ultimate arbitration of *acceptatio* to remind his readers of God's powerful mercy when human beings somehow fail to measure up to the preordained system or *communis lex*.[9]

In this chapter our aim is to show Holcot's interest in the latter perspective as visible in his commentary on the *Sentences*. To show this, we focus on the two key concepts of merit and faith. In answering this question Holcot asks his readers to think about faith—and the cognitive assent associated with faith—in a new light. More specifically, he asks us to see faith as something deeper and prior to cognitive assent. Accordingly, as this chapter and the following chapter show, he invites us to think of cognitive assent as its own kind of grace and ultimately as a result or sign of a previous merit earned by the will.

Merit and Divine *Acceptatio*

Meanings of Merit

To follow Holcot's earliest discussions of the nature of merit, some background information about this complex medieval debate is required. Merit is a concept that can be broken down into two specific species, which are sometimes called merit *de congruo* and merit *de condigno*, reflecting a complex vision of the pilgrim's path toward salvation.[10]

The first kind of merit (*de congruo*) is typically understood as a kind of half-merit—a reward, one could say, for a human being's attempts to do good. As such, this kind of merit represents God's gracious recognition of the fact that one has done the very best one can (*facere quod in se est*), no matter how inadequate this action might be. However, this merit and approval in no way suggest that the pilgrim is worthy (*dignus*) of beatitude and salvation.

Heiko Oberman explains it this way:

> No one holds, however that man's moral efforts unaided by grace are fully meritorious of God's rewards (*de condigno*) but rather that they are

graciously regarded by God as half merits or merits in a metaphorical sense (*de congruo*). The relationship between God's bestowal of grace and sinful man's best efforts rests on "contracted" rather than "actual" worth and is a result of God's liberality in giving "so much for so little." Man's own efforts have, in this sense, "congruity," but not "condignity."[11]

Merit *de condigno* can therefore be defined in contrast to merit *de congruo*. Merit *de condigno* is reserved, as Oberman says, for those actions that are "fully meritorious of God's rewards." It is generally agreed that no one can perform such actions through their best efforts alone. One must exist in the state of grace, which begins through the sacrament of baptism and loss of original sin and which is restored through the sacrament of penance. Through this infusion of grace, one is informed by the theological virtue of charity (often described as the grace making one good or *gratia gratum faciens*). Having been informed by this grace and the habit of divine charity (operative grace), one's actions, still assisted by God (through his continually cooperating grace), can be worthy of merit (i.e., they can be *condignus*). However, this too remains in dispute. What kinds of actions are we talking about? And must God necessarily accept them if they meet the aforementioned conditions? As we will see, the Augustinian Hermit Hugolino of Orvieto, writing a little more than a decade after Holcot, thinks that one of these actions is an assent to the articles of faith with God's assistance. But this is precisely what is at issue for Holcot. Further, does someone who performs the required actions (whatever they might be) assisted by God's grace earn merit *de condigno* necessarily? Can God's acceptance be necessitated at this point? Ultimately, the question is whether human beings can turn God into their debtor, such that divine *acceptatio* is owed rather than freely given?[12]

Holcot's Conditions of Merit de Condigno

Holcot's early discussion of merit begins in article 2 where he offers a careful and sometimes perplexing description of the conditions of merit. As the fourth condition will reveal, Holcot is here concerned with the kind of merit that makes human beings fully worthy (*dignus*) of salvation and divine *acceptatio* (i.e., merit *de condigno*).

The first condition of earning merit is that a meritorious act must conform to an extant divine law.[13] From this condition alone, Holcot can conclude that human action alone is never sufficient to earn merit. A meritorious act requires a divine law: a prescribed rule that God wants human beings to follow. But it is possible that God could have allowed creatures to exist without any laws, commands, or counsel. This happens to be the state of existence proper to brute animals, and thus it is impossible for animals to earn the kind of merit now under consideration.[14]

The second condition is that the act must be *accepted* by God.[15] The intrinsic "goodness" or "badness" of an act does not force God to accept or reject it. Thus even if we are willing to grant that acts have a moral value internal to themselves, these values of intrinsic good and bad need to be separated from ideas of merit and demerit. Here we can see that even obedience to the divine law (the fulfillment of condition 1) is not a sufficient condition. Once again, Holcot aims to show that properly human acts, even acts assisted by God's cooperative grace, are not sufficient to make those acts meritorious, no matter how "good" they may be.

As a third condition Holcot states that no act is meritorious of eternal life unless it is an act of the free will (*actus liberi arbitrii*).[16] This condition is of particular importance since it is the source of two problems. The first problem is whether the voluntariness of an action is a necessary condition of merit, such that God is unable to accept any act as meritorious without this condition. Though it seems like a necessary condition here in article 2, Holcot adds an important qualification in article 4 for particularly pastoral reasons that have often gone unnoticed. But the second and more central problem is the extent to which acts of belief or faith can or cannot be counted as acts of free will.

The fourth condition is that the act be done within the state of grace.[17] This condition confirms once and for all that in this question Holcot is primarily concerned with merit *de condigno*. For here he is concerned with the reception of one kind of grace on the condition of possessing a prior cooperating grace. This condition seems to demand that in order to be capable of doing those voluntary acts that both conform to the precepts of divine law and that God may choose to accept, one needs a certain kind of assistance. However, here we need to be particularly careful in light of a later assertion made by Holcot, namely that human beings are capable of genuinely loving God above all else by means of their own natural powers (i.e., outside the state of grace and without divine assistance or the infusion of charity).[18] But again Holcot insists that despite the fact that this is a genuinely good act, it has been done outside of the state of grace and thus cannot earn merit.[19] Therefore, while being in the state of grace is not considered necessary to truly love God above all else, it is required to fulfill the meaning of the biblical command that presumes that one possesses the habit of charity and exists within the state of grace. It is only within this context that one's voluntary acts can become candidates for divine acceptance.

Given the importance of being within the state of grace, we should not neglect Holcot's seemingly off-the-cuff comment implying that human beings are able to procure this state of grace for themselves. He writes that when a pact exists between God and humanity, then entrance into the state of grace is *de facto* within human power.[20] Within the context of contemporary debates and arguments this is a rather remarkable statement that aligns Holcot with a group of thinkers interested in emphasizing God's covenantal relationship with his people.[21] The suggestion is that God is not constrained to act by the metaphysical arrangement of things but is obliged by his fidelity to an agreement he made, whereby he is willing to respond to the pilgrim's best efforts to reach him. To some this is a comforting idea, but to others it is cause for increased anxiety over the certainty of one's ultimate salvation. One can understand this latter concern by simply looking at Holcot's caveat that immediately follows. He argues that if God were to annul that pact, then the entrance to the state of grace would no longer lie within human power.[22] The concern—voiced by many of Holcot's critics[23]—is that he makes God sound capricious in that he promises to behave in one way but always reserves the prerogative to do something else. A charitable reading, however, might reflect on Holcot's reason for adding this caveat. Is he attempting to assert that annulling this pact is something God might actually do? Or is Holcot attempting to show God's fidelity by reminding us that he *could* annul this agreement yet nevertheless remains faithful to it?

Merit and Acceptance Outside the Common Law

Nowhere does Holcot's relentless concern to preserve God's freedom against any and all claims of debt become more visible than in article 4, where he immediately qualifies the description of merit he formulated in article 2. The particular qualification in question regards condition 3 (i.e., that God can only accept as meritorious those actions that are done voluntarily). In article 4 Holcot develops what appears to be a blatant contradiction to his earlier position. He states that it is actually possible for God to accept natural acts rather than voluntary acts as meritorious and, vice versa, to reject voluntary acts as meritorious while accepting natural acts.[24] What he says here has been pointed to as another example of the capricious nature of Holcot's radically free God. Meissner, for instance, identifies this claim as an example of God's fickle nature, which threatens the stability of the moral order.[25]

However, little attention has been paid to the reason for Holcot's qualification of his original position. Scholars such as Meissner overlook the particular argument that Holcot employs to justify the exception. The argument Holcot formulates highlights his belief that if God's ultimate freedom on this issue were not preserved, very unloving and unmerciful results would follow. Holcot writes that God accepts the "death of the innocents" (referring to young children killed by Herod's soldiers in Luke 2:16–18) as meritorious despite the fact that there was no use of free will. To deny that God could accept those who have not earned merit through their voluntary actions would be to condemn these innocent children to damnation.[26] Here again we can see why a strict insistence on the causal role played by human agency in the economy of salvation leads to a rather brutal consequence. On such a view, God becomes constrained to reject those who never had the opportunity to freely earn merit. This is another example of why it is often appropriate to label Holcot's views, or the motivations for his views, as pastoral. Amidst the harsh realities of medieval life, the loss of a child was a common experience. Holcot appears fixed on establishing and defending a picture of God according to which God can accept these children, even though such an acceptance falls outside the normal order of things.

The exceptional circumstances noted here—and the use of such language as "in the normal order of things"—prompts us to note one final distinction frequently employed by Holcot, both implicitly and explicitly throughout his corpus. This is a distinction between the common law and normal order of things (*de lege communi, de lege statuata*)[27] on the one hand and the exceptional, which falls outside of this order, on the other. This distinction corresponds to Holcot's use of the distinction between God's ordained and absolute power.[28] God's ordained power worked with the common order of things, but God's absolute power always preserved his ability to act outside this normal arrangement of things. In its most extreme form, the distinction is often illustrated through the following example: while Saint Peter ought to be saved and Judas ought to be damned according to the common law and God's ordained power, it nevertheless remains possible for God, through his absolute power, to damn Peter and save Judas.[29]

Older scholarship has tended to focus negatively on Holcot's articulation of God's absolute power as a sign of an unpredictable and unstable moral order.[30] But, as we have seen, this negative spin has been countered by the more recent work of Paul Vignaux and Heiko Oberman. Recall that Holcot's distinction between the common order of things governed by God's ordained power and the exception made possible by God's absolute power is used to emphasize God's faithful commitment to the established order despite his ability to do otherwise.[31] Moreover, as our examples have already shown, Holcot's use of the exceptional order is typically employed not to insist that God really plans to damn Peter and save Judas but rather to preserve God's ability to be merciful to those who have done their best and yet remain unable to live up to the requirements of the common law.[32]

In short, the contemporary consensus is that Holcot is content to discuss and debate an economy of salvation that operates within the common law guided by God's ordained power. But his text remains permeated by caveats designed to remind us that God never becomes our debtor and is always free to act differently. However, as we have also seen in his concern for the *vetula* and the slaughtered innocents, his appeals to the exceptional are not designed to describe a mean and spiteful God who arbitrarily rejects those who seek him. Rather, he typically invokes God's freedom and absolute power in order to reveal a compassionate and merciful God, who desires to accept even those who somehow fall short of the demands of the common law.

Faith and Cognitive Assent

With this basic picture of merit in place—merit both within and outside of the common order of things—we can consider how Holcot answers his original question and in the process redefines the primary meaning of faith.

He begins by (in)famously denying that faith, understood as cognitive assent, is an act that lies within our free power. Given that, in the normal order of things, Holcot believes the voluntary nature of an act is a condition of its meritoriousness, he offers a predictable answer to the main question. Since our actual assent to the given propositions of faith is not a free act, it neither earns merit nor functions as a necessary condition of God's acceptance.[33] His most revealing response comes when he says:

> If it is posited that someone both exists in the state of grace and assents [to the truths of faith], it should be said that such a person does earn merit, but not because he believes, nor even precisely because he wishes to believe, but because he wishes to believe and God accepts his act of belief as worthy of a reward.[34]

We sort out many aspects of this answer later, but chief among them is Holcot's desire to separate the cognitive act of belief from the desire to believe. Holcot eventually uses this distinction to insist on a new focal meaning of faith, and it is with this new meaning that he asserts that human beings can still be commanded to believe despite the fact that our cognitive assent is not a voluntary act.

However, before we turn to his explicit definition of the meaning of "belief," we must first consider his prior and foundational claim that the will plays no role in the act of cognitive assent. This happens to be one of the most controversial aspects of his position. It is not particularly hard to find sympathetic readers who will agree that God is the ultimate arbiter of merit, nor is it hard to find agreement that voluntary actions are usually at least a condition of merit, but the idea that faith cannot be counted as one of these "voluntary actions" is a much harder claim to swallow. It seems to contradict the common-sense understanding of faith as a choice to believe what reason does not prove or a decision to assent even when evidence does not compel us. As the opening quotation from Hebrews suggests, it flies in the face of many biblical verses that command us to believe. If faith is not a choice, how can the biblical text command us to do something that is not within our power to control?

Assent Without Reason

Understanding Holcot's justification of his controversial claim involves making a number of clarifications. The first clarification required is a more precise understanding of the nature of the claim itself. The claim is not about whether someone who already possesses the habit of faith is able to voluntarily bring about or elicit an act of faith from that acquired habit. In other words, he argues that someone who has already given assent to certain truths in the past (habitually) is able to choose to call that habitual assent to mind, rather than leaving it dormant. This amounts to little more than the ability to direct our cognitive attention, and Holcot fully concedes that this is an act within the power of the will.[35] This, however, is not what the question is asking.

Holcot is interested in the first act of belief. All habits are established through the frequent repetition of acts, and Holcot is concerned with the first act of assent from which the habit originates. He gives us an example: imagine someone who has not yet been habituated into the faith. Then imagine that this person hears someone preaching that God is both three and one and that whoever believes this will have eternal life.[36] His question, in short, is: for the sake of eternal life, can this person choose or command herself to believe the required proposition?[37]

Let us consider a different example. Imagine you are in a room with a table in the center. From all appearances the table is completely empty. However, in the room with you is a person of great wealth, and she tells you that if you can believe that there is a dinosaur on top of the table she will give you $1 million. Holcot's response is: try as you might, you can never actually force yourself to truly believe there is a dinosaur on top of the table. You can certainly lie and tell the person you assent to this proposition. But in reality, you are only lying and not really believing. Your true mental state would be quickly revealed, for example, if you were first asked to believe that a cliff does not exist where it obviously does and then asked to prove that belief by walking off the edge of the cliff in question.

In short, that someone could command herself to believe something by sheer will power is, for Holcot, simply phenomenologically false. He gives at least three reasons, the first of which is sufficient to understand the gist of his response:

> It is not in the power of any human being to freely form an opinion about a proposition doubtful to him; therefore, it is not in the power of a human being to believe an article of faith or assent to a proposition that is doubtful to him.[38]

According to Holcot, even our opinions are not within our direct volitional control. His reasoning relies on the traditional scholastic view that faith, despite sharing with opinion a lack of demonstrative evidence, distinguishes itself from opinion by possessing a higher level of certainty on par with the kind of certainty enjoyed by scientific knowledge. On this model, if we cannot even command ourselves to grant this lower, dubitable, type of assent (i.e., opinionative assent), then how in the world can we command ourselves to give the kind of assent that is defined by complete commitment and the absence of any doubt whatsoever?[39] By rejecting the role of volition in assent, Holcot is charting a path toward the ultimate dissociation of faith from both opinion and science. Here he is insisting that it is actually a category mistake to put faith alongside opinion and science. As we will see, Holcot views this as a mistake because the kind of faith commanded by the biblical text does not actually belong under the genus of cognitive assent at all.

An Objection: Hugolino of Orvieto

The position of Robert Holcot did not go unnoticed or unchallenged. Lecturing on the *Sentences* at Paris between 1348 and 1349, the Augustinian Hermit Hugolino of Orvieto accused Holcot of making a specious argument. A brief look at Hugolino's argument helps clarify Holcot's position and highlights what is at stake in the argument.

Hugolino argues that in order for someone to believe that "something is thus" (*sic esse*) there are at least two conditions that are required. First, it must be entirely rational (*omnino rationabile*) that something existing in this way is true (*sic verum esse*). Second, it is required that "God moves and anticipates and assists the will" without compelling it. If these conditions hold, Hugolino concedes that there is indeed freedom to assent that "something is thus." Hugolino concludes his discussion by arguing that if Holcot's position amounts to simply asserting that these conditions must be present before intellectual assent can be given, then he really proves nothing (*nihil probat*).[40] In other words, Hugolino argues, no one *actually* thinks that the will by itself has the power to command our intellect to believe in things that are patently false. However, when certain conditions are present—notably probable reasons that support (but do not demonstrate) the claim in question and God's cooperative assistance—then we can *choose* or *command* our intellect to assent with the degree of conviction usually attributed to genuine faith (i.e., something more than a mere opinion). In fact, the will *must* be involved for us to assent at this level, since there is not enough evidence to compel our intellect to assent.

Let us imagine our dinosaur scenario again, but this time remove those details that make the scenario so obviously false. Pretend that you are no longer present in the room in question but that your trusted friend is giving you an account of the situation. And instead of a dinosaur, let us say that an elephant is in the room. Add to this the fact that you really trust your friend. She has never lied to you before and has always proved trustworthy. Likewise, you know that a circus has recently come to town, which is known for its elephant show. Suddenly, the claim appears possible or reasonable, albeit unusual. However, it remains true that you do not see this truth for yourself, and your friend has not *demonstrated* the truth of this statement to the point that it cannot be doubted. It is in this situation, Hugolino says, that the will comes into play. One has a choice of whether or not to believe. The will can command the intellect to either assent or dissent.[41]

Types of Volition: Actus Elicitus Versus Actus Imperatus

Before considering how Holcot would respond, it is helpful to introduce the scholastic distinction between an act elicited by the will *(actus elicitus)* and an act commanded by the will *(actus imperatus)*. This is a distinction used by the contemporary philosopher Roderick Chisholm to explain different senses of freedom, though it has plenty of scholastic precedent.[42] An *actus elicitus* is an act internal to the will. It is an act that is accomplished and executed, simply by the act of willing. For Chisholm this constitutes a kind of metaphysical freedom. An *actus imperatus* is an act executed by some other power but commanded by the will. This might be moving one's arm, jumping up and down, or performing some other action. For Chisholm this is a kind of physical or political freedom.[43]

Consider the difference between (a) loving someone and (b) performing certain acts of love, like serving at a soup kitchen or caring for the sick. The first is a kind of elicited act. No one can impede one from accomplishing it;

all that is needed to accomplish it is the will to do so. The second, however, is an act commanded by the will but executed by another power. This kind of act requires not only volition but also power or ability. It demands the power necessary to execute the desired action. If a man were locked in a prison cell, he would be free to love whomever he wishes, but his freedom to perform acts of love would be inhibited.

Hugolino employs this distinction to clarify his position vis-à-vis Holcot:

> "a freely commanded [act]" [happens] in two ways. In one way, since the soul is able to elicit or not elicit ... the soul habituated into some demonstrative science is able to freely elicit an act of knowing and is also freely able to occupy itself with something else and, as a consequence, to not elicit [an act of knowing].[44]

First, Hugolino acknowledges our ability to orient our attention through an elicited act of the will. We have the power to direct our attention somewhere, just by deciding to direct our attention somewhere. So if we have already assented to something as true, by directing our attention to it, we can reactualize that assent. On the other hand, by withdrawing our attention, we can withhold our assent. However, as we have seen, Holcot acknowledged this possibility by indicating that his claim is not about executing an act from an already existing habit but about executing the first act from which a habit is successively built.[45] Hugolino concedes this point and turns to the second:

> In another way, it happens that when all the required things are posited and when something believable, [e.g.] A, has been apprehended, the soul is able to freely assent to this A, and is also able to dissent [from it], or to doubt [it], or to disbelieve [it].[46]

What Hugolino affirms is the ability of the will to command the intellect (*actus imperatus*) in nonevidential cases and to give an unhesitating assent when the aforementioned conditions are present. For him, this is what separates belief from scientific knowledge. In the latter case, the will lacks the ability to command the intellect to withhold assent or to give assent because evidence necessitates the intellect to act.[47] In sum, Hugolino wants to defend the role of the will in acts of faith. After all, if the will is not involved, how is this kind of assent to be distinguished from scientific assent, where the will is by definition not involved?

Holcot's Radical Claim

Holcot's response to the preceding objection is simply a more radical reiteration of his original claim. Not only is it not in our power to assent to things that are manifestly false (like a dinosaur on a table where no dinosaur is visible), but the will is not even involved with those beliefs about propositions that have a great deal of support yet nevertheless fall short of demonstrative or scientific status.

Holcot's position is radical because he seems to say that our opinions and beliefs are necessitated just as scientific knowledge is necessitated. That is, nondemonstrative arguments, like probable arguments and trustworthy testimony, have compelling force. In short, all assent, when assent is given, is compelled by what appears to the intellect as true.

We can see this clearly when Holcot responds to the objection that, if his opinion were correct, then reasons (probable reasons and authoritative testimony) would be able to force an unbeliever to become a believer, whether she *wanted* to or not. Surprisingly, Holcot has no problem with this consequence:

> Thus I concede that a man, no matter how much of an unbeliever he might be, [would assent] if strange miracles were performed in his presence for the sake of showing the truth of those articles. For example, imagine that the dead were raised as foretold in those articles, and those very dead were similarly to testify to the truths of those articles. [In this case] I say that this would necessitate the unbeliever to believe. Similarly, if it were to become evident to him that there was a multitude of people, true in words, honest in life, and skilled and circumspect in natural or naturally knowable things, and that this multitude was constantly asserting that certain things should be believed, things to which natural reason neither does nor can reach at present. Then I say that it would indeed be possible to necessitate such an unbeliever of sound reason to assent to those things that should be believed. For to this end miracles and probable reasons, *which are sufficient for causing faith*, are useful. (our emphasis)[48]

In sum, let us imagine the difference between Holcot's analysis of your response to your friend's story about the elephant and Hugolino's counter. For Holcot, it may be true that through an *actus elicitus* you can turn your attention toward or away from a given matter or state of affairs. You can refuse to listen to your friend, after all. But if you listen, the resulting propositional-attitude you have with respect to your friend's story is not in your power. Her status of trustworthiness, the known circumstances, and the inherent plausibility of the account are all involved in how a proposition appears to your mind. It is the nature of this appearance that determines whether we dissent, assent, or cannot make up our mind. But we have no ability to volitionally control how a proposition appears or how our intellect responds to that appearance.

For Hugolino, this is where Holcot is wrong. Belief is distinguished from knowledge because, in cases of belief, our will has the final say. Hugolino makes it sound as though, faced with probable reasons and testimony, we still have to make a choice to believe our friend, or at least to believe with the conviction proper to religious faith. And if we have the freedom to assent, this means we also have the choice not to believe.

Defining Natural Reason

Before going a step further to see how Holcot deals with objections to his belief that assent to a proposition (whether opinion, faith, or knowledge) is not in our power, let us look at an immediate threat of internal inconsistency due to another of Holcot's controversial theses. His bold and infamous claim is that the articles of faith are not just above (*supra*) natural reason but are opposed (*contra*) to natural reason.

Why does this thesis threaten an internal contradiction? We have just seen that Holcot believes reasons or arguments, demonstrative or probable, affect our assent. The suggestion, then, that the articles of the faith are not just unable to be demonstrated by reason but actually contradict reason (i.e., they contradict what we know demonstrably to be true) makes it hard to see how our intellect, by itself, could ever assent to the articles of faith. The situation becomes somewhat akin to asking someone to believe that a dinosaur is on the empty table directly in front of him. Unlike the situation where you are being told by a trusted friend about the presence of an elephant in an unusual place, here you are being asked to assent to a proposition that is not only unlikely but is in manifest contradiction to your knowledge that dinosaurs do not exist as well as your experience that there is nothing on the table. If anything, Holcot's claim that the articles of faith contradict natural reason makes it seem more likely that he would argue for the opposite of the position we have just seen him defend. If the articles of the faith contradict reason, then would not the only recourse to assent be a pure command of the will, an absolute leap of faith? Yet we have seen that Holcot defends the very opposite position. It is the coupling of these two positions that has led Holcot's contemporaries[49] and modern readers to accuse him of inconsistency.[50]

To see how Holcot can avoid the inconsistency he is accused of, we must look at the rather unusual way he invokes the idea of natural reason. The easiest way to understand what Holcot means when he says that the articles of faith are "opposed to natural reason" is to look at the objections to his position and his subsequent responses. Four specific objections are listed in question 1, article 6.

The first objection attempts to show that Holcot's position leads to absurd consequences. The absurdity in this case is that, if the articles of faith were opposed to reason, the conclusions of a rational demonstration would be false. This consequence is considered absurd because a demonstration is defined in Aristotelian and scholastic philosophy as precisely that which can be trusted to be true. In the words of Aristotle, the conclusion of a demonstration signifies the recognition of a reality *that cannot be otherwise*.[51] The reasoning is fairly straightforward:

> P1. Everything that opposes faith is false.
> P2. The conclusion of natural reason [understood in the argument as a genuine demonstration] is contrary to faith.
> C. Therefore, the conclusion of a demonstration is false.[52]

Holcot's response lies in denying the consequence. That is, his response does not focus on disputing any one particular premise in isolation but rather on an equivocation that corrupts the reasoning and leads to a faulty conclusion.

Premise 2 identifies the "conclusion of natural reason" with the conclusion of a genuine demonstration. Holcot views this assimilation as the source of the problem, ultimately providing us with an idiosyncratic definition of natural reason. He writes: "therefore, what is concluded through natural reason, as I have said elsewhere often and frequently, is not a demonstration, but a sophism."[53] In this statement, he shows that in his mind "natural reason" and a "genuine (or true) demonstration" cannot be identified. The more common way to untangle the confusion would be to claim that the sophism in question is not a genuine instance of natural reason but only a kind of simulacrum. Holcot, instead, identifies natural reason with whatever "seems" or "appears" to be true and identifies a genuine demonstration more narrowly as only what is actually true. Thus he continues by arguing that a "demonstration concluding the opposite of faith, even if its error is not able to be exposed by a person of science [i.e., an expert], should be thought of as sophistical."[54] Holcot's advice is that anything that appears to be a demonstration but opposes faith should be distrusted. But, at the same time, what appears to be true, whether it turns out to be true or not, should be considered an instance of "natural reasoning."

From this response to the first objection we can conclude that Holcot's opinion is less radical than it first appears and less inflammatory than his successors make it seem.[55] Few thinkers are unwilling to admit that we make mistakes in reasoning. We can all recognize moments in which something appeared to be demonstratively true but actually turned out to be otherwise.[56]

Holcot, however, stands out as unique because of his desire to identify "natural reason" with what "appears" to be a true demonstration, rather than the more customary route of identifying "natural reason" only with those instances of human thinking that represent sound and valid thought. On this latter interpretation, sophisms would not count as actual instances of "natural reason."

Holcot, therefore, does not think that the articles of faith are opposed to genuine demonstrations. But he thinks that they are opposed and incompatible with those "sophisms" that he identifies with natural reason and that human beings often mistakenly believe to be genuine demonstrations. Few other scholastics would disagree with the substance of what Holcot is saying here, but most would express it in different terms.

In his response to the second stated objection, we can see the same terminological shift. Here he responds to the familiar Thomistic line that "grace does not destroy nature, but perfects nature."[57] Everything depends on what one means by "nature." Is "nature" meant to indicate what is *in principle* possible for the unerring natural intellect? Or is it something else?

Holcot pinpoints this ambiguity in his response by drawing attention to the two distinct roles for faith. If we understand faith as a supplement or addition over and above the proper functioning of natural reason, then it is indeed possible to think of faith as the perfection and perfect complement to nature.[58] But this supplemental knowing is not why we have faith in the present. He writes: "faith is instituted in the present time more for believing than for knowing."[59] Nature, understood as our present actual use of reason, is prone to error and therefore is often opposed by the correction that faith offers. Thus Holcot can, in the same breath, declare that faith both opposes nature and perfects nature:

> Therefore [faith] *does not perfect nature*, but rather the opposite, for nature, owing to the fact that it is imperfect without the grace of faith, errs or is able to err. And therefore *faith, by removing this error, perfects nature*.[60]

It would be nice if Holcot were a bit more precise here. Nevertheless, the ability of Holcot to seemingly contradict himself speaks to the ambiguous meaning of the word "nature": (a) nature as the actual reasoning habits of error prone humans or (b) nature as what is in principle possible within the limits of human natural power. With respect to the former, faith does indeed oppose nature, but with respect to the latter, faith and nature are perfectly compatible. This is a nuance glossed over in most of the subsequent presentations of Holcot's position.[61]

Holcot's response to the third and fourth objections continues along the same lines. The third objection states that, on Holcot's view, "natural reason" must necessitate unbelief.[62] The absurdity follows because demonstrations compel the intellect. But if these conclusions oppose faith, then the knower is compelled to assent to what opposes faith. Holcot's now predictable response is that those "demonstrations" that appear to compel us to assent to what contradicts faith are only sophisms that do not actually compel the intellect that can see the error. It is only the error of our reason that makes the sophism *appear* compelling.[63]

The fourth objection states that if natural reason errs, God is somehow responsible for the error.[64] Here we once again confront two senses of "nature." We have an "ideal" sense of nature as that which God originally created, and we have a "real" sense of nature representing a wounded and fallen nature.[65] The lesson is that faith does not contradict or oppose the first "ideal" sense of nature, but it does contradict and oppose the flawed and error-prone sense of natural reason. God, of course, can take credit for the "ideal" sense of nature but can point to human sin as the cause of the "real" sense of nature.

In response to the internal inconsistency noted by Albert Lang and others, Holcot can now offer a reply. He can maintain that the claims of faith often contradict what our error-prone natural reason mistakenly views as a genuine demonstration. But while holding this position, he is not obligated to hold that the only way faith becomes possible is through a choice of the will to overlook what appears to be true. On the contrary, Holcot can consistently maintain that the only way the intellect can assent to the claims of faith is when the claims themselves appear so true and convincing that one is compelled to see one's own natural reason as error prone and deficient. Once again, the key to belief (understood as cognitive assent) is how a proposition or state of affairs appears, and equally important is Holcot's claim that the manner of this appearance remains outside the control of the will.

The Meaning of Belief

With this potential internal inconsistency reconciled, the greatest external challenge to Holcot's position still remains. His position mandates that reason alone could cause someone unfaithful to become faithful. But this mandate raises two related concerns. First, if it is not in our power to believe and if reason alone compels assent, then why are Christians again and again commanded to believe? What has happened to the moral character of faith? It is common to believe that faith comes with a kind of merit, but this is in large part built on the assumption that faith is a decision that lies within the power of the will. It is for this very reason that scientific assent is devoid of merit, whereas faith is thought to be meritorious. Second, if belief is not in our power, to what extent is right belief important? If we cannot be praised or blamed for right belief, do infidelity and heresy become meaningless terms?

To have a complete position Holcot must be able to make sense of the many commands "to believe" within the biblical text and the Christian tradition at large. He develops a response by rigorously defining different senses of belief. According to Holcot, to believe or to have faith is said by the saints in three ways.

1. The most common (or broadest) definition is "to assent that reality is just as the proposition signifies it to be."[66] This definition applies as much to pure opinion as it does to the assent procured through a scientific demonstration.[67]
2. The second, stricter, definition is "to assent to propositions whose truth is only known through someone else's testimony."[68]

It is in this sense that we speak about belief as any kind of assent to a proposition about which we do not have a demonstration. However, this is still a broad category of belief that applies to all non-demonstrative beliefs and not simply religious beliefs. Thus belief in the historical resurrection through the testimony of others could be discussed in the same way that we speak of belief in the existence of a city we have never been to on the basis of the testimony of others.

3. The third and most strict definition adds the familiar religious overtones to the notion of faith. This definition reads: "to assent to what has been revealed by God and the testimony of miracles *and to wish to live and work according to these things*" (emphasis ours).[69]

It is here, in this third definition, that Holcot introduces a moral and volitional element. The volitional element, however, is not found in a command of the will to assent to what is supported by probable reasons (this is a mere belief in the second sense) but in the desire to live according to what the individual has come to believe. Thus it is through this definition that we can understand the command to believe, and we can restore the idea of merit to the notion of belief.[70] Peculiar to Holcot is the idea that this command is not really a command to *assent* to the articles of faith but a command to *desire to live according to them*.[71] It is this desire, and not the cognitive act of assent, that lies within our power and makes the pilgrim a candidate for divine acceptance.

He makes this point plain when he rephrases this third definition of belief: meritorious belief is "to wish to assent, or to accept assent, or to rejoice about assent."⁷² The volitional element of belief really has more to do with the disposition or response of the individual who is compelled to assent. How does one respond to what appears to be true? Is she disappointed, frustrated, or reluctant to follow the consequences of this appearance? Or is she happy, joyful, and eager to live out the implications of this apparent truth? This attitude is what lies within human power, and the biblical commands to believe are really commands to respond appropriately to one's natural (non-voluntary) act of assent.

It is here that we can understand how Holcot's notion of faith is distinguished from scientific knowledge. For Holcot, faith cannot be distinguished from scientific knowledge in the usual way—that is, by noting that the assent of faith is assisted by the will while the assent of scientific knowledge is not. Instead, faith and scientific knowledge are better differentiated by what is required in order to act on those respective beliefs. For example, it takes little courage to act on a belief that a person demonstrably knows cannot be otherwise—for example, a willingness to walk across a bridge that one knows *demonstrably* or scientifically will not fail. However, in the case of a bridge that someone believes will bear him on account of an apparently trustworthy but non-demonstrative testimony, the decision to walk across that bridge takes an extra effort, an effort we can reasonably assign to the will.

For Holcot, it is this act of belief that, in the normal course of things, both requires the cooperative assistance of divine grace (*meritum congruum*) to be achieved and, on completion, approaches a merit (*meritum condignum*) worthy (*dignum*) of salvation (*divina acceptatio*). It is undoubtedly this kind of eagerness to believe and to act on that belief that Holcot has in mind when he writes:

> If it is posited that someone assents and that person exists in the state of grace, it should be said that such a person does earn merit, but not because he believes, nor even precisely because he wishes to believe, but because he wishes to believe and God accepts his act of belief as worthy of a reward.⁷³

The (Un)Importance of Orthodoxy

Holcot's reinterpretation of religious belief as an aggregate composed of discrete parts certainly explains how he can both accept that the many biblical commands "to believe" are legitimate and, in the same breath, deny that direct assent to the articles of faith is something that the human will can command of the intellect. Holcot's insistence that the meritorious element of faith belongs to the attitude we have toward what appears to us as religious truth (rather than the assent itself) suggests that the two elements can be separated. In this way, it would appear that, we are morally or religiously culpable for the kind of attitude or disposition we have toward apparent religious truth but not culpable for the assent we give. Thus right belief per se is morally or salvifically unimportant, since it is not something within our power.

This concern must have also been an issue for Holcot's contemporaries since it is an objection Holcot explicitly acknowledges and attempts to combat.[74] But it is also a lingering concern with which later readers would continue to take issue.[75] The objection states that if Holcot were correct, then infidelity and heresy would not be a sin.[76] Holcot's response results in a redefinition of infidelity and heresy.

"Infidelity," he says, "is *to not wish* to believe what the Church believes."[77] Not stopping here, he immediately gives an alternative definition. "[Infidelity is] to not wish to live according to faith, that is according to the precepts of faith."[78] Still not content with these two definitions, he provides one further statement of clarification: "Thus, to hate the faith, customs, and rites of Christians is the sin of infidelity."[79] The consequence of this definition is that someone could be identified as an "infidel" who assents to all the correct propositions of faith. And, conversely, someone could be described as faithful who does not assent to the propositions of true religion but who wishes desperately to live according to the truths of the faith, whatever they might be.

Lo and behold, this is the ultimate conclusion that Holcot reaches:

> But not every error in these matters of faith is the sin of infidelity or heresy. Let us imagine that someone wishes to believe in general all the things which the Holy Spirit revealed to the Church as things that ought to be believed, but that under this faith [the third sense of belief] believes [the second sense of belief] by mistake that this faith contains something contrary to one of the subtle articles, such that in his explicit faith not everything is held [rightly], and as a consequence adheres to this mistaken proposition. [In this case] despite this mistake, as long as he has a

soul eager to believe only those things that the Church believes, such a person is not a heretic or an infidel.[80]

Holcot's pastoral concern is uncovered in his generous account of fidelity. There is a particular focus on the intention of the believer and a tendency to look past or even ignore the execution of that intention. For Holcot, the results of that intention are not in our power. If we are blessed with a quick intellect and the opportunity to witness compelling miracles, then we are fortunate but not morally praiseworthy. We earn merit not by assenting to the right propositions but by our intention to believe rightly and more specifically by our eagerness to subject ourselves to the apparent articles of faith. When the Apostle James notes (2:19), "even the demons believe, and tremble," Holcot's main point is made. Right belief is of course desirable, but it is not meritorious. Nor is it the central issue. For Holcot, it is how one approaches belief and how one responds to that belief that makes the difference.

Conclusion

It is here that Holcot's position on right intention and right belief and his position on merit and grace come full circle—a connection that will become our explicit theme in chapter 3. For Holcot, the intention of an eager and compliant will corresponds to Holcot's notion of "doing one's best" (*facere quod in se est*). However, as we have already seen, Holcot's notion of merit *de congruo* suggests that God responds graciously to those who do what they are capable of to the best of their ability. The implication is that those who are desirous of right belief are usually rewarded with right belief. But in this Holcot has reversed the commonly understood order of things. Holcot began by questioning the assumption that right belief was required for merit and salvation. In this light, belief was viewed as a kind of means to a different end. But when right belief is viewed as part of God's gracious response to our right intention, orthodoxy appears to be part of the end rather than a simple requirement one must meet in order to achieve salvation. The gift of orthodoxy is thus not a precondition of participation in divine life but part of the actual participation. One does not earn an invitation into this participation by acquiring right belief for oneself. Rather it comes from a volitional disposition that mirrors a kind of supplication. From Holcot's viewpoint, the person desirous of right belief is an example of the pilgrim whom the Gospels depict as *knocking at the door*. Right belief, therefore, rather than being a condition of merit, is a part of God's gracious response to every genuine seeker.

3

HUMAN KNOWLEDGE AND THE DIVINE NATURE

Introduction

In the previous chapter we learned that from the outset of Holcot's career he wanted to redefine belief and focus on the "merit of belief" found, not in the act of the assent, but in the attitude of the will toward those propositions that appear to be articles of true religion. This position, however, raises a number of questions. A cluster of these questions revolves around how the propositions of faith "appear to us." If we are not responsible for our assent, are we still responsible for how things appear to us, or is this too completely out of our hands? Stated differently, what is the use of intellectual effort regarding the matters of faith, and how far can natural intellectual powers take us?

Holcot begins to broach these questions when he discusses, in question 4 of book 1, whether or not it is naturally knowable that God should be loved above all else, and in question 5 of book 1, whether God is three distinct persons. Few places in Holcot's corpus have done as much to earn him the reputation of being a "skeptic" and "fideist" as questions 4 and 5. For this reason, we need to approach these questions with some background.

The charge that Robert Holcot is a skeptic or fideist is a modern accusation, and Hester Gelber has traced the historiography back to Carl von Prantl's *History of Logic in the West* published in the late nineteenth century.[1]

Prantl argued that the *Centiloquium theologicum*—which he attributed to Ockham—supported the incommensurability of theology and philosophy.[2] Further, he linked this development with the writings of Robert Holcot. He was the first to observe Holcot's twofold logic and the fact that Holcot denied the universal applicability of Aristotelian logic.[3] A similar approach, Gelber observes, is found in the writings of Konstantyn Michalski, who in the early twentieth century followed Prantl in labeling Holcot a skeptic.[4]

This picture of Holcot was further complicated when Philotheus Boehner argued in 1944 that the much maligned *Centiloquium* was written by Robert Holcot and not William Ockham. Boehner argued that "this so-called Ockhamist . . . denies the *distinctio formalis* in any sense, and also denies the formal [i.e., universal] character of Logic."[5] While Boehner succeeded in his vindication of Ockham, he did so by reassigning potential authorship of the *Centiloquium* to Holcot. Recently Hester Gelber has argued that Arnold Strelley is the author of the *Centiloquium*.[6] However, in the intervening period, the attribution of the *Centiloquium* to Holcot supported the preexisting narrative that he was a radical skeptic.[7]

A turn in Holcot scholarship began to emerge in the mid-twentieth century with the publications of Alois Meissner,[8] and, more significantly, Heiko Oberman, Heinrich Schepers, and Fritz Hoffmann.[9] Heiko Oberman confronted the charge of skepticism, following Meissner in arguing that "the supernatural articles of faith are *not contrary to reason* but go *beyond reason*."[10] This was evident in the previous chapter where we discussed Holcot's view of the articles of faith and their relationship to natural reason.[11] Further, in a series of articles, Heinrich Schepers argued that the radical nominalism (i.e., skepticism) one finds in Oxford around 1330 is actually an anti-Ockhamist movement and that Robert Holcot, in particular, was often a defender of Ockham's positions against radical anti-Ockhamists such as William Crathorn.[12] This puts distance between the more radical anti-Ockhamists and those who defended the positions of the Venerable Inceptor and links Holcot with a more moderate tradition.

The most precise and historical renarration of Holcot's thought can be found in Hoffmann, who argues that "what appears to be 'Fideism' in some Masters of the fourteenth century must be understood as resistance to the foreign infiltration of philosophy on theological thinking."[13] First, Hoffmann correctly argues that terms such as fideism (*Fideismus*) and skepticism (*Skeptizismus*) are only problematically—and one could add anachronistically—applied to late medieval authors.[14] The unhelpful label of "skeptic" is something that we return to throughout this book. Second, Hoffmann begins the process of reading Holcot historically and providing a positive understanding of his concept of the "logic of faith" as fundamentally rational.[15] On Hoffmann's reading, Holcot provides a rational basis for both theological and philosophical thought, such that there is no bifurcation of reason from faith or philosophy from theology. In fact, Hoffmann defends Holcot's logical approach to theological method, arguing that "Holcot's logical method [does not lead] to a destruction of theology, but instead certain theological insights emerge even sharper."[16] These insights of Hoffmann have led to a reevaluation of Holcot's thought. In what follows we contribute to this reevaluation by considering what Holcot has to say about the possibility of human knowledge of God's existence and the divine nature.

Human Reason and the Existence of God

Hypothetical Knowledge of God

Holcot's unique approach to the classical questions of natural theology is evident in the peripheral way he approaches the question of God's existence. While most medieval *Sentences* commentaries involve lengthy questions devoted to proofs for God's existence and the possibility of such proofs, Holcot's commentary is distinctive for approaching this issue tangentially and relatively briefly.

The main question in which this discussion takes place asks whether God alone should be enjoyed, a topic closely related to book 1, distinction 1 of Peter Lombard's *Sentences*.[17] Holcot divides the question into four parts.[18] The question of the proof of God's existence is broached in part 2. The issue of enjoyment of God in this life faces two obstacles. The first question treats whether or not human beings are able, by means of their natural ability, to love God above everything else. The second question asks whether or not human beings, by means of natural reason, are able to demonstrate that God should be loved above everything else. The first question is about the human capacity to execute its intention and the second about whether or not human beings can prove, by means of natural reason, that God should be loved above all else.

Holcot's official answer to the latter epistemological question is that categorically speaking we cannot demonstrate that God should be loved above all else. But his reasoning for this depends on the prior indemonstrability of God's existence. For Holcot it follows obviously that if we cannot prove that God exists, then "it is not able to be demonstrated that he should be loved above all else."[19] However, Holcot qualifies this final conclusion. Consistent with what we see throughout this book, Holcot actually believes that there is a strong place for the use of natural reason and natural investigation in matters of faith. However, for him this positive use of reason can only occur after we begin within the context of a firm faith. In this case, Holcot argues that while categorically it is impossible to prove that God should be loved above all else, natural reason can demonstrate the hypothetical conclusion that, if God exists, then it can be proved that humans should love God above all else.

Holcot's brief argument for the categorical indemonstrability of the fact that God should be loved above all else begins from a kind of analogy. It points out that any categorical affirmative proposition whose subject is "implicative" of something false (e.g., "All unicorns are mortal") can never be true. In the same way, any categorical affirmative proposition whose subject is implicative of something that is only believed can never be a naturally evident proposition.[20] Holcot—evidencing a certain form of nominalism here that denies that anything true can be known about a class if there are no members of that class—affirms the analogy by claiming, if there were no human beings, it would be false to say that a human being is a rational animal. Likewise, if there were no donkeys in the world, it is false to say that an ass runs because the subject of the proposition implies something false. In the same way, Holcot explains that if propositions like "God should be loved above all else" and "God is the first cause" or "God is the first mover" contain a subject implicative of belief, then clearly it cannot be demonstrated (i.e., made naturally evident) that God should be loved above all else.

Needless to say, the main burden of this proof lies in the minor premise— to show that the proposition that God should be loved above else really does contain a subject whose existence requires belief. Holcot's support for this important claim is unfortunately underwhelming. In nine lines, he explains that if we replace the term "God" for the definition of that term (*quid nominis*), we will understand that we are speaking about, at the very least, an infinite being, and if we believe in the Christian God—a much more demanding concept—it is left implied that such a concept clearly cannot be grasped, and therefore its existence must be believed.

While we will see later in our discussion of Holcot's assessment of Anselm's ontological argument that he has a bit more to say about why the existence of such a concept must be implicative of belief, it is important to momentarily set that aside and follow Holcot where he leads us. In this case, he guides us to the second conclusion, which asserts that once God's existence is believed, natural reason can prove (albeit conditionally) that God should be loved above all else. The thrust of the argument is that when God is understood as the Christian God, who intelligibly creates and freely conserves all things, and when we believe that this God exists, then reason can move forward to know that it necessarily follows that God should be loved above all else. Strictly speaking this is not a demonstrated truth because it relies on a believed supposition. However, Holcot calls it a conditional or hypothetical proof that reason can achieve once certain suppositions are in place.[21]

The larger and more important lesson here lies in how Holcot's shift from what is categorically demonstrated to what is conditionally demonstrated is illustrative of his larger valuation of reason. Again and again we see in Holcot a penchant to first demand the reasoner to be humbled by faith and to refrain from seeing human reasoning as the measure of possibility. At the same time, while many commentators have been tempted into thinking that Holcot has no room left for reason, Holcot shows that once reason is founded on the truths of faith, there is valuable intellectual work left to be done. Here the fact that God should be loved above all else is a truth that believers can procure and derive through thoughtful intellectual effort. In this sense, Gelber is correct that "Holcot's view of the relation between faith and reason was very much in the tradition of Anselm of faith seeking understanding."[22] While Holcot is quite cautious about what natural reason can achieve on its own, he, like Anselm, in no way thinks that this means there is no place for investigation into the truths of faith. This emphasis on the grounding of rational activity in prior belief is something that comes to the surface again in Holcot's analysis of Anselm's ontological argument.

Anselm Reconsidered

Anselm of Canterbury, the eleventh-century Benedictine monk, developed a complex argument for the existence of God in the second chapter of the *Proslogion*.[23] Anselm's argument (i.e., the *ratio Anselmi*)[24] has received numerous reconstructions; however, it is best here to recall his own words from chapter 2:

> Even the Fool, then, is forced to agree that something-than-which-nothing-greater-can-be-thought exists in the mind, since he understands this when he hears it, and whatever is understood is in the mind. And surely that-than-which-a-greater-cannot-be-thought cannot exist in the mind alone. For if it exists solely in the mind, it can be thought to exist in reality also, which is greater. If then that-than-which-a-greater-cannot-be-thought exists in the mind alone, this same that-than-which-a-greater-*cannot*-be-thought is that-than-which-a-greater-*can*-be-thought. But this is obviously impossible. Therefore there is absolutely no doubt that something-than-which-a-greater-cannot-be-thought exists both in the mind and in reality.[25]

Anselm's conclusion, of course, is that God exists both in the mind and in reality.

Anselm's argument was largely ignored in the twelfth century, only to be recovered by thirteenth- and fourteenth-century theologians. This process of recovery can be traced back to Alexander Nequam (†1217), who defended a version of the argument in the *Speculum speculationum*.[26] Positive articulations and variations of Anselm's argument can be found in William of Auxerre (†1231), Alexander of Hales (†1245), Richard Fishacre (†1248), Bonaventure (†1274), and others.[27] However, not all thirteenth-century scholastics were convinced by the argument, and one can trace a more critical reception of the argument in thinkers such as Richard Rufus (†c. 1260) and Thomas Aquinas.[28] In question 4 of book 1 of his commentary on the *Sentences*, Holcot joins those who reject the argument.[29]

In tracing the history of the reception of the *ratio Anselmi*, Holcot reproduces a summary of the argument for the existence of God as found in chapter 2 of the *Proslogion*, a discussion of the "Lost Island" objection found in Gaunilo's *Liber pro insipiente* (*Book in Defense of the Fool*), and Anselm's response to the objection.[30] Holcot, as one can anticipate, argues that the original argument of Anselm fails.[31]

Holcot begins his response to the *ratio Anselmi* by stating that Anselm's argument is sophistical and errs in the very truth (*in rei veritate*) of the matter.[32] This is clear, he thinks, because it is no more possible to understand the meaning of the term "that which nothing greater can be thought (*id quo maius cogitari non potest*)" than it is to understand an infinite magnitude.[33] Holcot is not arguing that an infinite magnitude (or Anselm's definition of God) is logically impossible, for example, as a round square is, but that one cannot have experiential knowledge of either. Thus Holcot argues that by means of natural reason alone one cannot understand the very terms of the argument. This is similar to Holcot's previous claim that in propositions such as "God exists," "God is the greatest good," or "God is an infinite being," the subject terms of the premises cannot be known by reason alone but only through faith. That is, the terms "God" and "that which is greater than can be thought" are both subject terms that can only be known through faith and not by means of natural reason.

However, aside from this basic epistemic claim, Holcot formulates a somewhat original response to Anselm's argument. Holcot argues that one can, by a similar argument, prove that "something better than God (*aliquid melius Deo est*)" exists. Following a similar logic to Anselm, Holcot argues that when we understand the term "something better than God," we have a concept of something better than God in our minds. However, this "something better than God" cannot exist in our minds alone (*tantum in intellectu tuo*), for if it did not exist in reality (*in re*), then "the [something] better than God is not better than God (*melius Deo non est melius Deo*)."[34] Therefore, there must exist in the mind and in reality (*in re*) something better than God.

While Holcot's argument from parity is perhaps initially persuasive, Ian Logan is correct in offering a rejoinder to Holcot. He observes that in Holcot's reconstruction of the argument, he fails to note that part of the definition of God, according to Anselm, is that he is "whatever it is better to be than not to be."[35] Thus there can be no such thing as "something greater than God," because otherwise God would be that thing. That said, it seems Holcot could retort by claiming that one can always imagine a greater being such that there is an infinite regression of maximal greatness. While such an argument would perhaps not satisfy a defender of the *ratio Anselmi*, Holcot sees it as support for the broader argument that the terms "God" and "that which is greater than can be thought" are beyond the limits of human reason and are therefore implicative of belief.

Intellectual Effort and the Search for God

This leads us back to the charge that Holcot is a skeptic and a fideist. Worse yet, he is considered someone who does not see a place for intellectual effort in the quest for God. This is a common charge.[36] However, as we have seen, Holcot thinks there is a place for reason in the investigation of the divine, once placed within the context of faith. Similarly, Holcot shows that there are reasons to value intellectual effort other than simply for its demonstrative or scientific achievement.

Oberman made precisely this point when responding to the broad and unnuanced charge of fideism. He begins with a puzzle. If Holcot is the skeptic he is claimed to be with respect to a natural knowledge of God, what explains his fascination with the work of Pagan philosophers such as Hermes Trismegistus, Plato, or Aristotle? Hermes Trismegistus, for example, was a pagan philosopher who recognized that humanity ought to give thanks to God because everything comes from God.[37] Holcot values the thought of Hermes and references him positively, despite the fact that Holcot denies that God can be demonstrated. The question arises in this case: what, according to Holcot, is the source of Hermes' knowledge of God? Further, if Hermes cannot demonstrate the existence of God, what does he have to offer the Christian theologian regarding the knowledge of God?

With respect to the former question, Fritz Hoffmann is correct to draw our attention to Holcot's discussion of Romans 1:19–20:

> because that which is known of God is manifest to them. For God has manifest it to them. For the invisible things of Him, from the creation

of the world, are clearly seen, being understood by the things that are made; his eternal power also, and divinity: so that they are inexcusable.[38]

This text, as Holcot understood it, refers to those who have not been given direct knowledge of God through the Scriptures. Thus the "them" in the first verse could potentially be read as referring to the Philosophers, such that Paul is arguing that the Philosophers have knowledge of God that originates from natural reason and, as Holcot says, from knowledge of creatures (*ex cognitione creaturarum*). Holcot rejects this simplistic reading of the passage and argues that the knowledge philosophers have—by means of the investigation of the natural order—is not such that it can lead to a demonstrative argument for the existence of God.[39]

However, Holcot complicates the picture by arguing that God will reward their intellectual and moral effort through a natural and revealed knowledge.[40] This is evident in his response to an objection examining how it is that the Gentiles seemed to follow the law without having knowledge of the law. The objection[41] appeals to Romans 2:14, which states: "For when the Gentiles, who have not the law, do by nature those things that are of the law; these, having not the law, are a law to themselves."[42] The Apostle Paul claims that these Gentiles followed the law, but the divine law or the Mosaic law demands that God be loved above all else. If the Gentiles really were able to follow this law, then they must have been able to recognize this precept through their natural reason alone. Thus the argument claims a space for a genuine natural theology, wherein natural reason can provide knowledge of certain divine laws.

As Oberman points out, Holcot's reply is not to deny the major premise. That is, he is not prepared to contradict the Apostle Paul and claim that the Gentiles were not able to fulfill the divine law. Holcot's reply becomes the basis on which to justify effort, even after he has claimed that such effort cannot reach the knowledge required. However, because they strove to live according to the principles of the natural law, they secured faith and grace from God without the law of Moses and for that reason they were able to follow the [divine] law and love God above all else.[43] Such Gentiles were instructed by God and not by natural demonstrations.[44] As Oberman argued, the gift of the knowledge of God is bestowed "on those who live according to principles of natural law."[45] Likewise, Hoffmann concludes, for the philosopher "all true knowledge of God has its origins in a divine, biblical, prophetic and inspired authority."[46]

As we have seen and will see again in subsequent chapters, Holcot emphasizes the need for the pilgrim to do his or her very best (*facere in se*), not because this will procure merit but because God will respond to that effort. In a similar way, the Gentiles did in fact know that God should be loved above all else, but this knowledge was not strictly speaking acquired by the Gentile philosophers. Rather, according to Holcot, it was due to the fact that, because they did their very best to find God, God revealed himself to them. God saw their effort and rewarded them with knowledge that natural reason cannot reach.

A further point of connection with what we saw in the previous chapter has emerged. Previously, Holcot's position on the meaning of "belief," "faith," and "infidelity" left us wondering to what degree orthodox belief was required for salvation. His emphasis on the commanded sense of belief as a desire to live according to what appears to be the truth of the faith suggested that salvation lies less in orthodox belief and more in the genuine desire to live according to whatever appears to be a proposition of true religion. Without denying any of that, Holcot's discussion of the possibility of a natural knowledge of God suggests that one can have it both ways. One can continue to insist that God's people are commanded to try to live according to the propositions of true religion, while recognizing that what appears to them as true is not directly within their power, and therefore they are not morally culpable if something false appears to be true. However, Holcot's view of God's covenantal relationship with his people suggests that he believes that God will grant a correspondence between the truth and the appearance of truth to those who obey the moral or "attitudinal" command to believe. Thus it can be true in the traditional scholastic way that explicit faith about certain creedal truths is required for salvation. But from Holcot's vantage point, orthodoxy should be viewed as a sign of acceptance by God (i.e., God's response to one's best efforts) and not as a condition of God's acceptance.

The Triune God

Question 5 of book 1 of Holcot's commentary on the *Sentences* of Peter Lombard has, since the sixteenth century, been a source of criticism and misunderstanding. Michael Servetus—the Spanish antitrinitarian polymath and condemned heretic—argued in his *On the Errors of the Trinity* that the incomprehensible nature of the doctrine of the Trinity was known to the medieval scholastic doctors; in particular, Servetus notes that in question 5 of book 1 Robert Holcot deduces 16 arguments against the divine Trinity, while failing to answer satisfactorily a single one of the objections except by sophistry (*sophistice*).[47] Further, as Servetus argues, Holcot seems to admit in question 5 that the divine Trinity is "opposed to all natural reason."

Servetus is not alone in his criticism of book 1, question 5, as it is here that Holcot starkly argues that there are two logics: a natural logic (*logica naturalis*) that pertains in the natural world and a logic of faith (*logica fidei*) that, by definition, extends beyond the natural order and governs specific supernatural truths such as the Trinity and incarnation. This twofold logic has been interpreted as evidence that Holcot denies the universality of Aristotelian logic as applied to theological truths, or worse, that he is a theological skeptic who denies the rational intelligibility of particular Christian doctrines.

William of Ockham and the Universality of Aristotelian Logic

In the *Summa logicae* William of Ockham examined the formality of Aristotelian logic (that is, its universal application to all sciences). While the majority of thirteenth-century scholastics defended the formality of Aristotelian logic, as Ockham recognized, to insist that Aristotle's logic was applicable to the divine Trinity was a difficult task.

Medieval philosophers understood Aristotle's theory of the syllogism to be the foundation of logic. As such, the universality of the syllogism was central to understanding the nature of Aristotelian logic broadly understood. In the *Summa logicae* Ockham defined the expository syllogism as a third-figure syllogism that contains two singular premises.[48] In a passage that had a strong influence on Holcot's definition of the expository syllogism,[49] Ockham argued that the expository syllogism is in the third figure and takes the following form (such that the middle term is the subject in both premises):

M is P
M is S

∴ S is P

Ockham clarified the condition of singularity by stating that the subject of the premises (i.e., the middle term) must supposit for something that is not several things (*plures res*) nor the same as something that is several things.⁵⁰ Returning to the question of formality and universality, we can note that for Ockham the expository syllogism would cease to be formal or universal if it would be possible to substitute the terms of a given inference with other terms that yield true premises but a false conclusion. This means that the expository syllogism would cease to be formal if it could be demonstrated that by substituting certain terms, one would get an argument that had all true premises but a false conclusion.

Here it is instructive to consider an example. Does the following argument demonstrate the informality of the expository syllogism?

Humanity is Socrates
Humanity is Plato

∴ Socrates is Plato⁵¹

In this argument both premises are true, but the conclusion is false. As such, it seems to render the expository syllogism informal. Ockham's response is that in this case the argument is not a true expository syllogism of the third figure, precisely because the middle term (i.e., humanity) is not singular. Humanity, Ockham argues, supposits for several things and therefore cannot be used as the middle term of a third-figure expository syllogism.

Ockham expands on this line of reasoning and considers several arguments with respect to the divine Trinity.

| This essence is the Father | *Haec essentia est Pater* |
This essence is the Son	*Haec essentia est Filius*
∴ the Son is the Father	∴ *Filius est Pater*⁵²

Ockham is clear that this is not an expository syllogism "because 'this essence' is several distinct persons." Similarly to the previous argument in which "humanity" was a middle term, this argument is not an expository syllogism because the middle term "this essence" supposits for more than one thing (i.e., the Father, Son, and Holy Spirit). Thus, as Gelber argues,

Ockham relies on the fallacy of accident (which originated with Aristotle) to argue that expository syllogisms containing the terms of the Trinity (e.g., essence) are in fact not syllogisms at all (instead, they are paralogisms: the products of illogical or fallacious argumentation).[53]

Ockham argues that the divine Trinity is particularly susceptible to paralogism given that "the divine essence, which is one God and a single essence, is several persons."[54] Thus Ockham states that the terms in trinitarian paralogisms are not necessarily problematic if used to speak about natural things, "because in creatures no one thing is really numerically several things."[55] It is not the terms themselves that are problematic, but the terms "God," "divine essence," "Father," "Son," and "Holy Spirit" when used to speak about the divine Trinity—and as such suppositing, often times, for more than one thing simultaneously—that are problematic. In his discussion of the fallacy of accident (*fallacia accidentis*), therefore, Ockham clarifies his position and guards against undermining the universality of Aristotelian logic by claiming that expository syllogisms employing trinitarian terms are not valid syllogisms but paralogisms.

The Sixteen Arguments and a Twofold Logic?

Holcot inherited the early-fourteenth-century question regarding the universality of Aristotelian logic, and in question 5 of the first book of his commentary on the *Sentences* he begins with 16 arguments or objections against the thesis that the one God is three distinct persons. These arguments range from arguments that deny that God is three persons (e.g., the first argument for the conclusion that "one God is not three persons")[56] to arguments examining the infinite/finite nature of God (e.g., the second argument claims that understanding the divine persons to be either infinite or finite is problematic).[57] Further, some of the arguments are directed toward implications that follow from the doctrine of the Trinity and are formally aspects of Christology (e.g., argument 7 treating the incarnation).[58] The reader who is familiar with a more traditional approach to trinitarian doctrine would perhaps find this barrage of arguments somewhat disconcerting.

In the body of this question, however, Holcot supports the argument that God is three distinct persons. He begins his response to the question by stating that God is three distinct persons "since this is the Catholic faith revealed to the holy Fathers, just as is sufficiently clear in the various creeds [of the Church]."[59] His subsequent claim, however, is somewhat striking: he argues that to demonstrate (*probare*) the Trinity "exceeds the faculty of human reason," and the attempt, as such, is presumptuous (*praesumptuosum*) and foolish (*fatuum*). While the majority of Christian theologians in the patristic and medieval period would agree that the Trinity exceeds human faculties, what is striking about Holcot is that he argues such an endeavor is not only impossible—it is simply foolish. Holcot supports this position with a lengthy quotation from Anselm of Canterbury's *Letter on the Incarnation of the Word*:

> I shall make a prefatory comment. I do so to curb the presumption of those who, since they are unable to understand intellectually things the Christian faith professes, and with foolish pride think that there cannot in any way be things that they cannot understand, with unspeakable rashness dare to argue against such things rather than with humble wisdom admit their possibility. Indeed, no Christian ought to argue how things that the Catholic Church sincerely believes and verbally professes are not so, but by always adhering to the same faith without hesitation, but loving it, and by humbly living according to it, a Christian ought to argue how they are, inasmuch as one can look for reasons. If one can understand, one should thank God; if one cannot, one should bow one's head in veneration rather than sound off trumpets.[60]

This lengthy quotation sets the tone for the remainder of Holcot's response to the 16 arguments and in many ways captures Holcot's broader outlook. His approach is not that of Ockham, who attempted to articulate precisely how Aristotelian logic remained formal despite arguments that appear to be both sound and valid.

In the fifth argument Holcot presents a series of syllogisms that point to the difficulty of harmonizing Aristotelian logic and the doctrine of the Trinity. He considers the following expository syllogism (*est enim syllogismus expositorius*):

This Father generates	*Hic Pater generat*
This Father is this divine essence	*Hic Pater est haec essentia divina*
∴ This divine essence generates	∴ *Haec essentia divina generat*[61]

As we saw earlier, Ockham would have stated that this syllogism is not an expository syllogism but a paralogism. In particular, Ockham would have argued that this argument is guilty of the fallacy of accident because the middle term (i.e., "Father") supposits for more than one thing. Regarding the nature of the expository syllogism and the divine Trinity, Holcot follows Ockham's approach in quodlibet 90. There he argues that an expository syllogism cannot be constructed "from terms suppositing for God or the divine essence or the divine persons, because the divine essence is essentially several things and each of them," further, "each divine person, or notion, or property, is the divine essence, which is several [things]."[62] But this is not Holcot's approach in the fifth question of book I.

Holcot's response to the fifth objection of question five has been discussed in numerous sources and is worth considering in some detail. He writes in response to this problematic syllogism:

> It is not unfitting that natural logic should be deficient in things of faith. And, therefore, just as faith is above natural philosophy in positing that things are produced through creation—to which natural philosophy does not reach—so the moral instruction of faith posits some principles that natural science (*scientia naturalis*) does not concede. In the same way, the rational logic of faith (*logica fidei*) must be different from natural logic (*logica naturali*). For the commentator [i.e., Averroes] says in the second book of the *Metaphysics*, comment 15, that there is a certain logic universal to all the sciences, and a certain [logic] proper to each one of the sciences; and if this is true, *a fortiori* it is necessary to posit a logic of faith.[63]

In this passage Holcot argues that there is a certain logic universal to all sciences and a particular logical proper to each science, such that it is necessary to posit a distinct logic for the science of faith. As Hoffmann observes, it is striking that Holcot relies on Averroes for justification of the claim that there is a universal logic that governs all of the sciences and individual logics that pertain to specific disciplines.[64] At any rate, Holcot relies on Averroes to argue that there is a logic of faith that is distinct from natural logic. In the same way that the faith teaches both a doctrine of creation and moral principles that exceed the natural or moral sciences, so too the divine Trinity exceeds the limitations of Aristotelian logic: in particular, the expository syllogism.[65]

A second intriguing aspect of Holcot's argument is that he returns to the obligational arts to provide an analogy for the *logica fidei*.⁶⁶ This is evident in a passage immediately following the previous quotation, where Holcot argues that the logician or theologian, practicing his art or science, is "obligated by a certain type of *obligatio*" to follow the rules of his science. Each discipline, Holcot argues, has an internal logic that one is obliged to follow as if responding to a proposed *positum*.

This passage has often been misunderstood and used to argue that Holcot was an intellectual skeptic who bifurcated reason and faith,⁶⁷ such that the Trinity is regulated to a matter of "faith alone" (*sola fide*) and as such is not a rational articulation of Christian belief. The problem with this interpretation is that Holcot is not arguing that the doctrine of the Trinity and incarnation are nonrational or not governed by an integral and coherent logic; he is arguing that Aristotelian logic is not capable of articulating the truth of the divine Trinity, given that the Trinity is something that is both three and one simultaneously. Thus Holcot posits a logic of faith (*logica fide*) that is, by definition, an independent and valid form of reasoning that examines the doctrines of the faith. But what is this logic of faith?

Holcot gives some indication of what he has in mind by positing two rules that govern the *logica fide* with respect to trinitarian theology:

Rule 1. Every absolute name is predicated in the singular of the three [divine persons], and not in the plural (*Quod omne absolutam [nomen] praedicatur in singuari de tribus, et non in plurali*).
Rule 2. [The divine] unity holds its consequence, where the opposition of relation does not intervene (*Quod unitas tenet suum consequens ubi non obviat relationis oppositio*).⁶⁸

The two rules, Holcot argues, constitute the logic of faith as it pertains to the Trinity. The rules are not original to Holcot but had been employed for centuries by theologians following the theological tradition of Augustine of Hippo and Anselm of Canterbury.

The first rule (every absolute name is predicated in the singular of the three divine persons) relies on Augustine's distinction between substantial (absolute) and relative predicates as elaborated in *The Trinity*, book 5.⁶⁹ There Augustine developed a trinitarian grammar according to which the various terms predicated of God are divided into two categories: (a) substantial terms (terms predicated *secundum substantiam*) that are predicated of the one God and of the three divine persons equally (e.g., God, good, true, eternal); and (b) relative or relational terms (terms predicated *secundum relativum*) that are predicated of the individual persons and indicate the distinctions between them (e.g., Father, Son, etc.). The substantial terms predicated of the divine, such as "God," are predicated of the undivided essence and the three divine persons in the singular; for example, the divine essence is God, the Father is God, the Son is God, and the Holy Spirit is God, and yet there are not three gods. All such substantial or absolute terms, Holcot argues, must be predicated of God in the singular. But how does this address the problems posed in the 16 objections? The answer becomes clear by considering the first objection that contains the following premise: "the three persons are three gods (*tres personae sunt tres dii*)." If this premise is examined according to the first rule, it can be rejected as inconsistent with the logic of faith because the absolute term "god" is used in the plural in this premise. As such, this premise violates Rule 1 and can be rejected.

The second rule (the divine unity holds its consequence, where the opposition of relation does not intervene) originates from Anselm of Canterbury's *On the Procession of the Holy Spirit* and is referred to by fourteenth-century theologians as the *regula Anselmi*.[70] Anselm's rule argues that within the simple divine nature the only distinction is the distinction by relation; stated conversely, there can be no distinction within the divine essence except for the distinction by relation. Like most fourteenth-century scholastics, Holcot references this rule throughout his writings on the Trinity, especially in his commentary on the *Sentences* and in quodlibet 90.[71] Again, how does this rule help address the objection at hand? In objection 4 of question 5, Holcot presents the following argument:

The Father is constituted through paternity	*Pater constituitur per paternitatem*
The Father is the essence	*Pater est essentia*
∴ There are four things in the divine	∴ *Sunt quatuor res in divinis*[72]

This argument concludes that there are four things in the divine: the Father, the Son, the Holy Spirit, and paternity. The problem, of course, is that the faith teaches that there are not four things in the divine, as was clarified at Lateran IV.[73] However, by following the *ratio Anselmi* one can reject such arguments simply because in God the only distinction is by relation (e.g., the distinction between the Father and Son) and the distinction implied in this argument—between *Pater* and *paternitas*—is not a distinction based on relation. Thus, one could reject this implied distinction and the argument as formulated.

While these two rules are probably not sufficient to address all of the problems posed by the expository syllogism, it is clear that Holcot had in mind certain theological rules that could supplement natural reason in the formulation of trinitarian propositions. These rules are not the product of a blind faith or theological skepticism; they are grounded in the theological works of Augustine and Anselm. And, once accepted, the rules become the basis for a rational investigation into the divine Trinity.

Holcot concludes his discussion of the *logica fidei* by returning to the question of whether or not Aristotle's logic is formal. He argues that Aristotelian logic is clearly not formal, if formality is to be understood in the sense that it holds in all matters (*in omnia materia*).[74] However, it is formal if formality means that it holds in the fields of natural science known to us through the senses (*a nobis sensibiliter notis*).[75] Thus Holcot redefines the term "formality" as applicable to Aristotelian logic and argues that it is formal in the sciences known by means of the senses; however, in matters of the faith, or when a science relies on revealed premises, it is clear that Aristotelian logic does not hold.[76]

The Trinity Beyond the Sentences

Robert Holcot's more robust treatment of the Trinity can be found in his quodlibetal questions. In the *Quodlibets* Holcot does not radically modify or change his opinion regarding the two logics, even if he employs different language. This is evident in his treatment of quodlibet 87: "Whether this is conceded: God is the Father, and the Son, and the Holy Spirit?" Holcot posits both a positive and a negative response to the question regarding whether or not a Christian can know the Trinity by means of a natural knowledge of God.[77] First, Holcot argues that knowledge of the Trinity is the domain of the theologian. Referencing Pseudo-Dionysius' *On The Divine Names*, he argues that the theologian has access to knowledge of the Trinity by means of authorities, revelation, and miracles, not by means of the natural light of reason (*lumen naturale*).[78] Second, Holcot argues that Christian theologians should not seek to respond scientifically (*scientifice*) to the arguments of heretics and philosophers by means of rebutting the individual propositions of their arguments (i.e., the *peccans in materia*).[79] To dispute the logical structure of an argument (i.e., the *peccans in forma*) would be possible, but if one were to debate the content of a proposition regarding the Trinity (*peccans in materia*), Holcot argues, it would not be possible for the believer to demonstrate that an individual proposition is either true or false. Therefore, it is not possible to argue with a philosopher regarding the material content of an argument for or against the Trinity.

As is evident in quodlibet 87, Holcot continues to defend the thesis that human beings have a limited knowledge of the divine Trinity and that Aristotelian logic, in particular, is not applicable to trinitarian theology in a formal way. However, this is not a position entirely new to Holcot.[80] A striking precursor to Holcot can be found in the *Enigma of Faith* written by the twelfth-century Cistercian William of St. Thierry.

> This way of speaking about God has its own discipline supported by the rules and limits of faith so as to teach a manner of speaking about God reasonably according to the reasoning of faith (*secundum rationem fidei*).[81] ... Now, we say "according to the reasoning of faith" because this manner of speaking about God has certain special words which are rational but not intelligible except in the reasoning of faith, not however in the reasoning of human understanding. What we said a little earlier—that the Father is God, the Son is God, and the Holy Spirit is God, but that there are not three gods but one God—is understood to some extent according to the reasoning of faith, but not at all according to the reasoning of human understanding. For, in human matters human reason acquires faith for itself, but in divine affairs faith comes first and then forms its own unique reasoning.[82]

Similar to Holcot, William defends the claim that the divine Trinity exceeds human reason and that there is a distinct "reasoning of faith" that is used to analyze the divine Trinity. Thus it is important to emphasize that Holcot probably understood himself to be grounded in a theological tradition that included not only the epistemically cautious approaches of Augustine and Pseudo-Dionysius[83] but also medieval thinkers such as William of St. Thierry.

Holcot's argument that human beings have a limited knowledge of the divine Trinity is consistent with the theology he develops in his later writings.[84] What emerges from the quodlibetal questions is a form of trinitarian minimalism that is consistent both with his previous discussion of the Trinity in his *Sentences* commentary and a general trend that emerged in Oxford in the early fourteenth century that emphasized the absolute simplicity of the divine nature.[85]

Latin trinitarian theology at the end of the thirteenth century was dominated by various explanatory models that accounted for the unity of God and the distinctions between the Father, Son, and Holy Spirit. All medieval theologians accepted that the Father generated the Son, and that the Father and Son spirated the Holy Spirit: thus, within God, there are two emanations (i.e., generation and spiration) and four relations indicating the active and passive aspects of the corresponding emanations (e.g., the Father actively generates the Son and thus *paternitas*, fatherhood, is proper to the Father). John Duns Scotus, for example, accepted that the divine persons are distinct by relations of origin and that the divine persons have individuating personal properties (e.g., again, the Father's personal property is *paternitas*). Further, Scotus argues that the persons are distinct by means of personal properties that, along with the divine essence, constitute the individual persons. The Father, therefore, shares the communicable entity of the divine essence with the Son and Holy Spirit, and has an individuating personal property that is formally distinct (i.e., a distinction less than a real distinction and more than a mere verbal distinction) from the essence.[86] And, while there was heated debate about the nature of those relations (i.e., whether the relations are opposed or disparate),[87] the majority of late thirteenth-century theologians held that each person has a personal property that is distinct, in some way, from the divine essence and individuates each person. While aspects of this theological model were hotly contested, underlying it was a generally accepted picture that posits some kind of distinction between the divine persons and their personal properties.

Robert Holcot's trinitarian thought builds on William of Ockham's emphasis on the absolute simplicity of the divine nature and is consistent with the theology of his contemporaries Walter Chatton and William Crathorn.[88] Holcot argues that theologians such as Aquinas and Scotus were wrong to posit a kind of distinction (rational, formal, or otherwise) between the persons and their individuating personal properties. Holcot argues explicitly that "the essence and relation in God are not distinguished really, nor modally, nor formally, nor by means of reason, nor convertibly, nor in any other way."[89] The formal distinction posited by Scotus, for example, is rejected by Holcot. He argues that the formal distinction is a distinction of some things (*distinctio aliquorum*) such that there is one thing and another thing, that is, two things (*duae res*)—on such a model, he writes, fatherhood and the essence are two things. However, this cannot be the case because it violates divine simplicity.[90]

Holcot argues, therefore, that the divine persons and their personal properties are identical, and he finds the claim that the divine persons are "constituted" by means of the divine essence and a personal property to be introducing some kind of aggregation (*aggregatio*) or constitution into the divine persons that is not fitting to the perfectly simple divine nature.[91] Holcot rejects such explanatory models and insists that the Father, Son, and Holy Spirit are distinct in and of themselves (*se ipsis*). He writes that "properly speaking, the Father is distinguished from the Son in and of himself (*se ipso*), and nothing distinguishes the Father from the Son."[92] The upshot is that according to Holcot the explanatory models employed by the previous generation of theologians violated divine simplicity and were not necessary to account for personal distinction. The persons, as persons, are distinct from one another and no further explanation can be given.

Conclusion

We return here, by way of conclusion, to the broader theme of this chapter—human knowledge and the search for God—as it relates to the moral life. In lecture 29 of his commentary on Wisdom, Holcot analyzes the claim that God's revelation (i.e., Scripture) is not needed because nature does nothing in vain.[93] Holcot agrees that nature does not want in necessary things, and he interprets God's provisions not as outfitting the human agent with the necessary means from the outset but rather in terms of God's pact, covenant, or agreement with humanity to provide the necessary means. Thus he writes, "if man does his best (*homo facit quod in se*), he will be sufficiently informed about things which are necessary for salvation."[94] This serves as a nice summary of what we have seen in his *Sentences* commentary. There we saw that, for Holcot, what appears to us as true is not directly in our power, and yet if we live rightly the required articles of belief will in fact appear to us as true.

Holcot's earlier exegesis suggests a link between doing one's best—the commanded sense of belief visible in question 1 of his *Sentences*—and intellectual effort. The relevant exegesis concerns the passage taken from Wisdom 2:21–22:

> These things they thought, and were deceived: for their own malice blinded them. And they knew not the secrets of God, nor hoped for the wages of justice, nor esteemed the honor of holy souls.

The line that begins "for their own malice blinded them" is the key assertion. For Holcot, this verse shows that the epistemic blindness is not the primary problem; the ignorance is the result of a previous mistake or it is no mistake at all. In his interpretation of this passage, Holcot shows that he has not abandoned his earlier position that intellectual assent is not directly in our power. Assent is simply the automatic result of what appears to us as true. If what appears to be true is not in fact true, and we remain culpable for this ignorance, then there must have been a prior mistake that caused the second.

As Holcot explains, there are two kinds of error or ignorance: *error vincibilis* (vincible error) and *error invincibilis* (invincible error). If the error in question were "invincible," then these people would not be blameworthy, for "God does not demand what man is not able to do well."[95] But if this error were conquerable, then people could have taken precautions to avoid it, and the fact that they do not suggests a moral failure.[96] Holcot argues that this failure is negligence—whether this comes from malice, stubbornness, or some other source—and concludes that negligence occurs when someone does not desire to know those things that one ought to know.

Here Holcot makes explicit the connection between the kind of moral failure of desire visible in his canonical definition of belief and intellectual effort. The suggestion is that the person who has the right desire naturally seeks to know the truth. Moral virtue and the desire for orthodox faith are not separable activities. The correct moral disposition will always lead people to *facere in se*—do their best—to know God. But it is important to see that "intellectual striving" is not contingent on our ability to discover what we want to know. On the contrary, irrespective of our ability, our desire to know impels us to strive without thinking of the outcome. This suggests that the value of intellectual striving is a moral value and therefore a practice that is valuable in itself: that is, a kind of activity that naturally flows out of love or adoration.

Such a description does not describe everyone, for one can also "desire not to know." Such a person is not merely lazy and indifferent to religious truth and truth generally but is actually a despiser of knowledge. In line with the verse Holcot is interpreting, Holcot identifies this as an unnatural malice. We should see this in light of Holcot's discussion of the sin of heresy and infidelity. There too sin is not found in an intellectual error but in the stubbornness and resistance to the truth itself.

4

GOD, CREATION, AND THE FUTURE

Introduction

We have already seen that Holcot is preoccupied with both divine and human fidelity. The nature of God's fidelity to his creation, the covenant he makes with them, and the corresponding fidelity required of creatures are perpetual concerns for Holcot. Nowhere does this issue rise to the surface more prominently and with more specificity in Holcot's corpus than in his discussion of God's relationship to the future. In what follows, we look first at how Holcot understands God's knowledge of the future and what this means for his power to change it. Second, we look at what this means for God's relationship to human beings: the extent to which he can and cannot deceive his creatures and what the possibility of divine deception means for creatures and their covenant with God.

Future Contingents and Divine Foreknowledge

The Problem of Future Contingents and the Principle of Bivalence

To understand Holcot's position on the compatibility of divine foreknowledge and a contingent future, we begin with a text from Holcot that engages with the thought of Aristotle, since Aristotle's discussion of future propositions is where every medieval discussion begins.

In developing an argument against the claim that "God knew from eternity that he would produce the world," Holcot illustrates the central concern: if God knew this, then it would follow that, before he created the world, the future proposition "God would produce the world" would be necessarily true. In other words, God's creation would not have been a truly free act of the divine will but an act of necessity.[1] The argument goes further to suppose an extreme hypothetical: suppose a man had been created before the world was created, and suppose that this man spoke the true proposition that God would create the world. On the supposition that this proposition exists and is true, God would have produced the world from necessity, compelled by the truth of the proposition about God's future act.[2] The argument states that this is clearly absurd and therefore proves that neither God, nor anyone else, knew from eternity that he would produce the world.

It is at this point that Holcot invokes the authority of Aristotle as a confirmation of the claim that God did not foreknow that he would produce the world before he produced it. The argument notes that—in concord with what has come to be known as the traditional interpretation of chapter 9 of Aristotle's *On Interpretation*[3]—the principle of bivalence should be suspended with respect to future contingent propositions. The principle of bivalence is the assertion that "every semantic statement is either true or false."[4] Aristotle affirms that the principle of bivalence applies to most propositions.[5] However, the traditional interpretation of Aristotle claims that he made an exception for statements about singular future contingents—an interpretation adopted by most fourteenth-century theologians.[6] The traditional interpretation reads chapter 9 of *On Interpretation* as a kind of concession that, if the principle of bivalence applied to future contingent propositions, then the future would become necessary. Thus, it is thought, to avoid such an unpalatable consequence Aristotle is willing to concede that propositions about future contingents do not yet have a truth-value and therefore escape the principle of bivalence.[7] Holcot's argument exploits this interpretation and draws the conclusion that because God's future contingent creation is neither true nor false, God could not foreknow that he would create the world until he actually did it.[8]

An extremely important and related Aristotelian position is also at work here: Aristotle's definition of "knowledge" or what it means "to know." When "knowledge" is understood as *epistēmē* or *scientia*, it is partially defined as the awareness that something cannot be otherwise.[9] If the contingent future is defined precisely as what can be otherwise, it follows naturally that there can be no "knowledge" of this future. Aristotle, however, was not particularly concerned with the problem that plagued most Christian theists. This was the belief that God was omniscient and that omniscience included not only knowledge of things past and present but also of all things future. In this way Aristotle's classical position introduces the two horns of the dilemma faced by all medieval theologians who attempted to wrestle with the problem of future contingents.

On the one hand, there is a theistic interest in preserving the freedom of divine action and therefore the contingency and indeterminacy of the future. It is this concern that we see front and center in the previous argument and the arguments willing to deny divine foreknowledge in the name of preserving God's omnipotence and freedom. In a related way, this concern is extended to the freedom of human action as well. As in the case of God, those who believe in the freedom of human action tend to correlatively insist, like Aristotle, on the indeterminacy and therefore unknowability of future contingent actions.

On the other hand, going at least as far back as Boethius, the Christian tradition repeatedly stressed the importance of defending divine omniscience. Above all Boethius was concerned with preserving and explaining the reality and efficacy of divine providence for which knowledge of the future appeared supremely important.[10] However, as Boethius explains in his work the *Consolation of Philosophy* and the previous argument makes clear, foreknowledge—understood to be an essential part of omniscience—seemingly threatens to render determinate precisely what needs to be indeterminate in order to preserve the freedom of God. Or, conversely, if this future could still turn out to be different than what God foreknows it to be, then this raises doubts about the reliability of God's knowledge and ultimately the efficacy of his providence. Katherine Tachau identifies this same tension as pervasive in Oxford during Holcot's tenure there: "The focal concern at their base lay in Oxford theologians' efforts to understand a wholly contingent created order with respect to an entirely benevolent, omnipotent, and omniscient divinity."[11]

As we have seen, Aristotle's commitment to the principle of bivalence or a two-valued logic presents us with two stark alternatives. One must choose one horn of this dilemma: either the future is indeterminate and genuine freedom (both human and divine) is preserved, or genuine foreknowledge is possible but on the condition that the future is determined and freedom (both human and divine) is an illusion.[12]

Holcot and the Opinio Communis: An Alternative to the Principle of Bivalence

Consistent with Holcot's outlook on most things, he gravitates toward a position that strongly defends God's freedom. Thus his challenge as a theologian is to explain how divine foreknowledge is possible. As we have seen, in Aristotle's two-value truth system, the preservation of divine freedom and future contingency would normally demand that he abandon the simultaneous possibility of divine foreknowledge or the belief that omniscience includes knowledge of future contingents.[13]

Holcot attempts to avoid this unsavory position by joining a larger movement of Oxford contemporaries who were rethinking the confines of Aristotle's two-valued logic system. In book 2, question 2, article 7 of his *Sentences* commentary, Holcot asks "whether in propositions about the future, in a contingent matter, there is *determinate* truth in one of the contradictories and falsity in the other" (emphasis ours).[14] The use of the word "determinate" is Holcot's way of asking whether or not genuinely knowable propositions about future contingent events exist—that is, propositions that have a definite truth value, either true or false.

Holcot first lists the predictable position of Aristotle, that there is indeed no determinate truth in future contingent propositions. Next he notes the opinion of the theologians who claim that there is indeed "determinate truth" in future contingent propositions. These two contrasting opinions nicely illustrate the central tension described earlier. Aristotle's position would preserve the possibility of freedom and contingency, while the position of the theologians is particularly concerned with preserving God's infallible knowledge of the future.[15]

In the midst of this dilemma, Holcot works to find a middle way by adopting what, in his *Sentences* commentary, he refers to as the common position.[16] Hester Gelber and Chris Schabel have shown that this common position can be found in William of Ockham and others. Speaking of Holcot's position in his *Sentences* commentary, Schabel writes:

> Basically following the *opinio communis*, Holcot accepts Ockham's distinction between true propositions about the past and present and those only vocally about the past or present which are equivalent to propositions about the future. True propositions about the past and present are necessarily true, but a proposition about the future is true in a way that it is able never to have been true.[17]

The distinguishing hallmark of this position is the idea that propositions about future contingents, even after they have come true, are distinguishable through the lingering possibility of a counterfactual past—a possibility that does not linger for truly necessary, non-contingent propositions.[18]

Here we should note that in adopting this more or less Ockhamist position, Holcot has not yet come to completely reject the two-valued logic system presumed by Aristotle and the source of the dilemma described earlier. As Schabel observes, Holcot would develop his position more fully in his quodlibetal questions, where he "followed his fellow Oxford Dominican Arnold of Strelley in attributing indeterminate truth and falsity to true and false propositions about the future, but not in his *Sentences* commentary."[19] Nevertheless, one can see that Holcot, like many of his contemporaries, is desperately searching for a middle way—a way to preserve the freedom of divine and human action but also to find some way to claim that God can have knowledge of the future, that providence is real, and that prophecy is a genuine possibility. In this way, the early but incomplete effort of the *Sentences* commentary should be seen as a preliminary stage in Holcot's journey toward the rejection of a two-valued logic system.[20]

In a later quodlibet, Holcot follows the position of Arnold of Strelley and fully embraces the multi-valued logic system. Here he asserts explicitly that future contingent propositions are "indeterminately true or false."[21] By following Strelley, Holcot rejects the idea that a proposition can *only* be determinately true or false or else—by lacking any truth value—completely unknowable.[22] Through this rejection he moves toward a multi-valued logic where he identifies *modality* (i.e., necessity, possibility, and impossibility) as the first and primary characteristic of a proposition, rather than truth or falsity.[23] As such, truth and falsity can be understood differently in each modal class. Hester Gelber explains:

> [Holcot's] position reflects a view of modality as primary. Necessity and contingency are fundamental, and judgments of truth mean something in each modal context, rather than truth being primary, and necessity and contingency providing a different valence to otherwise true propositions.[24]

Holcot describes his position in the following way:

> I say, just as it is commonly said, that a proposition about the future is necessarily true, even though it is possible that it never was true, and therefore it is *true in a different way* than those propositions which are strictly about the past or present (emphasis ours).[25]

The phrase "true in a different way," already present in his *Sentences* commentary, indicates the shift from a two-value logic to a multi-value logic. Suddenly, Holcot can talk about two different classes of truth: that which is determinately true (the only kind of truth that Aristotle acknowledges) and that which is *indeterminately* true. Further, Holcot can verbally agree with Aristotle that there is no determinate truth in future contingent propositions while still agreeing with the theologians that there is a knowable *indeterminate* truth regarding the future.

The critical point is that propositions can now be true in different ways. One proposition can be true necessarily and another can be true contingently. In fact, Holcot goes to some lengths to separate the idea of contingency and necessity from "what is sometimes the case" and "what is always the case."[26] To say that something "never has existed" and "never will exist" is not yet to say that it is impossible. Likewise, to say that something "has always existed" and "will always exist" is not yet to say that it is necessary.

This distinction allows Holcot to show the compatibility of infallible divine foreknowledge and freedom, both divine and human. If it is contingently true that some event will happen, then despite the fact that this is true and has always been true, at the moment when the event occurs it also remains true that it did not have to be this way. Here we see that the distinction between being "always the case" and "necessary" comes into play in a big way. Holcot frequently distinguishes this kind of truth by saying "though it is true, it nevertheless is able to never have been true (*licet vera, potest tamen numquam fuisse vera*)."[27] Gelber summarizes in the following way:

> Holcot contended that the common response of almost everyone to such an argument . . . was to pose the possibility of a counterfactual past: to say that the propositions "*a* will be" is true, yet contingently, and therefore, although it is true, it can never have been true. Thus Holcot maintained that the possibility of a counterfactual past differentiated propositions about the future on contingent matters and their equivalents—whether set in the past or present—from propositions about the past and present that are not about such contingent matters.[28]

In short, the possibility of a "counterfactual past" (i.e., that it is possible for that which will be true to never have been true) helps distinguish between those truths that are necessary and those that are just as true but contingently so.

In sum, the thrust of the response lies in correctly identifying what God foreknows. Before we were born God knew that it was true that we would be born. Nevertheless, he knew this both as something that most definitely would happen and as something that, strictly speaking, did not have to happen. As such, it is only a conditional necessity, necessitated by a larger conditional frame that God, in his omniscience, knows perfectly.

One might here worry that one's actions and choices still seem necessitated by the conditional set of circumstances in which one acts out one's life. But here we enter the realm of a kind of tautological necessity, wherein it is suggested "if I will act in this way, I will necessarily act this way" or "If I am a person who wants to sin and chooses to sin, then I will necessarily sin." The conditional frame compels these necessities and God knows these necessities because he knows the frames that have been constructed. But the actions themselves are not in any way necessitated by the fact that God knows what will result within these frames. This is the kind of mistake noted by Boethius, which was to mistake God's foreknowledge for the cause of an event rather than the simple awareness of an event that has been freely chosen.

Finally, the shift to a multivalent logic has understandable implications for what we mean by "knowledge." Recall that Aristotle's demonstrative sense of *epistēmē* or *scientia* demanded that one know that the truth in question cannot be otherwise, and there could only be knowledge where there was determinate truth. However, by insisting on the existence of "indeterminate truth," Strelley and Holcot can talk about knowing and foreknowing in two different ways. There is, of course, the kind of knowing that Aristotle has in mind, but this kind of knowing is only appropriate for determinate truth. A new kind of knowledge must now be admitted that is proper to indeterminate truth. It is for this reason that Holcot is willing to bite the bullet, embrace one horn of the original dilemma, and deny that God foreknows future contingents.[29] He is only willing to do this, however, when foreknowledge is understood in the strict Aristotelian sense proper to "determinate truth."

These implications are not merely conjecture. Already in his *Sentences* commentary Holcot distinguishes between different senses of "knowing" (*scire*) in order to differentiate between the proper and improper sense in which God is said to know the future.[30] Holcot identifies three senses of "knowing" (*scire*).[31] The first mode is the most general and is convertible with other, looser senses of knowing (*cognoscere*).[32] The second sense is stricter and refers to evident knowledge by which a person assents without doubt that something is in reality just as the proposition indicates.[33] The third sense is the most restrictive. It is in essence a restatement of the second sense of "to know," however, with the addition that one not only assents without doubt that the proposition is true but also knows that the reality signified by the proposition cannot be otherwise.[34] In the latter two senses of "knowing" (*scire*), Holcot separates the epistemological certainty from the ontological fact that something "cannot be otherwise."

Following this division, God is then understood "to know" future contingents with absolute certainty. However, this knowledge is also understood to make no claims about the ontological necessity of the proposition.[35] Accordingly, Holcot says that God knows future contingents in the second mode but not in the third, because "such propositions are true in such a way that they are able to never have been true."[36] In other words, God knows that these propositions are true but not in such a way that they could not have been otherwise.[37]

Revelation and Divine Deception

Having addressed Holcot's position on the nature of future contingents and the nature of God's foreknowledge of those propositions, a second related concern arises: can God communicate this knowledge of the future through prophecy and revelation?[38] In response to this question, the picture that gradually emerges is that Holcot is a pastorally minded thinker—even in his most academic works—and that his entire corpus is written with an eye for training clergy and preachers.[39]

Holcot's concern with the contingency of divine revelation continues the dilemma previously discussed, but now he presses the concern in a more acute and personal way. Joseph Incandela explains: "Both the freedom of the divine will and the freedom of the human will seem alternately imperiled depending on the sense one makes of prophecy and the contingency of revelation."[40] Once again the concern lingers about the possibility of both divine and human freedom. However, here the threat comes not from God's foreknowledge but from God's communication in time with his creatures. As such, the question becomes more acute. Where the threat comes from God's foreknowledge and impassible nature, this can be mitigated, as we have seen, by the recognition that God's knowledge can remain eternally infallible while the known propositions remain contingent; that is, God can eternally know that something will be false even though it could have been true. However, the assertions of revelation and prophecy are decidedly in time, and thus, on the supposition of the contingency of the future, carry with them the real possibility of turning out false. Further, in talking about revelation we are no longer just talking about the implications of God's nature for the created world order—we are now talking about God's active, intentional, and purposeful involvement in the world. To suggest that God's revelation could turn out to be false is to suggest something more than mere fallibility in God's nature. It is to suggest that God might be deceptive, unfaithful, and perhaps even malicious.[41]

In a quodlibetal question, Holcot asks "whether, once revelation of a future contingent has been made, that future remains contingent after its revelation." In this question he nicely summarizes the dilemma at hand.

> If the opposite of what was revealed is able to happen, God is able to deceive, lie, perjure, not fulfill what he promises, and be unfaithful and so on; which seem to oppose good morals. On the other hand, if we say that the opposite of what has been revealed, or promised, or asserted or swore by God is not able to happen, it seems to impair the divine power, which in no way is diminished through revelation, or an oath,

or a promise made to a creature. Moreover, it seems to impugn human liberty: because after revelation is made of something falling under the free faculty of the will, it would now make it necessary if the opposite could not happen.[42]

The goal then is to find some way to preserve both divine and human freedom and to save God from the charge of malice or anything unsuitable to his nature.

It is this charge of "unsuitability" that Holcot turns to first in his survey of those arguments claiming that God does have a binding obligation to fulfill what he promises. He specifically points to Anselm here, who suggests that such a failure is not in keeping with God's nature and therefore is impossible.[43] It is worth pointing out that Holcot refers to Anselm and the concern for "suitability" again in his discussion on baptism. In this context, Holcot suggests that baptism removes not only the guilt for sin but also the penalty. He then faces the objection that such a world is unordered and unsuitable where a correlative punishment is not enlisted to balance out the scales of justice. There, as here, Holcot pushes back with the general claim that God is not beholden to or necessitated by our notions of justice or the good. For Holcot, it is not the case that God is good or just because he does what is good or just; rather what God does is good and what God does is just. In the case of baptism, this allows him to say that God has the freedom to effect an ordered world in the manner he chooses, whether through penalty or through forgiveness.[44] Here on the question of fulfilling promises, the case is much the same. Holcot makes this point explicit: "God is no better when he acts justly than when he does nothing, and therefore God does not accrue goodness from any operation directed toward a creature."[45] This general principle is buttressed by the fact that Holcot takes seriously scriptural passages in which it appears obvious that God frequently deceives and misleads.

For example, Holcot points out that God can and frequently does deceive demons. Likewise, he points to God's deception of the Egyptians in the book of Exodus. In fact, Holcot regards the lack of ability to knowingly deceive as a real imperfection.[46]

Holcot's willingness to acknowledge these examples as instances of genuine divine deception stands in direct contrast with other ways that these biblical cases were approached. For Ockham, instances of apparent deception or erroneous prophecy could be explained by saying that what was revealed was a kind of conditional assertion. God declares this will happen (on the condition that X and Y are true), where the conditional is often left unstated. Revelation to Jonah that God would destroy Nineveh—a frequent example in debates about the veracity of prophecy—is a case in point. Did God reveal absolutely that he would destroy Nineveh and then not do it? This would be a case of genuine deception. Or did God reveal that he would destroy Nineveh on the condition that the Ninevites would not repent? Ockham takes the latter position.[47]

Similarly, Richard FitzRalph attempts to explain appearances of deception by drawing a distinction between accidental (*per accidens*) and essential (*per seipsum*) deception. For FitzRalph it is possible for God to speak in such a way that he is misunderstood and therefore deceives *per accidens*. But in such cases the error lies in the hearer and not directly with God. But FitzRalph denies that God can intentionally deceive someone or deceive them *per seipsum*.[48]

Holcot, in contrast, feels no need to mitigate or explain away apparent divine deception. It is something that happens frequently, and God would be a lesser being if he were not able to deceive intentionally. However, this admission demands that Holcot respond to the challenges of the initial dilemma. The dilemma, recall, is that if God's revelation could be false, God first might be a malicious God, and, second, his promises might not be certain and therefore worthy of our absolute trust and conviction. Holcot has a different response for each concern.

He first moves to dismiss the idea that the possibility of deceit mandates the possibility of a malicious God. He addresses this concern by making a very understandable distinction between two kinds of deceit. One kind of deceit proceeds from a good intention and another from a malicious intention. Of the former, one need only think of the nurturing lies that parents tell their children, or the lie that Plato envisions will help educate a disordered populace into virtue, or even the lie that one might tell a Nazi looking for Jews hiding in one's home. Holcot concedes that while it is more than possible for God to deceive in a nurturing, loving, or protecting way, it is contrary to his nature to deceive in the second way—that is, maliciously.[49]

There is an important corollary here about the kind of certainty an individual can have. Holcot is suggesting that natural reason can provide us with demonstrative certainty that God will never tell us anything maliciously because this is a contradiction of his nature. On the other hand, we retain no such demonstrative certainty about whether or not God is actually deceiving us. Thus we can be certain that whatever God reveals to us is done so benevolently, but we do not have any mechanisms or resources to certify demonstratively that what he has revealed to us is certain and cannot be otherwise.

This result, however, leads to the second, more pressing concern: what is the value of this divine communication, malicious or not, if it can turn out to be false? On what basis should it function as a guide for our lives and actions, if we know that the truth can be otherwise? Incandela himself notes that this admission by Holcot initially seems to go against the idea that Holcot is a particularly pastorally concerned thinker, always with one eye pointed toward the implications of his theoretical positions for the life of the faithful. When Holcot admits that it is a genuine possibility that all of Scripture is false,[50] one can hardly keep from wondering how this helps the faith of the ordinary believer.

The likely response to this query, suggested by Incandela as well as Gelber—and fitting with our earlier discussion of "belief" and Holcot's definition of true "heresy" in chapter 2—is that Holcot aims to rethink the source, meaning, and value of religious certainty. What Holcot is particularly worried about is a kind of religious certainty that approximates the kind of certainty one has in Aristotle's notion of a demonstrative science. Here, through logic and rigor, it is presumed that one can acquire absolute certainty of what cannot be otherwise. In such a case, assent in no way requires the kind of disposition of the will required by his definition of meritorious belief (seen in chapter 2).

Typically, belief based on authoritative testimony could never reach Aristotle's notion of *epistēmē* or *scientia* because the veracity of the speaker could always be problematized. However, what if the speaker was known to be God, and what if we were sure that what God promises could never be otherwise? Suddenly, this desired demonstrative certainty would seem possible, and the disposition of the will and the commitment and fidelity to that truth would once more appear superfluous.

Holcot's insistence on the possibility of divine deception is designed to wake up anyone who begins to rest on the notion that, once God has made his promises, his or her future is sealed and ensured. Instead, Holcot wants to emphasize a different kind of certainty—a certainty that shows an active and ongoing trust: an attitude of the will, rather than a cognitive awareness of what does or does not appear to be true. Holcot's understanding of this active, ongoing trust, is evident in the following passage:

> I say that the certitude that God causes in the blessed is not such that something will be so and impossible that it will not be so ... But he causes in them such certitude that they will always be blessed, and they cling to it so strongly and with such great assent, as if it is not able to be otherwise. They know nonetheless that it is able to be otherwise: because otherwise they would not know the condition of the creature's being always dependent on God.[51]

This quotation nicely captures many of the key points just asserted. First, starting from the very end of the passage, we can see Holcot's penchant to relieve the faithful from any sense of self-assurance and acquired certainty on which they can somehow rest, independent of God's continued cooperation (e.g., "because otherwise they would not know the condition of the creature's being always dependent on God"). A belief that God is somehow necessitated to fulfill his promises, independent of his ongoing desire to keep that promise, is a good way for such an independent certainty to fester.

Second and in contrast, we can notice the requirement of ongoing and active trust. Holcot uses an important phrase—"as if" (*ac sic*)—to suggest that the pilgrim is required to continue "to act" as if God's promises were certain. Here again are some parallels to what we have seen in chapter 2, namely that it is not the cognitive belief itself that is meritorious but the desire to live according to those promises that we believe to be true (whether they turn out to be true or not). We can see this active, striving, ongoing sense of certainty in the language Holcot uses, "cling[ing] to it so strongly and with such great assent."[52]

Conclusion

In concluding this chapter it is instructive to return to a broader understanding of what is meant by faith in relationship to God and revelation. Joseph Incandela, in a discussion of Holcot's understanding of prophecy, concludes: "There are no assurances, then, save the assurances of faith. Faith is the key."[53] While Incandela is on the right track, it is important to be precise about what is meant by faith. For at this point Holcot has carved out a couple of different meanings of faith. There is the kind of faith that can inoculate itself against doubt by first believing that God has spoken but then independently assuring itself of the certainty of these promises through the knowledge that God cannot fail to keep his promises. Then there is the other kind of faith: the kind of faith that emphasizes the ongoing desire to believe and trust in God's promises, knowing that God is in no way required to keep these promises. In the latter case, we see a kind of faith and trust grounded in love and ongoing devotion. In the former, we see a faith and certainty that wants to be possessed and owned in the way that certainty from a scientific demonstration is owned. But this certainty requires that God in a way becomes beholden to creatures, necessitated by human accusations of injustice. This is not the image of God Holcot wants the Christian flock to envision; he wants them to see a God not compelled by necessity but constantly faithful through his own volition.

5

THE SACRAMENTS

Baptism, Confession, and the Eucharist

Introduction

In this chapter we focus on what Holcot has to say about three crucially important sacraments for the life of the medieval Christian: baptism, confession and penance, and the eucharist. To understand this discussion and the kinds of claims Holcot makes, we begin with a brief description of the common medieval understanding of the sacraments and the role of the sacraments in the life of the Christian.

The seven sacraments of the late medieval Church (i.e., baptism, eucharist, penance, confirmation, marriage, holy orders, and last rites) consisted of both proper *form* and *matter*.[1] The *form* of the sacrament referred to the correct verbal formulation: for example, in baptism the priest must state "in the name of the Father, Son, and Holy Spirit." The *matter* of the sacrament referred to the material element or action: thus in baptism, the matter consists of water and the mode of applying the water (sprinkling, immersion, pouring, etc.). Sacraments consisting of the proper *form* and *matter*—when combined with the proper intention—confer grace.

One helpful way to think about the sacramental system is to consider the life of the medieval Christian as one of continual and successive conversion.[2]

This process brings with it a repeating threefold sequence that structures the life of the Christian: preparation for conversion, conversion, and post-conversion life.[3] Euan Cameron provides a helpful narrative of this cyclical process:

> Late medieval religion was, at least officially, about saving individual souls. Individual souls were saved, not in a once-and-for-all act of redemption, but by a lifelong course through a cycle of sin, absolution, and penance. This cycle was determined by the two great facts of religious life: human sin, that is, repeated breaking of the moral law of God, and the forgiveness of sins, offered through the Church in the sacrament of penance.[4]

The cycle began with birth and the incursion of original sin. This was followed by the cleansing and regenerative waters of baptism. It was then reenacted each time the pilgrim turned away from God (*aversio*) through sin and was then compelled to return to God (*conversio*) through confession and penance. Like baptism, the process of confession, absolution, and penance removes guilt and provides satisfaction for guilt through a sufficient penalty, which upon completion restores one to the state of grace immediately enjoyed after baptism. While the cyclical description of the Christian life is accurate with respect to the forgiveness of sins, it is important to recognize that the eucharist was also central to medieval Christianity. If placed within the sacramental picture described here, the medieval pilgrim would participate in eucharist after the confession and absolution of sins. Following the decree of Lateran IV (Canon 21), this took place at least once a year immediately following a yearly confession. Theologically, the eucharist was understood to nourish the pilgrim through God's grace.

As we will see, Holcot clearly sees baptism, confession, and the eucharist as essential aspects of the Christian life that should not be contemned or discarded. Nevertheless, in all three cases, Holcot believes that the ultimate efficacy of these sacraments lies in the hands of God rather than the work itself. In this way, Holcot's views on the sacraments remain strikingly pastoral. He is forever at pains to reassure pilgrims and genuine seekers that if they, in good faith, attempt to approach God in the way he has prescribed, they can rest assured that God will always respond.

Baptism

On the surface, Holcot maintains a classic medieval description of baptism as a sacrament. A valid and effective baptism generally requires a material element, a proper verbal form, and the correct intention on the part of its participants. However, it would be wrong to give the impression that Holcot holds a view that can fit into a purely mechanical view of the sacrament such that the conferral of grace by this sacrament is a necessary consequence of the act or compels God to bestow grace. Nor does he believe that the bestowal of baptismal grace cannot happen unless the constituted rite is perfectly performed. In short, Holcot takes the sacrament of baptism seriously as an important rite set aside by God; thus if anyone despises or looks down on this instituted means of grace, that person will surely be barred from its efficacy. However, he balances this by also claiming that the performance of the rite (or failure to perform the rite correctly) in no way compels God.[5]

Holcot's discussion of baptism is divided into eight main parts. The first six articles constitute his formal description of the sacrament and its requirements. We should note, however, that this makes up only a small portion of the discussion. The bulk of the question is taken up in articles 7 and 8 where Holcot responds to several problematic cases (*casus*) and then to several objections to the belief that baptism actually confers grace to the one being baptized. To clarify his position we first identify the formal criteria of baptism outlined by Holcot. Subsequently, we assess what those criteria look like in practice by following Holcot in his response to problematic cases and objections.

In article 1, Holcot lays out the three conditions that must be in place for a valid baptism: the proper matter, the proper form, and the proper intention of the one administering the baptism. Rather forcefully, Holcot asserts that "if one of these things is missing (*defuerit*), then there is no sacrament."[6] We will see the extent to which this assertion remains unqualified when Holcot faces the difficult cases and objections that arise from this position. At the outset, however, it is interesting to note that he does not mention the intention of the one being baptized as absolutely essential to the efficacy of the sacrament as he does for the intention of the one administering the sacrament. We will see a slight qualification to this later when Holcot discusses the requirements of adult baptism.

Article 2 focuses on the form of baptism. By "form" Holcot means the precise formula spoken during the act of immersion, namely, "I baptize you in the name of the Father, the Son, and the Holy Spirit" (cf. Matthew 28:19). The central discussion here is about the ways in which this form can be corrupted without becoming an obstacle to the sacrament.[7] Holcot regards certain changes to the formula as harmless, such as when a priest coughs or sneezes during the performance of the rite.[8] However, other kinds of insertions or omissions can disrupt the efficacy of the sacrament. Holcot identifies such a change in the added words introduced by Arius: "in the name of the *greater* father and *lesser son*."[9] The key to the distinction is to consider whether or not the altered spoken form shows a purposeful error or malice in the intention of the minister.[10] Does the minister intend to assert something heretical by this change? Or is the change merely accidental or motivated out of piety or devotion? If the former, the form is likely to impede the efficacy of the sacrament. But if the latter, it tends not to be a problem. Here we can see that the intention of the minster enjoys a kind of primacy over the form. And, as we will see later, the reason Holcot can hold this position is because, strictly speaking, it is actually God undertaking the baptism.[11] Thus, as in the case of meritorious belief, the verbal (or propositional) error is not in itself a problem. But a change to the form motivated by a malicious intention shows a kind of contempt for the sacrament as instituted. In the face of such contempt, God chooses not to respond.

In article 3, Holcot turns to the proper element of baptism and explains why water is the most appropriate element for baptism.[12] In this explanation, Holcot provides one of his most expansive discussions of what baptism symbolizes and enacts. First, he says that water is the most fitting material element for baptism because water is a kind of diaphanous material that can be illumined by light. In this way the water of baptism signifies the illumination through faith. Second, water is wet. The wetness symbolizes the cleaning power of baptism. Third, the water is cold, and the coldness symbolizes the extinguishing of tinder (*fomitis*; i.e., the tinder of sin [*fomes peccati*]). Fourth, he notes that, as Aristotle says, water is important for generation, and thus it symbolizes regeneration and the gathering of grace. Fifth and finally, the ubiquity of water signifies its necessity.[13]

This list answers the question of why water was chosen as the matter for the sacrament of baptism rather than another element. It also provides some indication of what Holcot thinks baptism accomplishes. A short while later, in article 6, Holcot clarifies the list by identifying four specific effects of baptism. In line with his view of water as a sign of cleansing, the first effect of baptism is identified here as the removal of sin.[14] This, coupled with his earlier claim that the coldness of water signifies the extinguishing of the tinder (*fomes*) of sin, suggests that he does not hold a theory whereby the traces of original sin are thought to linger after baptism. Rather, he believes that the cleansing of baptism is total and complete.

The second effect of baptism is the infusion of a new grace or, in the case of adult baptism, where some grace has already been acquired through other means, an increase of a preceding grace.[15] The conferral of grace is what distinguishes baptism from circumcision. Holcot follows the position of Peter Lombard, who affirms that, while both circumcision and baptism remove sin, baptism alone provides positive grace that guides and influences future action.[16]

The third effect of baptism is the remission of a penalty.[17] We should distinguish this removal of the penalty from the removal of the sin or guilt itself. This distinction is important because it raises a problem for Holcot. The sixth principal objection argues that there would be something unseemly and unordered about a world where wrongs were simply wiped away and were not balanced out by satisfaction-making penalties.[18] Holcot concedes that, through baptism, God does in fact accept the passion of Christ as an acceptable satisfaction-making penalty, and therefore it removes both the guilt and the need for any further penalty. However, in response to the accusation that this creates an unordered world, Holcot states that God "orders" guilt in two ways; one way is through punishing guilt but another is through removing guilt for his own honor and for a display of his goodness. Thus the world is well ordered whether God punishes or removes guilt.[19]

Finally, Holcot says there is the "impression of a character" (*impressio characteris*).[20] The baptismal character can be defined as

> a seal that guards the recipient's soul and sheds light on his regeneration. It disposes its recipient to faith and charity . . . The baptismal character insures the continuation of the grace of baptism in the recipient's soul after the water departs.[21]

Holcot has little to add to this. In fact, he provides no clear definition of the baptismal character itself. He simply takes the definition for granted and asserts that this is indeed an important effect of baptism that should not be overlooked. Nevertheless, this assertion without explanation offers us little in the way of distinguishing this "character" from the second effect of baptism, the new infusion of grace. Holcot, however, is not alone in being opaque about this difference. Speaking of William of Auxerre's account—which is one of the most substantial discussions of baptismal character—Marcia Colish writes "William's account does not fully succeed in explaining how baptismal character differs from the spiritual grace of the *res sacramenti*."[22] The only decisive difference she can identify is that baptized persons are capable of losing their baptismal grace through backsliding, while William insists that baptismal character is permanent and cannot be lost. Likewise, baptismal grace is salvific while baptismal character is not.[23] While Holcot does little to account for these differences, by asserting the infusion of grace and baptismal character as two separate effects he adopts and passes on this traditional, but somewhat opaque, distinction between baptismal effects.

Stepping back from the particular effects of baptism in general, we need to contextualize this within the larger scholastic debate about sacramental efficacy. In the third principal argument, the general problem is raised: if the sacrament of baptism really does produce the effect of grace, then it seems that a creature can give itself grace.[24]

In looking at how Holcot responds to this objection, we can position him more precisely within the debate about sacramental efficacy.[25] For instance, Bryan Spinks describes the difference between Aquinas and Scotus as follows:

> Scotus believed that Aquinas' view of sacramental causality was philosophically problematic, and sided with Bonaventure. He agreed with Aquinas that instrumental causes do not have intrinsic causal powers, but require a principle agent. Yet Scotus questioned the idea that a material object could have a supernatural causal power. In his view sacraments do not cause God's grace; rather, God has decided that whenever a sacrament is received, he will give the appropriate supernatural gift. This divine decision has been formalized in a covenant (*Pactio Divina*) with the Church. God's pact guarantees sacramental reliability.[26]

In answering the objection, Holcot demonstrates a clear preference for the kind of view attributed to Scotus, which ascribes the actual efficacy of the sacrament to the divine action at the performance of the sacramental rite rather than to the rite itself as an "instrumental cause."[27] He writes:

> When it is argued that if baptism were the effective cause of grace (*gratia effectiva gratiae*) then the creature would be able to cause [grace], it is able to be said that something is called an effective cause in two ways: properly and metaphorically. For, properly, the sacraments are not the efficient cause of grace, but only God [is the efficient cause of grace]. Metaphorically, our merits are called the causes of both grace and the increase of grace, and similarly in the case of the sacraments, because at the completion (*ad perfectionem*) of the sacraments God confers and causes grace.[28]

Holcot sees the sacrament of baptism as primarily an agreed-upon occasion in which God will act when the command has been followed. But there is little to suggest that Holcot thinks it is the rite itself that is somehow the instrumental cause directly causing the effects listed earlier.

With the effects of baptism identified, we can now return to its requirements. Besides the form (the verbal pronouncement) and the proper matter (water), a proper intention is also required. The central question here is what constitutes the right internal attitude to sufficiently fulfill the human side of the covenant with God, such that God will be pleased to honor his side of the bargain and confer grace.

The distinct concepts of "intention" and "faith" are particularly important here, though their difference is not always obvious. In describing the requirements placed on the one administering the sacrament, Holcot offers the following distinction. Normally, he says, the minister of the sacrament is the priest. Nevertheless, in times of necessity, nearly anyone can administer the rite of baptism, regardless of whether the person is a believer. As long as he has the intention of administering the sacrament according to the custom of the Church, then he can perform the rite.[29] Here we can see the difference between faith and intention. While ideally the minister believes the truths of the faith, the performance of the rite simply requires that one intends to perform the sacrament as God, through the Church, has commanded. The importance of this distinction should not be underestimated. During the Reformation, the question of whether or not faith is required for a baptism to be effective loomed large. Luther—at least the later Luther— argued that faith was not absolutely necessary for the efficacy of the sacrament.[30] He saw such a requirement as a way to turn the sacrament into another "work" wherein the efficacy of the sacrament was tied to human belief and human work, rather than to God's action and faithfulness.[31] In terms of this debate, Holcot and Luther are in agreement.

What then is required on the part of the one being baptized? Holcot gives this question some attention in article 4, and the answer varies depending on the candidate for baptism. There are two main types of candidates: children and adults. In the case of children, Holcot remarks that nothing is required except that the child is separated from its mother, either totally or in part.[32] Perhaps more remarkable than anything else is Holcot's lack of interest in any discussion or requirement of faith or *fides alienum,* whether on the part of the godparents or the faith community as a whole. What Holcot does seem particularly interested in is casuistically responding to all the exceptions that might occur if the death of an unbaptized child is imminent. For example, he explains that, in a moment of necessity where the death of the child is impending, it is permissible to sprinkle the head of the child as he emerges from the mother, because the head is the principal part of the person.[33] However, if the hand or foot emerges first, Holcot suggests that the child should not be so sprinkled.[34] Yet even here he qualifies the claim, saying that in the end it would not hurt if the hand or foot were sprinkled while the proper words are said because the "mercy of God should not be constrained (*arctanda*) in [times of] necessity."[35]

Holcot's consideration then shifts to the requirements of an adult candidate for baptism. He first considers the mental health of the adult. If the adult is permanently mentally incapacitated, then the person should be treated as if an infant or child.[36] If the candidate is only occasionally mentally impaired, Holcot says, it is required that the individual "intends to be baptized" during moments of mental soundness. Holcot compares this person to one who is asleep and says: "if before insanity or sleep they had a contrary will, then they do not receive the sacrament if they happened to be baptized [later] in sleep or madness."[37]

Finally, Holcot considers the adult catechumen who is of sound mind. Here Holcot asserts that not only must there be a right intention but there must also be right faith and either an "absolute or conditioned" will of undertaking the sacrament.[38] Holcot goes on to say that if the baptism is received with a mixed or conditioned will, then the candidate receives the sacrament but not the reality (*rem*) of the sacrament.[39] In common discussions of the *res et sacramentum*, the *res* is the grace conferred,[40] so it is possible that Holcot is saying the baptism is legitimate but the grace is withheld until the mixed will becomes pure or the conditioned will becomes absolute. Thus after this change there would be no need for rebaptism.[41] The requirement that the adult candidate have more than a right intention but also proper faith further distances Holcot from any extreme interpretation of the sacrament where grace is conferred automatically in absence of faith or a positive intention. Yet, at the same time, neither does Holcot's position seem to suggest that faith alone is sufficient to receive the intended grace and that the sacrament is merely an outward sign of that grace. Once more he holds a middle position in which, strictly speaking, it is God, not the sacrament, that confers grace, and yet God refuses to distribute that grace to those who despise the instituted mechanism and refuse to take part.

Following a formal clarification of the requirements of baptism and its effects, it is not unusual to provide an analysis of exceptional cases and to determine their validity. Holcot follows this custom in his seventh article. What may be a bit more exceptional—at least in comparison to his immediate contemporaries—is the space he devotes to this task and the number of cases he examines. Lecturing on book 4 one year after Holcot, Adam Wodeham engages in a similar task of resolving exceptional cases. However, where Wodeham focuses on 8 doubts (*dubia*), Holcot analyzes 16 different cases.[42] A number of these cases are traditional in origin and considered by both Holcot and Wodeham.

Such cases include many seemingly strange and often very specific scenarios. For instance, Holcot asks us to consider the following situation. Imagine that someone is carrying a child to a church to be baptized and becomes aware that the child will die before reaching the church. Given the high infant mortality rate of the time, this may have been a more common situation than it initially seems. Nevertheless, the situation becomes more specific. Imagine that the person carrying the child is crossing a high bridge and, in light of the immanent death of the child, decides to throw the child off the bridge into the river with the intention of baptizing the child while uttering the proper words. Holcot's response attempts to navigate between two extremes. One extreme says: yes, the child was baptized because the proper form and intention were present with the matter. Another extreme responds in the negative because baptism is meant to signify both the death, through immersion, and resurrection, through reemergence from the water. But in this case the child was only immersed in the water but was never lifted from it. To these extremes, Holcot simply replies: "I believe that the child will be saved, so long as God approves what is done by man however imperfectly."[43] The action itself is viewed by Holcot as imperfect and not recommended. Nevertheless, done in innocence and with the best intentions, God is likely to respond to such a gesture.

A second example shows, however, that despite his belief that it is God who truly confers grace and the work of the sacrament itself only confers grace metaphorically, Holcot still takes the requirements of the sacrament very seriously; these requirements are not to be ignored, partially observed, or divided. The case considered is certainly unique and extreme, but it comes with a substantial historically pedigree.[44] It considers the validity of a baptism conjointly performed by a unique pair of priests, one of whom is crippled and the other of whom is mute. The crippled priest is capable of uttering the words of baptism but cannot immerse the child. The mute priest, in contrast, is capable of lifting the child but cannot utter the words. Only together, it seems, can they fulfill the requirement of a valid baptism.

The concern in this case is the unification of the separate acts of uttering the words of the sacrament and performing the immersion. In response, Holcot argues that "ecclesiastical sacraments are sacraments of unity, and they are not able to be divided."[45] Further at issue is an apparent conflict between two statutes of canon law, primarily directed at the proper consecration of the eucharist. One canon in Gratian's *Decretum*—the twelfth-century collection of Church canons that, as evidenced here, wielded tremendous influence on later medieval theology and canon law—suggests that it is permissible for a person to assist another in the consecration of the eucharist. However, another canon suggests that it is not permissible for the bishop to raise the host while another priest says the words.[46] To solve this apparent contradiction, Holcot makes a distinction between essential requirements and the requirements of solemnity. Essential requirements, he says, cannot be divided. Thus if a priest begins to consecrate the host with the words *hoc est* (this is) but fails to keep going because of illness or some other reason, another priest should not simply add *corpus meum* (my body). Rather he should begin again.[47] However, there are many aspects of the rite that are not essential but are part of the solemnity of the occasion, and these can be divided. In this way Holcot can explain the allowance for assistance but can also deny division in the case of direct consecration or in the direct act of baptizing. Thus he concludes by saying that it would be better for the lame priest to say the words of the sacrament and merely sprinkle the water.

Confession and Penance

By far the most important and influential discussion of penance throughout the late Middle Ages is found in Gratian's *Decretum*.[48] Joseph Goering highlights two central poles or apparent *discordantia* that Gratian attempted to bring together in this work.[49] On the one hand, Gratian identifies several authorities that suggest that "contrition of the heart" and "secret confession" are sufficient for the forgiveness of sins.[50] At the same time, he acknowledges the existence of other authorities that suggest that contrition is not enough and forgiveness requires an oral confession. As Goering explains, Gratian is clear about the "primacy of internal contrition and of God's power in forgiving sins."[51] However, Gratian attempts to bring this position into harmony with the divergent tradition by emphasizing how important it is that confession of the mouth and the satisfaction of good works follow this sincere contrition. Any lack of effort to follow this contrition with confession and penance raises severe doubts about the genuineness of the private contrition and suggests contempt for the Church as a whole.[52]

Goering also notes that many authors try to explain Gratian's conciliatory efforts in the context of the debate between the followers of Bernard of Clairvaux and Peter Abelard. For example, Allen Frantzen writes:

> By the time Gratian published his concordance to the canons (1140) a serious disagreement about confession had arisen: the followers of Peter Abelard argued that sin could be forgiven so long as the sinner was genuinely sorry for it, but the followers of Bernard of Clairvaux insisted on oral confession, to be followed by penance and absolution ... Abelard

was seeking to prove that forgiveness depended not on the power of the keys, which Christ had given to the apostles, but on the sinner's interior disposition.[53]

Gratian, however, was not the only influential voice shaping the practice of penance. Peter Lombard's treatment also influenced future discussions of the topic.[54] Goering notes that a simple but extremely influential aspect of Peter Lombard's account was his decision to limit the discussion of sacraments to seven and his further decision to accord penance a place of centrality.[55] While Goering tends to downplay the differences between Gratian and Lombard,[56] other writers have emphasized that, where Gratian was ambiguous about the necessity of oral confession and public penance, Lombard was clear about its necessity.[57]

For all his ambiguity, Gratian's continued emphasis on the importance of oral confession—despite the sufficiency of inner contrition—and Lombard's continued insistence on its importance set the stage for the decision of the Fourth Lateran Council (Canon 21), which Holcot discusses in detail. The Canon mandates that every adult Christian of either sex should make a confession once a year to his proper priest.[58] This Canon sets the expectation that every Christian would confess once a year to a priest, who in turn would prepare himself to discern the health of souls and would make himself available for hearing confession. Without a doubt, the Canon of 1215 significantly shaped Christian penitential practice in dramatically new ways. Goering offers the following summary:

> Certainly by the end of the 13th century the practice of penance had given rise not only to a deep and lasting concern with contrition and the search of conscience but also to frequent confession to priests and friars, pilgrimages, indulgences, and many other types of popular devotion.[59]

It is within this context that Holcot's own account should be understood. First, there is the concern about the necessary and ancillary components of the sacrament. Is contrition sufficient? Will the grace conferred at contrition be lost if Canon 21 is not followed and yearly oral confession is not made? Second, what does this statute demand in practice? To whom exactly must this confession be made? Will any priest suffice, or must it be one's local parish priest? Both of these questions are considered in Holcot's account.

When it comes to Holcot's view on confession and penance perhaps no passage is more important than his direct response to the question regarding whether confession is necessary for salvation. To this question, Holcot responds

> I say that something is necessary for salvation in two ways. Either because without this it is impossible to have salvation or because it has been ordained thus (*sic ordinatum*) that it is not in the free power of the will to despise (*contemnere*) this and to have salvation. In the first mode, no sacrament is necessary for salvation ... In the second mode, confession is necessary for salvation, that is, confession is an ordained means for salvation, such that it is not in the power of man, having despised this, to obtain salvation.[60]

We can see this delicate stance at work in Holcot's reply to one of the first objections. The objection questions why contrition is not sufficient, and why further confession to a priest is also necessary. The traditional reason given is that confession is necessary for the dismissal of sin. But Ezekiel 18:21–22 says that, at the moment of contrition, grace is infused. Thus since grace and sin are incompatible, it follows that there is no longer guilt after the grace of contrition has been infused. There is no longer any sin remaining that confession to a priest would absolve.[61]

Holcot responds not by denying the argument's pivotal claims but by noting that the sacrament of confession is also important, and if it is viewed with contempt, the sin removed through contrition will be re-imputed.[62] Here we see Holcot showing a deep respect for the sacrament that has been prescribed, such that even while the contrite person has already been forgiven, sin will be re-imputed to that person if he suddenly chooses to despise the act of confession. This respect for the commanded sacrament is matched, however, by Holcot's recognition that confession is not absolutely necessary.[63] Once again, Holcot shows a preference for the supremacy of the intention and respect for the divine command rather than for its actual performance. Just as we have seen in other areas of Holcot's thought, although our actions do not compel God, they do reveal our intentions. God, we are reminded, has promised to respond only to those who faithfully and humbly do all that they can to follow his commands.

Beyond this concern for the necessity of confession as a whole, the main point that preoccupies Holcot is the question of whether confession must be made to a priest and, if so, whether any priest will suffice or whether Canon 21 meant something specific by the words "proper priest."

Regarding the first question, whether confession must be made to someone in ecclesiastical office, Holcot introduces an objection. The point is raised that confession should be made to a priest with the ability to discern between different types of sin and to proscribe proportionate responses. But sometimes it happens that a priest with sufficient ability cannot be found, and, in such cases, it certainly is permissible for an individual to proscribe the appropriate penance for himself.[64] Further, the objector points to James 5:16, "confess your sins to one another" and observes that there is no mention of the priestly office. Finally, Lombard says that "if a priest is lacking, confession is to be made to a neighbor or friend."[65] While conceding that confession to a priest is not absolutely necessary, Holcot clarifies that one is nevertheless required to confess to a priest if there is sufficient opportunity. The priest's license to hear confession does not come from a discerning skill or knowledge he possesses but an authority that a layperson does not have: an authority that comes through both ordination and commission by the Church.[66] In taking this position, Holcot joined a growing trend in the fourteenth century to discount lay confession. Here Holcot emphasizes the importance of the presence of an ecclesiastical authority in the sacrament of confession, such that ignoring its importance would be tantamount to contemning the sacrament itself. This reveals that Holcot also believes that the status of the priest in question is relevant for effective confession. However, there are two ways a priest can fail to have the required authority: either from lack of ordination or from lack of commission.

This discussion of priestly requirement is a useful introduction to the main issue that occupies Holcot in the following question:

> Whether it is necessary that a person, having confessed to and done penance for someone who is not their proper priest, but who nevertheless has a general commission of hearing confession, ought to confess those same sins again to his proper priest.[67]

At issue here is the assumption that in order to administer confession, a priest requires both the power of the order and the power of jurisdiction, and these two powers come by separate means. At ordination, the priest receives the power to consecrate and administer the eucharist. But this power of the order does not yet include the ecclesiastical power to judge, which is a power conferred through commission. The concern raised is about proper jurisdiction given to a priest through his commission and exactly what kind of jurisdiction Canon 21 intended by mandating every Christian confess their sins once a year to "their *proper priest*." The first argument listed in favor of demanding that one reconfess quotes this precept from Canon 21 in full and then points to the decisive bone of contention, stating that a "preacher" or a "minor" (presumably a Dominican preacher or Franciscan friar) is not a "proper priest" and therefore anyone confessing to one of these priests must confess these same sins again to their proper (understood as parish) priest.[68] This is a territorial dispute over the rights and jurisdiction granted to mendicant preachers through their commission and the rights and jurisdiction granted to parochial priests as a result of their assignment to a particular diocese and parish.

This is not an idiosyncratic concern unique to Holcot. Rather, Holcot is responding to a fairly recent controversy over the antifraternalist position of John of Pouilly that was condemned by Pope John XXII. Already in 1300 Pope Boniface VIII issued the papal bull *Super Cathedram* and granted mendicants the right to be licensed by the bishop to hear confession.[69] In the second decade of the fourteenth century, John of Pouilly reacted to this decision and argued that the pope did not have the power to relieve the laity of their obligation to confess to their parish or proper priests as mandated by Canon 21.[70] In response, Pope John XXII wrote the bull *Vas electionis* in 1321, which condemned the positions attributed to Pouilly and reaffirmed the power of the pope and other bishops to grant mendicant friars the license to hear confession.[71]

While this original conflict erupted in Paris and preceded Holcot by a generation, there is strong evidence to suggest that in England, at the time Holcot was writing, this issue continued to be contentious; moreover, it did not merely manifest itself in academic debate but was visible in the concrete political decisions affecting the daily lives of individuals. As early as 1329, the registers of the Bishop of Exeter, John Grandisson, show clashes and conflicts with unlicensed mendicants confessors.[72] Penn Szittya observes that these conflicts are visible up through 1360, culminating in a letter from Bishop Gandisson revealing the level of concern he had regarding these mendicant confessors.[73] In this letter Grandisson warns his diocese to be wary of seducers and hypocrites. But whom does he have in mind? He is at least in part referring to the friars who claim a legitimate license to hear confession. Szittya summarizes:

> Grandisson therefore counsels, exhorts, and commands under pain of excommunication that all curates under him beware and warn their parishioners to beware of these heralds of Antichrist (*Antichristi precones*). Among these are the friars, who falsely claim they have the bishop's license to confess. Grandisson ends with instructions for recognizing these false confessors, and commands that his letter be called to the attention of every person in the diocese.[74]

While this letter came several years after Holcot's discussion in his *Sentences* commentary, it is evidence of a broader climate in which this dispute was a present and pressing issue. Holcot, as a mendicant himself, enters this dispute and defends at length the rights of the mendicants to hear confession and argues that those confessing to a mendicant are relieved from any further obligation to confess to their parish priest.

Holcot begins by recounting the errors of Pouilly condemned in 1321.[75] First, Pouilly claims that anyone who confessed their sins to a friar with only a general license must confess those same sins again to their proper priest; second, the pope is not able to excuse the penitent from making confession to their proper priest; third, the pope is not able to grant a general license for hearing confession that would excuse a penitent from making confession to his proper priest.[76]

It is important to clarify here that the present debate is not over whether the "power of the order" is enough to hear confession and absolve sins. Holcot is not taking the position that any ordained priest automatically (by virtue of being ordained) has the power to hear confession and grant absolution of sin. In his next question (book 4, question 6), Holcot is sufficiently clear that one also needs the power of ecclesiastical jurisdiction acquired through a commission.[77] Holcot's debate with Pouilly is over whether the general license of hearing confession possessed by the mendicants is a sufficient license to allow those confessions to fulfill the obligation mandated in Canon 21 in 1215.

Holcot then notes the clear condemnation of these positions by Pope John XXII and concludes that the answer to the main question is clear: people do not need to reconfess their sins when they have already confessed to a priest who possesses a general license for hearing confession.[78] Despite his belief that the pope has made the answer to this question clear, Holcot aims to promote a greater understanding of this position by clarifying the true meaning of Canon 21.[79] He offers six arguments as to why "proper priest" was never meant to be restricted to one's parish priest alone. While we need not examine each of these arguments, a few colorful examples will help illustrate the general tenor of his response.

The arguments focus on showing the various absurdities that would follow if the statute literally meant that every faithful person were obliged to confess to his parish priest alone. The first argument states that if this were true, then a person who confessed to the pope himself would still be obliged to confess again to his parish priest, which is presumed to be absurd.[80] In a similar vein, the third argument points to other absurdities that would follow by looking at other uses of the phrase "proper priest." Holcot quotes a later portion of the statute that reads "if a subject wishes with just cause to confess to another priest he ought to seek and obtain a license from a 'proper priest.'"[81] Holcot then asks: did the statute mean parish priest here or not? If not, the position is conceded and the earlier use of "proper priest" cannot be restricted to parish priest alone. But, Holcot says, if the John of Pouilly camp insists that here too is meant parish priest, then this means that the parish priest alone has the power to commission the power of absolving, and therefore not even the pope would be able to commission someone without permission from the parochial priest, which is absurd.[82]

Holcot's most colorful example comes from critiquing what he sees as the extremely literal interpretation of the canon. If we are going to interpret it this narrowly, then the phrase "everyone of each sex" (*omnis utriusque sexus*) applies to a man who is of both sexes, such as a hermaphrodite, or it is intended to apply to all men and women everywhere. The former is dismissed as absurd. Therefore it must apply to everyone. But if it applies to everyone, this would seem to mandate that the pope himself, bishops, and their legates are required to confess to a parochial priest. This too Holcot suggests is absurd, therefore "the statute is not able to be understood according to the force of the words (*virtutem verborum*), just as experience sufficiently teaches."[83] In short, Holcot believes he is arguing for the common-sense position because the view of John of Pouilly leads to all kinds of absurdities that violate established Church practice and therefore cannot be what the authors of the statute intended.

Eucharist

Holcot's single question on the eucharist in his *Sentences* commentary asks a traditional question: whether the real body of Christ exists in the likeness or species of the bread. His fundamental answer is illustrative of a larger trend in his thought: on the one hand, he stresses the mystery of God's power and our inability to exhaustively comprehend his works. On the other hand, this recognition does not lead Holcot to silence. In one remarkable concluding line Holcot explains how the point of recognizing the mystery of God's power is not to drive us to abandon reason or the investigation of faith. Rather, the point is to temper our hubris and caution us against believing that our natural intellect should become the sole measure of possibility and credibility. A second point of emphasis lies in his continued concern for pious believers and his effort to relieve them of debilitating anxiety about whether the host has been consecrated correctly and is therefore truly nourishing to the spiritual life. Holcot, consistent with his larger view of the sacraments, continues to remind his reader that, above all, the eucharist is a work of God, not of man, and that if a believer comes piously to the place God has appointed, God will extend grace to him.

After surveying the principal arguments for and against the position that Christ's body is truly present, Holcot asserts strongly that we should believe that Christ's body is present. He then prefaces his breakdown of the different components and requirements of the sacrament with three conclusions. In the first conclusion he explains

> God is able to do more than we are able to understand and he is able to do things, the mode and cause of which we are not able to investigate. Therefore the following consequence is not valid: man is not able to declare sufficiently how the body of Christ really exists under the species of bread and wine, therefore it is not able to be so in reality or this ought not to be believed.[84]

A concrete instance of this conviction comes in his refutation of the first principal argument wherein it is said that the bread cannot really become

Christ's body because this would fundamentally violate the principles of ordered change. Since bread does not naturally generate or transform into flesh, for such a fundamental change to occur the bread would have to be annihilated while something new takes its place.[85] The objection points out that this would mean anything could become anything: the whole world could be present in a fly, or an ass could become a man.[86] Holcot's response is to explain that our common way of describing the sacrament as "the bread *becomes* the body" is an imperfect and analogous way of explaining what we cannot fully explain. We are familiar with other transformations where, without annihilation, one thing becomes another through ordered change, and so we use this language to describe what happens in the eucharist. However, the argument's hubris becomes apparent when it tries to argue from this imperfect analogical language to natural transformations to conclude that the annihilation of the bread and completely new presence of Christ *de novo* is impossible. Holcot explains that, strictly speaking, it is not true to say that the bread miraculously becomes the body. Rather, two separate miracles occur: the bread completely ceases to be and the body of Christ becomes present *de novo* under the likeness of bread.[87] Even though this is not how natural change occurs, Holcot views it as an error of presumption to conclude that the transformation of the bread into the body of Christ cannot work this way.

After warning us not to draw the conclusion that the eucharist is impossible because it does not fit our normal explanations of things, Holcot explains to his reader where the Christian must begin:

> For from the fact that we believe without a doubt that God is able to do more than we are able to understand through natural investigation, it follows that regarding those things which he tells us to believe, we ought to take our intellect captive. And this is the marvelous thing that God wishes, that we, in some individual matters instituted by Him, take our intellect captive.[88]

Holcot seems to be writing with more urgency and passion here than elsewhere. He clearly feels that the error of his time is to think too highly of reason's understanding of what is and is not possible, of what should count as warranted and what should not. Lahey, in his interpretation of the text, describes the position here as "markedly fideistic, suggesting that *moderni* reasoning has cordoned off yet another section of traditional scholastic theology as beyond rational analysis."[89] While Lahey's description certainly captures something of Holcot's position, nevertheless Holcot's final line in this same passage cautions us to temper any judgment that Holcot believes there is no place left for rational analysis. Holcot ends with quotations from Augustine, Gregory the Great, and Peter Lombard, all suggesting how the mysteries of the faith should be approached. He quotes Lombard as saying that the mysteries of the faith can be beneficially believed but not beneficially investigated. It is Holcot's advice on how to interpret this final Lombardian quotation that forces us to reevaluate the assessment of radical fideism. He writes:

> This [quotation] should [not be] understood such that man ought not to argue about those things that belong to faith, but rather [it should be understood as saying] that he ought not to affirm that he is able to achieve (*assignere*) perfect understanding (*rationem*).[90]

This final passage seems particularly important in light of the force of Holcot's previous remarks and the penchant in modern scholarship to label Holcot a skeptic. Holcot's goal is more nuanced; it is to encourage one to pursue the understanding and the investigation of faith but always with a humility that prevents him from claiming too much. This is a message Holcot goes on to put into practice in the rest of the question. Clearly, Holcot does not believe that nothing can be said about the eucharist because he subsequently explains the different components required for the sacrament to be properly performed and then responds, *with argumentation*, to the 10 principal arguments introduced at the outset.

Turning first to the form of the eucharist, Holcot claims, in accord with what he has said about baptism and confession, that, strictly speaking, none of the formal requirements of the sacraments are necessary because they are God's doing and not man's. Nevertheless, at this moment God has commanded that the sacrament be performed in a certain way and that we risk contemning the sacrament if we do not do our best to follow that command. This kind of balanced position is evident in Holcot's discussion of the language in which the eucharist is performed. He notes that it is not required that the words *hoc est corpus meum* (this is my body) be said in Latin, Greek, French, or English. However, some language is required.[91] Holcot is simultaneously criticizing those who are too strict in their conception of the sacrament and those who are too lax.

In addition to the form, Holcot discussed the matter of the sacrament and requirements of the priest. He handles the required material quickly, identifying wheat bread, wine, and water as the proper matter. The discussion of the requirements of the celebrating priest extend much further in length and echo Holcot's continual concern with the possibility of deception and his pastoral view that God recognizes and honors what is done with the best of intentions, whether or not the actual act lives up to that intention. The case in question is whether or not Christ's body is present to its partakers when the host is consecrated by someone who claims to be a priest but actually is not (e.g., perhaps they have not been baptized or ordained). Holcot, always sensitive to the pious laity, suggests that in such cases the eucharist is valid and Christ's body is indeed really present. He writes:

> I say that it would be hard to say that such a person [i.e., a fraudulent priest] did not absolve [sin] or consecrate [the host] because, if this were true, sinners would be cheated and many inconveniences would follow.[92]

To avoid such inconveniences, Holcot admits that either this fraudulent priest really did consecrate the host or God did it through him (such that the sacrament would be consecrated without a minister). He concludes without certainty: "which of these is more true, it is impossible to know without revelation."[93]

Holcot's responses to the principal arguments offer us several good examples of the two main emphases that emerge in this question: namely that the eucharist, while beyond comprehension, is not beyond investigation and that the eucharist is a work of God and not of man and therefore those who come to it piously will receive its grace no matter how flawed the circumstances of its performance. We close by looking at an example of each instance.

The fourth principal argument raised a particular concern, in response to which Holcot demonstrates that the eucharist is not beyond rational investigation. This argument suggests that the body of Christ is not truly present in the species of the bread because it is obviously not visible, and, therefore, since sight is the most noble sense, *a fortiori* it is not held or touched. Holcot responds by arguing that when people say that "they see the body of Christ" or "they touch the body of Christ," the statements are true in the sense that they are said; that is, the sense in which they are meant is that the body of Christ exists under the species of sight or touch. But these statements are not made in the sense that Christ's body actually changes or affects one's sight as an object of sight or touch does. The reason is because we hold by faith that the species are seen, touched, and broken and this vision and tangibility is in the species but not in our body. Thus these things are called sacraments because the Christian sees (and touches) one thing (i.e., the accidents of bread/wine) while understanding that the objects seen and touched are actually something else (i.e., the body of Christ). In short, the participants understand that Christ's body and blood are under the species of sight and touch even though they cannot see or touch them. With this clarification, Holcot helps his reader to be more precise with his words and ultimately, in doing so, resolves various difficulties. For example, Holcot concludes by stating that

> properly speaking it ought not to be conceded that "I touched the body of Christ" or "I saw the body of Christ," nor that "the body of Christ touched me" or "the body of Christ changed my sight" even though it is permissible to speak as many do as long as they have a sound intellect.[94]

The emphasis here on a sound intellect is a perfect reminder that Holcot does not think that the sacrament of the eucharist is a place for the intellect to be ignored or cast aside. On the contrary, it is only those of sound intellect—able to make sharp and rigorous distinctions—who are able to see through much of the verbal confusion and to liberate people's false conceptions of the sacrament from many of the contradictions of which it is accused.

The fifth principal argument raises several concerns about the required intention of the consecrating priest.[95] One such concern suggests that the requirement of a right intention should be abandoned altogether. The argument presumes that one could never truly know the intention of the priest, and, therefore, if the right intention on the part of the priest is required, then one should always be suspicious of the priest's intentions so as to ensure that one never wrongly worships an unconsecrated host. Holcot flips this objection on its head. He insists that one's obligation in this case of uncertainty is not to "doubt" but to "believe that the priest acts in good faith"[96] and therefore to worship in confidence. Holcot goes on to reassure worshipping pilgrims by helping them to see their worship as already understood conditionally. Namely, the pilgrim worships the host under the condition that this host was genuinely consecrated. Thus if it turns out that the host was not actually consecrated, no idolatry occurs. In this way, the pastorally minded Holcot reassures his reader that there is no danger of worshipping an unconsecrated host, and the pious pilgrim can worship freely without fear or suspicion.

Conclusion

Here we conclude both our discussion of Holcot's consideration of the sacraments and of Holcot's scholastic works. As we have seen in his discussion of baptism, confession, and the eucharist, Holcot shows repeated interest in a compassionate theology that makes concessions to the well-intentioned pilgrim. At the same, he also works to impress upon the reader that God expects and demands that the pious believer pursues him to the best of his or her ability. In the context of the sacraments, this means taking sacramental rites seriously as a divinely appointed meeting place between God and the believer that should not be despised, dismissed, or taken lightly. The distribution of grace, in the end, is always a divine act and never the necessary result of the performed right. At the same time, God only chooses to respond to those who do their best to meet him at the places he has appointed within a given covenant.

We have seen similar points of emphasis in Holcot's earlier discussions of faith, doctrine, and revelation. In each case, Holcot emphasizes that natural reason is never completely sufficient to reach God and, when accurate knowledge of God has been received, it is always due to God's choice to respond to an individual's search for him. Nevertheless, Holcot does not dismiss the value of rational investigation and inquiry. Rather he expects it and views this pursuit of knowledge as part of what it means to "do one's best." He sees such a pursuit as the obvious result of a genuine desire to know God and to follow the precepts of true religion; this is Holcot's interpretation of the Anselmian "faith seeking understanding."

Even Holcot's academic consideration of future continents and obligational theology reflect these pastoral interests. In a study of Holcot's obligational theology Hester Gelber concludes with a brief meditation on the theological and practical import of his understanding of human contingency. The bare fact that things could be other than they are is important, not only to speculative theology, but also to the pilgrim's lived experience. Gelber writes that a person's ability "to think about what is not now the case, and the allied belief that things could and can be other than they are, connect with some of our most profound experiences ... and ground the late medieval religious world view."[97]

The experiences that Holcot draws our attention to are those aspects of human life that transcend the present moment, the here and now. For example, without reflecting on the future Holcot wonders how we can properly mourn the death of a father (*dolere de morte patris*) or pray for his soul (*pro animi patris*). Holcot writes further that if we were not able to speculate about future contingents, "we would not be able to provide for the future, because we could not think about it." In the same way that an architect imagines the plans of a house or an artist the form of a sculpture, one must imagine a future that is different from the present.[98] As we have seen throughout the first part of this book, Holcot is not only interested in speculative theological debates; even in his most academic works he is concerned with how these debates work themselves out in various aspects of human life.

At this point, we leave behind Holcot's formal academic writing and turn to his biblical commentaries and sermons: two genres of writing more explicitly aimed at an audience of preachers and lay pilgrims with whom he is already quite concerned. While these texts will continue to include discussions of speculative theology and philosophy, the tone and tenor shifts even more dramatically to the practical and pastoral. Here Holcot's passion for guiding the life of the medieval pilgrim is on full display.

6

THE BIBLICAL COMMENTARY TRADITION

Introduction

This chapter begins a new section in the book and makes the transition from Holcot's purely speculative works to those works (biblical commentaries and sermons) written for an audience of preachers or potential preachers. The biblical commentaries and sermons were written primarily for those Dominicans who served the Church through preaching and dealt firsthand with the contingencies of human life. The chapter begins with a discussion of the texts in question, in particular the commentaries on Matthew, the Twelve Prophets, Ecclesiastes, Ecclesiasticus, the Apocalypse, and the Song of Songs. The second section of the chapter turns to the historical context of Holcot's commentaries, specifically considering the possible influence of Richard de Bury on Holcot's classicism. The following chapters examine in more detail Holcot's commentaries on the Twelve Prophets and the book of Wisdom.

Before turning to Holcot's extant works, it is important to observe just how unusual the preservation of Holcot's biblical commentaries is for a Dominican master in the mid-fourteenth century. In an instructive article on the Bible in the fourteenth century, William Courtenay observes that "the only notable mendicant commentators in the period between 1330 and 1370 were English, and of those only Robert Holcot's works were popular enough to survive in numerous manuscripts."[1] When compared with his near contemporaries, Holcot's production—and the preservation of these works—is staggering.[2] For example, we have no extant biblical commentaries for Durand of St. Pourçain, Francis Meyronnes, Thomas of Strasbourg, Gregory of Rimini, Hugolino of Orvieto, or John of Ripa at Paris; or William of Alnwick, John of Reading, John of Rodington, Walter Chatton, or Robert Halifax at Oxford. This basic fact makes the biblical commentaries of Holcot an important witness to the development of late medieval theology.

The Biblical Commentaries

The biblical commentaries and sermons of Robert Holcot are extant in numerous printings and manuscripts. Here we introduce each of Holcot's biblical commentaries (except for his commentary on Wisdom, which is discussed in chapters 8 and 9). These notes on each commentary are intended to provide some background information about the work in question and to serve as a guide (in the notes) to the primary and secondary sources.

Commentary on Matthew

Robert Holcot's commentary on Matthew was probably begun on February 10 (the feast of St. Scholastica), 1334, while he was a *baccalaureus biblicus* (bachelor of the Bible) and after he completed his lectures on the *Sentences*.[3] The commentary is no longer extant as a complete work; however, scholars have been able to discover parts of the work and, in other cases, reconstruct certain aspects of it. First, the inaugural sermon to the lectures that was preached when Holcot was a *baccalaureus biblicus* is preserved.[4] This sermon is relatively short and functions to introduce the series of lectures. Second, Heinrich Schepers argued that a careful study of Holcot's quodlibetal questions indicates that several of them probably originated from his commentary on Matthew.[5] Similar to his commentary on Wisdom, Holcot's Matthew commentary presumably contained both exegesis of the text and formal scholastic questions. The scholastic questions, imbedded throughout, were arguably preserved in the form of quodlibetal questions, while the surrounding exegesis was lost. Schepers originally identified three quodlibetal questions that probably originated with the commentary on Matthew.[6] William Courtenay, in a subsequent publication, expanded the methodology of Schepers and argued that 13 (less likely, up to 16) of the quodlibetal questions can be linked with the Matthew commentary.[7] Thus, as Courtenay concludes, while the explicitly exegetical aspects of the commentary have been lost, "some of Holcot's thoughts on Matthew" have been preserved.[8]

Finally, contemporaneous with his lectures on the book of Matthew Holcot could have also lectured on a book of the Old Testament. While the statutes of Oxford did not require the bachelors to lecture on two books of the Bible (as at Paris),[9] Thomas Kaeppeli observed that there is an *academic introitus* (a sermon functioning as an academic inaugural lecture) to the book of Genesis that was written by Holcot.[10] As Kaeppeli notes, the conclusion to the sermon states explicitly that the biblical book to be treated following the introduction is Genesis.[11] While there is no extant commentary on Genesis by Robert Holcot, this sermon is good evidence that he did lecture on the book of Genesis (perhaps as a bachelor at Oxford alongside his lectures on Matthew).

Commentary on the Twelve Prophets

The second biblical commentary that Robert Holcot wrote originated with his lectures on the Twelve Prophets.[12] This lecture series was given at Oxford while Holcot was regent master in theology (1336–1338). The lectures are interesting in that they have been preserved in a relatively unaltered state; as Smalley notes, "[Holcot] did not polish his notes on the Twelve Prophets enough to make them presentable."[13] The result is that, while the lectures never gained the fame of his other more polished commentaries, they do present us with a relatively pristine view of what was perhaps presented in the lectures themselves. Kimberly Rivers edited the book of Nahum and therefore provides a glimpse into Holcot's earliest scriptural exegesis.[14]

Commentary on Ecclesiastes

There is a partial commentary on the book of Ecclesiastes that is attributed to Robert Holcot.[15] The commentary in question is incomplete and terminates with Ecclesiastes 3:20. Smalley observes that the work contains "local allusions" (i.e., English allusions) and "is in Holcot's classicizing style."[16] Unfortunately, there has been almost no work on this incomplete commentary since Beryl Smalley identified it half a century ago.[17] However, since the initial work of Smalley, it has been discovered that there are other manuscript copies of this work.

Commentary on Ecclesiasticus

Robert Holcot also wrote a commentary on Ecclesiasticus (also known as Sirach or the Wisdom of Sirach).[18] The most accessible version of the work was published in Venice in 1509. The colophon of the Venice 1509 edition attributes it to Holcot and notes that the illustrious doctor was called by God while writing the work; there is a long tradition that Holcot died of the plague while working on this commentary.[19] When compared with the book of Wisdom, which contains 19 chapters, the book of Ecclesiasticus is quite substantial, including 51 chapters. Holcot only managed to complete his commentary on the first seven chapters; his work ends with lecture 88 on Ecclesiasticus 7:7–8.[20]

Commentary on the Apocalypse

According to Friedrich Stegmüller, there are five extant manuscripts containing a commentary on the Apocalypse by Holcot.[21] In her list of Holcot's works published in 1956, Smalley does not mention a commentary on the Apocalypse. However, at the time she was writing the Holcot article, Smalley did not have access to the fifth volume of Stegmüller's *Repertorium Biblicum* published in 1955, which contained the bibliography of Holcot.[22] Instead of Stegmüller, Smalley relies on the *Scriptores ordinis praedicatorum* by Jacques Quétif and Jacques Échard published in the early eighteenth century.[23] Further, at various points in her essay Smalley notes that she is in correspondence with Thomas Kaeppeli regarding the manuscripts of Robert Holcot. However, Kaeppeli's work also fails to mention the existence of the commentary on the Apocalypse noted by Stegmüller.[24] Thus it seems that in the 1956 essay Smalley was unaware of the existence of a commentary on the Apocalypse attributed to Holcot. In *English Friars and Antiquity*, published in 1960, Smalley does cite Stegmüller's work but again omits a discussion of a possible commentary on the Apocalypse.[25]

We have had the opportunity to examine a very readable copy (VC) of the commentary. In this witness Holcot's name appears at the end of the work in a distinct hand from the main text.[26] The front colophon attributes the work to Holcot but notes that "it has not been printed (*non est impressa*), nor is it among his works listed by Baleo [John Bale], but it is most especially of Holcot's style."[27] It is divided into lectures with the last lecture beginning with chapter 22 (the last chapter of the Apocalypse).

Commentary on the Song of Songs

The literature on Robert Holcot and late medieval biblical commentaries occasionally mentions a commentary on the Song of Songs by Robert Holcot. The origin of this attribution is probably Quétif and Échard's *Scriptores*, where they provide a brief entry for *In Cantica Canticorum* listing an incunabula produced in Venice in 1509 and, *cum sequenti*, in following years.[28] The *Cyclopaedia Bibliograhica* published in 1859 also makes reference to Quétif and Échard but records the title as *In cantica canticorum et in septem priora capita ecclesiastici* (Venice, 1509).[29] While these sources clearly ascribe a commentary on the Song of Songs to Robert Holcot—and modern sources continue to quote them with some authority—we have not been able to find any manuscript evidence for the work or any evidence (beyond the *Scriptores*) that such a work was produced in Venice in 1509 or anywhere in Europe during the sixteenth century.

The Historical Context and Holcot's Sources

Robert Holcot's exegetical works, like any literary texts, were shaped by the historical context in which they were written. With respect to the context of his commentaries on the Bible (and his sermons, treated in Part III), it is important to examine two topics: the relationship between Robert Holcot and Richard de Bury, the noted bibliophile and author of the *Philobiblon*, and the English classicizing friars discussed by Beryl Smalley in her work *English Friars and Antiquity*. In the third part of this section we also examine the sources referenced in Holcot's biblical commentaries.

Richard de Bury

Robert Holcot completed the majority of his scholastic works while serving as the regent master of Oxford and perhaps Cambridge University. If Holcot did serve as regent master of Cambridge, it was most likely during this period that he began a longstanding relationship with Richard de Bury. That said, understanding the intellectual context in which Holcot continued to develop his exegetical method is important for contextualizing his thought as it developed after the mid-1330s.

Richard de Bury was born in Bury St. Edmund's in the county of Suffolk, England, around 1285. He studied at Oxford University and entered the Benedictine order in Durham. However, despite being a member of a cloistered order, a series of ecclesial and political relationships had a significant influence on Richard de Bury's intellectual development. For example, he served as the tutor of Prince Edward, the Son of Edward II and Isabella of France; when the prince was crowned Edward III in 1327, Richard de Bury increasingly obtained positions of ecclesial and political significance. He became the Bishop of Durham in 1333, High Chancellor in 1334, and the treasurer of England in 1336. Interestingly, on a trip to Avignon around 1330 as an ambassador to Pope John XXII, Richard de Bury met the Italian scholar and poet Petrarch (1304–1374).[30] It is difficult not to speculate about Bury's meeting with Petrarch, as the two men shared a common passion and love—that of books, in particular the classics. Richard de Bury is best known for this aspect of his life and for writing the *Philobiblon*, or *The Love of Books*.

Richard de Bury's *Philobiblon* is important for understanding the intellectual context in which Robert Holcot worked. Holcot, as Beryl Smalley argued, can be classified as one of the "classicizing friars." The classicizing friars were Dominican or Franciscan friars who were intimately familiar with classical literature and who used this knowledge within biblical commentaries and in the art of preaching. However, Holcot shares more than just a common love of classical sources with Bury; in fact, seven of the extant manuscripts of the *Philobiblon* attribute authorship to Holcot. While the general scholarly consensus is that Holcot was not the author of the work, it is also agreed that Holcot was probably involved in the work as a scholar in the house of Richard de Bury. Because of this connection, it is useful to begin the second part of this work with a brief discussion of the *Philobiblon* as a way of contextualizing Holcot's approach to scriptural commentaries and preaching.

Richard de Bury concluded his prologue to the *Philobiblon* by stating that, in the manner of the ancient Romans, he would give his book a Greek name.[31] In so doing, he gestures at the Greek and Latin classical tradition. This tradition of the classics is central to Bury's work, as he wants to draw upon the full deposit of human wisdom recorded in books. This includes the knowledge of the Indians, Babylonians, Egyptians, Greeks, Arabians, and Latins.[32] In short, he invokes all of the known literature of the day, with a particular emphasis on Western classical literature and Christian writings.

The work is divided into 20 chapters, in which personified books often speak out in frustration against humanity. The books, that is, address specific classes of people who have neglected their duties to the books themselves. More than any other group of people the books' attention is focused on clerics: "all classes of men who are conspicuous by the tonsure or the sign of clerkship, against whom books lifted up their voices in the fourth, fifth, and sixth chapters, are bound to serve books with perpetual veneration."[33] As Bury understands things, those who are serving the Church as clerics, monks, or friars owe a special debt to books: a debt both in terms of what they know and how they understand things but also regarding what they should write. Here we turn briefly to chapters 4 through 6, focused on the clergy broadly conceived (ch. 4), the religious orders (ch. 5), and the mendicants (ch. 6).

The books begin their critique of those in the religious vocations by addressing the clergy. The books remind the clerics that everything they know is from them. They write,

> we clad you with the goodly garments of philosophy, rhetoric and dialectic, of which we had and have a store ... providing you with the fourfold wings of the quadrivials that you might be winged like the seraphs and so mount above the cherubim.[34]

Thus the books argue that they are the source of all knowledge for the clerics. Further, the clerics must continually call upon the books in their service to the Church, for "who ascends the pulpit or the rostrum without in some way consulting [the books]?"[35] The books argue that the clerics have neglected them and in doing so have neglected their office to preach and educate. Similarly, in the following chapter the books' indictment against the monks of the religious orders is that they have neglected their vocation. Augustine's rule strictly mandates that the books "be asked for each day at a given hour," but such rules are neglected.[36] Instead, the monks are emptying cups and worrying about flocks and fleece, crops and granaries, leeks and potherbs, drink and goblets.[37] As it happens, paid scribes have now replaced the monks, and the great treasure of books is suffering as a consequence.

Having strongly addressed the clerics and the monks, the books turn their criticism to the mendicant orders. The criticism here is a bit more focused, as the books address the Dominicans, the Order of Preachers.[38] The books criticize the mendicant orders for, like the clerics and monks, abandoning the love and use of books. One particular criticism pertains to preaching, as preaching is at the heart of the Dominican vocation. The books entreat the Order of Preachers to not behave as an ignorant parrot (*psittacus idiota*) or Balaam's ass (*asina Baalam*: see Numbers 22:21–38), which both repeat words without understanding.[39] The concluding argument of the books against the mendicants is the most interesting with respect to Robert Holcot. The books bring up Paul the Apostle—"preacher of the truth and excellent teacher of the nations"—who in his epistle to Timothy entreats him to bring three things: Paul's cloak, books, and parchment. These three objects, the books argue, are informative for mendicants: they are to be modestly dressed, they should have books as aids for study, and they should have parchment for writing. Paul's special entreaty for the parchment—especially the parchments, he writes—should indicate to the mendicants their special role in writing books.[40] In short, a mendicant who does not write is one who "beats the air with words and edifies only those who are present, but does nothing for those absent and for posterity."[41]

The *Philobiblon* presents a strong critique of clerics, monks, and mendicants, arguing that each group should be educated and should contribute to furthering the good news. In the case of the mendicants, the critique is twofold: the mendicants should both read and write. In particular, the Order of Preachers should continue to write religious texts for the instruction of other clerics. For Robert Holcot, this was advice that he took seriously, spending his later years writing scriptural commentaries and preaching manuals. In this respect, the *Philobiblon* sets the stage for Holcot's exegetical works. He exemplifies what the author of the *Philobiblon* entreated the mendicants to achieve: to produce literary works—in his case commentaries on Scripture, preaching aids, and sermons—that both educate the clergy in the things of God and transmit the wealth of ancient and modern learning in the process. The use of classical literature, so important to the author of the *Philobiblon*, is adopted by Robert Holcot and put to extraordinary use. Thus we turn to the group of classicizing friars who enjoyed the patronage of Bury and used his extensive collection of ancient books.

The Classicizing Friars

Based on her studies of early-fourteenth-century friars, Beryl Smalley coined the term "classicizing friars" as a "colourless name" that avoids the connotations of humanism or proto-humanism. In her *English Friars and Antiquity* she defined the term as one that has the "advantage of being noncommittal": "it points to fondness for classical literature, history and myth without suggesting that the group played any special part in the rise of humanism."[42] This interest in the classics, she argues, finds a home in the sermons, preaching aids, and biblical commentaries of this group of English friars. Before discussing this cohort of scholars, it is perhaps important to begin with Smalley's conclusion. Why, after all, is it not proper to refer to this group of classicizing friars as proto-humanists?

Smalley argues that the classicizing friars differed from the early Italian humanists in numerous ways; perhaps most important, the early humanists were lawyers, notaries, and jurists, while the classicizing friars were members of the mendicant religious orders (as recognized by the second council of Lyons in 1274, the Dominicans, Franciscans, Carmelites, and Augustinian Hermits).[43] When contrasted with the friars, early humanists "developed in a professional lay society, whose members tended to be rich or at least of moderate means."[44] Further, given that the Italian universities were secular (i.e., Italian universities had no higher faculty of theology, as there was, for example, in Oxford or Paris), the majority of the students of the arts and law were non-religious (i.e., not members of a religious order). Petrarch (†1374), for example, was non-religious and a student of law (like his father) at the Universities of Montpellier and Bologna. While Petrarch was in service of the Church throughout his life, his primary occupation, as such, was not hearing confessions, saying the mass, or preaching sermons. What this means, practically speaking, is that the type of classicism that developed in Italy in the fourteenth century emerged from a group of men who had radically different interests and life experiences when contrasted with the classicizing friars.

Many of the friars, of course, lived a life confined to a friary *studium* (house of study); as Smalley argues, this context could not have produced a "scholarly type of classicism" such as developed in Italy in the fourteenth century.[45] The friars could not travel Europe in search of manuscripts or spend their leisure time reading the classics. The friars were part of a Church culture in which their central job was to work as preachers and teachers. In Smalley's words, "their classical studies could only be marginal."[46] Thus, as we will notice throughout the subsequent chapters, the use of classical sources by the friars was in service of the Church and its central function of preaching the faith and teaching ethics. Robert Holcot, for example, was not a classicist but a friar who found in classical sources a resonance with the Gospel message. Such examples were also of interest to Holcot's audience. As Smalley observes,

> All the friars are moralists, responding to public demand for new and striking *exempla*. Women in Church want tales with a love interest; heraldry and lawsuits draw the attention of their menfolk. Every Englishman or woman has a stake in ancient history because Brutus came to Britain. The words "Greek" and "Roman" sound as magic on the preacher's lips. Fidelity to his classical sources would bore his congregation ... So he spreads truth and fiction about the ancients indiscriminately in such a way as to give pleasure.[47]

The classicizing friars, therefore, are a group of men who are interested in the use of classical sources for the furtherance of the Gospel through the art of preaching.

In her study, Smalley designated seven individuals as "classicizing friars": Thomas Waleys (O.P., †c. 1348–1349), John Ridevall (O.F.M., fl.

1330–1340), and John Lathbury (O.F.M., †1362) at Oxford; Robert Holcot and William Dencourt (Smalley prefers "D'Eyncourt" as the spelling; O.P, fl. 1330–1345) at Oxford and Cambridge; and Thomas Hopeman (O.P., fl. 1345–1355) and Thomas Ringstead (O.P., †1366) at Cambridge.[48] However, as Smalley noted, grouping them together as "classicizing friars" is in need of justification. Her argument is that, aside from sharing certain common methodological approaches to the use of classical sources, there is evidence in the manuscript tradition for treating these authors as a group. The manuscripts that preserve the shorter writings, she notes, often collect several of the texts together. Further, while the larger works (e.g., Holcot's Wisdom commentary) are often copied separately, this is not always the case. Balliol 27, for example, contains Holcot's commentary on Wisdom followed by William Dencourt's commentary on Ecclesiastes.[49] A further example—commissioned by the Lord John Beaver for the Monastery at St. Albans[50]—is found in the British Library. This manuscript includes substantial works by Robert Holcot (commentary on Wisdom) and Thomas Ringstead (commentary on Proverbs). Thus there is evidence that "bookmakers and librarians [e.g. John Beaver] grouped them as representatives of a classicizing type of pastoral literature."[51]

Further evidence that this collection of friars deserve to be treated as a distinct group can be found in the relationships that exist between the various writings of these authors. To summarize briefly, Ridevall uses the writings of Waleys, and Holcot the work of Ridevall;[52] in the later thinkers, Hopeman borrows from the work of Holcot while Dencourt and Ringstead engaged with the previous work of Waleys.[53] Thus as Smalley noted decades ago, there are clear lines of reception and influence between these seven scholars.

Holcot's Sources

We conclude with a discussion of Robert Holcot's sources, and while we have chosen to place this discussion in an introductory chapter on his biblical commentaries, it is equally applicable to all of his preaching tools (i.e., his commentaries, preaching aids, and sermons). The sources of late medieval authors are notoriously difficult to determine with precision, and the writings of Holcot and the other classicizing friars present a particular challenge.

In discussing Holcot's sources, Beryl Smalley said that "he took the whole of life as his library."[54] The problem, however, is that, given his extensive use of sources, it is often difficult to determine a particular source with any confidence. Holcot, as all medieval authors, relied on various types of sources. Further, once one has established the source, it is even more difficult to determine if Holcot read the work in question or simply found the quotation in one of his reference works.

First, medieval authors tended to quote passages from memory, as argued by Frances Yates and Mary Carruthers.[55] By the time Holcot was writing his own commentaries as a master, he would have had extensive instruction in the Bible; the fourteenth-century statutes required students at Oxford and Paris to attend three to four years of lectures on the Bible (as an *auditor* or hearer) and to lecture on the Bible (as a biblical cursor) another one to two years.[56] Drawing on this rich background, Holcot and his contemporaries developed citation practices or habits that relied on memory, and such practices are difficult to trace "textually." Second, medieval authors relied on extensive collections of excerpts or quotations called *florilegia*. As Richard and Mary Rouse argued in their study of Thomas of Ireland's *Manipulus florum*,[57] these collections of excerpts are diverse and highly organized. In their study, they argue that such *florilegia* collections in the thirteenth and fourteenth centuries "represent efforts to assimilate and organize inherited written authority in a systematic form" for the purpose of preaching.[58] These preaching aids functioned as rich sources for both secular and Christian citations from the period of Late Antiquity up through the early Middle Ages. However, while these collections were valuable to a medieval preacher, it means that if one encounters a quotation from Hermes Trismegistus, the Vatican Mythographers,[59] Seneca, or Augustine of Hippo in the writings of Holcot, one cannot assume that he read that source or even had access to a particular work. Finally, the magisterial twelfth-century works—the *Gloss* on Scripture, the *Sentences* of Peter Lombard, and Gratian's *Decretum*—are systematic collections of patristic and early medieval authorities that were known to every fourteenth-century theologian.

Although the sources of Robert Holcot have been studied by Beryl Smalley, the most exhaustive list of authors cited by Holcot is found in Welter's work on medieval *exemplum*. In his study of the commentary on the book of Wisdom, Jean-Thiébaut Welter observed that Holcot referenced the following classical authors: Hermes Trismegistus (the alleged author of the Hermetic Corpus), Homer, Aristotle, Cicero, Virgil, Horace, Titus Livius, Ovid, Varro, Valerius Maximus, Solon, Seneca, Pliny, Suetonius, Juvenal, Macrobius, Martial, Aulus Gellius, Plutarch, and Claudius.[60] As this list indicates, Holcot was familiar with a broad range of classical sources. However, Holcot's use of ancient sources was primarily for their moral content. Thomas Waleys, Holcot's contemporary, is useful here as a point of contrast, as Waleys took advantage of contacts with Avignon and Northern Italy (by means of Bury) and "developed an interest in ancient history and antiquities for themselves."[61] Further, while Waleys was a careful scholar who quoted his sources with great precision, Holcot could be "wildly wrong in his references" and even at times playfully added material to a particular passage.[62] For example, in his commentary on Wisdom, Holcot references "Alcyone, Calyce, and countless other women" as examples of faithful wives. However, as Smalley observes, these names originate from Ovid's epistle from Hero to Leander where they are noted as women who are loved by the sea-god; indeed, "they have no relevance as examples of faithful wives."[63] Examples like this can be produced by the dozens from Holcot's extant biblical commentaries.

Turning to Holcot's use of Christian sources, it is necessary to consider both his patristic and medieval references. Regarding patristic sources, Smalley observes that Holcot's use is "varied but unremarkable."[64] In his summary of patristic sources in Holcot's commentary on Wisdom, Welter catalogues quotations and references to Josephus, Lactantius, Ambrose, Jerome, Augustine, the *Vitae Patrum*, Fulgentius the Mythographer, Peter of Ravenna, Boethius, Cassiodorus, and Gregory the Great. Turning to the medieval sources, in the commentary on Wisdom Welter found references to John Damascene, Rabanus Maurus, Marbodius of Rennes, Anselm, Bernard Silvestris, the pseudo-Turpin Chronicle, Geoffrey Monmouth, Hugh of St. Victor, Peter Comestor, Alexander Nequam, Allan of Lille, Gerald of Wales, Hélinand of Froidmont, Gilbert of Tournai, William of Evange, Albert the Great, Gerald of Frachet, Martin of Opava, and Walter Burley.[65] However, this list is clearly incomplete; in the first 14 *lectiones* treating Wisdom 1 Holcot also references and directly quotes Augustine of Ireland (*De mirabilibus divinarum scripturarum*), Theodorus Lector

(*Historia tripartita*), Peter Lombard (*Sentences*), Eadmer of Canterbury (the *De similitudinibus*), and Thomas Aquinas (*Super tertium Sententiarum*).[66] However, a complete analysis of Holcot's sources is not possible until all of his biblical commentaries, preaching aids, and sermons are critically edited.

Conclusion

Robert Holcot's biblical commentaries shed light on a man who was creative, humorous, bitingly critical, and engaged with a wide variety of sources. Here we conclude the chapter by highlighting Holcot's use of humor and criticism.

Holcot's wit and criticism is revealed in his commentary on the Twelve Prophets (Amos 1:2, to be precise) where he satirizes the founding narratives of the Carmelites and the Hermits of St. Augustine (OESA). The Carmelites, who emerged as a religious order in the twelfth century, traced their origins to the Old Testament story of the Prophet Elijah on Mount Carmel (I Kings 18) and counted John the Baptist as a member of the order (e.g., Matthew 3). To this Holcot retorts that if the religious orders did exist at this time, they would have to be counted among the Pharisees, Sadducees, or Essenes as described by Josephus in the *Antiquities* and as such would be some of the first to oppose Christ. Clearly this would be nothing to be proud of. Further, Holcot pokes fun at the Augustinians for claiming a similarly ancient heritage and in particular for arguing that Augustine was a member of the Order at the age of 18. Holcot writes that if Augustine received the habit at the age of 18, then he received the habit while still a Manichee and an unbeliever (*Manicheus et infidelis*) and begat a son soon afterward. This paints an unflattering picture of the father of the Order. Holcot counters that Augustine converted to Christianity when he was 30 years of age (*30 annorum antequam ad fidem converteretur*). Holcot's criticism of the Carmelites and the Augustinians is focused on their claim to be more ancient than the Dominicans. However, it is also a great example of his creative use of historical arguments and his humorous criticism.

This approach to humor and criticism is not uncommon in Holcot's commentaries and sermons, and his use of puns in his final lecture (referred to as the *sermo finalis*) on Peter Lombard's *Sentences* is well known.[67] His *sermo finalis* is an interesting example of Holcot's playful use of language. As he introduces the man who will take his place as the lecturer on the *Sentences* of Peter Lombard at Oxford, Roger Gosford, Holcot plays with his English name (*in vulgari est Roger*). The name Roger indicates to English speakers two animals found in sacred Scripture: the roe deer and the common dog. The roe (i.e., the *Ro-* in *Roger*)—in Latin *caprea*—is known for its speed and swiftness, as indicated in II Samuel 2:18: "now Asael was a most swift runner, like one of the roes that abide in the woods (*porro Asael cursor velocissimus fuit, quasi unus de capreis quae morantur in silvis*)." Roger, the new lecturer, will run through the *Sentences* with the speed of the roe. Further, the name Roger recalls a dog, because the word "Roger" (*totum vocabulum*) is often used as a name for dogs (*convenit per appelationem*). The dog is also a swift animal like the roe but, more important, as Tobit 11:9 says, a dog often runs before its master: "Then the dog, which had been with them in the way, ran before, and coming as if he had brought the news, shewed his joy by his fawning and wagging his tail."[68] Referencing these two passages, Holcot links the English name Roger with two animals that indicate precisely how Roger will lecture on the *Sentences*: running swiftly through and leading his students. However, leading one's students by running ahead of them seems to be only one of the skills needed of a young bachelor of the *Sentences*, for theology contains great depth. Thus, turning to Roger's surname Gosford, Holcot relies on the English terms *goose* (i.e., *Gos-*; Latin *auca*) and *ford* (i.e., *-ford*; Latin *vado*) to note that Mr. Gosford has the ability to not only "run in the plains without stumbling" but to also "swim in the depths of theology" (much as a goose fords a stream).[69] This playful attention to both Latin and English terms is found throughout Holcot's biblical commentaries and preaching literature.

One final example captures Holcot's playfulness in the "vulgar tongue." In the introduction to his commentary on the book of Wisdom, he plays with his own surname (*cognomen*).[70] He introduces the discussion of his name with a passage from the Song of Solomon 2:14 that states "My dove in the clefts of the rock, in the hollow places of the wall (*Columba mea, in foraminibus petrae, in caverna maceriae*)." He offers two variants or readings of his surname that reference this passage: first observing that his name indicates a hole or window (*foramen*) in a cottage or house (*domunculae sive casae*);[71] second arguing that his name means a fissure in a rock (*foramine petrae*).[72] The second reading is close to the wording of the original passage from the Song of Solomon (*in foraminibus petrae*). Holcot further links this reading of the name *holcot* with Exodus 33:22, where God speaks to Moses and says that "when my glory shall pass, I will set you in a hole of the rock (*in foramine petrae*), and protect you with my right hand, till I pass."[73] While in Latin the term *holcot* has no obvious meaning, Holcot is again playing with an English reading of his name as a "hole cut" in the rock (or a cut in the rock). Of course, to his English-speaking audience this interpretation would make sense; if one attempts to read it as referencing a Latin etymology it borders on nonsense.

Holcot's humor, criticism, and wit are found throughout his biblical commentaries and sermons and add an unexpected human dimension to our image of the dry and boring scholastic. As we will see in the following chapters, through the study of Holcot's commentaries and sermons a broader image of this great medieval thinker begins to emerge.

7

THE TWELVE PROPHETS

Introduction

The Twelve Prophets is a collection of prophetic books found in the Jewish Scriptures and Christian Old Testament. The tradition of commenting on the Twelve Prophets as a single group originated in the early Christian era. The patristic authors Jerome (†420), Cyril of Alexandria (†444), Theodore of Mopsuestia (†428), Theodoret of Cyrus (†c. 457), and Isho'dad of Merv (fl. c. 850) each produced a commentary treating all 12 of the prophets.[1] The majority of early medieval commentators followed this practice—for example, a commentary on the Twelve Prophets was written by the Benedictine Remigius of Auxerre at the end of the ninth century (†908).[2]

Several medieval commentaries on the Twelve Prophets were written during the twelfth and thirteenth centuries. However, like Holcot's commentary, few of these works have been edited and as such exist only in manuscript form. Stephen Langton's (†1228) unedited commentary on the Twelve Prophets belongs to the late twelfth century.[3] Beryl Smalley notes that the text is composed "almost exclusively of extracts from Jerome's commentary" and is indicative of Langton's method of glossing.[4] The commentary by the Franciscan William of Middleton (†c. 1256)—to whom Pope Alexander IV appointed the task of completing Alexander of Hales's *Summa*—is also unedited and was written in the early thirteenth century.[5] Further, the

Dominican William of Luxi (fl. c. 1260–1275) composed a commentary on the Twelve Prophets between 1267 and 1275.[6] However, despite being written by a Dominican toward the end of the thirteenth century, William's commentary does not seem to have served as a source for Holcot's.

Smalley observes that Holcot's commentary on the Twelve Prophets refers six times to the mid-thirteenth-century English Dominican Simon of Hinton, whom Holcot refers to as the "expositor." Simon's commentary on the Twelve Prophets is the source for part of Holcot's literal exposition of the work (though not for the *quaestiones*).[7] As Smalley has shown, the citations of Simon's work correspond directly with Holcot's. Alongside Simon's commentary, four times Holcot followed the division of the biblical text according to Peter Aureoli's *Compendium on the Literal Sense of Scripture* (i.e., Joel 2, Amos 5, Zachariah 11 and 14).[8] However, as Smalley argues, Simon's unedited commentary served as the primary source for Holcot's gloss on the Twelve Prophets.

Smalley also notes that Holcot references Nicholas of Lyra in his commentary on Zachariah 13, although she was not able to locate the passage in Lyra.[9] Based on a reconstruction of when Nicholas of Lyra commented on the Old Testament (beginning in 1322–1323, reaching the Psalms by 1326, and covering Wisdom and Ecclesiasticus between 1330 and 1331),[10] Smalley argues that Holcot may not have had access to Lyra's comments on the Twelve Prophets, Wisdom, or Ecclesiasticus when he lectured on these books. Of course this all depends on when Holcot gave his lectures and whether or not he later added further quotations as he revised the works.[11]

Holcot's commentary on the Twelve Prophets is generally dated to the period of his regency at Oxford. As regent master, Holcot was expected to lecture simultaneously on one book of the Old Testament and one book of the New Testament.[12] Thus it is probable that besides the now-lost commentary on Matthew that is extant only in fragments, the commentary on the Twelve Prophets is Holcot's earliest biblical commentary. As was argued in the introduction, Holcot's commentary on the Twelve Prophets is the first text in which Holcot began using his method of "verbal pictures" or the picture technique. Here we focus on how this picture technique functioned in Holcot's commentary on the book of Nahum. We begin with a few observations about Holcot's exegesis before considering his commentary directly.

Holcot's Exegesis

Robert Holcot's exegetical method remains remarkably consistent throughout his commentaries on the Twelve Prophets, the book of Wisdom, and Ecclesiasticus. Holcot "divides his text, gives a brief note on the literal sense, and then moralizes, drawing out the moral content of the 'letter'.... sometimes as a supplement or alternative to moralizing he gives a number of *quaestiones* concerning theology or casuistry."[13] Methodologically the late medieval exegete follows a method of commenting on the text that is consistent with the structure of the late medieval sermons. As we will see in chapter 10, the late medieval sermon included a division of the text and a process of commenting on the discrete sections. However, what is unique to the biblical commentaries that emerged from a university setting is the place of theological questions embedded into the commentary that "have little bearing on the literal sense of the text."[14] This is particularly pronounced in the commentary on Wisdom, which includes over 80 theological questions.[15]

The habit of placing theological questions within a biblical commentary was developed in the late eleventh century by theologians such as Bruno of Chartreux (†1101) and Anselm of Laon (†1117). By the mid-twelfth century, the practice was extremely common, as is evidenced in Peter Abelard's (†1142) commentary on Romans or Peter Lombard's (†1164) *Magna glosatura* on the Pauline epistles; the questions belonging to Robert of Melun's commentary on the letters of the Apostle Paul became so popular that they circulated as a separate text (*Quaestiones de epistoli Pauli*).[16] However, with the development of Lombard's *Sentences* as the theological textbook at Paris and Oxford, a split emerged between scriptural commentaries and theological questions. Thus Smalley is correct to note that it was an uncommon practice in the first half of the fourteenth century. In speculating about probable reasons for Holcot's inclusion of these *quaestiones*, Smalley suggests that Holcot at the time was training young men to be preachers who would also have the responsibility of teaching theology at priory schools or "bishops' schools" within their diocese.[17] Thus a moral interpretation of the text was appropriate to the students as future preachers, and the doctrinal questions could prepare them for their duties as teachers. Holcot's lectures on Ecclesiasticus also emerged from such a context.

Medieval exegetes analyzed the biblical text according to its literal, tropological (moral), allegorical, and anagogical modes.[18] The Dominican Augustine of Dacia (†1282) captured the four senses thus.

The letter teaches events;	*Littera gesta docet*
allegory what you should believe;	*quid credas allegoria*
morality what you should do;	*moralis quid agas*
anagogy what mark you should be aiming for.	*quo tendas anagogia*.[19]

The tropological sense of Scripture treats the moral life of the Christian as instructed by Scripture and the Church and as exemplified in the sacramental system. Throughout his commentary on the Twelve Prophets Holcot offers a moral (or tropological) reading of the text that often builds dramatically on a few words or phrases understood in the literal sense.

The Pictures in Holcot's Commentary on Nahum

Holcot's exegetical method is generally consistent with other thirteenth- and fourteenth-century theologians with the exception of his picture technique. Holcot's unique picture technique is an exegetical method that relies on verbal descriptions (rhymed pictures) that are referred to as *picturae*.[20] The picture method was used in earnest by the early-fourteenth-century English mendicant preachers. However, by the end of the fourteenth century, such pictures or images were not the sole province of the friars. Siegfried Wenzel has studied sermons belonging to the end of the fourteenth and fifteenth centuries and concluded that "moralized *picturae* had become part of the *koiné* of pulpit rhetoric and [were] no longer a distinguishing feature of mendicant preaching."[21]

The fact that the picture technique was important to Holcot's late medieval readers is perhaps more evident in the manuscript tradition than in the printed versions of his works often consulted today. For example, in the Basel edition of the *Moralitates* printed in 1586, few of the individual moralizations are depicted as pictures. In fact, the editors of the early modern editions often gave individual moralizations a more descriptive title. However, in the manuscripts, the picture aspect of the *Moralitates* is often more present. For example, many manuscripts organize the moralizations by first listing the *picturae/imagines* (pictures/images) and subsequently listing the historical moralizations.[22]

Robert Holcot's picture method is found in various writings, including his Sermons,[23] the *Moralitates*, and his commentaries on Wisdom and the Twelve Prophets.[24] Smalley argues that while Holcot is interested in visual images in his commentary on Wisdom, Ecclesiasticus, and the partial commentary on Ecclesiastes, there are no "elaborate 'pictures'" in these later commentaries.[25] Accordingly, our focus here is on the picture technique as found in his commentary on the Twelve Prophets. Holcot's commentary on the Twelve Prophets includes 26 rhymed pictures (none of which are found in the *Moralitates*).[26] Somewhat surprisingly, despite the scholarly interest in the picture technique, there is to date no substantive description or exegesis of a single picture. While the pictures are discussed (and transcribed/translated) by both Smalley and Rivers, neither provides an actual discussion of a picture in detail. This is not intended as a criticism; both Smalley and Rivers focused on the sources, purpose, intent, or method of the pictures. Here we offer a fuller interpretation of one of Holcot's pictures.

Holcot and the Picture of Patience

The book of Nahum is a short work probably written during the seventh century BCE. This brief text consists of three chapters and contains the prophecy of Nahum against Nineveh, the great Mesopotamian city that functioned as the capital of the Assyrian Empire. The prophet Nahum proclaims in this work that the great city will be destroyed by the God of Israel. According to the third chapter, God's destruction of the great city will take place, in part, because of the "multitude of fornications of the harlot ... that made use of witchcraft (Nahum 3:4)." In one of the more memorable verses, God says: "Behold I have come against you ... I will discover your shame to your face, and will show your nakedness to the nations, and your shame to the kingdoms (Nahum 3:5)." This is significant because one of the themes running through this short prophetic book is the relationship between God's justice and mercy.[27] This is the theme on which Holcot chooses to focus.

Nahum 1:2 states that "the Lord is a jealous God, and a revenger: the Lord is a revenger, and has wrath: the Lord takes vengeance on his adversaries, and he is angry with his enemies." However, the following verse begins with a rather different tone, arguing that "the Lord is patient (*Dominus patiens*)." Holcot confronts this juxtaposition, noting that in the second verse Nahum "posits the vengeance and fury" of the Lord, while in the third verse he "posits his patience and strength."[28] First, Holcot begins with a short discussion of God's vengeance. Second, Holcot turns to the notion of patience and presents a lengthy discourse on patience. This section examines both discussions, with a particular focus on the picture of patience that Holcot paints in response to the claim that the God who is promising to destroy the great city of Nineveh is a patient God. What, after all, is patience?[29] Holcot's commentary on chapter 1 of Nahum is a theological meditation on the juxtaposition between God's vengeance and patience.

Holcot begins with a discussion of the phrase "the Lord takes vengeance on his adversaries (*ulciscens Dominus in hostes suos*)." He clarifies the phrase by pointing out that when it is said that the Lord takes vengeance on people it is a punishment for sin. Thus, despite the fact that God takes vengeance on sinners, Holcot advises Christians not to be quick to take vengeance on their enemies. In support of this argument, he quotes Seneca, who argued that "when you see that [your enemy] is in your power, you will think it vengeance enough to have had the power to avenge: know that to forgive is an honorable and great form of vengeance."[30] Holcot further supports his argument with additional passages from Seneca, Bernard of Clairvaux, the Justinian Code, and Scripture.[31] He concludes the argument with two appropriate passages from Scripture: Romans 12:19: "revenge is mine, I will repay, says the Lord" and Deuteronomy 32:43: "and he will render vengeance to their enemies, [and he will be merciful to the land of his people (*et propitius erit terrae populi sui*)]."[32] Thus Holcot concludes his relatively short analysis of vengeance with a word of caution: while vengeance is appropriate to God, the Christian should seek to be forgiving and leave the punishment of sin to God.

Following his relatively short discussion of vengeance, Holcot turns to his analysis of patience as found in Nahum 1:3. As a means of examining this particular biblical verse—that is, *Dominus patiens*—Holcot presents two verbal pictures: one of patience and the other of impatience. These two pictures bookend the remainder of his commentary on Nahum 1.

Structurally, therefore, Holcot presents a picture of patience—10 attributes of patience derived from this picture—and a concluding picture of impatience. We begin with the picture of patience (divided into 10 clauses). The patient man is:

(1) *sedens ditatus*, (2) *vilibus cibatus*	sitting satisfied, fed with common foods
(3) *vultu laetatus*, (4) *omnibus inclinatus*	of joyful countenance, turned toward all
(5) *purpura vestitus*, (6) *hostibus munitus*	clothed in purple, protected from enemies
(7) *cum manu arida et alia extenta*	with one hand shriveled and the other extended
(8) *sine pedibus*, (9) *sine lingua, et* (10) *[sine] auribus.*	without feet, without tongue and without ears.[33]

Holcot's analysis of patience builds on the 10 attributes noted in the picture. The first attribute states that the patient person is *sedens ditatus et quietatus* (sitting satisfied and content). Holcot glosses this passage by referencing Proverbs 15:18: "a passionate man stirs up strife, he that is patient appeases those that are stirred up;" Luke 21:19, "in your patience you will possess [master] your souls;" and Proverbs 16:32: "the patient man is better than the valiant, and he that rules his spirit, than he that takes cities." Therefore, Holcot argues, the patient person is his own master and is said to be satisfied and content (*ditatus et quietatus*).[34]

The second attribute states that the patient person is fed with common foods (*vilibus cibatus*).[35] These "common foods" represent the vices, insults, and injuries that are suffered in life and that nourish patience (*nutriunt patientiam*). In this sense, when properly nourished, patience ought to be as a nature (*quasi natura*) that does not fail. Further, as Holcot argues, following Scripture, patience is often linked with poverty—hence, the reference to common foods—for truly, *in paupertate patientia est habenda* (patience ought to be had in poverty). As Psalm 9:19 states, "The patience of the poor shall not perish forever." Thus the patient person is fed with the "common foods" of personal injury. Interestingly, Holcot concludes the second attribute with the realist observation that patience often fails when a person is in need of it. In support, he quotes Job 17:15: "Where, then, is my expectation, and who considers my patience."

The third attribute of the patient person is that he is "of joyful countenance."[36] In support of this claim Holcot cites Wisdom 7:12 "I rejoiced in all these [things] for this wisdom went before me"—a wisdom, Holcot writes, that produces patience. This is clear in Proverbs 14:29, which states that "he who is patient is governed by much wisdom, however whoever is impatient [exalts his folly]." The link between the wise person of joyful countenance and patience is defended in a series of quotations from Augustine's *Rule*, Seneca, and the Scriptures. Thus Holcot argues that the person who is patient has a happy or joyful countenance because he possesses wisdom.

The fourth attribute of the patient person is that he should be "turned toward all people" (*omnibus homo inclinatus*)—or, stated differently, the patient person is to be patient to all.[37] To explicate the point more fully, Holcot provides an example that indicates he still has in mind the biblical text in question (i.e., the book of Nahum and its broader context regarding sexual mores). He argues that some men are patient in specific situations but not with respect to all persons (*non quoad omnes*). Here Holcot gives an analogy of a snake attempting to have intercourse with an eel. In an effort to entice the eel the snake is patient and gently hisses at her; however, returning to his own mate and kind (*in natura*), the snake quickly resumes his venom. Such a snake is like many married men (*multis maritis*) who, when they approach their concubines, speak gently and sweetly. Like the snake, they exhibit patience to the concubine in all their words and deeds. However, when they return to their own spouses, they resume the poison of bitterness by means of curses, verbal threats, physical blows, and so forth. Holcot insists, therefore, that the patient person should be patient to all and not like the adulterer who is patient with his mistress but impatient with his spouse.

The fifth attribute of the patient person is that he should be "clothed in purple" (*purpura vestitus*) because he ought to have mercy, kindness, modesty, and humility.[38] These attributes are derived from Colossians 3:13 where the Apostle speaks of them as articles of clothing, stating that one ought to "put on" mercy, kindness, modesty, humility, and patience. Following the Scriptures, Holcot links these attributes of the patient person with the purple garment of salvation (*indumentum salutis*), making reference to Proverbs 31:22 and Judges 8:26. Finally, he concludes his discussion of the fifth attribute by stating that "all religious and clerics ought to have the robe of patience."[39]

The sixth attribute of the patient person is that he is "protected from enemies" (*hostibus munitus*).⁴⁰ To elucidate this attribute Holcot takes as his example the biblical character Job. The Bible states (Job 1–2) that God allowed Satan to bring a series of afflictions on Job. As a result, in the third chapter Job raises his voice and curses the day he was born. Because of this, Holcot notes, Job is questioned by his friend Eliphaz the Themanite: "where is your fear, your fortitude, your patience, and the perfection of your ways (Job 4:6)?" The response is that because of Job's silence and peace (*quia siluit, quievit*) in the face of suffering, God blessed him in all things. Patience, Holcot insists, is evident in Job's suffering because "he took from his friends and his enemies 'the armor of righteousness on the right hand and on his left'" (II Corinthians 6:7).⁴¹ The point here is that the patient person is protected from various tribulations and temptations. Holcot's elucidation of the sixth attribute is lengthy, and he continues his discussion with an analysis of passages from Ovid, the Bible, Agellius' *Noctium atticarum*, and St. Jerome.⁴²

Holcot alters the seventh attribute of the patient person, arguing that the patient person has "one hand closed (*clausa*) and the other extended to receive with patience."⁴³ This means that the patient person ought to be ready to bear the suffering that he sustains; the hand stretched out, in particular, symbolizes the reaching out to receive with patience (*suscipere cum patientia*). Here Holcot references Luke 6 in which Christ heals a man who had a withered hand; presumably, to reach out and be healed by Christ—in the passage Christ commands the man, *extende manum tuam*—is an act of receiving with patience. Further, Holcot references a passage where Christ commands the disciples (Luke 6:27–29) to love their enemies and to "pray for those who falsely accuse you." This kind of suffering assists the afflicted person in developing patience. Finally, Holcot concludes his discussion of Luke 6 by observing that after his tribulations with the Scribes and Pharisees regarding his healing of the man with the shriveled hand, Jesus ascended to a place of peace and quiet by means of the six steps of patience.⁴⁴

The description of the eighth attribute of patience is relatively brief. Holcot describes the patient person as one "sitting without feet" (*sedens sine pedibus*)—he glosses this by stating that the patient person "has the feet of patience in the heart (*pedem patientiae in corde*), because patience has a perfect work."⁴⁵ Following this description, Holcot references James 1:3–4: "Knowing that the trying of your faith works patience. And patience has a perfect work; that you may be perfect and whole, failing in nothing." The context for this passage (James 1:2) is important, as James writes that the Christian should consider diverse temptations a blessing because the trying of one's faith brings patience. That is, the struggles of the faith bring about patience, which will bring about the perfection and completion of the individual.

The ninth attribute of the patient person is that he is "without tongue" (*sine lingua*). This means that the patient person ought not to speak badly or respond to someone badly.[46] To support the claim that one should speak kind words at all times, Holcot tells a story of a robber and a hermit. The robber approached the hermit and said, "Greetings, my brother," to which the hermit responded, "You are the brother of demons!" Because of the hermits harsh words, the robber took out his sword and killed the hermit. When the Abbot heard about this he spoke to the robber and said, "Greetings, my brother." The robber responded to the Abbot, "I am not your brother, but [the brother] of demons." The Abbot replied, "Indeed, you are my brother, redeemed with the precious blood of Christ." In response the robber repented of his ways and became a devout hermit.

The final discussion of the ninth attribute considers more fully the notion of "without tongue." Holcot writes that a serpent is seen to have three tongues (or languages/*linguas*) just as impatience has three voices: (a) the voice of anger (*vocem iracundiae*), (b) the voice of envy and treachery (*vocem invidiae et perfidiae*), and (c) the voice of female stupidity (*feminae stultitiae*).[47] Holcot does not expand on this claim but concludes by observing that in Scripture women (Job 2:10), children (Genesis 21:17ff.), and the elderly (Daniel 13:14) are generally impatient. While one might be inclined to argue that Holcot himself is demonstrating impatience here with women, children, and the elderly, within the broader context of his argument the point seems to be that improper speech (by anyone) is not fitting of the patient person. The ninth attribute states, therefore, that the patient person ought to be "swift to hear, slow to speak, and slow to anger" (James 1:19).

The tenth and final attribute of patience is "without ears,"[48] meaning the patient person has the ability to ignore or forgive slights. In support of this claim Holcot cites several passages from Seneca's *De ira* (*On Anger*). The first passage is from *De ira*, book 2, where Seneca considers the claim that anger possesses a pleasure of its own, given that it is sweet to pay back wrongs (2.32.1).

Seneca argues that this is not the case, for revenge and retaliation are words that seem to imply righteousness but actually cover a multitude of sins. To further demonstrate the point, Seneca recalls a story—cited here by Holcot—involving Marcus Cato at the baths. While Cato was in the public bath someone struck him in ignorance. When the person later apologized, Cato replied to the person, "I do not remember being struck,"[49] for Cato thought it better to ignore the insult than to revenge it. For the great mind, Seneca writes, is able to despise the wrongs done to it; indeed, the most insulting kind of revenge is not to deem one's adversary worth taking revenge upon.[50]

Holcot provides further argumentation in favor of keeping silent in the face of wrongs. One further passage from Seneca is interesting, as it is the famous story of the courtier who managed to thrive in the court until old age. When asked how he was able to survive at court so long, he replied that he received wrongs and returned thanks.[51] In short, Holcot amasses four passages from Seneca and one from Jerome in support of the idea that one quality of a patient person is the ability to ignore and forgive faults.[52] Thus the patient person is at times "without ears" when he chooses to ignore the slights of others.

This concludes Holcot's verbal picture of patience and his analysis of the 10 distinct clauses or phrases that correlate to the 10 attributes. However, before ending his commentary on the first chapter Holcot closes with one further *pictura*: the picture of impatience.

(1) *homo pauper*, (2) *splendide cibatus*,	a poor man fed splendidly,
(3) *maestitia respersus*, (4) *omnibus adversus*,	sprinkled with the tears of grief, opposed to all,
(5) *vestibus nudatus*, (6) *aculeis vallatus*,	divested of clothing, defended by barbs,
(7) *cum manibus leprosis*, (8) *et pedibus vulpinis*,	with leprous hands and the feet of a fox,
(9) *cum lingua serpentina*, (10) *et auribus leoninis*.	with a serpentine tongue and the ears of a lion.[53]

Unlike the picture of patience, Holcot mercifully does not explicate the 10 corresponding attributes of impatience (lest he breed what he attempts to define). He simply writes at the conclusion of his commentary on chapter 1 that the explanation of the picture of impatience can be derived from the previous description of patience.[54] It is up to the reader, therefore, to imagine how the impatient person is naked and has leprous hands, the feet of a fox, a serpentine tongue, and the ears of a lion.

Having explicated Holcot's image of patience, it is hard not to sympathize with Smalley's judgment that the pictures "become tiresome as soon as the initial surprise has died down."[55] Smalley's concern is that after reading several of these pictures one comes away with the impression that they are an excessively rigid way of interpreting the biblical text. That is, they impose a structure that is not in any way intrinsic to the text itself. However, understanding the method discussed here is essential to appreciating the function of the pictures within Holcot's homiletical and exegetical method. Further, the themes discussed in these pictures are incorporated throughout Holcot's other commentaries. For example, Holcot focuses on patience in his commentary on Wisdom. In a moralization on a passage from Seneca involving a father and two sons—one of whom is disinherited—Holcot interprets the father as God the Father and Christ and humanity as the two brothers. Christ, speaking to his disinherited brother (i.e., humanity), says that the Father disinherits all of us many times since we all suffer adversity in this life. But what does Christ say to his brother who suffers? What does Christ say to the pilgrim sinner seeking God the Father?

> May you endure patiently and may you respond in no way harshly to our Father, and I will give to you my half of the inheritance, and at the same time with this I will stand with you in every fortune . . . because you did not murmur against the Father.[56]

Patience, therefore, is important throughout Holcot's corpus, and one must focus on both the theological content of the pictures as well as their unique methodology.

The Pictures as Memory Devices

This portrait of patience confirms Smalley's assessment of Holcot's picture method. She writes:

> He puts [the pictures] into preacher's rhythm; he lists the attributes of his subject and supports each one with a string of quotations to show its moral significance; sometimes, but not always, he gives his source for the "picture" as a whole.[57]

This is an accurate description of Holcot's basic method with respect to individual pictures, but it does not help explain the more pressing question of their purpose or function within the commentary.

In the manuscripts, these verbal images are called *picturae* (pictures/paintings) or *imagines* (images), and Holcot describes the production of such images as an act of painting (*depingens*).[58] This has led to debate regarding whether or not the pictures are intended to function as verbal or visual images. The visual aspects of the pictures were documented by Fritz Saxl, who observed that several manuscript illustrations depict the verbal images described by Holcot in the *Moralitates*:[59] one manuscript in particular originates from Germany sometime between 1425 and 1450.[60] However, the most important point with respect to Holcot is that there is no evidence of painted or drawn images being produced prior to the fifteenth century. As Saxl notes, "not a single English illuminated manuscript of [the *Moralitates*] is known"—for that matter, there is not a single illustrated Holcot manuscript known to modern researchers (English or Continental).[61] The illustrations of the verbal pictures taken from Holcot's *Moralitates*, Ridevall's *Fulgentius metaphoralis*, and the *Gesta Romanorum* are all later reconstructions that are not original to the fourteenth-century authors. Therefore, the two picture book manuscripts studied by Saxl ought to be understood as belonging to a uniquely fifteenth-century innovation that tells us more about the subsequent development of the woodcut than Holcot's pictures.

Accordingly, the majority of scholars have focused their attention on how these verbal pictures function as memory aids. Smalley argued that despite the language of pictures, the pictures serve as "aural aids to preaching." Her argument—despite the evidence provided by Saxl—is that many of the images are too abstract for visual depiction and as such do not lend themselves to painting or sketching.[62] Thus the function of the pictures is to create a memory aid by which the preacher could reconstruct the central point or argument of a homily.[63] In her study of memory in the Middle Ages, Mary Carruthers summarizes the function of the pictures thus:

> A textual picture is as good as a painted one in addressing memory work, for it can be painted by imagination without the constraints of paint and parchment. Holcot's are also emblematic pictures. They function as compositional aids, the use which their intended clerical audience would most readily have for them. Indeed, they are *imagines rerum*, which

related the parts of a theme like Faith or Sloth [or Patience] through a set of images, each of which is associated with one of its aspects (or divisions, in scholastic language).[64]

What this means practically for the picture of patience described earlier is that the friars would memorize the picture and employ it as a mnemonic device to recall the 10 aspects of patience described by Holcot. The friar who is contemplating (or preaching on) patience, therefore, could reflect on this particular rhymed picture and recall that the patient person (1) is satisfied and content (*sitting satisfied*); (2) suffers vices that nourish patience (*fed with common foods*); (3) is joyful (*of joyful countenance*); (4) is patient with all, including one's enemies (*turned toward all*); (5) is clothed in mercy, kindness, modesty, and humility (*clothed in purple*); (6) is given to silence and peace in times of trouble (*protected from enemies*); (7) is ready to bear troubles (*with one hand shriveled and the other [hand] extended*); (8) is brought to perfection and completion through the struggles of the faith (*without feet*); (9) speaks properly (*without tongue*); and (10) ignores or forgives insults (*without ears*). The 10 attributes, therefore, are attached to one of the 10 clauses. However, Holcot's memory method is not limited to the mapping of attributes with individual clauses.

One aspect of Holcot's pictures that is not discussed by Smalley or Rivers is the relationship between the 10 clauses (and corresponding attributes) and the scriptural passages Holcot quotes in support of them. What is clear is that often, though not always, Holcot links the words of a given clause with a passage from Scripture in a complex form of word association. Here it is instructive to consider a few examples.

The third attribute of patience is linked to the clause (3) *vult laetatus* (of joyful countenance). In his short description of this attribute of patience Holcot quotes Wisdom 7:12 to establish the relationship between patience, joy, and wisdom. Wisdom 7:12 states that "*Et laetatus sum in omnibus quoniam, antecedebat ista sapientia* (And I rejoiced in all these things, for this wisdom went before me)." Here Holcot links the clause *vult laetatus* with this particular passage from the book of Wisdom not only because the passage supports his general point but also because it will be easy for the preacher to recall this verse given the linking term *laetatus*. That is, if the preacher has dutifully memorized the picture and its 10 attributes (here *vult laetatus*), the individual attributes will recall for the preacher the biblical phrase that begins *et laetatus*.

The fifth attribute of patience, one will recall, is linked to the clause (5) *purpura vestitus* (clothed in purple). In support of this attribute Holcot makes reference to several passages that could support the present argument, but it is sufficient to consider Proverbs 31:22: "*Mem stragulam vestem fecit sibi byssus et purpura indumentum eius* (She has made for herself clothing of tapestry: fine linen, and purple, is her covering)." Proverbs 31 is an interesting choice because it is the famous passage in praise of the wise woman (or, alternatively, the wife of noble character). For Holcot's readers familiar with the biblical text, this passage is significant because the woman described in Proverbs 31 is the epitome of hard work, patience, planning, and wisdom. She is also, the passage notes, clothed in purple (*purpura*). Again, Holcot links the initial clause with this important passage from the book of Proverbs through a common term.

The use of individual terms is significant, however, in the seventh attribute Holcot links the clause (7) *cum manu arida et alia extenta* (with one hand shriveled and the other extended) even more intimately with Scripture. The seventh attribute of patience is that one is able to bear troubles (the shriveled hand) as an act of receiving patience (the extended hand). For Holcot's friar audience, this clause probably evoked the passage described previously regarding Jesus and the healing of the man with the crippled hand. The verses from Luke 6 that Holcot references are as follows:

> (v.6) *Factum est autem et in alio sabbato ut intraret in synagogam et doceret et erat ibi homo et manus eius dextra erat arida.* (v.10) *Et circumspectis omnibus dixit homini extende manum tuam et extendit et restituta est manus eius.*
>
> (v.6) And it came to pass also, on another Sabbath, that [Jesus] entered into the synagogue and taught. And there was a man whose right hand was withered. (v.10) And looking round about on them all, [Jesus] said to the man: "Stretch forth your hand." And he stretched it forth. And his hand was restored.

These verses from the Gospel of Luke are verbally linked with the initial clause. First, the phrase *manus arida* (crippled hand) recalls to mind the man with the crippled hand in Luke 6:6. Further, the original clause contains the term *extenta*, the perfect, passive participle of the verb *extendo* (to extend, to stretch forth) used twice in Luke 6:10.

For the medieval friar, such verbal links functioned as mnemonic devices. In the case of Holcot's picture of patience, it is clear that Holcot chose carefully the original words of the picture and sought to correlate those words with the language of the Scriptures. That is, if he could find a biblical text that used the same terms found in the picture, this would assist the friar in recalling both the attributes of the picture and the biblical text that supported a given attribute.

Thus Robert Holcot developed numerous verbal pictures in his biblical commentaries to function as mnemonic devices. The friars could easily memorize a rhymed picture and correlate that picture with specific content relevant to the interpretation of a given passage. Further, as argued here, Holcot also links the individual clauses of the picture with biblical quotations that employ the same language with the purpose of assisting the preacher in recalling the specific passages from the Scriptures that support his present interpretation. All of this would create a series of mnemonic patterns or connections that could be recalled through the verbal picture.

The Development of the Picture Technique

We conclude this chapter with a brief discussion of the development of the technique in Holcot's later works. Kimberly Rivers has argued that Robert Holcot's *picturae* can be divided into two groups: Type I pictures, which are made up of rhymed pictures (e.g., the pictures found in the commentary on the Twelve Prophets),[65] and Type II pictures, which are made up of non-rhymed pictures (e.g., the pictures found in the *Moralitates*).[66] Characteristic of Type I is a focus on rhymed pictures that contain lists of attributes, while Type II pictures largely abandon both the rhyming scheme and the list of attributes in favor of a "simpler image."[67] Holcot's picture technique in its final form (chronologically) can be found in the commentary on Wisdom and the *Moralitates*. In these later works, Rivers argues, Holcot has ceased creating the elaborate rhymed pictures of the commentary on the Twelve Prophets (Type I) in favor of short descriptive paragraphs (Type II).

Smalley considers an example of what Rivers calls a Type II picture in Holcot's picture of drunkenness from the commentary on Wisdom.[68] This picture of drunkenness is clearly recognized as one of Holcot's pictures by his medieval and early modern readers, as the margin of Balliol 27 notes (in another hand) that an image of drunkenness is portrayed (*imago ebrietatis depicta*), as does the margin of the 1586 Basel edition (here, *imago ebrietatis*). The picture of drunkenness is found in Holcot's commentary on Wisdom 2:7: "Let us fill ourselves with costly wine and ointments, and let not the flower of time pass us by." Smalley translates this particular image as:

> Someone imagines that the likeness of Drunkenness was painted thus: it had the likeness of a child, having a horn in his hand and a crown of glass on his head (*Fingitur a quodam imaginem ebrietatis sic fuisse depictam, imago puerilis, cornu habens in manu, et in capite coronam de vitreo.*)[69]

Unlike the image of patience discussed earlier, Holcot does not provide an extended gloss or interpretation of the picture beyond a few lines of text. He simply remarks that drunkenness is depicted as a child because the drunkard is childlike in being both speechless and irrational. By speechless, presumably, Holcot does not mean that either a child or a drunkard is quiet but that they both lack eloquent or rational speech. This idea is further depicted by the fact that the child has a blow horn, indicating that the drunkard is one who has no secrets (*nullum celat secretum*) and makes excessive noise. Finally, the drunkard has a crown of glass on his head for he considers himself to be glorious and rich (*gloriosum et divitem*) while in fact he has nothing.

This image of drunkenness is remarkably distinct from the image of patience considered in the previous section. First, the image itself is stylistically and structurally simple. Gone are the intricate rhymes and the 10 distinct clauses linked with various attributes. What has replaced the rhymed picture, as Rivers notes, is a "simpler image." Further, Rivers is correct in suggesting that these new pictures are perhaps more accessible to a lay audience.[70] These simpler pictures, Wenzel and Rivers have argued, are similar to the pictures used in the anonymous *Fasciculus morum*.[71] The image of drunkenness is also distinct from the earlier pictures with respect to its use of scriptural citations. The majority of the pictures found in the *Moralitates* and the commentary on the book of Wisdom are not linked with scriptural passages (through the use of common terms) and are often not supported with subsequent biblical references. For example, in the picture of drunkenness, Holcot does not use Scripture to interpret or support his picture of drunkenness. Of course Holcot is familiar with biblical images of the drunkard and cites in this lecture Noah's drunkenness in Genesis 9 and the lover of wine in Proverbs 21.[72] It is simply that these biblical verses are not linked verbally with his picture.

That said, the problem with a simple division between categorizing the various pictures as Type I and Type II is that this clear distinction does not adequately address the fact that some of the later pictures seem to be almost hybrids between Type I and Type II. For example, in *Moralitas* 33 Holcot offers the following picture of pride (*superbia*) described as three crowns:

Effluo, transcendo, quo quis privatur habendo	I pour out, I exceed, by which in the midst of having one is deprived,
Transmigrat genus exceditque homo, qui nec obedit.	A race passes on and a man falls away, who does not obey.
Turbor et affligor, perturbor, et undique laedor.[73]	I am disturbed and overthrown, I am confused, and I am wounded everywhere.

Holcot examines the first crown by focusing in particular on the term *effluo*, to pour out or pour forth. He observes that a scriptural example of this aspect of pride is found in II Maccabees 5, which records the struggle between Antiochus IV Epiphanes, the king of the Seleucid Empire (175–164 BCE), and Judas Maccabeus, the Jewish liberator. II Maccabees 5 recounts an incident where Antiochus pillaged the Jewish temple in Jerusalem and stole 1,800 talents. Following this incident, the text records that Antiochus attempted to return to Antioch, "thinking through pride that he might now make the land navigable, and the sea passable on foot. For such was the haughtiness of his mind."[74] According to Holcot, Antiochus is a perfect exemplar of this kind of pride, for he was arrogant enough to think he could change the landscape of God's creation.[75] Returning again to the biblical text, Holcot paraphrases God's punishment of Antiochus for his pride; II Maccabees 9:9 records that, as a result of his pride, Antiochus went mad, worms swarmed out of his body, his flesh fell off, and he was consumed with an awful stench.[76]

The second crown of pride, Holcot notes, is that "every man wants to be given preference to, and no man wants to obey."[77] He elucidates this aspect of pride by quoting two passages from a speech of King Rehoboam, the son of Solomon, on the day that he was anointed King of Israel (I Kings

12). According to I Kings, the people had petitioned Rehoboam because the yoke of his father Solomon was too heavy and they wanted relief. In this regard Rehoboam was instructed by the elders of Israel (Solomon's advisers) to be kind to the people and treat them fairly. Instead, Rehoboam sought the council of young men and said to the people: "My little finger is thicker than the back of my father ... my father beat you with whips, but I will beat you with scorpions."[78] Here, Holcot says, is an example of one whom the people would not obey, given his inexcusable pride.

Holcot turns to the final crown of pride and summarizes it by means of Genesis 16:12: "his hand is against all men, and the hand of all are against him."[79] To find an example of a prideful person who *is against all* and whom *all are against*, Holcot returns to the book of II Maccabees. Here Holcot recounts the complex story of Heliodorus—the chief advisor of Seleucus IV Philopator, king of Syria—and his attempt to take the money from the Jerusalem temple while Onias was high priest. According to II Maccabees 3, there was a man named Simon who worked in the temple as an administrative official. Simon, as it happened, remarked one day that the temple had a great treasure of wealth, and when this knowledge was made known to Seleucus, the king ordered Heliodorus, his advisor, to retrieve it for the royal treasury. However, what occurred when Heliodorus attempted to take the treasure is that, led by the High Priest Onias, the entire city rose up in prayer against him. In answer to the prayer, God sent a horse and a rider dressed in gold armor to protect the treasure, along with two young and beautiful men who beat Heliodorus incessantly until he was unconscious.[80] In response to this story Holcot explains that Heliodorus stood *against all men* and that they all *stood against him*. According to Holcot, Heliodorus acted out of pride when his evil acts were done throughout the entire city.

Having examined this picture of pride, it is difficult not to conclude that it is a pictorial hybrid somewhere between the Type I and Type II defined by Rivers. First, this picture is similar to the Type I pictures in that Holcot has returned to a rhymed schema. In particular, the first and third lines of the picture of pride have a rhythmic rhyming structure grounded in the use of repetitive verbs (often of identical form): *effluo*, *transcendo*, *habendo*, and *turbor*, *affligor perturbor*, and *laedor*. Of course one could object that such rhymes are simple to reproduce in Latin; however, this picture is distinct from the unrhymed picture of drunkenness found in the commentary on

Wisdom and discussed previously. Further, at some level, Holcot returns to the list of attributes in this picture of pride. The third crown is a useful example, for the four attributes of pride in this crown are four distinct verbs (all present passive indicative in form). One can almost hear the prideful person exclaiming, in a moment of self-reflection, "I am disturbed, I am overthrown, I am confused, I am wounded everywhere." Finally, this picture of pride also returns to the previous pattern of referencing Scripture in the development of the picture. Thus Holcot links each of these three crowns and their respective definition of pride with a particular figure from Scripture and quotes a lengthy section of the biblical text. In each aspect, therefore, it seems that the picture of pride found in *Moralitas* 33 is closer to a Type I picture than a Type II picture, although it is not as elaborate or strictly structured as what was seen in the Twelve Prophets.

In sum, therefore, while we agree with Rivers's basic distinction between the two types—as the distinction often does hold—it must be understood in a somewhat more fluid way. Holcot is not consistent in the commentary on Wisdom or in the *Moralitates* in how he paints these individual pictures: some return to the fuller picture method found in the commentary on the Twelve Prophets, whereas others break from this pattern and provide a simpler image.[81]

Conclusion

It is clear, therefore, that Holcot exhibits substantial diversity in his painting of verbal pictures. While they are not all consistent in form, content, or the use of previous exemplars, they all function, within the biblical commentary or preaching tool (e.g., the *Moralitates*), as a way of instructing the homilist or audience in how to remember a particular image or scriptural interpretation. While exegetes or readers who are interested in a literal commentary on the Twelve Prophets may be disappointed with Holcot's approach, it is clear that for Holcot the central aim of interpreting this text was moral instruction. The book of Nahum, one will recall, begins with the tension between God's justice and his mercy; for Holcot, this meant his mercy understood under the aspect of patience.

The other lesson that emerges for the patient reader of Holcot's commentary on Twelve Prophets or the *Moralitates* is that he had a remarkable grasp of the biblical text. When students of medieval philosophy and theology read the commentaries on the *Sentences* by Thomas Aquinas, John Duns Scotus, William of Ockham, or Robert Holcot, they often have the impression that these authors did not engage substantively with the biblical text. However, when one turns to the biblical commentaries, it is immediately evident that the friars possessed an intimate knowledge of the Scriptures. As demonstrated in this chapter, Holcot had a remarkable ability to find the perfect scriptural passage when elucidating a picture. For example, in his picture of humility Holcot notes that in I Samuel 16:12 the future King David was initially said to be ruddy, handsome, and noble (*rufus, pulcher, et decorus*), only to be described eight chapters later, when hunted by King Saul (24:15), as a dead dog (*canem mortuum*), a single flea (*pulicem unum*).[82] Here the future king is an outstanding exemplar of humility. With an almost encyclopedic knowledge of the biblical text, it is as if the perfect biblical story, person, image, or reference was ready at Holcot's fingertips to be painted into his picture.

8

THE BOOK OF WISDOM

Introduction

Holcot's commentary on the book of Wisdom is a long and structurally complex text. In this chapter we aim to provide the reader with an overview of the commentary as a whole before delving into some of the core themes of the book in the next chapter. In the first section, we survey Holcot's basic approach to the text, focusing on the style and conventions he adopts. Then we turn to the first crucial structural element of the text, the prologue (*prologus*), where we focus on his claims about the author of the text, its specific subject matter, and its purpose. Finally, we, at some length, guide the reader through Holcot's elaborate divisions of the commentary (the *divisio textus*), focusing on select literal and moralizing interpretations that follow.[1]

Our hope in following these basic divisions and Holcot's interpretation of their significance is first and foremost to provide the reader with the means to navigate the commentary. Second, however, we aim to provide support for an argument about Holcot's overall interpretation of the book's guiding principles and message. This argument is twofold. First, over and against rival interpretations and emphases,[2] Holcot sees this book as concerned with the acquisition of a particular type of moral wisdom acquired in society through the governance of wise rulers. Thus the book is addressed to people placed in positions of social responsibility and functions as an exhortation to acquire wisdom and consequently promote a wise society. Second, Holcot's glosses, interpretations, and moralizations repeatedly, within the larger address, reinforce the character of his thought. This will be seen most clearly in his characterization of the proper faith and piety required to attain wisdom and his evaluation of the utility and limits of natural reason in both the acquisition and use of that wisdom.

The Nature and Style of Holcot's Commentary on the Book of Wisdom

It is both predictable and remarkable how well the literary style of Holcot's commentary on the book of Wisdom fits the general pattern of a biblical commentary seen in earlier medieval works. It is predictable because Holcot was, after all, working within a genre and therefore was generally faithful to the requirements of that genre. However, it is also remarkable given that a scholar of medieval texts quickly becomes accustomed to finding medieval authors, especially fourteenth-century authors, breaking conventions previously established.

The most basic discernible structural element in Holcot's commentary is the lecture format. While this structure is slightly different from commentaries devoted to taking each verse individually—seen earlier in Ps.-Bonaventure's thirteenth-century commentary[3] and later in Jean de Lorin's (†1634) commentary printed in 1607[4]—it is generally in keeping with the genre.[5] Rather than strict verse divisions, Holcot's commentary is devoted to clear lecture divisions, which contain all subsequent structural divisions.[6] These lectures tend to take a few verses at a time, sometimes merely one or two but at other times four or five.[7] In the Basel edition there are 213 lectures covering the entire 19 chapters of the book.[8]

The lecture divisions are so strong that they, in a way, obscure a very common and important structural feature that is usually seen as preceding the lecture division. This is the prologue.[9] Holcot's prologue in the Basel edition and in some manuscripts (though not all)[10] is identified as lecture 1, yet it fits Timothy Bellamah's description of a traditional prologue almost exactly. Bellamah writes:

> Normally, the prologues of postills open with a biblical verse, generally from a book other than the one commented on, which serves as a theme

for what follows ... Another important feature of the prologues of the university commentaries is their orchestration around Aristotle's four causes.[11]

Holcot's first lecture does indeed introduce a biblical verse from another text—II Kings 22—and he uses this verse as the theme for his prologue. He also pays lip service to the convention of invoking the four causes by using this division to interpret the biblical verse he has introduced. Bellamah, however, hints that by the mid-thirteenth century this convention of invoking the four causes was used to replace an earlier practice of explicitly asking questions about the author, title, and intention of the work.[12] Not only does Holcot's invocation of the four causes not focus on concerns about the author, title, and intention of the work, but these themes are the explicit concern of lecture 2, suggesting that this lecture should also be considered part of the formal prologue. A surface glance would suggest that this lecture is not part of the prologue but rather part of the formal commentary. The Basel printing, for instance, identifies chapter 1, verse 1 as the direct concern of the section, and even the manuscripts that do not count the opening division as a lecture proper identify this second section as lecture 1. However, upon closer examination, Holcot appears to remain uninterested in the verse identified. Instead, he turns his attention to the book of Wisdom as a whole and points to three particular concerns: the name of the work, the author of the work, and the purpose of the work.[13] It seems likely that Holcot is continuing a trend seen in other prologues of different genres, namely to care less and less about structuring the prologue around Aristotle's four causes. The nature of his concern here in lecture 2 suggests that he finds this older schema either unhelpful or unnecessary. In any case, it cannot be denied that the concern of lecture 2 treats the topics that typically belong to a prologue[14] and therefore should be considered part of Holcot's own prologue. Further evidence of this inclusion is the fact that lecture 3 in the Basel edition repeats verse 1 as the title theme of the lecture (the only instance where this kind of repetition occurs).[15] Likewise, it is only in lecture 3 that the formal features of medieval exegesis become visible.

The first of the formal features is the *divisio textus* (division of the text). Bellamah rightly notes that, traditionally, it is here that "the text commented on is divided into component parts, not according to any preexisting set of principles, but according to the interpreter's own exegetical interests."[16] This is an accurate assessment of Holcot's own practice in his Wisdom commentary and, frankly, of the entire historical tradition of commentating on the book of Wisdom. Throughout the history of this tradition there exists a wide variety of ways that the book has been broken down, and each division would seem to reveal a great deal about the author's interests and agenda for the commentary. Accordingly, we focus in some detail on the elaborate breakdown that Holcot provides as a part of an attempt to identify his unique take on this biblical book.

Following the division of the text is the exposition. The exposition is formally composed of at least three parts: a line-by-line commentary, a literal interpretation, and a spiritual interpretation. With regularity these three features are present, but this does not mean they are necessarily easy to discern. Any line-by-line exposition of the text is typically interwoven within a literal interpretation. Nor is there any clear declaration of when and where the literal interpretation begins or ends. On the whole, this style of interpretation appears to be of only minor interest. Smalley observes that within each lecture Holcot shows a minimal concern for a literal exposition of the text. She summarizes his habit as follows: "He explained the general trend of his authors; the details of the literal exposition were a mere preliminary to the moral."[17]

The moral or tropological interpretation is one type of spiritual interpretation, and it is clearly the dominant concern.[18] In fact, in comparison to other commentaries (i.e., Ps.-Bonaventure or later sixteenth- and seventeenth-century commentaries), these extensive moralizing sections are one of the defining features of Holcot's commentary.[19] He takes every opportunity to provide a moralizing spin on a particular verse or set of verses. However, here again there is no obvious indication that a literal interpretation has been completed and a moral interpretation is beginning. Nevertheless, Holcot's style includes some important reoccurring patterns that tend to structure an individual lecture or at least alert the reader to a possible moralizing interpretation. Most noticeable are those sections of the text introduced by *notandum est* (it should be known) or *ubi notandum* (where it should be known). These sections tend to indicate an occasion where Holcot expands on an issue or topic, often in ways fairly tangential to the concern of the verses at hand. Anticipating these structural elements is often difficult. Since they are occasioned by the text and Holcot's own interests, their appearance, order, and content is hard to predict. Yet they are valuable because they often contain the core of Holcot's position on a given topic. Usually one will find within such a section a conceptual taxonomy. For example, in lecture 64 Holcot writes: "*Ubi notandum* according to the three types of sins, three shadows (*umbra*) follow."[20] The rest of the section tends to include a substantial explanation of the original assertion.[21] Sometimes the section takes its beginning from a particular clause, as is the case in lecture 163: "*Initium fornicationis est exquisitio idolorum* (it should be known that morally speaking [*moraliter loquendo*] we find four types of idols in the Church . . .)."[22] This latter example offers a rare instance— *moraliter loquendo*—where Holcot does hint that he is offering a tropological interpretation.

A final formal feature of a medieval biblical commentary, besides the *divisio* (division) and the *expositio* (exposition), is the *quaestio* (question). Holcot's Wisdom commentary stands out from his other commentaries because of the inclusion of numerous formal questions within the body of the text. While there are exceptions,[23] these questions are often introduced by the phrase *dubitatio litteralis* or simply *dubium* and, in good scholastic style, are followed by a section beginning with *videtur quod non* (it would seem that not) and then concluded with a short *responsio* (response).[24] Like the various discussions beginning with *ubi notandum*, these questions are occasioned by the verses, the exposition, and Holcot's apparent curiosity. They often, but again not always, appear at the end of a lecture. They do not appear in every lecture, and occasionally a lecture contains more than one such question.[25] As such these questions do not appear in any systematic fashion but rather at Holcot's caprice.[26]

Finally, a word should be said about Holcot's use of sources. Besides the elaborate moralizing interpretations, it is his extensive use of classical, Christian, and pagan sources that sets his commentary apart. As Smalley points out, the moralizing focus of Holcot's commentary affects his use of sources. She notes that there is a clear paucity of exegetical sources in proportion to others.[27] For example, references to previous commentaries of Rabanus, Hugh of St. Cher, and Ps.-Bonaventure are few and infrequent. In contrast, Holcot's commentary abounds with sources instrumental in making the relevant moralizing point. Smalley identifies at least three different categories of sources.[28] The commentary is filled with sources from histories and chronicles, literary and devotional writings, and political writings.

The commentary likewise abounds with colorful tales and stories designed to illustrate a point. One such story appears in lecture 91, where Holcot attempts to persuade his reader to prefer moral probity to worldly honors. Holcot compares worldly honor to a horse that carries one sweetly about—sweetly because "it is delightful to be honored through the service of men." Then Holcot warns, "let the honored ones beware because this is a truly sorrowful horse." All of this work to compare honor to a horse seems to be intentionally designed for the retelling of an anonymous story that was perhaps commonly known.[29]

> There is a story about a certain performer who had a small horse that he was accustomed to ride and who frequently performed with this horse at court. Among the games that he taught the horse to play, one was that whenever he said "bend your knees," the horse would obey and genuflect. But when he said, "get up," the horse would rise up. Therefore it happened that the minstrel performer was approaching the feast of some noble and his horse was collected in the stable with the horses of the other guests. But when the men had eaten, the minstrel, as was his custom, began performing a game before the court. Meanwhile, a certain squire hurried to the stable and, seeing the pleasant and handsome horse of the minstrel, left his own sickly horse and mounted the pleasant and healthy horse of the minstrel and departed. Immediately after the minstrel became aware of this, he left everyone else and followed swiftly after the squire. The squire, seeing that the minstrel had almost reached him and apprehended him, attempted to cross a river that no one on foot was able to cross. Then, the minstrel, seeing that the squire was about to hurt his horse, cried out loudly to his horse in his usual way, while the horse was standing in the middle of a river, "bend your knees." Immediately, the horse heard the voice of his master and bent his knees and threw the squire into the water. And when the minstrel had cried out, "get up," the horse rose up and returned to his master. The minstrel who plays tricks and mocks and deceives men is the world. The horse, with which he skillfully and expertly plays, is temporal honor.[30]

In her analysis of Dominican biblical commentaries, Michèle Mulchahey emphasizes that these commentaries were not just tools for biblical exegesis but were also "direct sources to which preachers turned for assistance."[31] The inclusion of elaborate moralizing stories like these makes her assessment all the more likely. The rich and colorful narrative details seen here are the perfect material for communicating moralizing messages to the masses. It is no wonder that this particular commentary went on to be a "medieval best-seller."

The Prologue

The Name and Subject of the Book

Having surveyed some of the basic features of Holcot's text, we can begin to look at his distinctive approach to the content of the book. It is helpful in this regard to begin where he begins: with an account of the central subject matter of this biblical book.

The history of interpretation has offered various accounts of the book's title and its core subject matter. The *Glossa ordinaria* offers a particularly Christological reading,[32] thought to be particularly influential on Meister Eckhart's own interpretation of the book.[33] Early modern commentators likewise began their commentaries with a discourse on the subject of the book and focused on the book's title. Cornelius de Lapide restricted the book's focus to a practical rather than speculative notion of wisdom.[34] In contrast, at least one modern commentary has pointed to the book's understanding of wisdom as encompassing "the entire range of natural science," "the human arts," and "all moral knowledge."[35]

Holcot himself recognizes a certain amount of ambiguity in the work's title and begins the second part of his prologue with a taxonomy of various possible meanings and a clear assertion of how the word should be understood in this context. He identifies three dominant meanings of the word "wisdom," only one of which is the focus of this book and therefore the focus of his commentary.

First, there is the definition of "wisdom" as defined by Aristotle in book 6 of the *Ethics* and likewise in *Metaphysics* book 1.[36] Here he has in mind a kind of speculative wisdom interested in the highest causes. It is a decidedly *theoretical* wisdom interested in pursuing these highest causes for their own sake.[37]

In contrast to this philosophical wisdom, there is a second meaning, which he attributes to the theologians. This is wisdom "understood as a supernatural or infused gift."[38] This, according to Holcot, is the kind of wisdom that Dionysius speaks of in the *Divine Names*. It is a special knowledge of human and divine things that cannot be achieved naturally and presupposes faith. Given that Holcot is commenting on a biblical book, a classic theological exercise, we might expect him to declare that the book of Wisdom is about wisdom understood in this theological sense. However, this turns out to be wrong. Holcot rejects both the speculative-philosophical and theological definitions of wisdom and points to a third, which he associates with stoic and moral philosophy. According to Holcot, this was the meaning of wisdom understood by Socrates, Seneca, and Boethius, and it means "nothing other than the collection of all intellectual and moral virtues" where the wise person is identifiable with the perfectly virtuous person.[39]

This third and final definition sets the stage for the rest of the commentary. Throughout the commentary Holcot is focused on the proper virtues, how to acquire them, and their benefits. This is not to say there is no discussion about speculative issues. There is in fact a great deal of abstract discussion about human nature, the nature of the cosmos, and even the combustion of the elements. However, the discussion of these issues never quite has the air of theoretical detachment seen in such an inquiry performed merely for its own sake. Rather Holcot's interest in these subjects is often related to some practical questions: how best do we guide and correct the tendencies of human nature; how do the movements of the celestial spheres affect climates and therefore the best places for settlement; or how and to what degree will the fires of hell inflict pain on those who refused to practice virtue in this life?

The Author of the Work

For most of its interpretative history there has been uncertainty and doubt about the true author of the book.[40] The book, through its title and resemblance to the biblical wisdom tradition, no doubt intended to give the impression that it was written by Solomon, thereby ensuring its status and readership.[41] The doubts about its authorship can be traced at least as far back as Jerome.[42] Thus, throughout its interpretative history, almost all commentators have initiated their prologue with some discussion of the author.[43] Medieval exegetes and commentators were not immune to such disagreement. Hugh of St. Victor, for example, following Jerome, doubts its attribution to Solomon,[44] while Ps.-Bonaventure affirms that it was written by Solomon but compiled by Philo.[45]

Holcot begins his own discussion of the author of this work with a survey of previous opinions. St. Jerome, he says, claims that the book was most excellently compiled by Philo from the many opinions of Solomon, and therefore Philo ought to be referred to as the author rather than Solomon.[46] Holcot disagrees. He points to several different arguments that support the view that Solomon is the genuine author. After marshalling these arguments, Holcot concedes: it is possible that the Jew Philo "edited the contents in Greek and his book was translated from Greek into Latin."[47] Nevertheless, he insists, "the Church ought to count this book among the canonical scriptures."[48]

The Purpose of the Book

In the words of Holcot, the purpose of wisdom—understood in the specific sense mentioned earlier—is "to prepare man and make him worthy specifically with respect to three things." First, it prepares us for governing the civil community. Second, wisdom prepares us to destroy hostile adversity. Here he points to the opening lines of Wisdom chapter 6: when it comes to defending one's community, "wisdom is better than strength, and a wise man is better than a strong man." Third and finally, the aim of the book is to prepare us to chastise the childish and foolish.[49] This final educational aim is particularly indicative of the political aspirations of the book and is echoed later in the commentary when Holcot chides negligent prelates for looking the other way at transgressions in order to maintain the appearance of peace and tranquility. The overall concern with training political leaders to guide their subjects stands squarely in line with the way Ps.-Bonaventure understood the book's central message. In his own commentary, Ps.-Bonaventure explains that, while the primary audience of the book of Wisdom is those individuals who find themselves in positions of power and authority, the goal is not simply to make them wise. Rather it is to make them wise in such a way that their own wisdom may trickle down to those below them,[50] ultimately building a community of wise people who are able to pass that wisdom on to each new generation. This fits well with the statement of purpose we see later in his commentary on chapter 6. There Holcot writes: "The true end of wisdom is to make man fit (*habilem*) for himself and virtuous for the governing of others."[51] The goal here is not simply to become happy or to reach immortality but also to become the kind of person who knows how to pass that wisdom on. The two aims are quite clearly not identical. The latter requires additional knowledge about the tendencies of human nature and the appropriate ways to guide and correct that nature in the proper direction. It is this extra knowledge that Holcot claims is the purpose of the book of Wisdom, and, consequently, it is the goal of his commentary to bring this teaching to light.

Holcot's Book of Wisdom in Outline

The dominance of the lecture format and the absence of a discernable guide to any other structure can make it appear to the casual reader that the commentary is entirely an ad hoc response to the verses as they appear. But a close reading of the text shows that Holcot is working hard throughout the commentary to expose for the reader the larger systematic argument of the book of Wisdom. Often we can see Holcot apologizing for the way the book itself fails to proceed systematically and therefore problematizes the general outline he is attempting to create. In the rest of this chapter, we attempt to guide the reader through the basic conceptual outline Holcot has in mind but nowhere describes in a single pass. Accordingly, the conceptual outline he is working with must be pieced together from the divisions he makes as he moves through the text.

It is worth noting that throughout the ages commentators have disagreed about the organization of the book to such an extent that one commentary remarked that the "author's method of composition defied system."[52] Despite this assessment, there has been no shortage of divergent attempts to schematize this book.[53] In particular, there is a great deal of disagreement about the initial divisions. Ps.-Bonaventure, for instance, wants to divide the book into two parts corresponding to chapters 1 to 6 and 7 to 19. In lecture 3, Holcot also claims that the book should be divided into two parts. However, he initially identifies the division beginning in chapter 9 rather than in chapter 6. He writes that in the first section (chapters 1–8), the author aims to show the nobility and excellence of wisdom. In the second section (chapter 9–19), he aims to show the utility and operation of wisdom.[54] However, at the outset of lecture 125, Holcot changes his mind and asserts that the second part of the book actually begins in chapter 10 and not chapter 9.[55]

It is also at this point that he clarifies the initial division in more detail. The first part of the book (now chapters 1–9), concerned with the excellence and nobility of wisdom, focuses on the "general effects" of wisdom. The second of part of this book (now chapters 10–19), concerned with the utility and operation of wisdom, focuses on the specific effects of wisdom. By specific effects he means how specific people who possessed wisdom received good results and how those who lacked wisdom found themselves in the midst of evil.[56] As Holcot further explains, within the division of the second part, only the first 15 verses (10:1–15) are dedicated to the benefits of wisdom accrued to specific people (e.g., Adam, Noah, Abraham, Lot, Jacob, and Joseph). The rest of the book (10:16–19:22) is about the effects of wisdom for a people as a whole: in other words, the political effects of wisdom. Here he has in mind the Israelites and the advantages they accrued because of their possession of true wisdom.[57] In light of these central divisions, we provide an overview of the critical subdivisions that follow. First, we consider what Holcot identifies as the general account of wisdom, and subsequently we consider the specific effects he identifies and why these can be seen as consequences flowing directly from the possession of wisdom.

The Nobility and Excellence of Wisdom (Chapters 1–9)

While the commentary tradition shows very little agreement on the main divisions of the book, there is more consensus about the discrete subsections that follow. Nearly every commentator recognizes an early unit of the text from chapter 1 to the end of chapter 5, though there remains disagreement about whether chapter 6 is the end of this section or the beginning of a new section.[58] Modern commentaries tend to focus on the theme of immortality and identify wisdom as a means of achieving immortality in some form.[59] Critical to these accounts is the focus in chapter 1 on the importance of justice and the idea that wisdom, and therefore immortality, cannot be achieved without justice.[60]

Within his first overarching division (chapters 1–9), Holcot is attentive to a further subdivision. First he argues for a division between chapters 5 and 6, therefore disagreeing with Ps.-Bonaventure and later commentators who place the division between chapter 6 and 7. Holcot claims that this first section (chapters 1–5) should be seen as an argument about how wisdom is acquired. The second section is usually described as a more general discussion of the "nature and power of wisdom,"[61] "in praise of wisdom," [62] or, in Ps.-Bonaventure's commentary, an "exhortation to acquire wisdom."[63] Holcot's own interpretation sees this section as a discussion about how someone who has just acquired wisdom is perfected by it.[64]

Amidst all these divisions, Holcot's caveat at the beginning of chapter 6 should be kept in mind throughout his commentary. Here he reminds his reader:

> It should be known that this division of the book or [its] development is not made precisely, such that in each part the other part occurs. For in the preceding section [1–5] it was sometimes said how wisdom is able to perfect man. And in what follows [6–9] it will sometimes be taught how man is able to acquire wisdom.[65]

Such a warning, which is echoed elsewhere, should alert us to two facts. First, Holcot is not completely satisfied with these divisions and is fully aware that the book of Wisdom is structurally difficult to describe. Second, such awareness is evidence of how interpretative these divisions are and therefore that they are highly representative of the unique interpretation for which Holcot wants to argue. In the following we highlight some of the key discussions that occur in each of these first two sections: discussions that will help us trace a coherent thread of interpretation through his commentary.

The Acquisition of Wisdom (Chapters 1–5)

In keeping with the dominant interpretation described earlier, the first precondition for the acquisition of wisdom is the love of justice. But just what Holcot means by "justice" and who especially is exhorted to love it relies on his earlier definition of wisdom. Recall that he is not concerned primarily with that science of metaphysics that Aristotle labels wisdom. Instead, he means a kind of practical wisdom that permeates one's entire individual and public existence. Thus the wisdom he has in mind demands a particular kind of social reality, and it is on this basis that the "love of justice" takes a central role. Holcot first explains why the book of Wisdom begins by addressing only those "who rule the earth" and commands them "to love justice."

> It should be known that in the generation of animals, nature does not begin from the finger or from the foot, but from the heart, the lungs, and the heads and the principal members, so the author of this book, wishing to inform the body of the Church in morals begins from the lords and prelates, who are responsible to order and judge. In this way, this moral teaching extends itself to everyone else.[66]

This provocative passage offers a clear vision of how Holcot approaches this book. The central message here is that for wisdom to be acquired by the population at large, it must be acquired in a well-ordered society. Thus the command to love justice is not directly addressed to the "individual" or "everyman" but rather to those who have found themselves in a position of political power and are therefore responsible for the moral education of society at large.

This direct and primary address to political leaders is echoed in Ps.-Bonaventure's commentary[67] and notably contrasts with some modern commentaries that go out of their way to stress that the reference to "rulers of the earth" in 1:1 should really be taken as an address to "everyman." Clarke for example writes:

> Certainly the real subject of the book is everyman ... It is unnecessary, therefore, to attempt an identification of the phrase *rulers of the earth*. The author was speaking to everyman and urged him to *love justice*.[68]

Holcot is opposed to such a view and is committed to the idea that wisdom is acquired by society at large through the wise and just rule of its governors. A few examples suffice to confirm this. In the same lecture, Holcot writes:

> For we see that that which is precious, cherished, or loved by the prince, in dress, action, or life, becomes an example for his subjects, whether it is useful or useless ... Whence if judges, lords, and prelates desire to love justice, there is no doubt that their subjects will also love it.[69]

Shortly thereafter, Holcot faces an objection: why do rulers need to love justice alone? As political leaders, do they not primarily need prudence?[70] In responding, Holcot takes a position on one of the central debates introduced in Augustine's *City of God*: whether a civil society requires the presence of a just law to be a true society or just effective coercive force. Holcot responds that any leader without justice is not a true lord but a tyrant and—quoting Augustine—no different than a leader of thieves.[71]

Having established that for a society to acquire wisdom its rulers must love justice and not merely be clever or prudent, Holcot turns, in lecture 4, to consider what it means to possess justice. For him, the discussion constitutes the rest of chapter 1. Dividing the chapter into three, Holcot explains that to love and possess justice is first to be rightly ordered to God in mind ("set your mind upon the lord" [1:1–4, lectures 4–6]), second in word ("Wisdom is a spirit devoted to man's good, and she will not hold a blasphemer blameless for his words" [1:6–11, lectures 7–11]), and third and finally in deed (*conversatione*) ("Do not stray from the path of life and court death" [1:12–16, lectures 12–14]).

In concord with most other commentators, Holcot identifies chapters 2 through 5 as a new unit. The general tenor of the unit, after chapter 1's praise and exhortation to pursue wisdom through the love of justice, is a refutation of the worldly-wise, who in view of their inevitable mortality claim that the pursuit of justice is the height of foolishness.[72] Chapter 5's discussion of the final judgment of the unjust and vindication of the just stands as a clear capstone to the central argument of this section, asserting fundamentally that, despite the protestations of the wicked, the pursuit of justice is not folly but the true path to wisdom. Such a capstone accounts for Holcot's decision to see a decisive break occurring between chapters 5 and 6.

The Perfection of Wisdom (Chapters 6–9)

At the outset of chapter 6, Holcot provides a general summary of the book of Wisdom up to this point and then indicates where he thinks the text will turn next:

> After it has been shown by the Holy Spirit, from the start of the book up until this point, how man is able *to acquire wisdom* through justice

and good morals, here consequently the Spirit declares how wisdom *once acquired is able to perfect man*.[73] Here we are told that the text shifts from a concern with the acquisition of wisdom to a concern for the effects or consequences of wisdom. Likewise, Holcot again reminds us that, while useful, this division is not precisely made.[74] The subsequent discussion is broken down further into two main parts. The intention of chapter 6 is a discussion of how kings, princes, judges, and prelates ought to govern themselves and others through the gift of wisdom.[75] The remainder of the section (chapters 7–9) is described in a couple of different ways, first at the outset of chapter 6 and then a second time at the beginning of chapter 7. At the outset of chapter 6, he states, without much clarity, that its aim is to show "how man is able to be granted (*impetrare*) wisdom."[76] The summary does not help us understand very clearly how this section should be distinguished from chapters 1 through 5, but of course this is likely one of the reasons Holcot reminds us that the text never perfectly conforms to his divisions. However, the use of the verb *impetrare* and its suggestion of "obtaining by request or entreaty"[77] hints at Holcot's awareness of the shift to the first person that begins in chapter 7 and persists through chapter 9. Holcot's summary at the outset of chapter 7 is more instructive about why he thinks this shift occurs. Here he writes that "after it was declared doctrinally, that it is possible that man acquires wisdom" what remains is for the same thing to be demonstrated through examples.[78] Holcot recognizes the shift to the first person and sees it as a kind of personal example or illustration of what was previously taught.

Holcot's claim that chapter 6 is specifically focused on the effects of wisdom on the rulers of the world fits well with his interpretation of this book as first and foremost directed at the rulers of the earth. The chapter begins with a reminder that "The true end of wisdom is to make man 'fit' (*habilem*) for himself and virtuous for the governing of others."[79] As such, Holcot, throughout the chapter, describes the requirements of a king (lecture 75), the various ways human judgment can be perverted (lecture 77), what it means to be a custodian of the law (lecture 84), and even the dangers that lie hidden in the office of the king (lecture 85). These themes are considered in the following chapter on Holcot's political philosophy. However, it is also worth pointing out that this is not always seen as the obvious interpretation. Clarke for instance is quick to see the appeal to rulers in chapter 6 as "an appeal to everyman"[80] and writes "the conclusion of all this is 'thus the desire of wisdom leads to kingly stature,' which is the goal intended for everyman in this life."[81] Holcot's focus is therefore more in line with the contemporary interpretation provided by Winston, who glosses verses 20 to 21 ("Thus the desire for wisdom leads to sovereignty. If, then, you take delight in your thrones and scepters, you rulers of the nations, honor wisdom so that you may reign forever") as "the obvious conclusion that if they [the actual and current political leaders] wish to retain their earthly sovereignty, they had better pursue wisdom."[82]

Because of the noticeable shift from the third to first person, modern commentators usually identify chapters 7 through 9 as a distinct unit.[83] Holcot too sees these chapters as a unit illustrating, by example, what was previously declared doctrinally. Commentators vary greatly about how to divide up this unit. As one reads through Holcot's commentary, it is clear that he further divides the section into two units; chapter 7 aims to identify those dispositions one must have if they are going to seek wisdom, and chapters 8 and 9 "narrate specifically how Solomon arrived at the marvelous wisdom he had come to possess."[84] Within this narration Holcot recognizes chapter 8 as a statement of Solomon's desire for wisdom, which he describes as a statement of "how Solomon possessed the desire and affection for acquiring wisdom."[85] Finally, in concord with other commentators, Holcot recognizes chapter 9 as an actual prayer, representing the very supplication or request for wisdom mentioned in 7:7 and recognized by Holcot in his use of the word *impetrare* at the beginning of chapter 6.[86] Evidence of this interpretation is seen when Holcot recaps chapters 7 and 8 and introduces chapter 9. He writes:

> After Solomon declared that wisdom, which is the true worship of God, is not able to be acquired, unless by seeking it from God with the insistence of the highest devotion: in this chapter he consequently explains the form and sequence of that supplication.[87]

As Holcot describes the sequence, it is clear that he sees the discrete sections of the book thus far as building on each other and progressively illustrating what came before. Chapters 7 through 9 offer an "experiential" illustration of what was taught doctrinally in 6 or even 1 through 6. Chapter 9 offers an illustration of the required disposition (chapter 7) and zeal (chapter 8) for wisdom put into action in the form of a prayer.

To get a sense of the doctrine Holcot sees chapters 7 through 9 illustrating and how Holcot uses these passages to create a moral interpretation, we look briefly at the breakdown of chapter 7 and the commentary offered. Here we can identify a few core themes that confirm his overall thesis: namely, that wisdom comes to the nations through a well-governed society that begins first and foremost with rulers who love justice and, as the recap in chapter 9 declares, "seek wisdom from God with the highest devotion." It is the nature of this seeking that, as we will see, is fully in line with Holcot's larger theological vision.[88]

Holcot divides chapter 7 into five parts (or rather attributes a fivefold division to the author of this book). The parts are divided around five dispositions that Solomon uses to tell his story about both the acquisition and use of wisdom. Once more, reminding us of the imperfection of the proposed division, Holcot says, "some of these dispositions preceded the acquisition of wisdom and some followed from its acquisition."[89] First, chapter 7 asserts the importance of humility as a requisite disposition for the acquisition of wisdom (7:1–6). Then the chapter describes a disposition of deprecation requesting wisdom (7:7). This is the verse, as noted earlier, that points forward to the actual prayer given in chapter 9. Third, it narrates the disposition of praise extolling wisdom (7:8–14). Fourth, the author treats the thanksgiving that comes when recognizing wisdom (7:15–21), and finally it ends with a disposition of commending wisdom (7:22–30).[90] Holcot sees each of these dispositions as illustrated in the particular case of Solomon's speech.

One point of interest in this chapter (especially with a view to the concern for the effects of an already acquired wisdom) is Holcot's exposition of the fourth disposition. Here Holcot calls attention to the distinct types of knowledge that flow from wisdom.[91] Verses 17–22 in particular are worth quoting in full because the various interpretations provided by commentators gesture toward their overall argument about the central message of the book and the nature of the wisdom under consideration.

> [17] For he has given me the true knowledge of the things that are: to know the disposition of the whole world, and the virtues of the elements. [18] The beginning, and ending, and midst of the times, the alterations of their courses, and the changes of seasons, [19] the revolutions of the year, and the dispositions of the stars, [20] the natures of living creatures, and

rage of wild beasts, the force of winds, and reasonings of men, the diversities of plants, and the virtues of roots. [21] And all such things as are hid and not foreseen, I have learned: for wisdom, which is the worker of all things, taught me.

These verses would seem to pose a particular challenge for Holcot and the dominant interpretation of wisdom that he has focused on since the opening lectures—namely, wisdom as a moral virtue rather than theoretical or metaphysical wisdom. Clarke, for instance, interprets verses 17–21 as follows:

> These verses contain a careful integration of Greek and Hebrew thought utilized to demonstrate the king's encyclopaedic knowledge obtained through associating with wisdom. It is no superficial synthesis but a valid demonstration of how the writer valued the Greek humanistic learning and culture in which he was educated and how he considered it to have contributed to the total revelation of God's uniqueness.[92]

Clarke's emphasis on "encyclopaedic" knowledge and the author's praise of Greek humanistic learning is at odds with Holcot's opening clarification that the wisdom of this book is not the *theoria* (theoretical knowledge) of Aristotle's philosophic wisdom but rather a moral and practical wisdom required for the pursuit of a life well lived.[93] However, while the passage in question details distinct types of knowledge that appear decidedly speculative and theoretical, Holcot provides an interpretation of each type of knowledge in such a way that it has a distinct connection to the moral life and political governance. Take, for example, the first type of knowledge: "the disposition of the whole world" (verse 17). While one could read this as indicating an acquired theoretical knowledge of the nature of the physical world—Clarke, for example, glosses it as a knowledge of "the construction of the physical word"[94]—Holcot ties it specifically to a knowledge of climate. More specifically, he interprets this verse as pointing to a specific knowledge of those places that are habitable and those that are inhabitable "according to their distance from the poles of the world and their nearness and remoteness from the path of the Sun."[95] Holcot provides a similar interpretation of the phrase *morum mutatio*, which the Douay-Rheims translates as simply the "alteration of their courses." He writes: "that is the diversity of customs and laws according to the situation, habituation (*assuefactionis*), and complexion (*complexionis*) of the time."[96] Again, Holcot shows the same interpretative bent when the text says that wisdom produces knowledge of the rage of wild beasts. This, Holcot says, means wisdom provides one with knowledge about the value of these animals for human utility and domestication (*ad utilitatem et domesticationem humanam*). Finally, where the text says wisdom provides knowledge of "the reasonings of men," Holcot interprets this as a knowledge of the different kinds of affections that men have.[97] Presumably, the wise political ruler is the one who is a student of human nature and understands the common tendencies and temptations that seduce human beings. Aware of these proclivities, the wise ruler can guide his subjects on the narrow path.

In sum, Holcot, in contrast to others who give perhaps more straightforward interpretations, is at pains to interpret this passage in such a way as to show that the main gifts of wisdom are politically useful types of knowledge, whether that means deciding where to found a city, what kinds of vegetation to plant or animals to domesticate, or how best to use the affections of human beings to unite them.

The Specific Effects of Wisdom (Chapters 10–19)

At the outset of his commentary, Holcot describes the second main section of this biblical book as a pivot to examine the "utility and operation" of wisdom.[98] However, as already noted, by the time he arrives at chapters 9 and 10, he has revised his understanding of the structure and now sees the decisive break beginning at chapter 10. The focus of this section, however, seems to remain fairly in line with the original designation. At the outset of 10, he identifies Solomon's intention to now begin considering the specific effects of wisdom. This consideration is itself broken into two parts. His consideration of 10:1–14, lectures 125 through 132, is a consideration of the special effects of wisdom visible in the Old Testament patriarchs Adam, Noah, Abraham, Lot, Jacob, and finally Joseph.

Beginning with verse 15 (lecture 133), Holcot notes that the focus of the book turns to the effects of wisdom not on specific rulers but on a people or society as a whole, namely the Israelites.[99] Here he seems to increasingly struggle with the organization of these final sections, continuing to note that the book does not always keep to the original organizational plan.

Nevertheless, he continues to try to divide the book into discrete units. For example, after completing his discussion of select patriarchs, the remainder of chapter 10 (10:15–22) is divided neatly into four sections, more or less retelling the story of the Israelites' flight from Egypt. First Holcot explains the role that wisdom plays in the liberation of the Israelites from the Egyptians (10:15–16), second in the enrichment of the Israelites from the Egyptians, third in the journey through the desert, and finally in the thanksgiving of good men.[100]

This fourth section in lecture 135 both offers a good example of the kind of moralizing exegesis he undertakes and, in the process of this interpretation, provides us with some coveted clues about his attitude toward the role of reason and philosophy in the overall pursuit of wisdom. In this section, Holcot discusses the acts of thanksgiving offered by the newly liberated Israelites. In the first part of this exposition he focuses on 10:19, which reads: "But their enemies she drowned in the sea, and from the depth of hell she brought them out. Therefore the just took the spoils of the wicked." Holcot by no means intends to offer a new interpretation of this famous verse. Instead, he points his reader directly to Augustine's famous interpretation of this passage in *On Christian Doctrine*, asserting that it is permissible to find truth in philosophy because, just as the Israelites were able to find many fine things amidst the detestable items that could be put to better use, so there are many fine truths to be found in philosophy. However, it is Holcot's memorable gloss on this passage that is worth quoting: "And therefore both in philosophy and in poetry the theologian ought to have studied for a season. Nor should the truth be despised, even if it is hidden in a box of vanity."[101] It is passages like this—and this will not be the last—that should repeatedly give us pause when we encounter the identification of Holcot as a skeptic. If "skeptic" is intended to mean a disdain for philosophy (or, for that matter, the wisdom latent in pagan poetry) and its utility or benefit for theology, then it clearly does not capture the "mind of Holcot."[102] Following Augustine, Holcot states explicitly that the theologian should engage in philosophy for a season. Clearly, he thinks philosophy by itself has problems, notably that it is veiled in vanity, just as the spoils of the Egyptians were mixed with idols and onerous things. Nevertheless, a theologian's education in philosophy and poetry is, in Holcot's eyes, worth the trouble.[103]

The remainder of Holcot's commentary, chapters 11 through 19, preserves the basic character described in our exposition so far. Here we can point to the main structural divisions and some of the key discussions that occur. According to Holcot, Solomon's continued desire to show Wisdom's marvelous governance of the people of Israel inspires him to demonstrate this by describing the antithesis, namely the fate of the reprobate.[104] This effort divides roughly into two parts. First, he attempts to describe the penalty inflicted on those who are not governed by wisdom. This is the concern of chapters 11 and 12.[105] Second, beginning in chapter 13, Solomon turns to the reason for their guilt, namely idolatry.[106] This second section beginning in chapter 13 is finally broken into two parts.[107] Chapters 13 through 15 focus on the origin of idolatry and its effects on a community. Chapter 16 to the end of the book is described as a concluding section about the appropriateness of God's punishment on those who engage in idolatry. He notes again that this final section (16:1–19:21) is fairly mixed, sometimes discussing the punishment inflicted on the Egyptians and sometimes the benefits conferred to the Jews.[108] Nevertheless, the goal remains one and the same: "to show that the idolaters were justly punished and that Jews were marvelously visited by God on account of their piety, since they faithfully worshipped the one true God."[109]

In this entire discussion, Holcot's exposition on the discussion of idolatry in chapters 13 through 15 is critical. Commentators have routinely identified these chapters as a tight unit.[110] Clarke describes them as "integral" to chapters 10 through 19,[111] and Winston explains that it is the intention of the author to show that "[idolatry] turned out to be the one great trap of human life, for idolatry is the source of every moral corruption." Beyond its importance for the structure and message of the book, the topic leads Holcot to a host of related social and political discussions. For example, when the text explains that one originating cause of the worship of idols was because a father, grieving the premature loss of a child, erected a monument in memory of his lost son that soon became an idol, Holcot takes the opportunity to explain why people grieve and when grief is appropriate and when it is not (lecture 164). When the text points to the desire for honor and glory as another cause of idolatry, Holcot constructs a social hierarchy and explains the different ways we should honor our neighbors, parents, and rulers (lecture 165). And when the text explains that, on account of idolatry, the people lived in ignorance of God and themselves, Holcot catalogues three kinds of political states that people, ignorant of genuine peace, mistake for a peaceful civil order (lecture 167). Here Holcot once more confirms his conviction that a wise political order—a political order that leads its individual citizens to wisdom—requires more than order and tranquility; it requires a just leadership of humble and faithful rulers.

The requirement for humble and faithful leaders to earnestly seek wisdom in the manner described in chapters 7 through 9 demands that we give final attention to the manner in which Holcot opens the discussion on idolatry in his commentary on 13:1. Here Holcot explains, in a manner consistent with his larger body of thought, what it means to be a faithful seeker and what this means for the utility of natural reason. This will help us see Holcot's biblical commentaries and his commentary on Wisdom as part of a unified worldview. Chapter 13:1 reads:

> But all men are vain, in whom there is not the knowledge (*scientia*) of God: and who by these good things that are seen, could not understand him that is, neither by attending to the works have acknowledged who was the workman.

The most striking characteristic of Holcot's interpretation of this verse is his gloss on the phrase "knowledge of God." The most obvious reading of this verse is that the Gentiles are without excuse because the natural world and natural reason are sufficient resources to arrive at a "knowledge of God." Such a reading stands in apparent concord with verses such as Psalm 18:2 ("The heavens show forth the glory of God, and the firmament declares the work of his hands") or Romans 1:20 ("For the invisible things of him, from the creation of the world, are clearly seen, being understood by the things that are made") and has been identified as the proper interpretation by other commentators.[112] However, as we will see—very much in keeping first with his interpretation of chapters 7 through 9 and the dispositions of humility and supplication required for the pursuit of wisdom, as well as with his larger corpus, stretching back to book 1 of his commentary on the *Sentences*—Holcot goes out of his way to offer a decisively different and counterintuitive interpretation.

He begins his interpretation by invoking Aristotle and Anselm to assert that human beings exist for a purpose, to both know and worship God.

Therefore, our lives truly would be "vain," as verse one says, without a knowledge or *scientia* of God. Holcot, however, immediately follows this recognition with the claim: "This science is faith, revealed to the ancient fathers through the prophets, and later preached to us through the Son."[113] In keeping with his proclivity for paradoxical statements, Holcot equates terms that are usually contrasted. In doing so, he changes the reading of the verse significantly. No longer is this about the failure of the Gentiles to attain a natural knowledge of God; instead it is about their lack of a very different kind of knowledge that comes through faith. Without faith, they are rightly called "vain" or "empty" because their life is unable to achieve its purpose. He colorfully writes: "Therefore the unfaithful build nothing good, as long as they persist in their infidelity."[114]

The impression that Holcot is taking an extremely skeptical and dismissive attitude toward natural reason and its ability to help us reach our natural end is only furthered in a subsequent section when it is asked: how could it be that philosophers could demonstrate that God is good and the creator of the world when even a Christian could not?[115] Holcot's response is to insist on a claim that he has made throughout his career: "that God exists" and that "God is the creator of the world" are not actually able to be demonstrated by reason.[116] This response has been understandably identified as further confirmation of Holcot's status as a skeptic.[117] But, once again, what do we mean by "skeptic"? If by skeptic we mean that Holcot believes that God's existence cannot be absolutely demonstrated, then there is no denying that the label fits Holcot. Holcot denies this possibility here in this passage just as he had done previously. However, usually the word "skeptic" connotes something more—namely an attitude of dismissal toward the overall utility of natural reason. We hope that it has become clear up to this point that Holcot's attitude toward natural reason is much more nuanced than this. A closer look at a few more passages in this same discussion surrounding the error of the idolaters will serve to reaffirm this nuanced understanding.

First, in summing up why the Gentile idolaters are reprimanded, Holcot writes: "They are reprimanded because they do not have faith in God as the foundation of their inquisition."[118] This passage simply serves as evidence that Holcot is not dismissive of natural reason or inquiry absolutely. Rather, the error he points to is the context of this inquisition. Does this inquiry begin from an attitude or disposition of piety and faith? While not identical, there is a good deal of similarity in the way Holcot interprets Solomon's speech in chapter 7, beginning with the dispositions of humility and supplication that were required to obtain wisdom.

Still, this passage continues to insist that faith must come first. One can certainly wonder how the Gentiles, removed and untouched by the historical revelation through the prophets or Christ, can really be blamed for their idolatry, as this passage from Wisdom clearly suggests. To answer this, we must look closer at what Holcot means by "infidelity" when he says "the unfaithful build nothing good, as long they persist in their infidelity." This question, the reader will recall, was asked before in book 1 of his *Sentences* commentary. The answer visible here in his Wisdom commentary, while less extensive, is remarkably similar and consistent with his earlier statement. Immediately after declaring that God's existence cannot be demonstrated by natural reason, Holcot writes:

> But whoever innocently disposes themselves to God, *exercises their natural reason through study*, and does not present an obstacle to divine grace, God sufficiently communicates the knowledge of himself to them, [knowledge] which is sufficient for salvation.[119]

This statement is remarkable for a couple of reasons. First it adds some clarity to what it might mean to let "faith" be the foundation of one's investigation. As was the case in book 1 of the *Sentences*, "faith," here described as an innocent disposition toward God, sounds similar to the depiction of faith as the "desire to believe correctly"[120] located primarily in the will rather than a cognitive state of perfectly correct doctrinal belief. Thus, on this elaborate interpretation, the Gentile idolaters were at fault not because they lacked an "explicit" belief in the revelation of the Mosaic law or the coming of Christ but because they lacked an innocent disposition. In short, they lacked a requisite purity of heart, the kind of disposition of humility and supplication seen at work in Solomon's own pursuit of wisdom.[121]

Second, this statement directly contradicts the suggestion that Holcot is a skeptic in the sense that he thinks the use of natural reason in study and inquiry should be set aside. Many years ago, Smalley wrote regarding what she perceived to be the skeptical themes in Holcot's work:

> If we remember the extraordinary diffusion of his Wisdom commentary, we realise how important this simple statement could be. How

many readers were introduced to the scepticism of the schools through Holcot's plain speaking on Wisdom?[122]

But is skepticism really the dominant message one would take away from the previous lines? Is it obvious that the genuine seeker of God would read these lines and decide that formal education and investigation of the natural world is a worthless and futile endeavor? On the contrary, it seems more probable that the reader would read in these lines an imperative to use his natural reason humbly and honestly. Nor does this come to us as a mere recommendation, but, as stated here, it is a prior condition of receiving grace. Consistent with Holcot's covenantal description of our relationship with God and the requirement that one must do their best before God will respond, the inquisitive use of natural reason actually appears to be a requisite part of this pact.[123] After all, how genuine can "one's desire to believe" be if it does not translate into the honest pursuit of God using every resource available? In sum, this imperative to use "natural reason" is consistent with Holcot's earlier encouragement to use the "spoils of the Egyptians," his continual use of pagan and classical sources throughout his corpus, and his positive estimation of genuine natural reason against sophistic "natural reason."

Conclusion

The intention of this chapter has been to give the reader an overview and basic guide to the mammoth text that is Holcot's commentary on the book of Wisdom. Central to this overview is a clear declaration of the form and style of Holcot's commentary on Wisdom, so that, within the arc traced here, a reader can be attentive to the different formal and structural elements present in the commentary. Here we outlined four key structural elements. The first and most obvious structural feature is the lecture format. Second, each lecture contains early on a small literal exposition focusing on explaining the divisions of the text and the various meanings of key words. Following this, structural features became less predictable, but at least two stand out. The first is a moral or tropological interpretation typically using a theme from the verses in question to make a moralizing point often only tangentially related to the text itself. Such discussions are frequently introduced with some version of the phrase *notandum est* or "it should be known." Finally, scattered through the text are inserted *dubitationes litterales*, which are formal academic questions occasioned by the discussion, including a *pro*, *contra*, and *responsio*. Given their scattered nature, these questions are hard to anticipate, but we have provided a list of these questions and where they can be found in Appendix C.

Second, our goal in outlining Holcot's prologue was to point out that the perceived subject matter of this book is neither philosophical nor theological wisdom but moral wisdom. It is equally important to understand both who Holcot thought the intended audience of the book of Wisdom was and who Holcot saw as the intended audience of his own commentary. Regarding the former, Holcot clearly believes the book of Wisdom was written by Solomon and intended for rulers and anyone in a position of social power. As we noted at the outset, Holcot sees his commentary as a tool intended for future sermon writers and preachers—those who occupy a teaching role in society and are in a position to instruct both rulers and subjects about how they should relate and behave in a wisely ordered society.

Third, this chapter intended to provide a sense of the structure and content of the commentary so that an interested reader could navigate this text. There is no denying that Holcot does see the book of Wisdom as organized around a discernible narrative and arc. Holcot works hard to identify this structure and communicate it to his reader. Central to this arc is the early discussion about the acquisition of wisdom (1:1–5:23), followed by an account of the general effects of wisdom (6:1–9:19). The second half of the book (10:1–19:21) focuses on the specific historical effects of wisdom, including both its benefits and the evils that follow from its absence. The focus of these chapters is on tracing the historical benefits that accrued to the people of Israel as they were governed by wisdom and contrasting this with the errors, deceptions, and evils that befell those historical groups—most notably the Egyptians—who were not governed by genuine wisdom. The survey provided here is in no way exhaustive of the themes present in Holcot's commentary. However, when the overall arc of the commentary is kept in mind, along with a solid understanding of its formal structures and divisions, the novice reader will be in a good position to track down discussions of interest and to understand their place in the context of the commentary as a whole.

Finally, throughout the entirety of this structure we have seen that Holcot remains focused on the book of Wisdom as directed primarily to the leaders of the world through whom wisdom will visit the masses. Furthermore, in the discussion of the ruler's acquisition of wisdom, his use of natural reason, and the required disposition before God, we have seen an interpretation reoccur that is consistent with our larger understanding of Holcot. Central to this understanding is the idea that faith first and foremost refers to the disposition of the genuine seeker. With this disposition as the foundation, Holcot does not advise rulers to abandon their use of natural reason but actually exhorts them to use every resource available in the pursuit of God. The caveat, however, is that pious rulers must remember that it is never their efforts that lead them directly to God. Rather it is through God's response to their best efforts that they receive the required wisdom and the knowledge to govern well.

9

HOLCOT'S POLITICAL PHILOSOPHY

Introduction

In light of the overview of Holcot's commentary on Wisdom in the previous chapter, there should be little doubt that this book is first and foremost a political treatise.[1] As such, Holcot's commentary provides us with an excellent opportunity to examine his political philosophy and theology. Because much of this material is found in the form of a biblical commentary, we have nothing like a systematic treatise; Holcot's ad hoc way of introducing various notes and *dubitationes* considerably heightens the unsystematic presentation of his political thought. Therefore, in this chapter we attempt to extract a picture of Holcot's vision of a properly ordered political life and society, always aware that we are choosing and arranging material from a scattered collection of ideas.

The Goal of Life

Holcot's view of political institutions can be examined only within the broader context of his understanding of the purpose or end of an individual life and the obstacles that typically prevent one from realizing that end. What, then, does he see as the supreme end of human life? A critical passage is found in lecture 47, where Holcot declares: "The consummation and completion of man is to be united to God through cognition and love."[2] And, conversely, "Every man divided from God is imperfect and incomplete. And therefore bad and undisciplined children are divided from God, therefore they are rightly called unfinished branches, and these branches will be broken."[3]

Holcot's primary exegetical responsibility at this juncture is to explain why the author of the book of Wisdom claims "unfinished branches will be broken," while, presumably, the finished branches—signifying the future blessed—remain whole (cf. John 15:6). His answer has to do with the affection of the soul at the moment of death. The wicked are marked by their desire to "live here always and to never see another life."[4] For both the wicked and the good, the moment of death is a moment of division, a division of body and soul. The wicked experience this division as something violent and painful because their affect remains attached to the material world. In contrast, the blessed are marked by their desire to be with Christ, and therefore they experience the division at death as something sweet.[5]

One possible description, therefore, of the proper aim of the individual earthly life is to become the kind of people for whom the division at death is voluntary and sweet. For Holcot, it is the goal of political leadership to produce such a person. But what does it take to meet death in such a way, and why is this so often a difficult and arduous process?

In the same lecture Holcot turns to an important analogy between the life of trees and the life of human beings culminating in the moment of death. Paraphrasing Mark 8:24, Holcot says that "Human beings are like trees . . . for they have the same likeness in living, growing, bearing fruit, and finally dying."[6] Here we can glimpse some of the formal features that he believes are necessary to meet death in the sweet and voluntary way just described.

First, he explains what it means to live like a tree. A tree lives through the provisions of the soil and the light of the sun; in the same way, a human being lives a moral life only through the nourishment of humility and charity.[7] "Humility," he says, "arises from the earth, that is from the intense consideration that we are of the earth and that we will return to earth in a brief time."[8] It is important to linger on the importance of the virtue of humility, for as we have already noted in the previous chapter and will see again,[9] it is one of the first characteristics Holcot associates with a good and effective political ruler. Here one can see why he thinks this is a politically valuable virtue. He describes those nourished by the deep roots of humility as those who refuse dignities and honors and are content with their simplicity.[10] Those who refuse to care about such honors, he believes, live a much longer and more stable life.[11] They live with a quieter conscience than those who throw themselves into positions of honor and the ambitions of the world.[12] Finally, such a person lives more perfectly within the life of grace and withstands more firmly the trials of human guilt (*culpae*);[13] like a tree with deep roots, such a person is more able to withstand the vicissitudes of life.

Continuing the analogy, Holcot remarks that the life of a human being is similar to the tree in the way it grows or matures. When a tree grows, Holcot says, the lower part remains rooted, while the better and more beautiful part rises up above the earth, reaching toward the sky. So it is in the case of the human life. While it is necessary to have some care for our earthly existence—for example, the need to secure food and shelter—nevertheless, the point of such an earthly concern is to support the straining of the higher part of our will toward the heavens.[14] Here we learn a political lesson. The earthly, productive life is instrumental. Like the roots and trunk of a tree, it is designed to support a higher and more important activity. A social or political life that supports our continued physical existence—but does so by jeopardizing the higher growth—would be inadequate no matter how well it took care of our earthly needs.[15]

Third, Holcot claims that human life is comparable to a tree because in maturity it is supposed to bear fruit. Quoting John Chrysostom (†407), Holcot states that as the tree first sprouts, then flowers, then bears fruit, the good works of a human life should result from the sprouts of good thoughts and the flowers of good volitions.[16] The point is that "right action" by itself is not enough to lead us to the "sweet" kind of death. The fruit of a full human life must involve a harmony between thought, intention, and action, and this is the kind of life that rulers and the broader society have a responsibility to promote (cf. Matthew 3:8; Luke 3:8).[17]

Finally, the human being is like a tree in death. When a tree dies, Holcot says, it falls in the direction that, during its life, it extended its many branches. Thus it is the same for human beings. When humans die, they fall toward what they spent their life pursuing: "he falls in the direction to which while living he sent many thoughts and affectations, whether he falls into heaven, earth, or the fire."[18] This, in sum, is the portrait of the good life: the life that fulfills its purpose and the life that society is instituted to produce. A life without the support of a strong political structure will produce branches that will experience death as a painful breaking because in life they reached toward the earth rather than heaven.

The State of Innocence and the State of Nature

A description of the aim, function, or purpose of human life is not in itself sufficient to explain the need for society. Political philosophy, before considering the origins of laws, political institutions, and the characteristics of good government, must begin by explaining why society is necessary in the first place. Whether society is understood as natural or artificial, its role and place in the pursuit of the good must be clarified before laws, institutions, and governments can be designed and evaluated.

The pursuit of such an explanation has time and again led thinkers to imagine the state of innocence or the state of nature. Was there a political order from the very beginning? Was such an order and hierarchy of power naturally ordained? If not, then what happened to require the imposition of a new order, and to what degree does this new order attempt to restore what was lost?

These are questions that we must approach indirectly, as Holcot does not address them directly. Yet he does have something to say about the state of innocence.[19] He also has plenty to say about the many corrupting tendencies of human nature that follow from the loss of that innocence and then require social correction. Finally, he discusses what is required in ordered for individuals to become virtuous, given the new postlapsarian order.[20] By examining these discussions, we can create a sketch of why Holcot thinks the sociopolitical order is necessary for individuals to bear good fruit and meet a "sweet death" and why the acquisition of virtue is only possible within a particular kind of social context.

Holcot asks directly whether God was protecting Adam in the state of innocence.[21] The arguments to the contrary stem from the rather understandable notion that if God was protecting Adam, then Adam would not have been tempted. He responds that God was protecting Adam by providing him with an original justice and grace, through which he had previously been able to protect himself if he had wished to do so.[22] This answer clues us into a couple of things. First, as we have seen already, the goal and perfection of human life is not simply right action but right action freely chosen. Holcot makes this point in response to the question: Why did God not simply make Adam in such a way that he could not sin? He writes that it is part of God's ordained order to create humanity is such a way that "it is part of the nature of man that he reach beatitude through the good use of his free will."[23] Second, it is precisely this unique kind of protection—that is, original justice that enabled Adam to choose the good—that was lost through the fall. The loss of an ability to perservere in the good is what requires a new political order.

Holcot provides more clues about how humanity has changed as a result of the fall in an early formal question (*dubitatio*) in which he asks if Adam and Eve would not have died if they had not sinned.[24] As usual, there are two sides to this question. On the one hand, there is the basic Aristotelian position that all composites are subject to change. On the other hand, one must confront the authority of St. Paul, who states that death is the result of sin (Romans 6). In response, Holcot makes two assertions. First, immortality is not natural. Second, because Adam and Eve existed in a special state of grace—enjoying external protection through the grace of providence and inner protection through the grace of original justice[25]—the corruptible body was perpetually sustained.[26] Thus he concludes that despite the fact that immortality is not, strictly speaking, natural, immortality was nevertheless the operative state in the prelapsarian world. The loss of this state of grace generated a radically new environment for human beings, one in which death must be faced as a real reality for the first time.

The impact of the fall and the new state of existence can be clearly seen in a passage where Holcot compares sin to death. The comparison is worth quoting in full:

> [sin] is similar to death in aspect, for however much man was lovable, beautiful, and fine, immediately after death he is horrible, ugly, and abominable, and is set apart and separated from the society of men. In the same way the soul before sin appears most beautiful and renowned ... [but] through sin it is truly stripped of grace and made vulnerable in natural things, and it becomes beastly and abominable before God ... And then

through sin the miserable soul is separated from the society of the faithful, the friendship of God, and the good angels.[27]

One clear feature of this comparison is the emphasis on the resulting social antagonism. A dominant feature of the world of sin is one of social hostility that separates human beings from one another and from God: the very communion that we have already seen as the goal of human life and human striving.

The resulting social dysfunction is fairly predictable when we look once more at what Holcot points to as the dominant cause tempting Adam and Eve to abandon the original justice provided by God. The decisive motivation is envy. The desire for social superiority is what motivates the initial loss of the state of grace, the onset of mortality, and the social separation and discord described earlier.

In light of the loss of the state of grace and the onset of all the vices that result from the sudden onset of mortality, we can now look at why Holcot thinks a new social or political apparatus is necessary. While under the protection of the gift of original justice, the pursuit of a "sweet death" is seamless and without complication. The loss of this protection introduces new challenges, engendered by mankind's new envious and socially divisive nature. Late in the commentary Holcot identifies those conditions that are now necessary to overcome these new challenges. Many of these conditions are clearly political in nature. First, Holcot states that becoming virtuous requires a good disposition (*consuetudo*).[28] But such a *consuetudo* is no longer immediately available as it was in the state of grace; it is something that has to be cultivated through instruction. Further, Holcot says, this instruction comes through good laws, which require good legislators.[29] Next, good laws require the utility of secure or safe cohabitation.[30] And finally, laws require some kind of authority ensuring a lasting obligation (*mansurae obligationis*).[31]

In short, Holcot's position is that after the loss of the original state of grace, which preserved and protected the natural self from corruption— and after the indulgence in envy, the onset of mortality, and the vices that follow in their wake—a political order (laws, legislators, security, and authority) is necessary. This order is necessary not just to create a manageable peace within the chaos of sin[32] but to create a society where people can be weaned off of their bad disposition and return to the good disposition that will lead them back to their natural end.

Laws

Given the central pedagogical and reforming role assigned to laws, it is no wonder that the topics of law and custom frequently reappear throughout Holcot's commentary. Here we focus on two such important discussions from lectures 46 and 199.

In lecture 46, Holcot states that the laws of every well-ordered city must meet three conditions. First, the laws must be in harmony with themselves (*leges concorditer ordinatae*). Second, the laws must be observed habitually. Third, the laws must be founded on natural reason.[33] It is the third of these criteria that firmly establishes Holcot within the natural law tradition. In the modern field of the philosophy of law, the debate continues over whether the prudential criteria typified in Holcot's first two mandates—internally coherent and regularly enforced—are really indicative of a moral and just society ruled by law or whether they can just as easily be found in unjust and tyrannical regimes. H. L. A. Hart, for instance, explains that if coercion were the primary indicator of law, it would be extremely hard to distinguish the obligation one has to society from an obligation to respond to a gunman's demands, where those demands, however unjust, are without contradiction and habitually enforced.[34] Thus there would be few resources to distinguish between the rule of law and the rule of men.

Holcot enters this debate decidedly in the natural law camp. The consistency of laws is not by itself a sufficient condition of the rule of law. The positive or human laws constructed by any society must be able to be traced back to a foundation in natural law or those laws universally and immediately recognized through the use of natural reason. His position here, once again, works against the common characterization of Holcot as a skeptic. A skeptic would likely eschew any definition of law founded on natural reason and, like modern-day legal positivists, would emphasize a definition of law built on the factual presence of command and coercion, whether by a human or divine ruler.

Moving on from lecture 46, Holcot turns to a more detailed discussion of law in lecture 199. Here he is explicating the verse "they unanimously ordered a law of justice" (Wisdom 18:9). This verse becomes the occasion for Holcot to identify four characteristics of the founders of a genuine republic (*res publica*). According to Holcot, the founders and legislators of any true society—a society ruled by law rather than caprice—must meet four conditions. They must (1) possess the subtlety of mature deliberation, (2) enjoy the utility of secure cohabitation, (3) have the authority of enduring obligation, and (4) possess an equality of measure and distribution.[35]

In his explanation of the first requirement of legislation, Holcot further grounds his understanding of law within the natural law tradition. He compares law to medicine. Law is to the soul what medicine is to the body.[36] Thus genuine laws cannot be identified solely by the presence of coercive enforcement. Further, they must also be precepts that direct or guide action in a certain direction and toward an assumed or implicit understanding of spiritual health. As any reader of the Plato's *Gorgias* knows, the ability to lead one to the good requires more than just power; it requires the knowledge of what the good is and the means to achieve it. Accordingly, Holcot believes that a legislator, in addition to executive power, must have a knowledge of the good and be skilled in deliberation.[37]

With this in place, Holcot turns to the criterion that good laws require the utility of secure cohabitation. Here the discussion is about what unites a city and binds it to its laws. However, there is also some ambiguity about what secure cohabitation (or concord) means and whether it should be seen as the end result of good laws or as a prerequisite of the proper function of laws. When he begins this section, claiming that secure cohabitation is required, it seems like the latter is more probable. However, he then refers to this as the final cause of laws, stating that the purpose of the law is to help individuals "live together in harmony (*concorditer habitare*)."[38] The answer to this ambiguity may be that concord is both a prerequisite and the goal. Because it is the goal of the political state to educate the youth into this state of harmony, this unity and harmonious devotion to the present laws must be found among the society's founders so that the laws can function in their pedagogic capacity.

Importantly, Holcot recognizes two distinct answers as to how this unity can be affected. First, he offers several definitions from Aristotle that emphasize the civic importance of friendship, including a quotation that reads "Friendship seems to hold states together, and lawgivers to care more for it than for justice."[39] In a similar vein, Holcot cites Augustine's quotation of Cicero in book 19 of the *City of God*, which identifies a true city as one where the people are "joined together by a common sense of right and a community of interest."⁴⁰ However, Holcot is also aware that Augustine identifies a second possible definition of a city, which understands a people as a "multitude of rational beings joined together by common agreement on the objects of their love" and not by a common conception of what is right or good.⁴¹

These two rival definitions have occupied a great amount of discussion in political philosophy. They lead to divergent visions of political life: a view of the city as a community that aims to achieve a particular conception of justice or a view of the city as a community content to let its members pursue divergent visions of the good but united by their common need for peace to pursue this good. True to the vision of the city and its purpose that we have already seen in Holcot's text, he further declares his preference for the Ciceronian definition of a society and rejects the more modest and politically realist definition of Augustine. Elsewhere, and in concord with this preference, Holcot distinguishes false notions of peace from true peace, which can only be found in the context of true justice.⁴² Nevertheless, even here, Holcot points out that on either definition it remains true that there can be no "people" unless they somehow live in concord.⁴³ This concord is a required utility. It is required for the city to meet the less demanding definition of a "people" and *a fortiori* it is required for the stronger sense wherein laws are intended to guide members to a common conception of the just and good.

Holcot's third requirement is that a society ruled by laws must have laws that enjoy a certain amount of permanence. This requirement leads him into an elaborate discussion about when and if laws should be changed, which becomes especially acute in cases where a society has discovered new and better laws or that they have inherited bad or unjust laws. Such discoveries have been a stubborn and perpetual problem for most natural law theorists who want to simultaneously emphasize the stability of law and also claim that all genuine laws—and our obligations to them—are grounded in justice. The discovery of an unjust law poses a particular problem because the moment a law is discovered to be unjust, it seems that it should no longer hold any obligatory force, even if it has not been officially repealed.

As we will see, Holcot's response to this problem has a modern analogue in a parallel discussion provided by modern natural law theorist John

Finnis, who struggles with the same problem. Holcot first offers four possible reasons why laws should be changed—reasons that are routinely cited by critics of natural law theory as evidence that, in a natural law system, laws would be in a continuous state of flux and the status of our obligation would be continually in doubt.

> It seems like [laws] should [be changed] for four reasons: (1) because it happens this way in other arts, like in medicine and in music, that things approved by the ancient doctors are changed; (2) because many things that come from such laws are truly barbaric and irrational, such as that citizens were able to sell their wives for a sword; (3) because ancient men were brutal and without feeling; and (4) because the laws of Scripture are [applied] universally, but the acts of men are particular and varied, and they are not able to be ruled through one law.[44]

The disconcerting consequence of this argument is that—given the inevitably of error and corruption in any system of laws—if the laws are not changed, then many people will seem either obligated to unjust laws or without obligation to the laws enforced by the state. The latter alternative is what John Austin finds so nonsensical about the natural law tradition. He writes:

> Now, to say that human laws which conflict with the divine law are not binding, that is to say, are not laws, is to talk nonsense. The most pernicious laws, and therefore those which are opposed to the will of God, have been and are continually enforced as laws by judicial tribunals.[45]

Whether just or not, right or wrong, a law is factually obligatory when it is coercively enforced. However, if the natural theorist wants to claim that we are never obligated to unjust laws, then a conflict arises because Holcot seems to openly acknowledge that, often, bad or unjust laws are included in the state's set of enforced precepts, and, despite this, these laws should not always be changed. Likewise, when they are not changed, citizens remain obliged.

Unraveling this apparent contradiction in obligation (the obligation to just laws and the obligation to the unjust laws of the state) simply requires some clarification on the nature of legal obligation and its consequences. Here John Finnis is quite helpful. Finnis identifies four distinct senses of obligation, the last two of which are most relevant for our discussion. For convenience sake, we can call these the moral obligation to positive laws and the moral obligation to law, understood as the institution of law itself.

That we have an actual *moral* obligation to positive human laws is distinctive of the natural law tradition. Unlike Austin, we are not obliged to positive laws simply because someone in authority demands it or because of our fear of reprisal or punishment. Rather we are obligated on account the rationality or "practical reasonableness" of the command. It is important that we all drive on one side of the road. Whether this is the left side or the right side is, at the moment of ruling, arbitrary and morally insignificant. But once this has been decided, it becomes a moral obligation because it is supremely rational to act in this coordinated way.[46] Accordingly, Finnis goes on to say that strictly speaking we do not have any direct moral obligation to obey those positive laws that, while commanded by legitimate authority, make no contribution to the common good but actively work against it.[47] That Holcot holds a position more or less in line with this is already evident in his insistence that genuine laws (morally obligatory laws) must be founded on reason, the product of mature deliberation, and created by a community united by a common sense of right or good.

With the moral obligation to positive laws clarified, Finnis turns to the second kind of obligation: the obligation to the institution of law. Finnis explains that deciding whether or not one has a moral obligation to a given positive law is not sufficient to decide whether or not one has a moral obligation to obey that particular law in question.[48] In other words, while I may not have a moral obligation to this particular positive law, practical reasonableness continues to obligate me to uphold the institution of law with all of its procedural demands—including the redress of injustice through a court of appeals rather than protest or disobedience—designed to ensure its stability and predictability: a feature that practical reasonableness recognizes as essential for the common good.[49]

In response to the question at hand, whether laws should be changed frequently—that is, whenever a flaw, error, or corruption, is noticed—Holcot provides a response similar to that offered by Finnis, albeit from the perspective of the legislator rather than the citizen. Holcot does not deny that there can be many bad or unjust laws in a city's legal code. Nor does he claim that they are obligatory simply because they have been commanded. Instead, he appeals to the same kind of collateral damage to the positive aspects of the institution of law and raises a concern about what would happen to the stability of laws in general if they were changed the moment they were suspected of missing the mark of justice. Holcot writes:

> To easily create new laws and to change old ones is harmful in many ways, because this is nothing other than to habituate men to destroying laws and to paying little attention to the obligation of the law, and therefore it is better to permit small and light errors, than to destroy the ancient laws. Because one who frequently changes the law does more harm than good, because he habituates the citizens to ignore the statutes and commands of the prince. Whence Aristotle holds that the one who easily changes the law weakens the virtue of the law.[50]

Finally, as if gesturing at the very same conclusion that Finnis reaches, Holcot notes that many positive laws do not have any obligatory force within themselves but nevertheless for the sake of the good of the institution of law remain morally obligatory. He writes: "But positive laws do not have obligation in many matters except from custom, observance, and tradition and therefore to weaken the custom is to weaken the law."[51]

Does this mean that Holcot thinks laws should never be changed? That a society or its legislator should never work to improve the moral purity of its laws or that an individual should never break a society's law? The answer is no. As Holcot says: "If there were truly ancient laws which manifestly contained the ruin of the city, they ought to be removed through mature council, but this would not happen without consent nor would it be common."[52]

In sum, when faced with the existence of an unjust law, legislators are always forced to perform a cost-benefit analysis about their obligation to change this law, just as the citizens—as Finnis explains—are required to perform a similar analysis about whether the resulting collateral damage to the institution is sufficient to morally bind them to obey an unjust law.

Justice and Equity

The centrality of the promotion of the common good is consistent with one of the only explicitly political discussions that appears in Holcot's *Sentences* commentary. In the *Sentences* commentary tradition of the fourteenth century and after, distinction 15 of book 4 became the customary place for an analysis of rights and justice issues.[53] One particular case study often considered is a special kind of prisoner's dilemma: whether it is licit for a person, justly condemned to death, to escape from prison if he can do so without injuring his neighbor.[54]

Traditional answers to this question—which trace their lineage back to Socrates in the *Crito*—are usually grounded in a right to self-preservation such that one is never obliged to submit to death. As Brian Tierney notes, such a dilemma creates a kind of rights discourse where the sovereign and criminal have competing rights.[55]

In the scholastic tradition preceding Robert Holcot, Henry of Ghent offered a substantial discussion of this unique dilemma in question 26 of his 9th Quodlibet.[56] In answering, Henry focuses explicitly on the rights of the condemned prisoner to self-preservation. By contrast, Holcot makes no such reference to individual rights. Instead, his response—consistent with his appraisal of law—is focused on the common good, and the situation is judged entirely in terms of its contribution to or detraction from the promotion of that common good.

Henry of Ghent's account begins with an objection recognizing the apparent conflict between rights that would occur if it were licit for the condemned prisoner to flee. The rest of Henry's argument for why the prisoner can licitly flee constitutes, as Tierney says, "an elaborate inquiry into the different kinds of rights that the judge and the criminal possessed in the body of the criminal."[57]

The reason Henry of Ghent's discussion is worth noting is not because of any noticeable influence on Holcot's account but rather because of the absence of any similar approach. Besides a brief mention of the fact that no one is obliged to kill themselves,[58] Holcot's strategy is different. As we will see, while still attempting to negotiate a middle way between the conflict between the prisoner and the sovereign, Holcot's focus is on the concept of the common good and its relationship to legal and natural justice. His focus, then, is not to establish who has the greater claim right but rather to consider the demands of natural justice and the status of legal justice relative to those demands.

Holcot's discussion of the case begins in the third principal argument of book 4, question 7. The principal argument asks whether humans can make satisfaction for their sins. The objection asserts that the sinner would have to atone for his sins according to the instituted laws. The objector thinks this is clearly false because it would demand that a justly condemned person ought to wish to be killed. The argument then takes a turn because Holcot acknowledges that some people fully embrace this consequence and believe that a person justly condemned to death should not flee prison even if there is the opportunity to do so without injury to anyone else. Holcot's response is no longer explicitly about whether condign satisfaction must be made for sin but whether someone could flee from his legal punishment without violating the instituted laws. On the surface, of course, it seems obvious that, in running from legal punishment, the instituted law is violated. Holcot's involved response clarifies the nature of the instituted laws and their relationship to justice.

This initial objection is not entirely dissimilar from the objection entertained by Henry: namely, that to flee would be to rob the sovereign of a rightfully obtained possession. Again, what is notable, however, is that, unlike Henry, Holcot's response is not couched in terms of rights and uses but in terms of the good, natural justice, and legal justice. He writes:

> A person is not obliged to death on account of the judgment given, any more than a person is obliged to something through a licit vow or licit oath. But it is possible for someone, after justly making an obligation through a licit vow or oath, to do something else for the sake of a greater good.[59]

The claim that a prisoner can in some cases licitly flee is supported by Holcot's belief that it is perfectly reasonable and licit for a person who made a vow to travel to the Holy Land to suddenly cease from his or her pilgrimage and join a religious order instead.[60] The key condition in the legitimacy of breaking an original vow does not lie in a consideration of the individual's subjective rights but in the fact that he intends to exchange a lesser good for a greater good. Holcot offers another example where the consideration of the greater good is the decisive criteria. He asks the reader to suppose that there is a man whose death would cause a schism in the Church or a war between two kingdoms. In such a case, if the man can escape without causing injury, then it is licit for him to flee due to the greater good that will be achieved through his escape.[61] The same logic underlying his view of the flexible and uncategorical nature of positive laws is at work in his account of the prisoner's licit escape.

This view clearly met some challenges from Holcot's colleague, William Chitterne, because Holcot returned to the position a second time in book 3.[62] In readdressing the issue he takes a slightly new approach, this time focusing on the character of laws.

This is a discussion that can be illuminated by a brief consideration of the way laws and rules are sometimes discussed in contemporary ethics. In *After Virtue*, Alasdair MacIntyre pays particular attention to the changing function of rules and laws in classical and modern ethical theories. Central to what he calls the classical Aristotelian account is the notion that rules and laws play a secondary, supportive role in moral thinking. Rules, he notes, function as an important pedagogical tool in shaping the habits and qualities of individuals. However, obedience to those rules is not the end goal. The rules exist for the sake of the excellences they promote.[63] MacIntyre contrasts this view to rival moral theories—those he explicitly identifies as representing a kind of decline—where the sense of *what it is all for* has been lost and rules no longer point toward a larger goal but instead become the primary focal point of moral thought. Virtues or excellences, then, instead of being the goal that rules aim to produce, become the singular habit or quality of being well-disposed toward rules, such that the person with virtue is the person who is good at following the rules.[64]

One wishes MacIntyre had access to Holcot's reinvigorated discussion in book 3, because he would have found there a shining example of the classical view of rules and laws that he celebrates. Holcot's argument for why it is licit for a prisoner, justly condemned, to flee when he can do so without injury to his neighbor focuses not on the nature of individual rights but on the nature of punishment and the purpose of laws.

"Punishments," he says, "ought to be medicinal, and imposed, not for their own sake, but on account of the good of the republic, which results from the goodness of each individual."[65] This view is confirmed by looking at the precepts of the legislator. "The law," he says, "never commands a person to die, unless on account of the good of the republic."[66] Thus it is quite possible that someone who has justly been condemned may feel a separate command of conscience to flee because "he wishes thereafter to become good and to abstain from vice."[67] When such a person has such a command of conscience, he can licitly and even meritoriously flee.

Two pertinent details should be stressed here. First, the flight from prison is not justified in terms of a "right to survival" or "right to dominion over self and body." Rather, as we saw in Holcot's original response, the legitimacy of this flight is based on the exchange of a lesser good for a greater good. Such an evaluation requires more than a moral framework of rules and rights—it requires a communal consensus about what the good of the republic is and in turn what the good for an individual human being is.

Second, Holcot's response relies heavily on the role of conscience. An easily anticipated objection is: who gets to decide what is a better good for the community? Any political realist of the Hobbesian stripe would see this as a recipe for chaos. Where each person is left to define the good, there can only be war. To avoid war, a single will must be appointed to decide what is rational and what is good. One can easily see the sentencing judge as fulfilling this role. By his sentence of execution, he has already declared that a death will be the best thing for the good republic. Holcot, therefore, must see conscience as something more than a private preference but a rational faculty that allows an individual to recognize a dimension of the good not accessible from the point of view of the state.

This division between the point of view of the sentencing judge and the individual conscience is further addressed by Holcot's clarification of two ways of considering the matter: from the perspective of "legal" justice and the perspective of "natural" justice. Holcot explains this difference and its application in the present case by introducing the Aristotelian notion of *epieikeia*. *Epieikeia*, roughly translated as "equity," was frequently employed in later political debates, particularly in arguments about how to end the Western schism. Scholars working in this area have generally seen this concept employed as a kind of bludgeon to be employed when legal methods to a desired route appear exhausted.[68] In short, in these debates *epieikeia* appears as a shorthand for the "ends justify the means." This, however, is not at all what Holcot means. In fact, in the discussion from book 4 he cites Romans 8:3 and explicitly denies that a bad thing should be done for the sake of something good.[69]

Holcot suggests that the difference between natural justice and legal justice (what we might, in this case, think about as the positive law) is that natural justice holds in every case without exception. Legal justice, while nevertheless "universally established," is not expedient in particular cases.

Epieikeia is then introduced as a kind of judicial prudence—Holcot at one point speaks of the person with *epieikeia* as the *epieikeins* suggesting that this is a quality possessed by individuals. The person with *epieikeia* is defined as the person who is able to direct or adjust the laws of legal justice according to the dictates of natural justice. Such a person, Holcot remarks, is able to rearrange things just as the original legislator would have if he had been aware of the particular circumstances of the situation.

Holcot further identifies the reason why this kind of adjustment is needed. The need for adjustment, and therefore *epieikeia*, is due neither to the law nor the legislator. Rather, it is due to the nature of the material about which the laws are made. Following Aristotle, Holcot says that it is simply the nature of human operation that often produces exceptions that mandate this kind of legal fine-tuning.

In the case of our conscience-plagued prisoner, this is a development that a legislator cannot predict, and yet it is a circumstance that natural justice demands we take into account. *Epieikeia* is precisely the virtue that should allow us to recognize a licit exception in this case and should allow for a lessening of punishment on the part of the escaped prisoner, precisely because, as Holcot reminds us one last time, "penalties are not done for their own sake, but as if a kind of medicine."

In sum, we reiterate (as Holcot does at the very end of his main response)[70] that the justification of this flight is not based on rights or self-ownership possessed by the prisoner. Rather it is only licit when the prisoner, through the direction of conscience, intends to exchange one good, the good of exacted legal justice, for a greater good for the community. Here it is the sense of an "objective right" rather a "subjective right" that is driving the exception. As such, Holcot cannot yet be seen as a bearer of the modern notion of possessed individual rights. Rather he continues to discuss licit and illicit behavior in terms of a dialectic between legal and natural, particular and general justice.

Authority

Key to the success of the legal order is its execution and therefore the wisdom of those who are in charge of executing the law. Accordingly, the requirements of kingship and leadership in general are dominant themes in Holcot's commentary on Wisdom. Lecture 75—part of his commentary on Wisdom 6, which Holcot understands to be addressed to the rulers of the world—offers one of the clearest declarations of what it takes to be a genuine king rather than a tyrant. Wisdom 6:2 reads: "Hear therefore, you kings, and understand: learn you that are judges of the ends of the earth." Holcot identifies in this passage four disciplines that are required for wise kingship:[71]

> Therefore the Holy Spirit explains in this text four things, namely the humility of learning (*hear therefore you kings*); the subtlety of attention (*understand*); a zeal for inquiry (*learn*); and the severity of execution (*judges of the ends of the earth*).[72]

Holcot's exposition is consistent with what we have already seen:[73] a humble disposition is an absolute must for a king to be a wise ruler. He explains: "Every king ought to worship God and know the law of God." This requirement leads him to an extended discussion of the symbols used in coronation that are designed to reinforce the disposition of humility.[74] By the time he arrives at the second discipline, Holcot wants his reader to know that these required disciplines extend beyond secular rulers and apply to clerics as well.[75] Both the second and third discipline appear to be focused on making a similar point: the wise ruler must be informed. "To understand is to read internally, that is, to ponder, to record, and to retain in memory."[76] Those who refuse are considered useless.[77] Likewise, the third discipline requires that rulers be zealous in the pursuit of knowledge. Invoking both biblical precedent and the historical example of Aristotle's tutelage of Alexander the Great,[78] Holcot advises the wise ruler to seek knowledge. Here again we see a consistency with the larger message of Holcot's commentary: namely, rather than discourage the use of natural reason, Holcot advises us to use it to the best of our abilities, once it is rooted in the proper disposition of faith and humility.

The emphasis on knowledge required for a person of political power to "rule themselves and others well"[79] is also consistent with Holcot's position on natural law. It even leads him to a provocative related question: which is better—a good king or a good law? His answer reveals that he is a realist about the inability to ever perfectly instantiate just laws. He writes:

"A good king is better, because it is impossible to invent a law which does not need application, interpretation, and management, which is able to be provided by a good king."[80] Here he demonstrates an understanding that the perfectly conceived natural laws will never be enough for a successful social order; equity and wise judgment are required to fully achieve the common good and for legal justice to approach natural justice. This kind of equity and judgment requires that kings and prelates not only be faithful and humble but also knowledgeable of the actual good and sufficiently skillful in executing it.

Finally, Holcot insists that rulers must have the discipline and severity to execute that which is just.[81] By this he means that the judges of the world need to exercise severity with the morally base. Here he particularly warns about the dangers of bribes, which he says "blind the eyes of judges and alter the words of justice."[82] This warning is representative of a dominant concern that reoccurs throughout the commentary. This is the negligence of rulers, especially ecclesiastical prelates, to discipline bad morals. While in this passage the reason for this negligence is identified as bribery, in later passages Holcot identifies other reasons as well. In one such passage, he discusses the temptation to settle for the false peace that comes as a result of ecclesiastical prelates turning a blind eye to bad behavior rather than confronting it.[83] Holcot's rejection of this false peace is consistent with his overall expectation of a good political order. The job of the social order is to do more than simply promote peace or lack of conflict. Rather, the social order is an apparatus designed to lead citizens back to God. Thus the peace that comes from neglecting vice can never be anything other than a false peace and an impediment to the peace enjoyed in the knowledge and worship of God.

Beyond his description of the requirements of good leadership, Holcot is also attentive to the practical questions of how to achieve it. In lecture 120, he asks: which is better—that the king should be chosen or that he should be selected through hereditary succession? In answering, Holcot reminds us of Aristotle's answer to this question. In book 3 of the *Politics*, Aristotle argues that appointment to the throne should not come from hereditary succession because it often happens that a good ruler has a bad son. In such cases, the rule ought to be given to one who is good.[84] With respect to this response, Holcot is initially incredulous.[85] His disbelief seems to come less from any disagreement with Aristotle's theoretical point of view and more from a politically realistic outlook. Here again Holcot shows himself to be attentive to the difficulties of actual governance and the challenges of implementing the natural law. He writes:

> [succession by choice] would be difficult and something beyond human nature, since he would hand over the kingdom to the one he loves most, and [since] a son is like another self, it would seem necessary that he would hand it over to his son. This question Aristotle does not solve.[86]

Despite all of Holcot's insistence on the need for moral probity in a good ruler, he continues to acknowledge the inevitable imperfection of actual rulers. This is evident as he further surveys and affirms the solutions of other expositors. The answer comes in the form of a distinction between the best way to transfer power *per se* and the best way *per accidens*. The best way *per se*—or in an ideal world—is through choice because it allows us to choose the best successor and to avoid the problem of having power pass to a bad heir. However, in practice this does not work out very well.[87] Holcot lists three reasons:

> First, because of the disagreement between those doing the choosing; second because of the custom of ruling in one house; and third because no one wishes, without good reason, to be subject to their equal. Therefore the changing of power through election is dangerous for the common peace.[88]

Once again, all of Holcot's practical exceptions are guided by the overall goal of promoting the common good or natural justice at which all legal justice aims. At the same time, Holcot also reminds us that this argument identifies hereditary succession as the best practice only *per accidens*, that is, given the flaws and weaknesses of human nature. He concludes that in an ideal world—where everyone is "rational and has zeal for the republic"—election would be the best means of choosing a new king.[89]

Family

The family has loomed large in many political philosophies, and Holcot's Wisdom commentary is no exception. Here our focus is on the family unit as a further example of Holcot's emphasis on the importance of stability and predictable social structures such that good laws can foster the kind of society in which people can "become good" and "live together in harmony (*concorditer*)."

At the start of lecture 44—as part of an extended explication of the book of Wisdom's praise of a "chaste generation"—Holcot outlines the basic requirements of the proper family unit. Recalling the words of Augustine, Holcot explains that three goods flow from matrimony: faith, offspring, and sacrament (*fides, proles, et sacramentum*).[90]

He begins his exposition by explaining that the notion of faith (*fides*) that he has in mind is not the theological virtue of faith but the virtue of fidelity, which is a part of justice. One of the reasons why a chaste marriage is so desirable is because it instills in its participants the capacity for loyalty or, as Holcot says: "a moral virtue ... through which a man effectively fulfills that which he promised."[91] Here we see at least one reason Holcot views marriage as a cornerstone of a healthy political life. It instills in its participants a virtue that is central to the city's survival and the success of the law's pedagogical aims: namely, a habit of commitment and promise keeping.

Offspring are the second good that flows from a chaste marriage. However, it is not sufficient to say simply that the good in question is offspring. Holcot is quite aware that both married and unmarried couples are equally capable of producing offspring. Accordingly, he says, "those who have many and badly educated children, have offspring, but they do not have the good of offspring."[92] What Holcot emphasizes here is that a chaste marriage is uniquely capable of morally educating offspring in a way that unchaste unions cannot. And, importantly, he notes that this is a unique education that can lead children to the worship of God. In this way he connects the institution of marriage and offspring back to the political function of training others for their true and proper end.[93]

Third and finally, Holcot describes the good of sacrament. Even here his focus stays predominantly on the political and social consequences of a chaste marriage. First and most explicitly, the "good of the sacrament" is the inseparability of the joined partners, a union symbolizing the inseparability of Christ to the Church. Once again, the importance of stability and fidelity are stressed. However, Holcot goes further; in expositing why the biblical author praises chastity, he notes that men and women do not live together merely for the sake of producing children but also for the sake of those things that contribute to the active life. The point stressed here is that the chaste couple is conceived of as an important economic unit in its own right. Each member occupies a special role in the division of household labor that ultimately contributes to the advance of the faith. His claim is that the joined couple can do more for the faith together than they can apart.[94] Thus he closes by stating that the good of a "chaste generation" is not merely the procreation of children within a stable household but also the protection and keeping of the faith.[95]

Holcot is so preoccupied with the goods that a properly arranged family produces that he goes to great lengths to provide instruction for how a man should select, direct, correct, and love his wife. However unegalitarian such instruction appears, the details suggest a rather countercultural view of how a husband should select his wife. Consider, for instance, Holcot's advice on how a wife should be chosen. Flying in the face of what must have been perceived as the common practice, Holcot declares that a spouse should not be chosen for money or for her parents but for good morals.[96] Describing at some length Aristotle's description of three kinds of friendships, Holcot— always concerned for the stability of the institution—argues that a marriage ought to be the greatest kind of friendship because only this kind of friendships lasts.[97] Such a friendship, he notes, cannot be based on corporeal beauty but only on virtue or integrity (*honestas*).[98] His subsequent advice on how a husband should direct his spouse is similar in tone: "a wife should be directed sweetly, not with tyrannical authority or rigor, with words, not with blows, with love, not with fear, with sweetness, not with bitterness."[99] Holcot advises correction be done privately so as to avoid public humiliation. Finally, he advises that a wife should be loved completely, in the manner first of God's love for the Church, second of a man's love for his own body, and third of a man's love for his own self.

The real political force of Holcot's praise of marital fidelity in the previous two lectures (44 and 45) can be seen in the opening of lecture 46. As he moves from the goods of marital fidelity to the defects of fornication, he reasserts the central political message:

> In this mode, it was earlier shown that generally persons generated from fornication are not well adjusted, nor personally good on account of the defects of [their] personal education. Therefore the Holy Spirit shows,

consequently, that these persons are not prepared for the civil society . . . Then [the Holy Spirit] shows that generation produced in a marriage (*generatio coniugalis*) is most well suited for continuing the permanence of the earthly kingdom . . . Here [in this lecture] he shows that an adulterous generation destroys the civility of the earthly kingdom.[100]

The context that introduces this claim brings the point home. Just before making the previous claim, Holcot notes that there are two different ways something can be called good, either through personal virtue or through living "civilly in the republic."[101] He then goes on to say:

> Whence it is not the same thing to be a good man and a good citizen. The reason is because a person is called "good" who lives in conformity to the law given commonly to all. But a good citizen is nothing other than one who lives usefully for the city of which he is a part.[102]

The point of this brief introductory passage is, whether one cares about being personally good or not, if one merely cares about the health of the city or republic of which one is a part, then one should care about marital fidelity and thus care about discouraging fornication. The health of the city is at stake, and, at a minimum, we need to ensure that citizens are behaving in a manner that is "useful" to the survival of the city. Marital fidelity and the generation of offspring within its confines are seen as two such useful activities. Procreation outside of this institution is seen as harmful. Holcot examines the nature of this particular harm in the first part of lecture 46.

His specific thesis is twofold. First, as long as a generation persists in fornication, such a generation will never be able to arrange just laws for the republic.[103] Second, "granted that rational laws were able to be arranged, such laws would not be able to last due to the wickedness [of the citizens]."[104]

It is no accident that his argument for these claims leads him directly to his discussion of the three requirements of law discussed previously. These requirements, again, are that laws must be (1) harmoniously ordered, (2) habitually observed (*per consuetudinem observatae*), and (3) founded through natural reason.[105] It is Holcot's position that weak and fractured families make it increasingly difficult for a society to meet these requirements.

With respect to the first condition of law he writes:

> That civil laws have never been able to be well ordered by such people, it is proved in the following way: no law is able to be established from

an agreement by the will of this type of people; but such people, some of whom are irreverent [towards the law] in themselves, and others are irreverent on account of their diverse heritage (that is, educated in separate and diverse households), will never agree on the law that should be established. Therefore such people [i.e., people generated from adulterous relationships] are not useful for constituting civil laws.[106]

Holcot further supports this claim by pointing to the fact that societies of "diverse blood" rarely get along sufficiently to establish compatible laws. He asks his reader to think of the Romans, French, English, and Britons as clear examples of groups who, untethered by any blood tie, are unable to form a useful society. As a counterexample Holcot turns once more to the family. He writes that a union formed from six or seven legitimate brothers will always be able to establish stronger laws and institutions than a union of just two people born from illegitimate blood.[107]

Second, on the subject of the required habituation to law and consistent application, Holcot doubts the ability of children raised in unstable households with untraceable lineages to achieve this kind of stability. He writes: "It is necessary that laws have been well thought out, rooted through long approval and custom. But this is not able to happen among people that arise from indifferent fornication, concubinage, and adultery."[108] The reason he gives is that the descendants of illegitimate unions "will not make high roots." In other words, they will not be able to trace back their lineage to a common ancestor. They will not be able to say, "my grandfather did this," "my great-grandfather did that," or "my ancestors acted in such and such a way."[109] This perceived lack of a common heritage is of great concern to Holcot. He believes it will damage the stability of a society and consequently its ability to apply the laws consistently and predictably.

Third, Holcot criticizes the practical reasoning ability of those who cannot be chaste within the confines of the institution of marriage. He writes: "In the third place it is necessary that laws are well thought out, established through sound reason. But the inconstant and carnal are never able to do this."[110] For Holcot, those who are able to restrict their sexual desire to the confines of marriage show the ability to control and restrain the body. This kind of control is seen as required for sound law-making, and it is something those who cannot remain chaste in marriage appear to lack.

Finally, Holcot stresses that even in a society that has been gifted a perfectly just set of laws, these laws will not be able to remain intact because the ability to preserve them is something that comes through the stability of parental education. He colorfully writes:

> no law will last while this goes on, even if it has originally been set up by the elders. The reason is that such sons do not receive the advice of fathers. For just as branches receiving weak nourishment from their roots are able to germinate and flower but not bear fruit, so neither are these sons [able to bear fruit]; even though they are able to begin to live virtuously, nevertheless they are not able to continue.[111]

In short, throughout his commentary on Wisdom, Holcot sees the stability of the monogamous family as a required institution for a society ruled by law rather than men. Because the law requires the harmonious cooperation of citizens, the blood tie of the family creates a natural inclination for this cooperation that is extremely difficult to invent. Moreover, the family unit provides a traceable lineage that encourages the respect for tradition and habituation for custom that a functioning legal system requires. Finally, the chaste family unit promotes the kind of virtue and self-mastery required for laws to be well-reasoned, impartial, and long-lasting.

Conclusion

We opened this chapter with a discussion of Holcot's understanding of the end of human life by following his comparison of human life to the growth of a tree. Fittingly, we find him reusing the analogy of branches in consideration of the growth and development of the young. This is not altogether surprising as it is an analogy with plenty of biblical precedent. Nevertheless, it is an image that provides us with a helpful way to organize and conceptualize Holcot's remarks about political life.

In Holcot's mind, the city and its founders are responsible for a great deal more than the continued existence of its members. Human life is intended to grow in a particular direction, and in a postlapsarian world natural momentum is no longer sufficient to ensure this directional growth. The emergence, in particular, of envy and mortality increasingly bind human beings to the temporal world, drawing the branches of humanity away from heaven and down to the earth. The political order, first and foremost the rule of law, is designed to reverse this downward fall. However, Holcot is also a sufficient realist to recognize that laws by themselves—even very good laws—are not enough to accomplish their aim. They must be buttressed by humble and wise kings and strong family units. Without these institutions the "branches grow weak" and we become unable to flower and bear fruit. Without such institutions, even the good laws that we do have will grow weak, become ineffective, and will ultimately be forgotten. Such oblivion, in Holcot's mind, is a catastrophe. Human flourishing requires the guidance of the law, and, without these laws, no matter how peaceful a society is, its members will fail to realize their true and ultimate purpose.

10

LATE MEDIEVAL PREACHING

Introduction

Perhaps the best guide to understanding the life and thought of Robert Holcot is the simple fact that he was a Dominican and belonged to an order dedicated to preaching. While it is common knowledge among students of medieval history that the Dominicans were and are a preaching order, it is less well known that at the time St. Dominic traveled to Rome to petition Pope Honorius III for approval of a new order, it was unprecedented to dedicate the religious life—much less an entire religious order—to the art of preaching. For example, Benedict of Nursia's *Rule*, which guided the Benedictine Order (*Ordo Sancti Benedicti*) since the sixth century and the Cistercian Order (*Ordo Cisterciensis*) since the twelfth, makes no mention of preaching. It is not simply that preaching is not emphasized in Benedict's *Rule*; it is that it is omitted completely. Thus when Dominic petitioned the pope to approve an order dedicated solely to preaching, it was without precedent. In response to the request, Pope Honorius III was forced to ask himself, "who is this man, who wants to found an Order consisting entirely of Bishops."[1]

Influenced by Bishop Diego, Dominic had caught the missionary's zeal. He traveled to Denmark with Diego around the turn of the thirteenth century and witnessed the Archbishop of Lund organizing mission trips to

Livonia (modern-day Latvia) and Estonia.[2] These mission trips had a lasting impression on both Diego and Dominic. After the death of Diego in 1207, Dominic attended the Fourth Lateran Council in 1215 and heard of "the need for auxiliary preachers and for the proper training of the clergy."[3] Following the council, Dominic petitioned the pope with his extraordinary request to found an order of preachers. The pope granted the request, and the Order of Preachers was founded in 1216.

The missionary mentality of Diego and Dominic had a strong influence on the centrality of preaching within the Dominican Order. Perhaps this is best exemplified in the work of Humbert of Romans, who served as the fifth Master General of the Order from 1254 until 1263.[4] Humbert published numerous tracts on preaching and argued that it should be the very heart and soul of the religious life.[5] In his treatise *On the Formation* he examines in detail the nature of preaching—but, perhaps more significantly, he makes an impassioned plea for the need of good preaching. In this, one could say, he is closest to the spirit of Dominic. Humbert writes:

> Without preaching the whole world would be in darkness, everything would be choked by the abundance of wickedness, a most dangerous famine would prevail universally, a plague of diseases would bring countless men to their death, cities would become desolate, the lack of the water of saving wisdom would lead to an unbearable drought, and no one on earth would be able to identify the ways that lead to salvation.[6]

For Humbert, preaching was central not just to the Order of Preachers but was necessary for the good of Christendom and the entirety of the natural world. This mentality is fostered throughout the early history of the Dominican Order and gave it a distinct focus.

While Robert Holcot resided at Blackfriars, Simon of Boraston—the Prior Provincial from 1327 to 1336—had a significant influence on the Oxford Dominicans. Simon resided in the Shrewsbury convent. He was licensed to hear confessions at Oxford in 1318 and completed his doctorate between 1318 and 1322.[7] Throughout his fruitful career Simon published several works on the Church, a substantial collection of sermons, and a preaching aid called the *Distinctiones*.[8] Blackfriars flourished under Simon and produced theologians and preachers such as Hugh of Lawton, William Crathorn, Robert Holcot, John Grafton, Roger Gosford, Nicholas of Lee, and others.[9] Holcot is perhaps the most influential preacher of the group; however, it is important to recall that his focus on preaching and preaching aids was grounded in the Dominican tradition and embodied in his Provincial Prior Simon Boraston. Because of this, it is fitting that the present volume concludes with a section dedicated to the preaching of Robert Holcot.

The Late Medieval Sermon

Late medieval preaching is a dense and complicated subject. This is the case because sermon collections remain remarkably diverse given their distinct provenance.[10] Here we introduce late medieval preaching through a discussion of four related topics: the occasion, audience, structure, and content of a medieval sermon. While this allows for a systematic presentation of the matter at hand, it should be noted that the precedent for this organization is Humbert of Roman's treatise *On the Formation of Preachers*.[11]

The Occasion of the Late Medieval Sermon

Fourteenth-century sermons were composed for a variety of occasions and audiences. First, it is helpful to analyze several occasions that generated distinct styles and content within a given sermon. The four broad areas to be considered here are (a) sermons preached for a given Sunday in ordinary time, (b) feast days, (c) saints' days, and (d) special occasions (e.g., a sermon preached during a bishop's visitation).[12] Each of these occasions generated a specific kind of sermon, and to understand medieval preaching is, at least in part, to understand these various occasions and their influence on the preached word.

The broadest and most general occasion for a medieval preacher was the average Sunday sermon. Such sermons were generally focused on a particular reading for the day, found in a medieval lectionary. The lectionary is in its broadest sense a list of liturgical texts to be read during a church service; when a reading refers explicitly to a text from Scripture, it is referred to as a *lectio divina*, a divine reading.[13] Thus for each Sunday of the liturgical year there would be a Gospel reading assigned for the day. In the absence of another specific context (e.g., a feast day or saints' day), the sermon would often provide a reflection on the Gospel reading for the day.

However, medieval lectionaries are far from uniform and differ widely by region and diocese.

One of the most common liturgical rites of the high Middle Ages was the Roman Rite followed by the Diocese of Rome. However, the Roman Rite was subject to variation within the numerous dioceses: for example, in England there was the Sarum Use associated with Salisbury Cathedral and the York Use associated with northern England. Further, there was the separate Durham Rite practiced in the Diocese of Durham.[14] Over time the Sarum Use gradually became the dominant use of the Roman rite within southern England. With respect to Robert Holcot, it is also important to note that the mendicant orders established their own lectionaries.[15] The Catholic Order rites (e.g., the rites of the Carmelites, Dominicans, Franciscans, Benedictines, etc.) introduces a complexity that is difficult to track. A given friar could preach numerous sermons throughout his lifetime, following the rite, or use, appropriate for a given context. Hence if Holcot was preaching to his fellow friars at a Dominican *studium* (house of study), he would have followed the Gospel reading established in the rite of the Dominicans, whereas if he were to preach to a lay audience at a local Oxford parish, he would have followed the Sarum Use of the Roman Rite.[16] This would potentially influence a given sermon because the readings from Holy Scripture could be distinct within the various rites.

Because there are distinct rites—and various uses within the rites—it is important to attend to how the readings of a given Sunday are divided within the missal. The mass consists of the Order (the *ordo missae*, or Ordinary) and the Proper, with the Order being the texts and readings that remain unchanged from service to service (e.g., the *Kyrie, Gloria*) and the Proper being the readings that changed from service to service (e.g., the epistle and Gospel readings).[17] The Proper is our focus here, as it is the Gospel reading for a given Sunday that is generally the focus of a preacher's sermon. The Proper can be understood as consisting of two distinct ways of tracking the calendar year, the *Temporale* and the *Sanctorale*. The *Temporale* is the "temporal cycle" that consists of the Christmas cycle, the Easter cycle, and ordinary time. It begins the Church year with Advent and proceeds through the five major Church festivals of Christmas, Epiphany, Easter, Ascension, and Pentecost: Advent, Christmas, and Epiphany occupy December and part of January; Lent, Easter, Ascension, and Pentecost occupy March, April, and May; leaving part of January, February, and June through November as ordinary time. While a complete description of the *Temporale* is not necessary here, it is important to observe that the daily readings changed from year to year given the changing date of Easter.[18] Finally, the *Sanctorale* is the complimentary accounting of the Church's calendar year by the marking of saints' days.

We can return here to the four types of sermons preached and locate them within the previous discussion. Beginning with the second category—sermons preached on a feast day—we can recall that these are *sermones de tempore* (i.e., sermons belonging to the "temporal cycle"). These are sermons that are preached on the readings from the Proper and correspond to the *Temporale*. To give a concrete example, the Gospel readings of the *Temporale* assigned to the season of Advent would include the traditional Christmas readings taken from the Gospels. Hence, on the fourth Sunday of Advent, the Gospel reading is taken from Luke and speaks of the birth of Jesus (1:39–45). Second, we can note that the third category—sermons preached in response to saints' days—are classified as *sermones de sanctis* (i.e., sermons belonging to the cycle of saints' days). These are sermons that also follow the Proper and correspond to the *Sanctorale*. Again, to give a specific example, within the Latin West the feast day of St. Stephen was celebrated on December 26 and included specific readings taken from the Acts of the Apostles and the Gospel of Matthew. The readings from Acts recall Stephen's qualities as a preacher (6:8–10) and his subsequent martyrdom (7:54–59), while the reading from Matthew (10:17–22) is taken from Jesus' speech upon sending out the 12 disciples and includes his warning that they will be persecuted "for my sake." As such, the readings from Acts are specific to the feast of St. Stephen, while the reading from Matthew could be recited for any saint who died as a martyr.

Two classifications of sermons can, therefore, be noted: *sermones de temporibus* and *sermones de sanctis*. In both cases, the Gospel reading of a given Sunday would have influenced the sermon simply because homilists often preached on the texts assigned for that day. We noted earlier that there were also sermons that were not preached on a feast day or saints' day—these include sermons preached during ordinary time (i.e., not a feast day) and those preached for a special occasion. First, sermons preached during ordinary time and not falling on a given saints' day would tend to follow the Gospel reading assigned for that day. Second, sermons preached on a special occasion—for example, upon the visit of a bishop—would follow the Gospel reading for the day but can be designated as a separate category because such sermons exhibit basic patterns that are unique to the context. In sum, medieval sermons were preached for various occasions, including Sunday sermons in ordinary time, feast day sermons, saints' day sermons, and sermons preached for special occasions. Attending to the liturgical order of the given rites allows a reader to identify the specific occasion of a particular sermon; that said, it is important to recall the council of Siegfried Wenzel, who observes that "individual preachers many times chose their *themata* from biblical texts other than those prescribed for a given occasion."[19] Medieval preachers, Wenzel reminds us, did not follow the lectionary slavishly.

The Audience

Having described the various occasions of a late medieval sermon, here we discuss the related question of audience. The problem, as one can anticipate, is that there is precious little evidence of who the audience of a late medieval sermon was (i.e., who attended the services and how often). That said, based on the evidence found in the sermons themselves, it is possible to make a few distinctions between those preached (a) to the people (*ad populum*), (b) to religious audiences (*ad clerum*), and (c) to academic audiences (*ad studentes*). As Wenzel notes, many medieval manuscripts contain rubrics indicating the audience of a particular sermon.[20]

Sermons preached *ad populum* can often be determined by examining their content. For example, sermons preached to a lay audience often include information about how to raise children or how to treat one's spouse. Such sermons are clearly not intended for a religious or academic audience given that both religious and academic audiences tended to be comprised of individuals who did not have spouses or children (either because they were members of a religious order or because they were students and did not yet have a family). Further, sermons preached to the people could include religious information—for example, persuasive arguments to make regular confession, or even instructions on how to confess—that was not necessarily specific to a lay audience but was in all probability intended for one. It has also been argued that it is possible to determine what specific sermons were preached *ad populum* based on their use of language. For example, it has often been argued that sermons preached in Latin were intended for an educated audience (e.g., a clerical or university audience) while sermons preached in the vernacular were intended for the uneducated laity.[21] However, such a simplistic distinction is complicated by two general points: first, many sermons recorded and preserved in Latin were preached in English by preachers adept at translating them on the fly, and, second, by the end of the fourteenth century the distinction breaks down, as sermons to the laity were often delivered in Latin. For an example of the first point, Leith Spencer observes that the Irish scholastic Richard FitzRalph writes in his "sermon diary" that he preached the majority of his sermons (preserved in Latin) in English.[22] For an example of the second point, Wenzel notes that the English bishop William Lyndwood (†1446) wrote that he would preach to the clergy and the laity in both Latin and English.[23] Thus while it is probable that a Latin sermon was intended for an educated audience, one cannot rule out that such sermons were also preached to the laity. This is important as one approaches Holcot's sermons, as they are all preserved in Latin with English words and phrases occasionally interspersed.[24]

The second group of sermons are those preached *ad clerum* (to the clergy) or *ad religiosos* (to members of the religious orders). These sermons often indicate, in the margin of the manuscript or otherwise, that they are addressed to clerics through the phrases *Reverendi* (reverends), *Reverendi mei* (my reverends), or *Reverendi domini* (reverend lords).[25] Examples of this are found in Holcot's Cambridge collection of sermons, where the scribe marked sermon 109 as a sermon *ad curatos* (to the curates) and 111 as a sermon *ad religiosos*.[26] Sermons for the clergy, as Wenzel has argued, often include information that is specific to the religious life or the life of a priest. Thus one can expect a sermon to clerics to include exhortations proclaiming the virtues of delivering a sermon or specific advice on how to craft or deliver a sermon. In particular, Wenzel notes that the address *Carissimi* (dear, or beloved) is employed for either a lay or clerical audience, while the more specific address of *Carissimi fratres* (dear brothers) designates members of a religious order or a monastic context.[27] As useful as this distinction is in some sermon collections, Holcot's sermons preserved in Peterhouse 210 are all addressed to *Carissimi*, despite the fact that sermon 111 is designated specifically as a *sermo ad religiosos*.[28] One also observes that some sermons present a profound critique of the clerics and admonish them to reform their life; this type of late medieval sermon is often found in sermons preached both to the laity and the clerics themselves.[29] There are numerous examples of such sermons; Katherine Walsh notes that in his sermons preached at Avignon, Richard FitzRalph preached several sermons that were directed to the Dominican Order. For example, on May 27, 1341, he preached to the general chapter of the Dominicans, exhorting the virtues of Saint Dominic.[30] Similarly, Robert Holcot begins sermon 42—treating the *thema* (Revelation 2:5), "Be mindful therefore from whence you have fallen: and do penance and do the first works"—with the bold claim that "those words can be applied to the preacher!"[31] Such sermons directed to clerics can most easily be discerned by their specific content and the fact that the manuscripts often indicate the intended audience.

The third and final group of sermons are those preached *ad studentes* (to students). Despite the name, however, such sermons were not preached just to students but often to the broader university audience. Further, within this context the term "sermon" is a bit of a misnomer, as fourteenth-century academic sermons often functioned less as homilies or sermons in a modern sense and more as inaugural lectures. Medieval students of theology were referred to as bachelors of the *Sentences* during the period in which they were required to lecture on Peter Lombard's four books of *Sentences* (at Oxford, this occurred before they lectured on the Bible).[32] In fourteenth-century Oxford this period would last for two years, and at the beginning of this process the student would preach a sermon prior to lecturing on each of the four books. In technical terms, the student would provide what is called a *principium* (a beginning) that consisted of a sermon, called a *collatio* (collation), and an inaugural disputation (called a *quaestio collativa*).[33] These formal academic sermons functioned more as lectures than sermons but are an interesting subgenre of sermons preached specifically within an academic context.[34] Other sermons—such as sermon 47 of Holcot's Cambridge collection—were clearly given in an academic setting and make numerous references to the university context and students.[35]

The majority of the extant sermons preached by Robert Holcot were preached either to the people or to the clergy. First, one can note that many of his sermons indicate that they were delivered to a clerical audience—in many cases, presumably, to his Dominican brothers. That said, there is also evidence that many of the sermons were preached, or intended, for a non-clerical audience. It is important, in conclusion, to recall that in some ways the division is artificial: all of Holcot's sermons, as preserved in Latin, are highly structured pieces of formal writing that are designed to serve as a model for other preachers. Thus regardless of the intended audience, it is almost certain that Holcot's sermon collection was preserved for a clerical audience in that they were intended to be used as examples in preaching. We can also note that one of Holcot's sermons *ad studentes* (to the students) has been preserved: his famous "final sermon" (*sermo finalis*) that was preached at Oxford University upon the completion of his commentary on the *Sentences*, as he passed the torch to the next Dominican lecturer.[36]

Holcot has an interesting remark in his commentary on Wisdom regarding the relationship between the preacher and the intended audience. He notes a distinction between the "teachers who feed the people with the word of God (*docentes qui pascunt populum verbo Dei*)" by means of five loaves of bread and those who feed them with seven loaves.[37] Those who preach according to the "five loaves" are simple preachers who are less educated in the schools (*minus eruditi in scholastica eruditione*). Such preachers preach the five loaves: that is, (a) the 12 articles of faith, (b) the Ten Commandments, (c) the seven deadly sins, (d) the pains of hell, and (e) the joys of paradise.[38] This is contrasted with those who preach the seven loaves, for "seven is the number of universality/the University (*septenarius est numerus universitatis*)."[39] Holcot is not precise about the nature of the seven loaves, although he observes that such subtle doctors preach in a way that extends beyond the five loaves because they have been instructed in what is concealed within the mystical book sealed with seven seals (Revelation 5:1). Presumably, therefore, not all preachers preach to the same audiences; those who are less educated preach primarily to the people, while those who are better educated, the subtle doctors, are more suited to preach to a clerical or university audience. Holcot, of course, fed his audience with seven loaves.

The Structure and Form

Students of medieval preaching have long recognized that there is a basic distinction between medieval sermons belonging to the early and high medieval period (c. 500–1200) and those belonging to the late medieval period (c. 1200–1550). Scholars have traditionally referred to these two types of sermons as the ancient form and the modern form; the latter, which is the focus of attention here, is variously referred to as either a school, university, or scholastic sermon.[40] The ancient from of the medieval sermon developed during the early Christian era and is rather straightforward in treating the liturgically determined reading (*lectio*) for the day and offering a narrative summary of the text followed by a moral interpretation.[41] The scholastic sermon, by contrast, is a highly structured work that tends to follow a determined pattern.

The distinction between the ancient form and the scholastic or modern form of the medieval sermon originated with the English Dominican Thomas Waleys' (†c. 1349) work *On the Method for Composing Sermons*.[42] This work is dated to the 1340s, when Holcot was composing his own preaching aids (i.e., the *Convertimini* and the *Moralitates*).[43] Mulchahey nicely describes Waley's understanding of the distinction between the two forms:

> The difference between the two techniques, as Waleys describes it, was this: the *modus antiques* consisted in a complete verse-by-verse commentary on the Gospel reading of the day, while a modern sermon was based on the careful elaboration of a single select *thema*, an individual line from Scripture, analogous to the *lemma* of biblical exegesis.[44]

Hence, while the structure of the ancient sermon was generally quite straightforward, the scholastic or modern sermon is much more structured and focused.[45] The structure can broadly be described as follows:[46]

1. *Thema*[47]
    The *thema* is the focus of a given homily and consists of a few words taken from Scripture (often the Gospel reading for the day). For example, in Holcot's sermon 50 the *thema* is *Dic ut lapides isti panes fiant* (command that these stones be made bread).[48] This *thema* is taken from Matthew 4:3 in which the devil says to Jesus, "If you are the Son of God, command that these stones be made bread."
2. Protheme (*prothema/antithema*)
    The protheme is a short introductory section in which the preacher introduces the central topic of the sermon.

3. Prayer
   The protheme is followed by a prayer invoking God to guide the preacher and to open the ears of his audience.
4. Restatement of the *thema*
   Following the prayer, the *thema* is repeated to remind the audience of the particular passage of Scripture that is the focus of the sermon.
5. Introduction of the *thema* (*introductio thematis*)
   In the *introductio thematis* the preacher repeats the *thema* and offers a brief literal commentary on the text. Further, the preacher would generally relate the given text to the saint's day or feast day in question, or to the broader Gospel reading for the day. This often functioned as a brief literal commentary on the text so as to place it within its broader textual and liturgical context.
6. Restatement of the *thema*
   The *thema* is again repeated, this time just prior to the division of the text.
7. Division of the *thema* (*divisio thematis*)
   The division of the *thema* was the heart of the scholastic sermon. Here the preacher divided up the *thema* both textually and thematically prior to preaching on the various sections. Fourteenth-century preaching handbooks noted two kinds of divisions: (a) division from within (*divisio ab intus*) that divides the *thema* by the words themselves (i.e., a textual division) and (b) division from without (*divisio ab extra*) that divides the *thema* conceptually by various ideas suggested in the text.[49]

The *divisio ab intus* and *divisio ab extra* are best described by considering a specific example. Returning to Holcot's sermon 50 we recall that the *thema* is *Dic ut lapides isti panes fiant* (command that these stones be made bread). In the division of the *thema* Holcot's focus is initially on three terms: *dic* (say), *lapides* (stones), and *panes* (bread). The command *dic*, "to say," Holcot notes, refers to the work of the virtuous who bring about a change; *lapides*, or stones, refer to sinners; *panes*, or bread, refer to the good, just, and virtuous (*iustos et bonos sive virtuosos*).[50] Therefore, we can observe that Holcot here follows a *divisio ab intus* that follows upon the precise terms used in the *thema*. Having established this textual division, Holcot maps this threefold division onto a more thematic one, according to which the three terms (*dic*, *lapides*, and *panes*) are related to three developments in the Christian life: (a) a conversion of miraculous work or operation (*dic* as *miraculosa operatio*), (b) the painful process of dealing with and assimilating sin (*lapides* as *dolorosa assimilatio*), and (c) the conversion of the sinner into a virtuous person (*panes* as *perfectuosa conversio*). Holcot expands this threefold division by means of a *divisio ab extra* that analyzes the three stages noted earlier through the lens of the seven deadly sins.[51]

8. Development of the announced parts
Having established the *divisio ab intus* and the *divisio ab extra* of the *thema*, the preacher proceeds to develop the sermon around these divisions. In Holcot's sermon 50 he preaches a lengthy sermon following the threefold division by means of the *divisio ab intus* and the broader thematic discussion of the seven deadly sins. This is the heart of the sermon and occupies the majority of the text. This is often referred to as the expansion (*dilatatio*) of the text: the skeleton of the sermon articulated through the division of the *thema* is fleshed out.[52]

9. Closing formula
In the closing formula the preacher returns again to the *thema* and repeats the central message of the sermon. The sermon usually closes with a prayer.

The scholastic sermon of the fourteenth century followed a carefully defined structure.[53] That said, late medieval preachers often deviated from the structure described here. Preachers exercised considerable freedom in developing a sermon and often chose to deviate from the form described.

Having discussed briefly the occasion, audience, and structure of a medieval sermon, it is important to conclude with a cautionary note made by Wenzel. He writes:

> All [medieval sermons] must be considered to be the result of a literary effort and activity that reflects the form of their actual delivery at best dimly. In the absence of unedited verbatim transcripts of the preacher's words, we can only guess at what was actually said in the pulpit and heard by the congregation.[54]

The point is well taken. The sermons of late medieval preachers that have been preserved were probably not intended as an actual *record* of what was said. Instead, these sermon collections functioned as examples of sermons that could be informative for other preachers. Each sermon, in that sense, is a particular literary construct that resembles, perhaps quite loosely, the actual sermons that were preached.

The Content

The canons of Lateran IV demanded a renewed focus on the art of preaching and the proper education of preachers.[55] These educational reforms had an impact on preaching, as it was now required that every preacher have a basic knowledge of the faith. The literature that grew up around these educational developments is referred to as *pastoralia*.[56]

Within the English context the most influential *pastoralis* of the early thirteenth century was Robert Grosseteste's (†1253) *Constitutions*. As Bishop of Lincoln, Grosseteste was responsible not only for the local diocese but for the education of the Franciscans. His *Constitutions* (c. 1239) states that every preacher should have a basic knowledge of (a) the Decalogue and the broader Mosaic law; (b) the seven deadly sins; (c) the seven sacraments of the Church, including the baptismal formula (in Latin and the common tongue); and (d) and the faith broadly understood as put forth in the creeds (the Athanasian Creed is noted specifically).[57] These educational requirements had a significant influence on the content of medieval sermons. Thus there are numerous sermons focusing on the Ten Commandments, the seven deadly sins, or the seven sacraments. While these theological topics do not exhaust the themes discussed in medieval sermons, the educational reforms had a clear impact on sermon content. Evidence of this, the reader will recall, is found in Holcot's commentary on Wisdom where he notes the five loaves of preaching, including three of the four noted earlier (the 12 articles [i.e., the creed], the Ten Commandments, and the seven deadly sins).

The *Constitutions* of Robert Grosseteste was reinforced by the subsequent *Constitutions* of John Peckham (†1292), Archbishop of Canterbury, issued in 1281 at the Council of Lambeth (known also as *The Ignorance of Priests*). The ignorance of priests, Peckham argues, "casts the people into the pit of error," and the only remedy is the proper education of the clergy.[58] Peckham prescribes a sevenfold educational platform that includes the proper instruction in (a) the 14 articles of the faith found in the *Apostles' Creed*, (b) the Decalogue, (c) Jesus' twofold summary of the law (i.e.,

Matthew 22:35–40: love of God and love of neighbor), (d) the seven works of mercy taken from the life of Christ, (e) the seven deadly sins, (f) the seven virtues, and (g) the seven sacraments. Besides expanding the general educational platform of Grosseteste, the Lambeth *Constitutions* is also significant, as Wenzel argues, for mandating that the basic tenets of Christian belief (called the *pastoralia*) are taught four times a year in the vernacular tongue and without excessive subtlety.[59]

These educational reforms generated numerous handbooks—the most popular being William of Pagula's *Oculus sacerdotis* (*The Eye of the Priest*)[60]—and had a significant influence on late medieval preaching. Robert Holcot's sermons and preaching manuals are an excellent example of the pervasive influence of the preaching reforms.

The *Artes Praedicandi*: Preaching Manuals

One response to the educational reforms described here (and in the 10th and 33rd canons of the Fourth Lateran Council) was the production of preaching manuals for the instruction in the arts of preaching (*Artes praedicandi*).[61] Preaching aids originated in the twelfth century and became incredibly popular beginning in the middle of the thirteenth.

The preaching aids that developed in the thirteenth and fourteenth centuries were incredibly diverse and included sermon collections,[62] *florilegia* (collections of sayings by the Fathers arranged topically),[63] *postillae* (running glosses on a text), preaching manuals, *distinctiones* (alphabetized lists of scriptural terms given specific definitions), and *exempla* (examples of vices, virtues, etc.). Robert Holcot's *Moralitates* is an outstanding example of an *exempla* collection and is considered in the following chapter. Here we focus on the art of preaching.

There are numerous extant preaching manuals from the thirteenth and fourteenth centuries that are instructive in establishing the context of Holcot's work.[64] Here we focus on two examples taken from the Dominican tradition: Humbert of Romans' *On the Formation of Preachers* and Thomas Waley's *On the Method of Composing Sermons*.[65] Following this discussion we turn to a recently discovered sermon on the art of preaching that is arguably by Holcot.[66]

Humbert of Romans wrote *On the Formation of Preachers* for his Dominican brothers sometime between 1266 and 1277.[67] The work consists of seven parts.[68] The first part discusses at length the need for quality preaching, and Humbert makes an impassioned three pronged plea to his audience: (a) preaching is apostolic in that Christ's apostles preached (Mark 3:14), (b) preaching is angelic in that the angels in heaven preached (Revelation 5:2), and (c) preaching is divine in that Jesus preached (Mark 1:38). Therefore, Humbert concludes, any job which is "apostolic, angelic and divine must indeed be outstanding!" More important, Humbert argues throughout the first part that preaching is necessary both for the good of the Church and the entire cosmos. The second and third parts turn to the preacher, looking in detail at the qualities that a preacher needs (i.e., knowledge, quality of speech, moral merit, etc.) and the right and wrong ways of becoming a preacher. Having treated the need for preaching and the nature of the preacher, the fourth section begins a discussion of the performance of preaching. Here, among other things, Humbert is concerned with what makes a quality performance, particularly with respect to the mental state and moral focus of the preacher. Related to this discussion, the fifth section examines those things that impede the preacher. Humbert pays particular attention to the situations in a preacher's life that keep him from doing his job. The final two parts treat the results of preaching (e.g., whether there are good or bad results of preaching in the form of lives changed negatively or positively) and the other things that go with preaching (i.e., various aspects of the preacher's life, such as travel). Throughout the seven parts of the treatise, the focus is on the preacher and not the organization or content of sermons. As Mulchahey and others have noted, this is not a work focused on the structure or content of scholastic sermons.[69] What Humbert presents is a manual for preachers that encourages and instructs them in their vocation. That is, he continually encouraged his fellow Dominicans not only in *how* they should preach but in *that* they should preach.

On the Formation of Preachers is instructive for understanding the mentality that informed the Order of Preachers in the thirteenth century. The Dominicans, following the canons of Lateran IV, took seriously the command to preach the Gospel to the people. While Humbert's work is not particularly useful in establishing the structure or content of a medieval sermon, it is perhaps the best work for understanding the particular "missionary zeal" that informed the mission and mentality of the Order. Preaching, as understood by Humbert, speeds the second coming of Christ, fills the earth with knowledge, and teaches men and women the way of life.[70]

By contrast, Thomas Waleys' *On the Method of Composing Sermons* is a work that focuses on the actual method of composing a scholastic sermon. He writes in the epistolary prologue that the work is written for clergy who are "sitting at the table of Scripture continually" (*ad mensam residens Scripturam continue*) and are preparing spiritual food for the people.[71] Thus the work was probably written for non-Dominican preachers with the intention of communicating a knowledge of preaching to a broader audience.

On the Method of Composing Sermons is divided into nine chapters, the first of which is an introductory section in praise of preaching that elucidates the qualities of the preacher.[72] In this short introductory section, Waleys provides practical advice to young preachers. One charming piece of advice is that new preachers should practice their craft in a quiet and undisturbed setting; perhaps even preaching to trees and rocks in private, until one gains confidence.[73] However, this type of practical advice is not the central focus of the work. In the remaining eight chapters Waleys analyzes the modern or scholastic sermon in contrast to the ancient sermon (*modus antiquus*).[74] The modern sermon is described in detail by Waleys, and he divides his work into a discussion of the identification or assumption of the *thema*, the division of the *thema*, and the amplification of the *thema*. Throughout the nine chapters, Waleys articulates the structure of the scholastic sermon described earlier in exquisite detail.

The preaching manuals of Humbert of Romans and Thomas Waleys contain two distinct features: (a) instruction and motivation in the art of preaching (in Humbert), and (b) technical information on how to construct a scholastic sermon (Waleys). Intriguingly, these two aspects of the manual tradition are preserved in a sermon on the art of preaching that Siegfried Wenzel suggests is by Robert Holcot.[75] This is a scholastic sermon of English provenance on the art of preaching. The *thema* of the sermon is Matthew 22:16, "*dic nobis quid tibi videtur* (tell us, what do you think)." Holcot divides the *thema* by means of the four Aristotelian causes. Thus the art of preaching is said to be praiseworthy by means of an efficient, formal, material, and final cause. Schematically, therefore, the four causes of the art of preaching can be related to the *thema* and organized as such:

Dic	The efficient cause	The able teacher
Tibi videtur	The formal cause	The splendor that illuminates the mind
Quid	The material cause	The concrete matter of the sermon
Nobis	The final cause	The profit for its audience[76]

The sermon proceeds by examining each of the four causes of the art of preaching, with a particular focus on the material cause (i.e., the concrete matter of the sermon). In this section Holcot argues that the matter of the sermon must contain: (a) a solid base (i.e., a scriptural *thema*), (b) a lucid presentation, and (c) an appropriate confirmation. The solid base must be chosen from the Scriptures, complete in meaning, edifying, and non-offensive.[77] The lucid presentation requires an introduction, a "placing of the foot" (*pedis positio*) or explanation of the introduction, a division of the *thema*, and a subdivision that examines the subject of the sermon by means of the four senses of Scripture.[78] Finally, the appropriate confirmation of the sermon consists of the proper use of scriptural authorities, reason, examples of the saints, and quotations from the Doctors of the Church.[79] Thus Holcot provides an account of how to structure a sermon and how to develop the various parts by means of authorities. However, this examination of the four causes of the sermon is not the end of the matter. Similar to Humbert of Romans, Holcot encourages the preacher by means of rhetorical strategies that commend and praise the art of preaching.[80] Therefore, what we find in Holcot's sermon on the art of preaching is a complex blending of the rhetorical emphasis developed by Humbert of Romans and the technical and formal aspects developed by Thomas Waleys.[81]

Conclusion

The Dominican Order began as a preaching order largely because of the missionary vocation of St. Dominic and his Bishop Diego. Dominic, in particular, imagined a religious order that was focused on the apostolic life:

this, in his view, was a commitment to apostolic poverty and preaching. Inspired by Christ's last words to the Apostles (Mark 16:15) to "go into all the world and preach the Gospel to everyone," Dominic was influential in bringing about a renewal of preaching in the thirteenth century. Building on Lateran IV, this passion for preaching informed the newly founded mendicant orders.

Holcot was inculcated by a culture of preaching. He was, first and foremost, a preacher by training. This is evident in the fact that much of his work—after his university career was over—was dedicated to the art of preaching. This is an art that

> was not drunk in a single draught from one manual or two or three, or in a gulp at a medieval university, but was something inculcated in him every day of his life as he listened and watched, and read and re-read the sermons of the great ones and studied the theology which formed their substance.[82]

Like many Dominicans of his time, Holcot was completely dedicated to this particular calling of the Order. This is evident in sermon 106 on the *thema* from Philippians 3:18—"for many walk" (*multi enim ambulant*) who are enemies of the cross of Christ—where he notes that perhaps the apostle should have written *many run* (*currunt*) instead of *many walk*, for the enemies of Christ run after many false things. People, Holcot observes, run to the wrong things—such as taverns or dances—"but they hardly go to church."[83] Further, when they do make it to church, they often show up late, chatter too much, and gossip. If Holcot had had his way, the churches would be full, and those in the churches would show up on time, listen respectfully in silence, and focus their attention on the sermon.

11

THE *MORALITATES*

Introduction

In the previous chapter we touched upon various kinds of preaching manuals, and here we explore in greater depth the *Moralitates*. This is a work that is often referenced and mentioned in passing but has received limited scholarly analysis. Holcot's *Moralitates* is categorized as an *exemplum* (an example or pattern) and in his magisterial study of the genre, Jean-Thiébaut Welter offered the following definition:

> By the word *exemplum*, one understood, in a broad sense of the term, a report or a short story, a fable or a parable, a moralization or a description, that could be used in support of a doctrinal, religious, or moral point.[1]

The *Moralitates*, therefore, is a work that interprets a history, fable, or parable to serve a doctrinal, religious, or moral purpose.

The genre of medieval *exempla* includes a diversity of texts. Homiletic *exempla* can be found in sermon collections in which the author employs them as a model of preaching. These collections exist throughout the high and late Middle Ages, extending from Guibert of Nogent (†c. 1125) to Olivier Maillard (†1502).[2] Medieval authors also employ *exempla* in biblical commentaries, and Robert Holcot's commentary on Wisdom and Ecclesiasticus contain numerous *exempla* that function both as an interpretation of the text and as a collection or repository. Holcot's *Moralitates* (and the anonymous *Gesta Romanorum*) constitutes a third group that can be termed moralized *exempla*. These works present a passage or *exemplum* that is moralized or "interpreted allegorically point by point."[3]

Contextualizing the *Moralitates*

Holcot's *Moralitates* is a striking work in that it offends and insults modern sensibilities with respect to the historical relationship between ancient culture and Christian truth. Yet it is also a work that intrigues and entices. Holcot—the reader soon realizes—thinks that a Christian allegorical or moral reading of Marcus Tullius Cicero's (†43 BCE) *Academica*, Ovid's (†17/18 CE) *Metamorphoses* (*De Transformatis*, for Holcot), or even Aesop's (†564 BCE) *Fables* is a legitimate reading of the text.[4] And by allegorical we do not mean a generic reading in which a character or event in a piece of literature represents or symbolizes something else: for Holcot, as for the previous Christian tradition, the allegorical interpretation of texts involved "the things of the old law signifying the things of the new law."[5] This definition, taken from Thomas Aquinas' *Summa theologiae*, is used to define a Christian allegorical reading of the Old Testament (in Thomas' words, the old law), and this definition is easily extrapolated to include Christian allegorical readings of non-Christian texts (e.g., texts by classical authors).

The above description of Holcot's approach to non-Christian texts is confirmed by Judson Boyce Allen, who observes that Holcot and the "classicizing friars"

> read literature in precisely the same way that was traditional for scripture. That is, they applied to the fictions of the classical poets, which they retold and quoted in their religious writings with great frequency and obvious delight, the same allegorical method of interpretation that they used for scripture.[6]

In the *Moralitates*, Holcot embarks on an adventure of Christian—or, perhaps more properly, christological—exegesis of texts that predate the coming of Christ.

In fourteenth-century England, Holcot was not alone in his approach to classical texts. Thus one realizes that this "spiritual sense of fiction"[7] found in Holcot's text was common to authors such as John Bromyard, John Ridevall, Thomas Ringstead, Nicholas Trevet, and Thomas Waleys. However, this fourteenth-century approach to pre-Christian or pagan texts was not novel, as it built upon a patristic and early medieval tradition of incorporating pagan truth into Christianity.

Since the second century, Christian theologians and apologists argued that there was a unique relationship between Christian truth as revealed in the person of Jesus Christ and the antecedent (by definition, non-Christian) truth revealed in the texts of classical antiquity. In his *First Apology*, Justin Martyr (†165) writes that there is a deep harmony between some of the ideas of Plato—for example, the idea that "God, having altered matter which was shapeless, made the world"—and the Christian belief that God created the world as described in Genesis 1–3. Justin argues that in fact Plato borrowed this idea from Moses, who was the first prophet and who was of "greater antiquity than the Greek writers."[8] As Justin sees things, there is a profound agreement between the Christian truth revealed in Scripture and the teachings of Plato.

The approach of Justin Martyr was typical of the patristic era, and thinkers such as Origen of Alexandria (†254), Ambrose of Milan (†397), and Augustine of Hippo explored in great depth the relationship between Christian truth and classical antiquity. In his commentary on the Song of Songs Origen developed an allegory in which the Christian soul approached Christ, the Bridegroom, equipped with two wedding gifts: the Mosaic law and the Hebrew Prophets, on the one hand, and natural law and reason, on the other. This latter category contains the truths Christians gleaned from pagan wisdom.[9] In a letter to Gregory of Thaumaturgus, Origen famously called the Christian borrowing of classical learning the "despoiling of the Egyptians"—a phrase that would be retained throughout the patristic and medieval period.[10] A century and a half later, Augustine of Hippo wrote in the *Confessions* that among the Egyptians (i.e., the classical authors) he found a desire for idols and perishable things, and as such he "did not eat that food (i.e., the noneternal and thus perishable aspects of pagan thought)." However, Augustine states that instead of the "food" of the pagans, "I set my heart upon the gold which at your [i.e., God's] bidding your people had brought out of Egypt, because wherever it was, it belonged to you."[11] For Augustine, the gold that was brought out of Egypt included the eternal truths of natural law and reason studied and uncovered by pre-Christian cultures.

Justin, Origen, and Augustine all argued that Christians ought to adopt the truths of pagan teaching where it was not opposed to Scripture. This became a common assumption of medieval Christian exegetes and preachers. In his *Summa on the Art of Preaching*, Alan of Lille argues that the preacher should make use of both Christian and pagan examples to get his point across.[12] While this approach to pagan literature was not universally accepted, it was supported by Thomas Waleys in the *De modo componendi sermones* and Robert Holcot in his commentary on Wisdom.[13] In the Wisdom commentary Holcot approaches the subject by discussing Augustine's teaching on the matter in *On Christian Doctrine* and addressing the general idea of spoiling the Egyptians. He summarizes by stating that "the teachings of the gentiles, which, though they contain many superfluous things, nevertheless have many extremely useful things for seeking the truth."[14] Thus Holcot follows prior Christian tradition in accepting that pagan texts contain truths that are worth examining and retaining.[15]

Given this basic assumption, Holcot and the classicizing friars took the next logical step in arguing that texts of pagan authors should be interpreted according to the same methods that one employs in interpreting Scripture. Medieval Christians had long used the New Testament as a lens by which to interpret the Old Testament: for example, Christian exegetes interpreted the "Spirit" hovering over the waters in Genesis 1:2 as the Holy Spirit revealed in the New Testament and Abraham's "sacrifice" of his son Isaac in Genesis 22 as prefiguring the sacrifice of Jesus Christ, the lamb of God. In these instances, the revelation of Christ found in the Gospels was used to interpret the passages of Scripture that predated the coming of Christ. In his *Moralitates*, Holcot similarly employs the New Testament message of the good news of Jesus Christ to interpret the literature of Cicero, Seneca, and Aesop.

The Text of the *Moralitates*

Having considered the hermeneutical assumptions informing Christian moralizations of classical fables, we need to explore the textual origin of the *Moralitates*. The practice of moralizing ancient texts is found in the early Christian tradition but comes to fruition in the late-fifth- and early-sixth-century scholar Fulgentius the Mythographer.[16] Fulgentius wrote an influential work, divided into three books, called the *Mythologies*, in which he examined the moral implications of classical myths. Thus he presented Christian allegories of classical myths, such as the fable of Saturn (I.2), the fable of Ceres (I.11), and the fable of the Swan and Leda (II.13). The work of Fulgentius was influential in the medieval period, and John Ridevall, a contemporary of Holcot (†c. 1340), composed a similar work called the *Fulgentius metaforalis*.[17]

The most extensive analysis of the manuscripts of the *Moralitates* is by Welter in *L'exemplum dans la littérature religieuse et didactique du Moyen Âge*.[18] Welter provides a provisional list that includes 41 manuscripts and 10 incunabula or early modern editions of the *Moralitates*.[19] However, a complete list extends to almost 130 extant manuscripts.[20] Given the number and geographical disbursement of the manuscripts and the early printed editions, one can surmise that the *Moralitates* had a strong readership in the fifteenth and early sixteenth centuries.[21] Further, among the numerous *exemplum* collections he studied, Welter argues that Holcot's *Moralitates* marks the final development of the genre: in many ways, the *Moralitates* became the model of the *exemplum* literature.[22]

The *Convertimini* is a work that is similar to the *Moralitates* and should be discussed here with other spurious works misattributed to Holcot. Speaking about Holcot's relationship with the *exemplum* literature, Smalley wrote that "Holcot's shoulders were broad enough to carry any amount of *spuria*"[23]—meaning, of course, that numerous texts were misattributed to Holcot in the late fourteenth and early fifteenth centuries. The *Convertimini* was never published in an early printed edition, and there are at least 21 extant manuscripts. One of the manuscripts tentatively attributes the work to Holcot;[24] however, scholars remain divided on whether or not it can be attributed to him.[25] Similarly, the *Tractatus de septem vitiis*—a work on the seven deadly sins—is occasionally attributed to Holcot. Smalley notes that a London manuscript indicates that the work is by Holcot.[26] This manuscript is not the only instance, as it is found in an Austrian manuscript and was printed by Regnault Chaudière in Paris in 1517 (under the title *Heptalogus . . . de origine diffinitione et remediis peccatorum*).[27] Smalley somewhat convincingly argues that the text is modeled after William of Lavicea's (OFM) *Dieta salutis* and that, had Holcot written such a text, he would have probably chosen the Dominican William of Peraldus' *Summa de vitiis et virtutibus* as an exemplar given the authority of the Dominican's text and Holcot's familiarity with the work.[28] While both the *Convertimini* and the *Tractatus* are probably not authentic to Holcot, they clearly demonstrate a similar interest in providing examples and resources for preaching.[29]

Finally, when discussing the *Moralitates* one of the more problematic questions regarding the historical provenance is whether it predates or postdates the *Gesta Romanorum* (the *Deeds of the Romans*). The date and authorship of the *Gesta*—perhaps most famous as a source for William Shakespeare's *The Merchant of Venice*[30]—remains highly disputed. Smalley states that the *Gesta* probably originated from an English Franciscan milieu and that the earliest manuscript dates it to 1342. Welter argued that the *Gesta* borrowed from Holcot, and Smalley followed Welter's argument.[31] Further, as Smalley notes, this places the *terminus ante quem* of the *Moralitates* to just before 1342. Because the *Moralitates* were probably written after the commentary on the Twelve Prophets, this places the *terminus post quem* sometime after 1334. Like the *Moralitates* and the commentary on Wisdom, the *Gesta* was a popular work existing in at least 165 extant manuscripts.[32]

Concluding our discussion of the *Gesta*, it is interesting as a historiographical curiosity to peruse the edition and translation of the *Gesta* produced by Thomas Wright and published in London in 1824. The title and subtitle indicate Wright's basic approach: *Gesta Romanorum, or, Entertaining Stories Invented by the Monks as a Fire-Side Recreation; and Commonly Applied in their Discourses from the Pulpit* ... While the title perhaps summarizes Wright's basic approach—that is, that the work is an oddity worthy of being read by friars sitting around a campfire—he is more explicit in the preface to the 1871 edition. According to Wright, the *Gesta* is "one of the most curious of those collections of tales which are found in the popular literature of most peoples."[33] Thus he categorizes the work alongside the fables of the Greeks, Latins, Orientals, Celts, and Teutons. The *Gesta*, and Holcot's *Moralitates*, by extension, are to be read alongside the *1001 Arabian Nights* as a source of entertainment. The present reading of Holcot's *Moralitates* takes an alternative approach, considering in detail Holcot's presentation of Christ throughout the work.

Reading the *Moralitates*

This section considers the structure and content of *Moralitates* 11, 12, 35, and 8. The purpose here is not to give an exhaustive account of the themes discussed throughout this work but to provide a broader appreciation for Holcot's exegetical method. As we will show, throughout the *Moralitates* Holcot interprets classical and traditional myths through the lens of the Gospel. More specifically, these *Moralitates* demonstrate the christological center of Holcot's exegesis. We begin with three instances of moral exposition (*moralis expositio*) in *Moralitates* 11, 12, and 35 and conclude with an instance of tropological exposition (*tropologica expositio*) in *Moralitas* 8.

Moralitas 11: The Fight Between Christ and the Devil

Moralitas 11 of the 1586 edition is titled "the history of the battle between Christ and the devil."[34] In this *Moralitas* Holcot examines a story that he found in the history of the Romans about Romulus attempting to retain control over the city of Rome against an aggressor. In this account both Romulus and his aggressors send three soldiers into battle to fight for the rights of the city. Thus, instead of whole armies fighting in pitched battle, the three individuals represent their respective armies, and the fate of both sides is contingent on the three individuals who are sent into the duel.

In his moralization of this story, Holcot relates an elaborate account of the fight between God and the devil. In the story, Romulus represents God (*per Romulum ... intelligo Deum*), Rome represents the human soul (*per Romam ... intelligo animam humanam*), and the wall of Rome represents the human body (*muro fortissimo: id est, corpore humano*). God, naturally, desires to retain dominion over his city (i.e., the human soul), while the devil seeks to penetrate the walls of the city and to take control of it. In his attempt to retain control of the human soul (i.e., the city), God establishes three defensive soldiers: the law of nature (*lex naturae*), the Mosaic law (*lex Mosaica*), and the law of the Gospel (*lex evangelica*). As observed in chapter 1, Holcot relies on a division of world history into (a) a time before the Mosaic law, (b) a time under the Mosaic law, and (c) a time under grace. In Holcot's account of the siege of the human soul, the devil is on the offensive and attacks the human person with three warriors of his own: lust (*luxuria*), pride (*superbia*), and greed (*avaritia*).[35] In the first battle, the law of nature confronts lust and is killed; in the second battle, the law of Moses confronts pride and is also killed. Finally, in the third battle, the law of the Gospel confronts greed and not only conquers and kills this third solider but also kills the first two soldiers of the devil. Thus Holcot moralizes the siege of Rome as an elaborate fight between the soldiers of God and the soldiers of the devil for the right to govern the human soul. Having outlined the basic structure, it is instructive to reflect on how Holcot describes these battles.

The first battle is between the law of nature and lust. According to Holcot, this conflict takes place in what is described as the prehistory of the Old Testament (Genesis 1–11) prior to God's covenant with Abraham and the Jewish people. During this time period, human nature was not protected by the law of Moses or the law of the Gospels (i.e., the second and third soldiers) but only the law of nature. As a result of the weakness of the law of nature, humanity succumbed to lust; Holcot writes that "on account of lust God destroyed the entire human race by means of the flood, except for eight souls (i.e., Moses and his family)."[36] The second battle takes place between the law of Moses and pride. According to Holcot's account of human history, the law of Moses (i.e., the second solider) was supposed to protect the human soul during the period from Abraham up until the time of Christ. However, this second law was not sufficient: the "law of Moses, which was the second soldier of God, was killed by means of the pride of the Jews."[37] As a result, Holcot argues, "God destroyed that law." The third soldier, the law of the Gospel, pretended to flee from the battle and, as it were, to succumb to death with Christ. However, this solider did not die, and once the solider (i.e., the law of the Gospel) was given to humanity, this soldier entered into conflict with the devil's soldiers and vanquished them all.[38] Thus the law of the Gospel succeeded in conquering lust through continence, pride through humility, and greed through the giving of alms and generosity.[39] For any human soul governed by the three soldiers of God, therefore, Christ will have complete dominion over his soul just as Romulus did over the city of Rome.[40]

At first glance, when one encounters Holcot's moralization of the battle between the three soldiers of Romulus and the three soldiers of the aggressor, one is perhaps inclined to view such an outlandish interpretation of the text with skepticism. The original passage as recorded in Holcot makes no mention of the human soul, Christ, or the devil. In fact, the passage clearly depicts an event that was alleged to take place in pre-Christian history and one is left to question how Holcot's Christian moralization of this passage is justified in any sense. What are the hermeneutical parameters (if any) that govern such an interpretation?

To better understand Holcot's analysis of this text, it is important to recall just how common this historical and theological vision was to his late medieval audience (both clerical and secular). Holcot's intended audience here was probably clerics who were using this material as a preaching aid and would have been familiar with the Christian view of history articulated in this text. First, the basic narrative of the three ages—*ante legem* (before the law), *sub lege* (under the law), and *sub gratia* (under grace)—was common to almost all medieval preachers. The tradition originated from Augustine's interpretation of the letters of Paul the Apostle and, by the twelfth century, was a common way of articulating the relationship between the laws of Moses and the Gospel of Christ. Holcot makes use of this division of history throughout his writings, including a slightly modified version in *Moralitas* 2.[41] Second, the moral life was central to late medieval preaching; as Siegfried Wenzel and others have argued, the study of the virtues and vices was at the heart of the early-fourteenth-century sermon. A fine example is the *Fasciculus morum* (discussed earlier), which is a handbook for preachers focused on the seven deadly sins. In the *Moralitates*, when Holcot pits the two armies against each other and narrates a battle between pride, lechery, and avarice against humility, continence, and the giving of alms, he is repeating a theological paradigm common to the *Fasciculus morum* and almost all late medieval preachers. In the *Fasciculus*, the discussion of pride (I.i–I.vii) is followed by a discussion of humility (I.viii–I.xi);[42] lechery or lust (VII.i–VII.xvi) is followed by a discussion of chastity or continence (*castitas sive continencia*) (VII.xvii–VII.xx);[43] and avarice (IV.i–IV.ix) is followed by a short discussion of the giving of alms (IV.xi–xii).[44] From the late medieval perspective, therefore, Holcot's reading of this particular story was completely consistent with the Christian theology of salvation history and the moral life. Further, a moralized story—such as the account here involving the soldiers of Christ and the soldiers of the devil fighting for the human soul—presents the preacher with a narrative structure, or memory device, for recalling the various aspects of the theological vision being offered. Thus while Holcot's moralization may seem forced or strained to a modern reader, at each step he is relying on a prior Christian exegetical tradition and theological worldview that would have been shared by all who heard or read the *Moralitates* in the fourteenth century.

Moralitas 12: The History of the Ascension of Our Lord Jesus Christ

Moralitas 12 continues the discussion of Jesus Christ and in the 1586 edition is titled "The History of the Ascension of our Lord Jesus Christ."[45] This moralization is marked explicitly as a moral exposition. Holcot begins by recalling a story in the history of the Athenians about a king and a group of persons of noble birth who offended him and transgressed his precepts. As a result, the king sentences the individuals who offended him. However, the king's son, out of love and piety, binds himself to those sentenced and, as a consequence, receives the same sentencing. The son accepts the sentence to be exiled with the offenders and in response changes his [coat of] arms: "the son made himself a shield of black as a sign of great pain and sadness." In the middle of the shield (the fess) was written the word "VITA" (life); on the middle and highest point of the shield (the chief) was written the word "MORS" (death); on the right point was written the word "INFORTUNIUM" (misfortune); and on the left point was written "REMEDIUM" (remedy). Finally, around the shield was written "Surely, one does not find that in all things death, life, and misfortune are changed into 'BONUM' (good)."[46] After some time—during which the son conducted himself well in exile—he is called home by his father and restored to his former inheritance. Thereafter the son fashions a new coat of arms: in the middle of the shield was written the word "ODIUM" (hatred); on the middle and highest point of the shield was written "AMOR" (love); on the right point was written the word "OFFENSA" (resentment); and on the left point was written the word "PAX" (peace). Finally, around the shield was written "In time, pain and misery cease. For now hatred is converted into love and resentment into reconciliation."[47]

For one familiar with the Christian narrative of human salvation, it is not difficult to anticipate Holcot's moralization of this particular story. First, Holcot discusses the three main characters in this narrative. He states that by the king he understands God the Father, creator of heaven and earth. By those banished from the kingdom, he understands Adam, who was originally exalted in paradise but subsequently banished. Finally, by the son Holcot understands the Son of God, who by means of his compassion for Adam is condemned and exiled, thus being banished from heaven to earth. Focusing on the Son of God, Holcot argues that the initial change of arms signifies Christ assuming our human nature and with it life, death, misfortune, and the potential remedy for sin. The Son—having faithfully completed his work of salvation on earth—was recalled to heaven to his former inheritance. Thus, returning to heaven, Christ takes up a new shield with the four words *hatred, love, resentment,* and *peace,* because for the faithful, hatred is changed into love and resentment into peace.

Moralitas 12, therefore, presents a christological analysis of a traditional Athenian narrative. The emphasis is placed on the person of Jesus Christ, who first sympathizes with those the Father justly exiled from the Garden of Eden because of their sins and subsequently offers himself as one to be exiled as well. As a result of this exile, Jesus takes on human flesh (i.e., changes his coat of arms) and enters into the human process of life and death, misfortune and remedy. Ultimately, though, as a result of his taking up human flesh, Jesus is called home by the Father and reconciled along with the other exiles. The final message of Jesus, on his new coat of arms, is that hatred is conquered by love and resentment by peace. As with *Moralitas* 11, Holcot's emphasis throughout is on the narrative of salvation offered through the person of Jesus Christ—a theme fitting for an audience of preachers seeking material to enliven and inform their sermons.

Moralitas 35: The Fable of the Ass and the Lion Skin

Alongside the more explicitly "historical" narratives, Holcot also includes moralizations of Aesop's fables. The fable in *Moralitas* 35 is a variation of the classical fable of the ass and the lion skin.[48] This moralization is labeled as a moral exposition of the text and is titled against pride (*contra superbiam*). In Holcot's version, the story begins as usual with an ass who, out of an act of pride, chooses to wear the skin of a lion to elevate himself above the other animals. Here it is not a farmer or a fox who discovers the true identity of the ass but the lord of the ass (*dominus asini*). The lord of the ass identifies the ass in the end, for "He knew him through his long ears."[49]

Holcot's moralization of Aesop's fable about the ass and the lion skin is significantly distinct from the two moralizations discussed previously. The two central differences are, first, that this moralization is not focused on doctrinal issues but questions of moral theology, and second, in his analysis of this fable Holcot interjects several passages of Scripture. By the ass, Holcot says, he means to indicate anyone who has the sense of an ass and has abandoned his reason and knowledge. The lion skin is understood to represent the grace of Christ, and Holcot cites a passage from Scripture as evidence, in which Jesus is called the lion of the tribe of Judah (Cf. Genesis 49:9 and, esp. Revelation 5:5). The skin of the lion, therefore, is not Christ himself but his grace infused into creatures "which covers or clothes, and decorates, [the person] through internal goods in the manner of a skin by means of the generosity of the gifts, some great, some small" (Cf. I Corinthians 12 on the diversity of graces/gifts).[50] However, it happens that man-ass (*homo asinus*, i.e., the person who rejects reason on account of pride) elevates himself above others and does not understand or comprehend the source of this grace (which is Christ). Such individuals neither fear God nor respect their fellow human beings. Finally, the lord of the ass, Jesus Christ, seeks out the ass but does not recognize him because of his pride. Here—quoting a paraphrase of the magnificat—Holcot writes that Christ does not recognize them, "because he despised the proud in the conceit of their hearts" (Luke 1:51).[51] However, at the final judgment the *homo asinus* will finally be known by his two massive ears: the sins of disobedience and obstinance, which are the ways of the devil.

While Holcot's moralization here is a bit strained (as it is odd that the lion skin is the grace of Christ and that Christ is the lord of the ass), his broader argument is a Christian allegorization examining the relationship between human pride and the gifts of grace. In the 1586 edition *Moralitas* 35 is labeled "against pride," and the general theme is that the grace of God that is infused into the believer should not be a source of pride. In Holcot's reading, the *homo asinus* is the person who puts on the skin of the lion—the infused grace given to a Christian—and takes that as a source of individual accomplishment and pride. By not recognizing the true source of grace, the *homo asinus* is not recognized by Christ and is ultimately rejected at the last judgment. This moralization, therefore, is a statement about human salvation and the proper sense of humility that is to accompany the gift of grace. Returning to the two points mentioned earlier, it is significant that this moralization is distinct from the two previously discussed as the focus is on moral theology and not questions of doctrine. This is notable because it expands the thematic range of this work and, as such, broadens the potential impact it could have within the context of late medieval preaching. Second, unlike the two moralizations discussed previously, *Moralitas* 35 makes explicit use of Scripture to assist in interpreting this passage. This is evident not only in the margins of the 1586 edition (which lists Psalms 21 and 31, Genesis 18 and 49, Revelation 5, and Luke 1) but in the body of the text.[52] This is also the case with *Moralitas* 8.

Moralitas 8: On the Love of Christ in the Passion

Holcot's *Moralitas* 8 is labeled a tropological exposition and differs from the previous three *moralitates* in that the analysis is substantially longer and more complex. The passage Holcot moralizes in *Moralitas* 8 originates, according to him, with a description of love found in Fulgentius the Mythographer and Isidore of Seville. Love is depicted here as a boy with four wings, each wing representing different aspects of love found in Scripture. In brief, true love is understood in four ways: (a) love is strong, (b) love is not self-seeking, (c) love seeks to mitigate troubles and anguish, and (d) love is young at heart (i.e., it is eternal and never dies).[53] These four wings of love are not elaborated, and Holcot follows this short passage with a lengthy moralization.

Holcot begins his analysis of love by addressing the first claim that love is strong. He argues that we have an example of this in the love of Jesus Christ. Holcot directs his reader's attention to the story of Jesus' passion described in John 18. In John's Gospel account, Jesus, on the night he would be betrayed, entered into a garden with the disciples and confronted Judas and a band of soldiers. Jesus approached Judas and the soldiers and asked them "Whom do you seek?" And they responded to him, "Jesus of Nazareth." Following his recounting of this Gospel story, Holcot responds

"Oh! What a great flame of love burned in the heart of Christ."[54] Holcot argues that Jesus is an example of the strength of love because, through great love and ardor, Jesus sought out those who would oppress and ultimately kill him. It was the strength of love, Holcot implies, that allowed Jesus to confront his own suffering and death. Finally, Holcot includes a note or brief addition to the discussion by observing that there are four signs of heat: sweating, thirst, casting off one's clothes, and appearing red. Jesus showed all four signs: "the first in [his] scourging, the second in [his] crowning (i.e., the crown of thorns), the third in [his] crucifixion, and the fourth in [his] piercing."[55] Jesus, therefore, displays a great heat or flame of love through this fourfold suffering.

The second quality of love is that love is not self-seeking. As an example, Holcot returns to Jesus to argue that during the crucifixion (Luke 22–23) Jesus, out of generosity, gave himself up: "he gave his body and blood to his disciples, his soul to the Father, and paradise to the thief."[56] These three images build upon the account of Christ's death in Luke chapters 22 and 23. According to Holcot's reading of Luke, Jesus gave his body and blood to the disciples during the last supper, saying (22:19–20), "this is my body . . ." and "this is the chalice, the new testament in my blood;" he gave his spirit or soul to the Father (23:46) when he spoke the words, "Father, into your hands I commend my Spirit;" and he gave of his inheritance (paradise) to the thief on the cross by stating that (23:43) "this day you will be with me in paradise."

Holcot continues to gloss this second definition of love by noting that perfect love or charity requires one to give of one's self, to forgive debts, to remit injuries, and to excuse offenses. All of these things, Holcot argues, Jesus does throughout his interactions with humanity. He gives of himself completely (as noted previously), forgives sins, remits injuries, and excuses offenses. In this sense, therefore, Jesus is the complete fulfillment of the second aspect of true love—he gives of himself completely for another.[57]

Jesus is also the perfect example of the third aspect of love, which is to mitigate the troubles and anguish of another. Christ not only demonstrated his love through his grief, but he also took the "handwriting of the decree" and nailed it to the cross.[58] This reference is to Colossians 2:14, which states that Jesus "Blott[ed] out the handwriting of the decree that was against us, which was contrary to us." He has taken this decree and "fastening it to the cross" has addressed God's judgment. The decree—that is, God's judgment against humanity—is nullified and blotted out because the sins of humanity were nailed to the cross. In this way, Jesus actively demonstrates his love by mitigating the troubles and anguish (i.e., sin and sin's consequences) of the human race. Further, not only do the works of Jesus function as a mitigation of troubles, Holcot also argues that Jesus provides for humanity because "we have an advocate with the Father" (I John 2:1) "who continually prays (intercedes) for us with unspeakable groanings" (Romans 8:26–27).[59] This advocate, of course, is the Holy Spirit who was sent from the Father to be the advocate and comforter of the people of God. Further, while Holcot does not quote directly from John 14:26, it is a passage that has strong resonances with the language he has chosen—that is, the language of the Holy Spirit as an advocate who Jesus says the Father will send in his name.

The fourth and final quality of love is that it never grows old but is always young. Here Holcot argues that love is eternal. Love never dies. Holcot attempts to capture this meaning with reference to Jesus by arguing that we have an example of the love of Christ, "who not only loved us when he lived on the earth, but now loves us greater since he reigns [with the Father] in Heaven."[60] In particular, Jesus loves human beings eternally by not only loving them during his time on earth but also in his time in heaven. This time in heaven is eternal; Jesus ascended into heaven to prepare a place for humanity (cf. John 14:3) and to restore peace "between God and man." Thus Holcot concludes his discussion of the four aspects of love as found in the person of Jesus Christ. Jesus, as Holcot argues, demonstrates throughout his life, death, and resurrection that love is strong, is not self-seeking, mitigates against troubles and anguish, and is eternal. However, this does not conclude Holcot's analysis of this particular passage.

Holcot continues his discussion of the love of Jesus by means of an interpretation of the seven cries (*septem clamores*) from the cross.[61] In the Gospel accounts of Jesus' death, there are seven cries (spread throughout the Gospels) that he utters while hanging on the cross: three of the passages are from Luke (23:34, 43, and 46), three from John (19:26–27, 28, and 29–30), and one from Mark (15:34) and Matthew (27:46).[62] The seven cries from the cross are one of the traditional medieval heptads (sets of seven) found throughout Scripture and analyzed by medieval preachers. For example, medieval authors such as Alan of Lille discussed[63] the seven trips the Israelites made around the city of Jericho (Joshua 6), the seven gifts [of the Spirit] in Isaiah (11:1–2), the seven virtues and vices, the seven evil spirits mentioned by Jesus (Matthew 12:45/Luke 11:25), the seven devils driven out of Mary Magdalene (Mark 16:9), the seven petitions of the Lord's prayer (Matthew 6:9–13/Luke 11:2–4), and the seven heads of the Dragon of the Apocalypse (Revelation 12:3). The use of heptads in Christian preaching is a medieval development that emerged in the tenth or eleventh century.[64]

Holcot writes that Jesus gave himself up humbly and that this is manifest in the seven cries from the cross. The first cry from the cross (Matthew 27:46: "My God, My God, why have you forsaken me?") is an indication of Jesus' great humility. As Holcot writes, "is this not great humility,"[65] for God may be said to be omnipotent and yet Jesus is forsaken or abandoned by God and destitute of help. The humility is evident, of course, because Jesus is the eternal Son of the Father, and yet in his omnipotence and love the Father has forsaken his only Son. The second cry from the cross (Luke 23:45: "Father, into your hands I commend [*commendo*] my spirit") again indicates great humility. For, as Holcot observes, the Son is equal to the Father, and yet he "re-commends" (*recommendare*)—he re-entrusts or re-commits—his spirit to the Father. This intratrinitarian *recommendare* is itself an act of humility, as the equality of Father and Son can only be breached by means of an intratrinitarian act (i.e., the Son's sacrifice of himself). The third cry from the cross (Luke 23:34: "Father, forgive them, for they do not know what they do") indicates the humility of Jesus because here he offers a prayer for those who are crucifying him. In Holcot's language, Jesus renders good for evil through this act of humility. The fourth cry from the cross (John 19:27: "Behold, your mother") was spoken to the apostle John; this cry indicates the profound humility of Jesus as he gives his mother—the Queen of Heaven—to one who is poor and despised. The fifth cry (Luke 23:43: "Amen, I say to you, this day you will be with me in paradise") will, as Holcot notes, comfort those who are desperate. In response to the request of the thief on the cross, Christ displays his humility and piety by granting such a request. The sixth cry from the cross (John 19:28: "I thirst") demonstrates Christ's humility because in this moment God is suffering the infirmities of the body and experiencing human anguish. Finally, the seventh cry from the cross (John 19:39: "It is finished") displays Christ's humility because here, at the end of his life, the *alpha* and the *omega*, the beginning and the end, has as his ending the gibbet of the cross.

Following the four qualities of love, Holcot moralizes this particular text by examining the ways in which Christ's love is evident in the seven cries from the cross. This particular heptad displays the love of Christ as he humbles himself in love. Interestingly, Holcot continues this moralization with another heptad displaying the love of Christ. This particular heptad is somewhat more condensed, and we can mention it briefly. Matthew 11:4–6 states:

> And Jesus making answer said to them: "Go and relate to John what you have heard and seen. The blind see, the lame walk, the lepers are cleansed, the deaf hear, the dead rise again, the poor have the Gospel preached to them. And blessed is he that shall not be scandalized by me."

Holcot argues that in this passage there are seven ways in which Christ displays his love: he illuminates sight, heals the lame, cleanses lepers, heals the deaf, raises the dead, gives the Gospel to the poor, and blesses those not scandalized by himself.[66]

What stands out in *Moralitas* 8 is Holcot's strong christological reading of the text. In contrast, Robrecht Lievens has shown that Dirc van Delf († 1404) interprets the same *exemplum* without any mention of Christ.[67] While Dirc connects the four wings to four characters of the Hebrew Bible known for great acts of love (i.e., Jacob, Jonathan, Ruth, and David), Holcot links all four wings with the person of Jesus Christ.

Conclusion

In the introduction to this chapter we argued that Holcot's *Moralitates* is a work that provides a Christian allegorical reading of select non-Christian works from late antiquity. Holcot reads these texts in the same way that Christians read the Old Testament in the medieval period: as an allegorical work that points to the future coming of Christ or as interpreted through the lens of his life and work. It is not surprising, therefore, that Holcot's reading of the boy with four wings is more christological than the interpretation of Dirc van Delf. The *Moralitates* is first and foremost a christological work providing future preachers with non-Christian material interpreted through a Christian framework.

12

HOLCOT AS PREACHER

Introduction

The German Reformer Martin Luther was educated in the theology of the "modern way" (*via moderna*) at the University of Erfurt where he studied the great scholastic thinkers William of Ockham (†1347), Pierre d'Ailly (†1420), and Gabriel Biel (†1495). During the year 1532, Luther wrote in his *Table Talk* (*Tischreden*) that "Ockham, my teacher, was the greatest of the dialecticians, but he was not skilled in the preaching [of the Gospel]" or, again, "Ockham alone understood dialectic ... but he was no preacher."[1] What is interesting about Luther's pronouncement here is that there is no evidence to either endorse or oppose it. There is no extant record of William of Ockham's preaching or that of his near contemporaries Henry Harclay, Walter Chatton, or Adam Wodeham. By contrast, Robert Holcot is relatively unique among fourteenth-century English scholastics in that we have an extensive collection of his sermons. This body of literature allows one to sketch a broader portrait of Holcot the thinker.

Robert Holcot's sermons are collected in five manuscripts found in England, France,[2] and Italy.[3] This study of Holcot's sermons is based on Cambridge, Peterhouse 210: a late-fourteenth-century manuscript that contains a collection of 119 Latin sermons.[4] Both the sermons and the manuscript originate from an English context. As Alan Fletcher has observed, four of the sermons contain an English division of the text (i.e., sermons 1 [1ʳ], 24 [32ʳᵃ], 80 [128ʳᵇ], and 86 [139ʳᵃ⁻ʳᵇ]).[5] Further, as argued by Smalley, the sermons follow the Sarum Use.[6] The sermons are almost certainly by Holcot: the flyleaf contains an attribution to Holcot written in the hand of Thomas James, the man chosen in 1602 as the first librarian of the Bodleian library.[7] James was surely following a further attribution in a fifteenth-century hand stating that the manuscript contains a collection of sermons by Robert Holcot for Sundays and weekdays.[8]

This chapter examines Holcot's preaching as found in the Peterhouse manuscript. The first section discusses the broader structure and content of the sermons contained in Peterhouse 210. Here we cover the occasions of the sermons and their relationship to the church calendar. In the second section we turn to the content of one of Holcot's exemplary sermons to give the reader some sense of his practical theology and preaching.

Peterhouse 210: A Systematic Overview

Sermon collections are categorized into two basic groups: random sermon collections and regular cycles. Random sermon collections "gather sermons haphazardly from a variety of occasions," thus intermixing regular Sunday sermons and feast day sermons.[9] Regular cycles, by contrast, are "quite evidently products of scholarly study, systematic expositions of the lections for Sundays, feast days, or saints' feasts in homiletic form, made to be consulted with ease."[10] In many ways, the random collections preserve a text that is perhaps closer to a "real" sermon than was actually preached; although Wenzel is correct to urge caution here, as the line between these two groups in this regard is far from clear.[11] Holcot's sermons preserved in the Peterhouse manuscript constitute a regular cycle. Thus we can begin with the basic organization of the sermons in the manuscript and their correspondence with the *Temporale* (temporal cycle) of the Proper.

The *Temporale*, we will recall, progresses through the five major Church festivals: Advent/Christmas (December), Epiphany (January), Easter, Ascension, and Pentecost (March through May). Holcot's sermons are organized according to the *Temporale* and begin, in sermon 1, with the first Sunday of Advent. In Peterhouse 210, this information—that is, the occasion of every sermon—is given in the top right corner of the first folio of the sermon. This marginal header indicates the occasion of all 119 sermons. Relying on the information preserved in the marginal headers, the first (sermons 1, 2), second (sermons 3–10, 14), third (11–13, 15) and fourth (16–18) Sundays of Advent occupied the first 18 sermons.[12] Following the Advent sermons, Holcot includes two sermons (i.e., 19, 20) dedicated to the Sunday in the octave of Christmas—or the Sunday that falls between Christmas and January 1 (this period is referred to as the octave, as it consists of eight days). Following the octave are two sermons (i.e., 21, 22) on the day of Christ's circumcision, or January 1. The next nine sermons (i.e., sermons 23–31) are marked from the first Sunday after the octave of the twelfth night, commonly referred to as Epiphany Sunday. They are accordingly listed as the first (23–26), second (27), third (28, 29), and fourth (30, 31) Sundays after the octave of the twelfth night.

Turning from Christmas to Easter, the following 68 sermons (i.e., 32–98 and 107) are all marked according to the Easter festival. The dating from Easter begins with the ninth (32–36), eighth (37–39), and seventh (40, 41) Sundays before Easter. Following the seventh Sunday before Easter is Ash Wednesday (42–44), and the first through fifth Sundays in Lent (45–73 and 107). Turning to Holy Week and the first week of the Easter season, Holcot's collection includes sermons for Palm Sunday, Good Friday, and the Monday and Tuesday of Easter week. Finally, the sermons marked from Easter conclude with the first through fifth Sundays after Easter (88–97) as well as the Sunday after Ascension Day (98). This concludes the sermons marked by the Easter holiday, which constitute over half of Holcot's sermons.

The third group of 17 sermons consists of those marked after the feast of the Holy Trinity, beginning with the first Sunday and concluding with the twenty-third Sunday following the feast of the Holy Trinity.[13] Finally, there are two sermons that do not fit within the regular cycle: sermon 109, marked as a sermon preached to the curates/priests (*sermo ad curatos*), and sermon 111, preached to the religious (*sermo ad religiosos*).

Robert Holcot's sermon collection in Peterhouse 210 is, like so many regular cycles, a highly organized and structured work that progresses through the Church calendar. With only a few exceptions, the sermons are organized according to the Church year. One aspect this analysis brings forth is the centrality of Lent and Holy Week in late medieval preaching, for over a third of the sermons are dedicated to this period of the Church year.

Holcot the Homilist

The sermons of Robert Holcot collected in Peterhouse 210 present a refreshing entry point into his thought. It was argued previously that the *Moralitates* demonstrate Holcot's focus on Christ and salvation, despite the fact that his *Sentences* commentary has little formal discussion of christology. Similarly, Holcot's sermons provide a glimpse into his broader christocentric theology and his emphasis on human redemption.

Sermon 76 is one of the seven sermons in the collection dedicated to Palm Sunday: a highpoint of the liturgical year within late medieval Christianity.[14] The Palm Sunday liturgy was rich with symbolism, and by the twelfth century it was common to celebrate with a procession that began outside the church with the collecting of palm branches (and often the *Palmesel*, or wooden figure of Christ seated on a donkey) and processed into the sanctuary.[15] This particular sermon is exemplary according to one medieval reader or scribe who wrote in the bottom margin, "note, here is a good sermon (*Nota bonum sermonem hic*)."[16]

The passion of Christ has been central to Christian theology and preaching since the patristic era. It was related, first and foremost, to Christian theories of salvation. Early Christians argued that the suffering of Christ recorded in the Gospels was a necessary part of God's redemptive plan. Christ suffered with and for humanity. The theology of the passion is exemplified in the weeks preceding Easter. The heart of the passion week—and by extension the Christian Gospel—is the sorrow of Christ at being betrayed, abandoned, denied, and forsaken: he was betrayed by Judas (Matthew 26:14–16), abandoned and by his disciples (26:40–42), denied by Peter (26:69–75), and forsaken by his Father (27:46). The passion is the heart of Christianity, therefore, because in the moment that God the Father forsook God the Son, Christ took upon himself the sins of humanity. This is the basic message that has been preached within the Church since the patristic era.

Holcot's examination of the suffering of Christ is focused on Christ's suffering and its relationship to Christian salvation, as well as the suffering of the pining earthly pilgrim and the sinner.[17] This examination of divine and human suffering proceeds through an analysis of the words of Christ, "*tristis est anima mea* (my soul is sorrowful)" (Matthew 26:38).

The Suffering of Christ

Holcot begins his analysis of the suffering of Christ by referencing Augustine's argument in the *City of God* that the body does not feel pain without the soul, while the soul can experience pain without the body.[18] From this it follows, Holcot argues, that "true pain is the sorrow of the soul."[19] Returning to Christ's pain, it is evident, Holcot writes, that his pain in the Garden of Gethsemane is the result of his anticipation of his future passion. That is, Christ foresaw the suffering that was to befall him and cried out in the garden *tristis est anima mea*. As Holcot observes, this passion is clearly not the result of bodily suffering but rather originates from the suffering of the soul—for, while in the Garden of Gethsemane, Christ had not yet undergone any physical affliction or suffering. Here Holcot turns to an analysis of Christ's suffering that occupies a central place in the sermon: what, in particular, is the cause of Christ's suffering if it is not physical affliction? He concludes that Christ felt pain due to three causes that are common to human beings.

The first cause of Christ's pain is the "grievous loss of something loved."[20] The thing loved by God more than all created things, Holcot argues, is the human soul. Further, there is evidence that Christ greatly loves the human soul, for the wise man does not feel great pain for the loss of things that are loved only moderately. Evidence of God's love for the soul of humanity can be found in the book of Job. In the story of Job, God first gave the devil permission to destroy all of the possessions of Job (1:12) without touching his person. In response, Job did not sin or cease to love God. The devil returned to God, saying "skin for skin (*pellem pro pelle*)"—if you allow me to hurt his person, he will abandon you. In response God permits Satan to hurt Job's person without killing him or striking his soul.[21] What, Holcot asks, can we learn from this, except that God loves the human soul more than the body and the human body more than possessions. For in the same way that a noble man guards the possessions that are most dear to him and assigns the care of lesser possessions to his servants, in the case of Job God protected that which was most dear to him.[22]

Thus the first cause of Christ's pain is the grief at losing the human soul. However, it remains unclear precisely for which human souls Holcot imagines Christ to be sorrowful. Is Christ sorrowful for the souls of the elect who fell but would ultimately be saved, or for those of the damned? Is Christ sorrowful for all human souls? While Holcot gives no precise answer to this question, he writes that "Since, therefore, God loved the human soul so much, it should not be wondered at if he vehemently felt pain when he lost this thing so dear to him through sin, for he showed that he felt more pain at the loss of a few souls than if he lost the entire world."[23] It seems, therefore, that the sorrow of Christ is for the souls who would be lost through sin. Christ cried out in the garden—*tristis est anima mea*—for the souls lost in sin.

The second cause of Christ's pain is the "painstaking search for something desired."[24] The something desired is again the human soul. Holcot argues that Christ laboriously and painfully (*laboriose et dolorose*) sought the human soul for more than 30 years, living his entire life in poverty and pain.[25] He here likens Christ's search for the soul of humanity to the wild ass who seeks his mate at the top of a mountain and when he arrives finds her. So Christ lived in the wilderness of this world and ultimately ascended the mount of Calvary (where he would be crucified) and having arrived found his mate (the human soul). However, the ascent of the mountain is really a descent, for Christ did not find his mate in this world, "but he found her in hell" (*sed in inferno eam invenit*).[26]

Holcot captures Christ's search for the human soul through the memorable image of the *Christus falco*, the Christ falcon. Here he switches his point of address and instead of discussing the human soul in the abstract focuses his attention on the audience, addressing them in the second person. The Christ falcon hunts for *your* souls (*animae tuae*) by flying from heaven into the womb of the virgin, from the womb of the virgin into the world, and from the world into hell. This descent of the *Christus falco* from heaven to hell is a 33-year search for the thing he loves and on account of which he says, *tristis est anima mea*.

The third cause of Christ's pain is the suffering of a penalty or painful affliction.[27] Here Holcot recalls that according to Cassiodorus there are three opinions regarding the location of the soul. The soul is said to be located (a) in the head, (b) in the heart, or (c) spread throughout the body in all of its parts.[28] The latter position (held by Cassiodorus) was also, according to Holcot, the opinion of the Jews who, seeking to punish the soul of Christ, subjected his entire body to punishment. Christ, therefore, repeated the words *tristis est anima mea* while he was in the garden because he was contemplating the future suffering of his flesh and soul.[29] Because Christ's soul is spread equally throughout his body and is not located specifically in one place, the physical suffering of his whole person was simultaneously a suffering of the soul.

The Sorrow of the Just

In the second section of the sermon Holcot observes that the cry *tristis est anima mea* not only captures the "words of our redeemer" but is also the cry of the just pilgrim who suffers in this life. Following the teaching of Gregory the Great, Holcot writes that there are three causes of suffering for the just: (a) the sin he commits, (b) the world in which he lives, and (c) the kingdom to which he tends.

Holcot begins by arguing that not only Christians suffer on account of their sins but that even pagan philosophers such as Heraclitus were accustomed to crying over the punishments and miseries in the world. The grief of the just person, Holcot argues, is not simply for the sins that he has committed but is a response to the sins of the world. And if the philosophers—who live only according to reason (not the Mosaic law or Gospel)—grieve over the sins of the world, how much more should the Christian grieve the sins of others? The Christian, of course, should also grieve over his own sins, given that true contrition is necessary for the forgiveness of sins.

The second reason that the just person suffers is on account of the world in which he lives. The just person, Holcot writes, cannot help but confront difficulty and tribulation in the world. This is manifestly evident in the biblical figure of Elijah, who when being pursued by Jezebel fled into the wilderness, sat under the broom tree, and begged that God might take his soul (I Kings 19:4). Elijah underwent such suffering "because this life which [the just] lead does not exist without pain and the affliction of spirit."[30] Holcot recognizes that in response to an unjust world, the just person can either resist or capitulate. If he resists the injustice of the world, he will do so at great cost because he can protect himself only through extreme labors of the mind. Conversely, if he capitulates, deforms himself, and oppresses the poor and afflicts the weak, he will also suffer on account of the oppression he has brought upon others. Thus, however the just person navigates the world, he will confront pain and suffering. This is evident, Holcot concludes, in both Job and Jonah: two Old Testament figures who sought death on account of their suffering, for, as Jonah remarks, "it is better for me to die than to live."[31]

The third reason the just person suffers is on account of the tension between the suffering of this world and the desire for the next. The just person, Holcot says, looks to the promised eternal life where "the virtues of the soul are not difficult or laborious" and the highest happiness is the love of what one has.[32] The just person, therefore, repeats the words of the Psalmist (Psalm 41:3), "my soul has thirsted after the strong living God." However, despite the passionate desire for the next life, "no one reaches this place except through the way of tribulation" as is evident in the life of Christ, Mary, and the saints.[33] This tension between the present state of suffering and future blessedness "compels one to sadness in the present life."[34] For this reason, the just person says *tristis est anima mea*.

The Sorrow of the Pilgrim Sinner

Holcot completes the sermon by arguing that the words *tristis est anima mea* are applicable not only to Christ and the just but also to any pilgrim sinner making her way through the world. The sinner held in the trap of the devil, Holcot argues, ought to groan until the point of death, or at least until she suffers to the point of feeling herself loosened from the trap of the devil. These feelings of suffering are identified as true devotion, compunction, and contrition, and they are found near the river of paradise because they are the appropriate response to sin.[35] The pilgrim sinner, therefore, suffers greatly in this life on account of the challenges of sin. The pilgrim sinners can be divided into three distinct groups: (a) those who sell their souls, (b) those who lose their souls, and (c) those who give their souls away for nothing.

The first category of pilgrim sinners includes the merchants who expose themselves to "plunder, theft, perjury, and false dealings for the riches of this life."[36] These individuals sell their soul to the devil for the riches of this world. Some are so greedy, Holcot observes, that they sell their soul for very little; as a parenthetical note, he observes that "many modern people sell their souls" in such a way.[37] These kinds of pilgrim sinners lament that their soul is sorrowful, for when they sell their soul they do not know if they will ever recover it.

The second category of pilgrim sinner is comprised of those who, instead of selling their soul, simply lose it. These sinners are lazy and idle and have no desire to do any good work nor care if they remain mired in sin. Holcot likens these sinners to a sea monster who desires the society of both the fish (the unjust) and the birds (the just). The sea monster first searches the deep sea (symbolizing the life of sin) for society, but when it has grown tired of the water it rises on its wings to seek the society of the birds (symbolizing the life of the just). However, the sea monster cannot sustain flight for long, for it is beaten back by the wind and returns to glide in the sea. The idle sinner is like the sea monster who ebbs and flows through life. Such sinners spend most of their life gliding in the depths of sin and despair. That is, until sometime just before Easter when they attempt to raise themselves out of the depths of sin through fasting and prayer. These sinners cannot remain at such a height, for they are tempted by "their old ways" and revert to their former misery and remain there for the rest of the year.[38] Such idle persons—Holcot warns on this Palm Sunday—"ought to attend to how they lose their souls from negligence" and, so reflecting, ought to cry out, *tristis est anima mea*.[39]

The final category of pilgrim sinners includes the worldly and angry who give their souls to the devil for nothing. This stands in contrast to those who give their souls away for some material gain. For example, in exchange for their souls, the desirous receive riches, the inconstant receive delights, the prideful receive honors, and the gluttonous receive the pleasure of food and drink. However, the worldly and the angry, by contrast, receive nothing delightful and give their souls to the devil for free (*animas suas gratis dant diabolo*).[40]

Here Holcot observes that such a person is spoken of in Judges 9:17,[41] and it is worth lingering over his reference to this passage. Judges 9 records the story of the coronation of Abimelech (son of the prophet Gideon), in which he murders his 70 "brothers" on a single stone. One brother, Jotham, escaped the carnage and goes to Mount Gerizim where he delivers the "parable of the trees" to the people. Jotham said: one day the trees went to anoint a king. They went to the olive tree and asked it to reign over them. The olive answered, "How can I leave my fatness to be promoted king of the trees?" They went to the fig tree and asked it to reign over them. The fig answered, "How can I leave my sweetness to be promoted king of the trees?" They went to the grape vine and asked it to reign over them. The grape vine answered, "How can I leave my wine to be promoted king of the trees?" Finally, they asked the bramble (*ramnum*) who had nothing to give up. The bramble responded, "If you mean to make me king, come rest under my shadow: but if you mean it not, let fire come from the bramble and devour the cedars of Lebanon." The pilgrim sinner who remains worldly and angry is likened to the bramble, who was worldly and angry and had nothing to lose. These sinners, Holcot argues, receive no earthly delight in exchange for their sin. Such persons cry out, *tristis est anima mea.*

Concluding the sermon, Holcot switches again to a second-person address and entreats his listeners: "let [this] not be, beloved (*Carissimi*), but instead give your souls to God."[42] There are four things that desire the human soul: the flesh, the world, God, and the devil. The flesh wishes that your soul desires the flesh more than everything else; the world wishes that your soul would give itself to riches and possessions; the devil simply asks that you give your soul to him. God, by contrast, "asks from you the love of your soul." You must choose, Holcot argues, to whom you will give your soul. While the flesh, the world, and the devil give you nothing in return beyond punishment and eternal death, God "will give you eternal delight in the heavenly kingdom."[43]

Conclusion

The core message of sermon 76 is a fitting way to conclude our book on the thought of Robert Holcot. In this sermon Holcot is attentive to God's pining and suffering for his creatures. Accordingly, he also focuses on the expected response of the faithful pilgrim and the ways that human beings fail to respond to God's invitation. In these themes, much of Holcot's life work has been captured and distilled.

Throughout his corpus, whether in his most academic work, his biblical commentaries, or his sermons, Holcot has shown a noticeable pastoral concern. There is no denying the fact that Holcot's work is preoccupied with issues of merit and salvation. He takes every opportunity to encourage his reader to put purity of heart and the genuine desire to follow God's commands above all else. His message to other pastors is that God is beholden to no master and therefore God may accept whom he pleases. His message to every seeker is to replace the fear of failing to believe correctly or worship correctly with an honest and genuine search for God. The Christ falcon will never fail to find those who seek God in this way.

But lest we forget, Holcot is also attentive to the fact that the capacity to seek God takes training and education: a training and education that requires a wise and just community with equally wise and just rulers. Only this education can prevent the seeker from foolishly selling his soul—a most precious possession—to the devil. Only this education helps the tree of life to grow tall and strong toward heaven, rather than downward toward the brutish earth. It is to the growth and survival of such a community that Holcot devoted his life. Through the labor of teaching, writing, and debating, he worked to send this message throughout Christendom. Spending his final days in parish ministry, Holcot attended to the victims of the plague and most likely succumbed to the plague as a result. In this final vocation, Holcot worked to ease the sorrow on earth and to direct that sorrow toward its heavenly redemption.

APPENDICES

Appendix A: Holcot's Commentary on the *Sentences*

Robert Holcot's commentary on the *Sentences* presents a challenge because the early modern printings of the text are unreliable[1] and the manuscript tradition preserves the individual questions of the work in different orders. The manuscripts consulted in preparation for the book have preserved various orderings of the questions. Because of this situation—and in order to establish a workable method of citation—we offer a table of questions based on the more accessible Lyon 1518 edition with references to other possible orderings.

Until a critical edition of Holcot's commentary on the *Sentences* is completed, many of the questions concerning the relationships between the various manuscripts will remain undetermined. However, for purely practical purposes an order of the questions had to be adopted. One's first inclination is to follow the historical order of the lectures. However, identifying this order has proved difficult because of the varied state of the manuscript witnesses. Paul Streveler and Katherine Tachau have attempted to provide a historical reconstruction of the questions.[2] While this reconstruction has proved useful for identifying the principal questions often excluded from surviving witnesses of the commentary, there are reasons this list cannot be taken as final. The most important of these is that internal references within the manuscript tradition suggest that Holcot probably lectured on book 3 after book 4; therefore, in this respect Streveler and Tachau's list needs to be adjusted.[3]

The most important evidence for the reordering of book 3 and book 4 is the presence of internal references within book 3, q.1 that implicitly refer to and depend on book 4. As scholars have noted,[4] book 3 begins an engagement with Holcot's *socius* William Chitterne. The later articles of book 3, q.1—which demonstrate dependence on earlier discussions in the *Six Articles* and even earlier in book 1—have been the primary interest. It is these references that prompted scholars to see the *Six Articles* as being given at the end of Holcot's first year of lecturing (during the summer after completing his lectures on book 2 and before lecturing on books 3 and 4).[5] However, less attention has been given to book 3, q.1, aa.1–4. Articles 1 through 4 focus on a selection of seemingly unrelated issues: article 1 examines the difference between a vow and an oath; articles 2 and 3 consider whether it is possible for people to will their own annihilation; and article 4 asks whether it is licit for an unjustly condemned prisoner to flee from prison. Each of these discussions is clearly a response to the criticisms of the *socius* who in turn is responding to an initial position of Holcot. The question, however, is where? Unlike the later articles—which refer to discussions that can be identified in book 1 and the *Six Articles*—Holcot's references to his previous arguments cannot be found there.

These questions are found in book 4, q.7 of Lyon 1518, which asks "Whether it is possible for a sinner to make satisfaction for a mortal sin." In Streveler and Tachau's list, this is book 4, q.5 and is positioned after book 3. This question contains extended principal arguments, and it is here we find discussions paralleling those in book 3: the second principal argument focuses on the difference between vows and oaths; the fifth principal argument raises issues about the ability to will one's annihilation; the third principal argument asks the question of whether it is licit for someone justly condemned to flee from prison. Each of these discussions gets referenced and alluded to in the corresponding passages in book 3, showing clearly that these discussions in book 3 follow the discussions taking place within book 4. The most striking parallels can be found in the discussion of oaths and vows in book 4, q.7, arg.2 and resumed in book 3, q.1, a.1.

In book 3, q.1, a.1 Holcot says that he will recite some arguments of a *socius*. However, it is only in the body of this article that we gain any real confirmation that Holcot is picking up in the middle of an ongoing debate with the *socius*. Here Holcot argues that vows and oaths require equal deliberation and consent, such that a vow by itself does not oblige one more than an oath does.[6] At this point he references a prior discussion not found in books

1 or 2 or in the *Six Articles*. He writes that he already defended this position with four distinct arguments, but someone has gone on to add new arguments.[7] Here it is evident that the *socius* has responded to Holcot's previous four arguments, and now Holcot turns to address the matter a second time. The original four arguments are found in book 4, q.7. But can we be sure that these four arguments are the same ones he is referring to in book 3? The discussion in book 3 offers some clarification. After listing and responding to nine new arguments in book 3, Holcot returns to review at least three of the initial arguments that he developed previously in book 4, noting explicitly that he would like "to reintroduce" (*reducere*) his arguments.[8] The textual parallels between the questions from book 4 and book 3 can be seen in the following. Notice the uses of the past tense in the passages from book 3 (i.e., *arguebam* and *arguebatur*) suggesting that these are arguments Holcot has already made.

Book 4, q.7, arg.2 (L)	Book 3, a.1, a.3 (L)
1. Sed contra arguitur sic, tota ratio obligationis quae est in voto, est in iuramento, aliqua est in iuramento, quae non est in voto, ergo obligatio iuramenti est fortior (L p.6va; O 199va).	1. Arguebam enim sic: omnis ratio obligationis quae est in voto, est in iuramento et non econtrario, quia aliqua est in iuramento quae non est in voto, ergo iuramentum est maioris obligationis (L m.2vb; O 172vb).
2. Praeterea plus de irreverentia fit Deo in periurio quam in transgressione voti simplicis, quia sponte transgrediens iuramentum licitum, imponit Deo quantum in ipso est crimen falsitatis, et hoc est interpretative blasphemare Deum et significare Deum falsum esse quia factum hominis habet suam significationem veritatem et falsitatem sicut verba, sicut docet Anselmus *De veritate*, c. IX ... (L p.6va; O 199va).	2. Secundo arguebam[9] sic: plus irreverentiae fit Deo in transgressione iuramenti quam in trangressione voti privati, nam talis interpretative est blasphemus, quia quantum in eo est falsificat seipsum et Deum, transgressor voti non nisi se, ergo maiorem facit Deo irreverentiam (L m.2vb–m.3ra; O 172vb).
4. Quarto sic: votum non obligat nisi quia ex veritate humana, sed iuramentum obligat ex veritate divina et humana, ergo plus obligat et hoc nunc apparet mihi verum (L p.6vb; O 199va).	3. Tertio arguebatur sic: iuramentum ligat ex veritate et divina et humana, votum tantum ex veritate humana (L m.3ra; O 172vb).

Similar parallels can be found on the subject of willing one's own annihilation in book 4, q.7, arg.5 (L p.7^{ra-rb}; O 199vb) and book 3, q.1, aa.2–3 (L m.3va–m.7rb; O 173ra–175ra). Likewise, one can see parallels in the discussion of whether it is licit for an unjustly condemned person to flee from prison in book 4, q.7, arg.3 (L p.6vb; O 199va) and book 3, q.1, a.4 (L m.7rb; O 175ra).[10] This textual evidence for dating book 3 prior to book 4 is corroborated by a few other factors. First, as William Courtenay and Chris Schabel observe, it was common in the first half of the fourteenth century for bachelors to lecture on the *Sentences* out of order, such that the sequence 1, 4, 2, 3 was common.[11] Second, Pascale Farago-Bermon—in her survey of the seven manuscripts at the Bibliothèque Nationale (Paris)—notes that six witnesses place book 4 before book 3.[12] To her list should be added Troyes 634, Merton 113, and perhaps others. Finally, the peculiar nature of book 3 (it is a single question, with eight diverse articles only tangentially related to the explicit question) is consistent with the notion that Holcot was giving lip service to the requirement to lecture on book 3 at the end of the second year of lecturing, when the schedule was becoming increasingly tight and he simply wanted to follow up on previous discussions.

Given the present state of research and the fact that a historical ordering of the questions awaits further inquiry, for purely practical reasons we follow the order of the Lyon 1518 edition. In the table S-T refers to the order presented by Streveler-Tachau.

L Question Number	L Folio	Question	S-T Question Number	S-T Order
I, q.1	a.1ra	Utrum quilibet viator existens in gratia, assentiendo articulis fidei, mereatur vitam aeternam.	I, q.1	2
I, q.2	b.2ra	De obiecto actus credendi: utrum sit ipsum complexum an res significata per complexum.	Principia 1	1
I, q.3	b.2rb	Utrum voluntas creata in utendo ut fruendo sit libera libertate contradictionis.	I, q.2	3
I, q.4	d.4rb	Utrum viator tenatur frui soli Deo.	I, q.3	4
I, q.5	e.8va	Utrum Deus sit tres personae distinctae.	I, q.4	5

(*continued*)

L Question Number	L Folio	Question	S-T Question Number	S-T Order
I, q.5	f.2va	Utrum aliqua res simpliciter simplex sit in genere.	I, q.5	6
II, q.1	f.5rb	Utrum creator generis humani iuste gubernat genus humanum.	II, q.1	8
II, q.2	h.1ra	Utrum Deus ab aeterno sciverit se producturum mundum.	II, q.2	9
II, q.3	i.8vb	Utrum daemones libere peccaverunt.	II, q.4	11
II, q.4	k.3ra	Utrum angelo confirmato conveniat deputari ad custodiendum hominem viatorem.	II, q.3	10
III, q.un	m.1ra	Utrum filius Dei incarnari potuit.	III, q.un	14(23)
IV, q.1	n.4va	Utrum baptismus rite susceptus conferat gratiam baptizato.	IV, q.1	16(14)
IV, q.2	o.2ra	Utrum confirmatio sit sacramentum.	IV, q.3^{13}	17(15)
IV, q.3	o.2vb	Utrum in sacramento eucharistiae sub speciebus panis vere et realiter existat corpus Christi.	IV, q.4	18(16)
IV, q.4	p.1rb	Utrum confessio sacerdoti facienda sit homini necessaria ad salutem.	IV, q.7	21(19)
IV, q.5	p.2ra	Utrum poenitenti et confesso non proprio sacerdoti, habenti tamen commissionem generalem audiendi confessiones necesse sit eadem peccata iterum confiteri proprio sacerdoti.	IV, q.8	22(20)
IV, q.6	p.4va	Utrum quilibet sacerdos posset quemlibet absolvere a quocumque peccato.	IV, q.6	20(18)
IV, q.7	p.5vb	Utrum peccator possit satisfacere Deo pro peccato mortali.	IV, q.5	19(17)
IV, q.8	p.8ra	Utrum finale praemium boni viatoris sit aeterna beatitudo.	IV, q.9	23(21)
OTHER PARTS OF THE COMMENTARY				
Sex Articuli	q.5ra	Sex sunt articuli quos in diversis materiis dixi.		12.5^{14}

(continued)

L Question Number	L Folio	Question	S-T Question Number	S-T Order
		Circa principium secundi libri in quo arguitur de causalitate Dei respectu creaturae, quaero istam quaestionem: utrum Deus sit causa effectiva omnium aliorum a se.	Principia 2	7
		Utrum stellae sint creatae ut per lumen et motuum sint in signa et tempora.	II, q.5	12
		Utrum Filius Dei assumpsit naturam humani in unitatem suppositi *or* Utrum viae vivendi, quas Christus docuit, sint meritoriae vitae aeternae.[15]	Principia 3	13(22)
		Utrum viator existens in gratia ordinate utendo et fruendo posset vitare omne peccatum *or* Utrum cum omni sacramento debito modo suscepto recipienti sacramentum informans gratia conferatur.[16]	Principia 4	15(13)
		Sermo finalis: 'Cursum consummavi, fidem servavi,' Tim. 4. Sollicitudo scolastica studiosissima circa sacrae theologiae notitiam adquirendam comparatur amicitae amatoris qui per laboriosam militiam nititur quaerere sibi sponsam.	Sermo finalis	24

Appendix B: The Quodlibetal Questions

The first significant study of Holcot's quodlibets was Palémon Glorieux's *La littérature quodlibétique de 1260 à 1320* published in 1935. Glorieux's research was followed by more recent work, including studies by E. A. Moody (1964); Paolo Molteni (1967); Fritz Hoffmann (1972); Richard Gillespie (1971 and 1974); Hester G. Gelber (1983); Heikki Kirjavainen (1986); Leonard Kennedy (1993); Paul Streveler, Katherine Tachau, William J. Courtenay, and Hester G. Gelber (1995); and Rondo Keele (2007).[17]

Here we present a table of questions for each of Holcot's extant quodlibetal questions. The list prioritizes the Pembroke manuscript (P) in terms of the order of presentation. Further, William Courtenay has argued that Robert Holcot's lost commentary on the book of Matthew is extant (in part) in various quodlibetal questions and in the commentary on the *Sentences*,[18] and we have noted such questions with an asterisk (*). The table includes endnotes indicating which of the extant questions have been edited.

Finally, in his recent study of Oxford quodlibets, Rondo Keele observes that there is a fourth manuscript (i.e., D) that "apparently includes *Determinationes* on ff. 239^v–325^r" and should be included in subsequent editions of the quodlibets.[19] It is important to note that D is of no use for reconstructing Holcot's quodlibetal questions. According to the colophon (D 325rb), the manuscript dates from 1512 and is simply a manuscript copy of the editions printed in Lyon in 1505/1510 (or a copy of the exemplar used to produce those editions).

Quaestio	P	B	R	L
1 Utrum stellae sint creatae ut per motum et lumen sint in figura et tempora.	117ra	—	—	—
2* Utrum Filius Dei assumpsit naturam humanam in unitatem suppositi (Matthew 1:18–25).	132rb	—	—	—
3* Utrum beatus Matthaeus convenienter narravit Christi genealogiam (Matthew 1:1–17).	141vb	211va	—	—
4* Utrum historia conceptionis Christi sit in toto vera (Matthew 1:18–25).	143ra	212vb	—	—
5* Utrum virginitas beatae Virginis fuit laudabilior quam eius fecunditas (Matthew 1:18–25).	143vb	202va	—	—
6* Utrum beata Virgo fuit concepta in originali peccato (Matthew 1:18–25).	144va	—	—	—
7* Utrum Christus convenienter redemit genus humanum (Matthew 1:18–25).	146va	216rb	—	D.13 K3^{rb}
8* Utrum divinitas sit pars Christi (Matthew 1:18–25).	146vb	218rb	—	—
9 Utrum Christus incarnatus fuisset dato quod homo non peccasset.	147ra	256rb	149va	—
10* Utrum voluntas humana in Christo fuit divinae voluntati conformis (Matthew 26:39).	147rb	218va	—	—
11* Utrum Deus propter beneficium redemptionis sit amplius diligendus ab homine quam si nunquam hominem ab inferno redemisset (Matthew 27).	147vb	209va	—	—
12* Utrum Christus probavit resurrectionem suam convenientibus argumentis (Matthew 28).	148rb	208ra	—	—
13* Utrum motus ascensus Christi in caelum fuit sensibiliter successivus (Matthew 28).	148vb	208va	—	—
14* Utrum doctrina evangelica beati Matthaei de Christo sit generaliter tota vera.[20]	149ra	—	—	D.15 K5^{va}

(*continued*)

Quaestio		P	B	R	L
15*	Utrum beatus Matthaeus gaudeat in caelo de conversione suae a teloneo ad apostolatum (Matthew 9:9).²¹	151vb	205rb	—	—
16	Utrum sapientia increata obligando viatorem ad aliquod antecedens obliget eum eoipso ad quodlibet suum consequens.	152ra	206ra	152ra	—
17	Utrum in quolibet poenitente virtuose pro peccatis virtute passionis Christi praeveniat gratia gratum faciens.	152va	206va	—	—
18	Utrum quilibet viator existens in mortali peccato tenetur quam cito poterit poenitere.	153ra	207ra	—	—
19	Utrum in quolibet poenitente requiritur spes veniae ad hoc quod meritorie poeniteat de peccato.	153va	207va	—	—
20	Utrum cuilibet viatori deputetur ad custodiam aliquis angelus confirmatus.	154ra	208vb	—	—
21	Utrum angelus confirmatus libere operetur circa hominem quem custodit.	154rb	209rb	—	—
22	Utrum septem vitia capitalia specie distinguantur.	154va	203va	151vb	—
23	Utrum qualitas suscipiat magis aut minus.	154vb	203vb	—	—
24	Utrum contraria possunt esse in eodem subiecto coextensa.	155rb	204va	—	—
25	Utrum homo possit peccare.	155rb	204va	—	—
26	Utrum alicuius peccati mortalis possit esse aliqua circumstantia venialis.	155vb	210ra	—	—
27	Utrum aliqua virtus create possit in actum suum absque hoc quod immediate a Deo applicetur.	156ra	210rb	—	—
28	Utrum Deus possit esse causa peccati.	156ra	210va	—	—
29²²	Utrum Deus velit fieri voluntate efficienti quod fit contra eius praeceptum vel prohibitionem.	156rb	210va	—	—
30	Utrum ad operationes licitas sequitur necessario peccatum mortale.	156rb	210vb	—	—
31	Utrum gratuite diligens Deum plus se possit pro eadem mensura mereri et demereri.	156va	210vb	—	—

(continued)

Quaestio		P	B	R	L
32[23]	Utrum Sortes deberet peccare mortaliter pro vita aeterna consequenda.	156va	210vb	—	—
33	Utrum sine recta ratione in intellectu possit voluntas elicere actum rectum et virtuosum.	156va	211ra	—	—
34	Utrum ultra omnem gradum possibilem haberi in via possit caritas augeri ex merito hominis.	156vb	211ra	—	—
35	Utrum respectu dilectionis gratuitae caritas habeat efficaciam in mente.	156vb	211rb	—	—
36	Utrum perfectio vitae praesentis sit potissime in actu contemplationis.[24]	156vb	211rb	—	—
37	Utrum Deus posset dare potentiam creandi cuicumque creaturae.	157ra	211va	—	—
38*	Utrum oratio sit ab ecclesia convenienter usitata (Matthew 6:7–15).	157ra	213va	—	—
39*	Utrum oratio dominica sit rationabiliter ordinata (Matthew 6:7–15).	157ra	213va	—	—
40	Utrum Deus secundum exigentiam meritorum vel demeritorum distribuat poenas et praemia.	157va	214rb	—	—
41	Utrum omne peccatum sit voluntati hominis debite imputandum.	157vb	214rb	—	—
42[25]	Utrum voluntas creata sit causa principalis cuiuslibet sui demeriti actualis.	157vb	214va	—	—
43	Utrum anima beata retardetur a plenitudine suae beatitudinis propter appetitum ad corpus.	158ra	214vb	—	—
44	Utrum David peccavit quando tenebatur non peccare.	158va	215rb	—	—
45	Utrum animae existentes in purgatorio delectentur de poenis quas ibi patiuntur.	158va	215va	—	—
46	Utrum sacerdos qui tenetur ex voto ad castitatem incidens in fornicationem gravius peccet quam laicus coniugatus committens adulterium.	158va	215va	—	—
47	Utrum vovens ingressum religionis et intrans cum proposito exeundi adimpleat votum.	158vb	215vb	—	—

(*continued*)

	Quaestio	P	B	R	L
48	Utrum periurium sit gravius peccatum quam homicidium.	159ra	216ra	—	—
49	Utrum licitum sit fidelibus ponere in ecclesiis et venerari imagines illorum qui non sunt adscripti ab Ecclesia Romana catalogo sanctorum.	159ra	216ra	—	—
50	Utrum aliqua propositio possit componi ex intentionibus et speciebus in anima naturaliter significantibus rem extra.	159ra	216va	—	—
51	Utrum doctrina venerabilis Anselmi rationabiliter debeat reprobari.	160rb	219ra	—	—
52	Utrum viae vivendi quas Christus docuit sint meritoriae aeternae.	160vb	219va	—	D.2 E7^{ra}
53	Utrum voluntas humana in utendo creaturis sit libera.	165va	225rb	—	D.3 F7^{vb}
54	Utrum anima Christi fruens Deo fruatur eo ipso necessario quodlibet quod est Deus.	168ra	228va	—	D.5 G5^{vb}
55	Utrum creatura rationalis sit a Deo facta ad fruendum finaliter solo Deo.	170va	231ra	—	D.6 G8^{vb}
56	Utrum obiectum fruitionis beatificae sit Deus vel aliud a Deo.	172va	233ra	—	D.7 H3^{ra}
57	Utrum viator existens in gratia ordinate utendo et fruendo posset vitare omne peccatum.	173rb	234ra	—	D.4 G3^{rb}
58[26]	Utrum Deus possit facere creaturam rationalem impeccabilem.	175rb	257va	152rb	—
59	Utrum voluntas peccabilis in qualibet temptatione sua sufficiat ex se a peccato declinare ita quod excludatur gratia vel habitus.	175vb	258rb	153ra	—
60	Utrum meritum viatoris consistat solum in actu voluntatis.	176ra	258va	153va	—
61	Utrum actus exterior habeat propriam bonitatem vel malitiam super actum interiorem.	176va	259ra	153vb	—
62	Utrum imperium voluntatis possit impediri per aliquam virtutem intellectivam vel sensitivam.	177rb	260rb	155ra	—

(*continued*)

272 APPENDIX B

Quaestio		P	B	R	L
63[27]	Utrum creator rationalis creaturae iuste operatur vel operabatur in omni operatione et in omni tempore suo.	177vb	261ra	155va	—
64	Utrum aureola doctoris debeator solis doctoribus sacrae theologiae qui in ea incipiunt in universitate approbata iuxta modum et formam universitatis.	178rb	261rb	156ra	—
65[28]	Utrum dilectio Dei aeterna sit homini possibilis.	178vb	262rb	156vb	—
66	Utrum quolibet peccatum veniale diminuat habitum caritatis.	179ra	262va	157ra	—
67	Utrum adultus rite baptizatus possit per tempus vitare omne peccatum.	179rb	238ra	157va	—
68[29]	Utrum clare videns Deum videat omnia futura contingentia.	179rb	263ra	157va	—
69[30]	Utrum ista consequentia sit necessaria: "Deus scit *a* fore ergo *a* erit." Significet *a* unum futurum contingens.	180rb	264rb	158vb	—
70[31]	Utrum, facta revelatione alicuius futuri contingentis, ipsum maneat contingens post revelationem.	180rb	255va	159ra	—
71	Utrum Deus possit aliquem punire de condigno.	180vb	256vb	159vb	—
72[32]	Utrum observantia legis mosaycae fuit judaeis meritoria vitae aeternae.	181ra	242vb	168ra	—
73[33]	Utrum generalis resurrectio necessario sit futura.	183vb	245rb	161vb	—
74	Utrum sapientia increata disponat suaviter universa.	188ra	248vb	163rb	—
75	Utrum lex sapientiae increatae obliget viatorem ad impossibilia.	192va	238ra	166va	—
76	Utrum sapientia increata beatificet hominem virtuosum secundum merita.	193rb	238va	167rb	—
77	Utrum perfectio vitae praesentis sit potissime in actu contemplationis.	193rb	239ra	167rb	—
78	Utrum Deus possit punire peccantem mortaliter ad condignum.	194ra	239va	169rb	—
79	Utrum homo de necessitate salutis teneatur ad opus supererogationis quod voco omne opus sine quo potest homo salvari.	194rb	239vb	169va	—

(*continued*)

APPENDIX B   273

	Quaestio	P	B	R	L
80	Utrum male agentes sint a legislatoribus puniendi.	194rb	239vb	169vb	—
81	Utrum voluntas possit agere contra iudicium suae rationis.	195va	241ra	170vb	—
82	Utrum voluntas possit libere educere intentionem in intellectu de actu primo in actum secundum.	196rb	241vb	171va	—
83	Utrum peccans mereatur punire.	197ra	242va	172vb	—
84	Utrum discedens omne peccato possit iuste damnari.	197rb	—	173ra	—
85	Utrum sapientia increata iuste puniat peccatores iuxta demerita.	197va	236rb	160va	—
86[34]	Utrum theologia sit scientia.	199ra	182ra	141vb	—
87[35]	Utrum haec sit concedanda: Deus est Pater et Filius et Spiritus Sanctus.	202vb	192ra	148ra	—
88	Utrum fruitio possit manere in voluntate et non esse fruitio.	205rb	—	—	D.8 H4^{vb}
89	Utrum angelus non confirmatus clare videns Deum posset Deum non diligere stante illa vision.	207ra	—	—	D.9 H6^{vb}
90[36]	Utrum cum unitate essentiae divinae stet pluralitas personarum.	209ra	—	—	D.10 J2^{va}
91[37]	Utrum perfectiones attributales essentiales in divinis indistincte praecedant omnem operationem intellectus.	214va	194ra	146rb	—
92	Utrum Deus sit causa effectiva omnium aliorum a se.	215rb	—	—	D.11 I8^{va}
93	Utrum circumstantia aggravet <peccatum>.	217va	—	—	—
94	Utrum unio naturae humanae ad Verbum sit una res distincta absoluta vel respectiva.	218ra	195va	149ra	—
95	Utrum Deus possit facere quodlibet de quolibet.	218vb	198ra	149vb	—
96[38]	Utrum Deus possit scire plura quam scit.	218vb	198rb	150ra	—
97	Utrum in beato Paulo fuerunt virtutes theologicae pro tempore raptus sui.	220va	199vb	151vb	—
98[39]	Utrum caritas beatorum in patria possit corrumpi.	220vb	200ra	—	—

(continued)

Quaestio	P	B	R	L
99^{40} Utrum per potentiam Dei absolutam possit aliquis acceptari sine caritate eidem formaliter inhaerente.	221rb	200vb	—	—
— Utrum omnis amor quo Deus dilexit homines fuit moraliter virtuosus.	—	218vb	—	—
—* Utrum beatus Iohannes Baptista testimonium perhibendo de Christo placuit Deo (Matthew 3).	—	264rb	—	—
— Utrum Deus fuerit causa effectiva mundi per creationem.	—	—	—	D.12 $K3^{vb}$
— Utrum Deus sit a nobis cognoscibilis.	—	—	—	D.14 $K5^{rb}$
— Utrum haec sit concedenda: Christus est creatura.	—	—	173rb	—

Appendix C: The Wisdom Commentary: *Dubitationes*

Robert Holcot's commentary on Wisdom contains numerous formal *dubitationes*. As these questions are not easily identifiable in the 1586 edition, we present here a list of questions compiled from the tables of questions found in the manuscript tradition (B2 314vb–315rb, T 193vb–194ra, VO 216rb–216va, and VP 489ra–490rb) and based on our own reading of the text. Smalley is correct that as time progresses the tables of questions become more elaborate and complex. For example, B2 presents a simple and unalphabetized table while the table in VP is organized according to an alphabetical index.[41]

As noted, some of the *dubitationes* in the master list are not found in the various tables. Here we have not listed every time Holcot includes an interrogative in his text or every use of the word *dubium*. We have identified only those questions that have the feel of a formal *quaestio* or *dubitatio litterales*. That said, we cannot simply limit ourselves to times that Holcot explicitly prefaces a discussion with *dubitatio litterales* because there are many questions, often recognized within the manuscript lists, where such an introduction does not exist. The following table records the question, *lectio*, and pagination/foliation for B1 and B2, respectively.

Lect. No.	B1	B2	Quaestio
3	12	6va	Quare principibus et praelatis potius dicitur, diligite iusticiam quam diligite prudentiam.
3	12	6vb	Quae est magis necessaria reipublicae, vel iusticia, vel amicitia.
4	15	7va	Utrum praeter virtutes morales acquisitas necesse sit ponere theologicas.

(*continued*)

Lect. No.	B1	B2	Quaestio
6	23	11ra	An Spiritus Sanctus detestetur et fugiat omnem fictionem.
8	32	14ra	Utrum peccata per poenitentiam condonata sint revelanda in iudicio generali.
14	51	24ra	Utrum virtutes cardinales manebunt in patriam.
14	52	24va	An iustitia originalis includat aliquod donum supernaturale.
15	54	25vb	Utrum anima sit immortalis.
15	54	25vb	An [quod anima sit immortalis] possit probari evidenter ratione naturali.
16	59	27vb	Utrum omne corpus humanum sit de lege communi in cineres redigendum.
17	62	29rb	Quomodo dicunt quod nubes sive nebula per calorem solis aggravatur, cum calor non sit causa gravitatis, nec descensus, sed magis causa levitatis et ascensus.
17	62	29va	Utrum vita humana sit denuo reparanda.
18	69	32ra	Utrum sit homini virtuosum negligere famam suam.
19	69	32va	Utrum resurrectio omnium generaliter sit futura.
20	73	34ra	Utrum homo ex caritate teneatur plus diligere Deum quam seipsum.
21	76	35va	Utrum usus vini sit homini licitus.
22	78	36vb	Utrum fornicatio simplex sit peccatum mortale.
23	82	38rb	An liceat per potentiam[42] opprimere proximum.
25	89	41rb	Utrum aliquis teneatur ex praecepto sui iudicis revelare secretum fidei suae commissum.
27	96	44va	An persecutores[43] Christi cognoverunt eum esse Deum.
28	99	46ra	An Christus fuerit violenter occisus.
29	103	47^{va-vb}	Utrum aliqua credenda supernaturalia fuerunt homini revelanda necessario ad salutem.
30	106	49^{ra-rb}	Utrum corpus primi hominis fuisset incorruptibile dato quod in statu innocentiae perstitisset.
31	111	51ra	Utrum animae defunctorum habeant distincta receptacula post hanc vitam sibi divinitus deputata.
34	121	56ra	Utrum corpus gloriosum istis quatuor dotibus sit dotandum.

(*continued*)

Lect. No.	B1	B2	Quaestio
35	124	57rb	Utrum sancti[44] homines in iudicio generali participabunt aliquo modo actum iudicandi.
36	126	58va	Utrum homo adiutus gratia possit mereri vitam aeternam ex condigno.
37	131	61ra	Utrum omnis negligentia sit peccatum mortale.
39	137	63vb	Utrum virginitas sit virtus moralis.
40	140	65ra	Utrum liceat alicui seipsum castrare propter continentiam servandam.
40	141	65va	Utrum virginitati debeatur aureola.
42	147	68vb	Utrum filii debeant aliquod damnum propter defectum natalium[45] reportare.
43	153	70rb	Utrum filius teneatur per omnia parentibus obedire.
44	157	72vb	Utrum actus matrimonialis fieri posset virtuose.
45	159	73vb	Utrum coniugatus resuscitatus a morte teneatur iterato uxori coniugi.
46	164	76rb	Utrum in actu adulterii gravius peccet vir quam uxor.
46	165	76va	Utrum fornicando caeteris paribus plus peccet vir quam mulier.
46	165	76vb	Utrum plus peccet caeteris paribus vir adulterando quam sacerdos fornicando.
48	171	79va	Utrum mors sit poena inflicta pro peccato primi parentis.
49	174	81ra	Utrum malus senex possit in articulo mortis utiliter poenitere.
53	188	87rb	Utrum omni opere Dei misericordia et iusticia coniungantur.
57	202	94rb	Utrum vox tubalis praecedens iudicium erit aliquo modo causa resurrectionis corporum.
58	205	95rb	Utrum in iudicio generali erit aliquam disceptatio vocalis.
59	208	96va	Utrum dolor poenitentis possit esse nimius.
66	233	107vb	Utrum licitum sit et meritorium alicui Christiano, aliquem infidelem, sicut paganum invadendo per vim,[46] occidere.
66	236	109rb	Utrum glaudium extrahendo peccavit Petrus tempore passionis Christi.[47]
68	242	112ra	Utrum damnati in inferno agant poenitentiam de eo quod peccaverunt.

(continued)

Lect. No.	B1	B2	Quaestio
71[48]	251	115va	Utrum beati post diem iudicii gaudebunt de poenis damnatorum.
71	252	*om.*	Utrum ignis purgatorius involvet reprobos.
71	253	*om.*	Utrum damnati puniantur per corporales tenebras.
72	256	117ra	Utrum mundus purgabitur per ignem.
73	259	118rb	Utrum poena damnatorum debeat dici corporalis.
79[49]	275	125rb	Utrum personarum acceptio sit peccatum.
79	*om.*	125rb	Utrum liceat iudici condemnari ad mortem propter allegata et probata coram se in fora iuris illum quem scit penitus esse innocentem.
88	301	133vb	Utrum in Christo fuit necessitas moriendi.
96	323	145ra	Utrum liceat religiosis intendere studio Scripturarum.
99	336	151ra	Utrum de motibus stellarum[50] possit esse scientia.
101	344	154va	An Deus sit in qualibet creatura adorandus.[51]
103	348	156va	Utrum solis amicis Dei conservatur donum prophetiae.[52]
104 ·	353	158va	An sol illuminet infra terram.
104	353	158va	An sol illuminet stellas superiores.
105	356	159vb	An omnia subdentur gubernationi divinae.[53]
105	356	159vb	An Deus disponat omnia misericorditer.
106	359	161va	Utrum proles sequi debeat conditiones patris in libertate et servitute.
109	369	165va	An virtutes morales sint connexae sic quod nullus possit habere unam nisi omnes habeat.
114	384	172va	Utrum bellum possit esse licitum Christiano.
120	402	180rb	An electores praelatorum[54] teneantur eligere meliorum.
120	403	180va	An melius sit habere reges per electionem quam per haereditariam successionem.
120	403	180va	An melius sit regi optima lege, vel optimo rege.
125	421	188ra	Utrum Adam in statu innocentiae fuit a Deo rationabiliter custoditus.
133	448	200ra	Quare modernis temporibus non fiunt miracula ita passim, sicut olim in primitiva ecclesia.
146	492	220^{ra-rb}	Utrum gratia Spiritus Sancti detur necessario homini se quantum potest ad gratiam praeparanti.
158	524	234va	Utrum licet Christianis aliquas imagines adorare.

(*continued*)

Lect. No.	B1	B2	Quaestio
160	529	237ra	Utrum observatio signorum ad praecognoscendum eventus futuros sit licita, vel superstitiosa.
160	530	237rb	An liceat tales imagines facere, et tales factis uti, sicut temporibus meis quidam in Londonia dicebatur curari a quartana per imaginem leonis auream, secundum certam constellationem factam.[55]
189	621	278va	Utrum ignis corporalis puniet in inferno damnatos.
190	625	280vb	Utrum ars magica sit hominibus rationabiliter interdicta.
199	657	295ra	Utrum civitati semper expediat mutare patrias leges pro melioribus legibus, noviter adinventis.
201	662	297rb	Utrum angelus exterminator Aegypti fuerit bonus.
201	663	297vb	Utrum animae in purgatorio puniuntur per angelos bonos, vel per malos.
202	665	298vb	Utrum divinatio per somnia sit licita.
203	671	301vb	Utrum in Christi passione fuerit mala grammatica.[56]

NOTES

INTRODUCTION

1. On Dominican education, see Mulchahey (1998).
2. With respect to dating, we have followed Gelber (2004), 92–98. See also Schepers (1970, 1972); Courtenay (1978), 96–100; and Tachau (1995), 25–27.
3. Gelber (2004), 93–94, esp. n107.
4. See Schepers (1970), 320–354.
5. See Appendix A.
6. Schepers (1970), 325.
7. Courtenay (1980), 103–112.
8. Gelber (2004), 94.
9. For a discussion of the manuscripts, see Appendix A.
10. Gelber (2004), 94; see Smalley (1960), 139ff; and Rivers (1993), 5.
11. For a discussion of the quodlibetal material see later in this chapter and Appendix B; for information on *De Stellis*, see Thorndike (1957), 227–235. *De imputabilitate peccati* is attributed to Holcot by the editors of L and is found at A.1ra–C.8vb.
12. See de Ghellinck (1922), 491–500; Neal (1976), 229–257; and Martin (1964), 194–230, esp. 217–219.
13. Smalley (1960), 143–145.
14. The evidence is largely conjectural, although there is good textual support for the claim that in his writings after 1335 Holcot increasingly engages with classical sources. See chapter 6.

15. Courtenay (1987), 106.
16. For an introduction to the Calculators, see Sylla (1982), 540–563.
17. Martin (1964), 218. See also Courtenay (1987), 133–137.
18. Courtenay (1987), 134; Martin (1964), 219. Chambre, *Continuatio historiae Dunelmensis*, 128.
19. Gelber (2004), 97, esp. n126; Smalley (1960), 141. As Gelber notes, Quétif-Échard (1719–1721), I, 630, observe that two of the Paris manuscripts of the Wisdom commentary designate Holcot as from Cambridge.
20. Throughout this book we use the Latin titles for the *Convertimini* and *Moralitates* as there are no clear English equivalents.
21. Gelber (2004), 98.
22. See Smalley (1960), 142. See also chapter 6.
23. The tradition is recorded in Johannes Trithemius, *Liber de scriptoribus ecclesiasticis*, 90^v.
24. Ecclesiasticus 7:37–40.
25. Lecturing on the *Sentences* was part of the formal degree requirements at Oxford University during the fourteenth century. On the place of the *Sentences* within the university curriculum, see Courtenay (1987), 41–48. On Peter Lombard's *Sentences*, see Colish (1994) and Rosemann (2004). For a useful introduction to the *Sentences* commentary tradition, see Rosemann (2007, 2010, 2015) and Evans (2002).
26. See Brady (1965).
27. In this respect, the commentaries on the *Sentences* of Peter Lombard eventually took the place of *quodlibetal* questions in the sense that it was in the commentaries that medieval theologians engaged in sustained philosophical and theological analysis.
28. On Arnold of Strelley, see Gelber (2004), 79–83. On Richard FitzRalph, see Dunne (2010). On Crathorn, see Aurélien (2011).
29. See Slotemaker-Witt (2012).
30. See Hallamaa (2010).
31. See Appendix A.
32. Five of the six articles are published in Hoffmann (1993), 65–127. For a discussion of Hoffmann's editon, see Gelber (2004), 297, n77.
33. Gelber (2004), 295–306. Regarding his debate with Chitterne, see Tachau (1994), 157–196.
34. See Glorieux (1925, 1935) and Schabel (2006, 2007).
35. See Courtenay (2007), 693–699.
36. See note 2.
37. While there are numerous disagreements between the views of Schepers, Courtenay, and Tachau, both arguments place the quodlibetal disputes between 1333 and 1334. See the literature cited in Appendix B.
38. Gelber (2004), 91–95.
39. Keele (2007), 680.

40. See the literature cited in Appendix B.
41. See Appendix B.
42. The editors of L and L1 surmise that the *Determinationes* are perhaps the product of Holcot's students or of the schools: "verumtamen non desunt qui eas a discipulis Holcot collectas putent, aut ab ispso inter profitendum in gymnasio publico dictatas." See L1 D.1ra; L D.1ra. Note that the initial quodlibet recorded in L and L1 is by Roger Rosetus. Cf. Gelber (1983), 19, n53.
43. See Gillespie (1974), 121–124; Gelber (1983), 18–23; Tachau (1995), 20–27; and Appendix B.
44. There is evidence that Holcot wrote a now-lost work on the art of preaching (*De predicationis officio opusculum*). See Mulchahey (1998), 475, n475. The incipit is recorded as *A sacro canone tanquam a fonte* . . .
45. See chapter 6 for further information on the other commentaries, the manuscripts, and the early printings.
46. Smalley (1956), 10.
47. See Smalley (1949, 1950, 1950–1951).
48. *PL* 28, 1242–1243.
49. *PL* 70, 1117.
50. See *PL* 109, 671–762.
51. For Eckhart, see Duclow (1987). Eckhart's *Expositio libri Sapientiae* is found in the second volume of the Latin Works in *Die deutschen und lateinischen Werke* (1992), 301–643. See Ps.-Bonaventure, *Commentarius in librum Sapientiae*. The authorship of this work is currently in dispute and is attributed by Bellamah (2011) to William of Alton. See also Bougerol (2014), 185, who attributes it to John of Varzy (†1277). We have referenced this work as Ps.-Bonaventure throughout.
52. Tachau (1995), 2–3; Gelber (2004), 47.
53. See note 6.
54. See Rivers (1993) for a study of the commentary on the Twelve Prophets.
55. See chapter 7. On classical sources in late medieval preaching, see Wenzel (1995b).
56. The *Moralitates* is readily available in B1 508–550. For a valuable discussion of the *Convertimini*, see Ward and Herbert (1883–1910), III, 116–155. For further textual information, see the introduction to chapter 11.
57. See P1. There are also a few other manuscripts that contain sermons attributed to Holcot. See Slotemaker-Witt (in press).
58. Though see Slotemaker (2014) and Slotemaker-Witt (in press).
59. Smalley (1956), 5–6.
60. Chenu (2005), 19.
61. Pelikan (1959), 23. While historians of Christian thought working in patristic and Reformation theology have recently attended to Pelikan's critique, it is still far too common for medievalists to ignore both the exegetical writings

of scholastic authors and the use of Scripture within scholastic treatises on theology per se (e.g., commentaries on the *Sentences*).

62. Pelikan (1959), 23.

CHAPTER 1

1. See the later discussion of Isidore and Augustine.
2. See Augustine, *De Trin.* 4.4.7 (*CCCM* 50, 170$^{26-27}$; *WSA* 1.5; 147). See Fredriksen (1991) and Armitage (2008).
3. See Isidore, *Etymologies* 6.17.16 (Barney 144b); Anselm of Havelberg, *Anticimenon* I. 3.13 (*PL* 188, 1138–1252); Hugh of St. Victor, *De Sacramentis legis naturalis et scriptae* (*PL* 176, 32); id., *De archa Noe, Libellus de formatione arche* (*CCCM* 176, 119–162); Rupert of Deutz, *De Trinitate et operibus suis* 3.36 (*PL* 167, 324–326); and Robert Grosseteste, *De cessatione legalium* 4.7 (Dales-King 179–199).
4. See Armitage (2008).
5. Cf. Holcot, *Moralitas* 2 (B1 710); *Moralitas* 11 (B1 720); and *Sup. Eccl.*, lec.1 (V1 2rb; BA3 1rb).
6. Isidore, *Etymologies* 5.39.9 (Barney 131a) and 5.1.1 (Barney 117a).
7. Isidore, *Etymologies* 6.17.16 (Barney 144b).
8. Isidore, *Etymologies* 1.38.11 (Barney 65a).
9. Isidore, *Etymologies* 9.2.3 (Barney 192b).
10. See Fredriksen (2010), 163 and 243.
11. Augustine, *Propositionum ex epistolae ad Romanos*, in Fredriksen (1982), 30.
12. Fredriksen (2010), 243.
13. Cited in Fredriksen (2010), 243.
14. Fredriksen (2010), 245.
15. Augustine, *The Spirit and the Letter* 48.28 (*WSA* 1.23, 174).
16. Augustine, *Contra Faustum* 12.2–3 (*WSA* 1.20, 126–127).
17. Holcot, *Sap.* lec.13 (B1 49; B2 23^{ra-va}).
18. Hugh, *De archa Noe* (*CCCM* 176, 137).
19. Hugh, *De archa Noe* (*CCCM* 176, 133–135).
20. Rorem (2009), 85.
21. Augustine, *City of God* 4.33 and 16.26 (*WSA* 1.6, 141; 1.7, 217). See also id., *Contra Faustum* 6.9 (*WSA* 1.20, 103).
22. See Augustine, *Contra Faustum* 11.5–6 (*WSA* 1.20, 118–120). For a useful summary of the medieval understanding of the relationship between the Old and New Testaments, see de Lubac (1998), I, 225–267. See also Oberman (2000), 112–119.
23. This quodlibet is a complex argument between Holcot and an unnamed *socius*. For further analysis see Gillespie (1974), 232–297. On this quodlibet see also Turner's corrective (2002), 144 to Dahan (1990).
24. Augustine, *Contra Faustum* 11.5 (*WSA* 1.20, 119).

25. These propositions are found throughout the quodlibet and are not quoted directly from Holcot.
26. Holcot, *Quodl.* 72 (Molteni 174$^{7-12}$).
27. Holcot, *Quodl.* 72 (Molteni 183$^{23-31}$).
28. Lombard, *Sent.* IV, d.1, c.4 (Brady II, 233$^{17-20}$; Silano IV, 4).
29. Colish (1994), II, 510–514 and 528, here 511.
30. Holcot, *Quodl.* 72 (Molteni 179$^{30-33}$).
31. Holcot, *Quodl.* 72 (Molteni 180$^{7-11}$).
32. Holcot, *Quodl.* 72 (Molteni 176$^{16-22}$).
33. Holcot, *Quodl.* 72 (Molteni 176$^{23-35}$). This argument is reminiscent of Thomas Aquinas, who argued in his discussion of circumcision that "guilt is not remitted except by grace." Thomas, *ST* III, q.70 a.4 (Leonine XII, 119–120). Thomas' theology of the law and Judaism is a highly disputed topic. See Cohen (1984) and in particular (1999), 364–389. For a list of scholarship critical of his position, see Cohen (1999), 364, n1. Boguslawski (2008) offers an unconvincing (in our opinion) critique of Cohen.
34. Holcot, *Quodl.* 72 (Molteni 177$^{1-14}$).
35. Holcot, *Quodl.* 72 (Molteni 203$^{7-10}$).
36. Holcot, *Quodl.* 72 (Molteni 202$^{26-31}$).
37. Holcot, *Quodl.* 72 (Molteni 174$^{26-35}$; 202^{31}–203^{3}).
38. See also Holcot, *Sent.* I, q.1 (L a.7rb; O 123ra): *Unde quidam ducti sunt ad fidem.*
39. Holcot, *Quodl.* 72 (Molteni 203$^{3-7}$). Arnold of Strelley and Walter Burley (†1344) held a similar position (Gelber [2004], 194–195). Pope John XXII condemned this view (c. 1330–1333), arguing that baptism was necessary for salvation (Courtenay [1990], 147–154). See also Oberman (2000), 243–248.
40. Cf. Gelber (2004), 294.
41. Cf. Holcot, *Sent.* III, q.1 (L n.i^{va}; O 176rb): *Quarto, dico, quod de istis...*
42. Henry Harclay, citing William of Auvergne, mentions (and rejects) similar cases involving both pagans and those who follow other religions. See Harclay, *Ordinary Questions* VII (Henninger I, 303).
43. Minnis (2009), 38–39 brought this text to our attention.
44. Hilton, *The Scale* II, c.3 (Bestul 138$^{115-118}$; Clark-Dorward 196).
45. Hilton, *The Scale* II, c.3 (Bestul 139$^{125-128}$; Clark-Dorward 197).
46. Minnis (2009), 38.
47. This section follows closely Gelber (2004), 151–190. Her transcriptions (and translations) of several key passages are followed (with occasional silent modifications).
48. Hoffmann (1972), 18–19, 276–277, 280–281, and 346–355. Gelber (2004), 151–190; and (in press).
49. Spade (2014).
50. Bradwardine, *Insolubilia* 9.1, 9.5.1, and 9.7 (Read 137, 143–45, 149), and Read's discussion at 44–45.

51. See Ockham, *Summa logicae* III-3, 39 (Gál-Brown 732[12–13]).
52. See also Novaes (2007), 145–214 (including discussions of Walter Burley, Roger Swyneshed, and Ralph Strode).
53. See Spade (1992) and King (1991).
54. Holcot, *Sent*. I, q.3 (L d.2^{rb-va}; O 132rb), trans. in Gelber (2004), 182.
55. These rules are found in Holcot, *Sent*. II, q.2, a.9 (Streveler-Tachau-Courtenay-Gelber 158^{1000}–159^{1019}), trans. in Gelber (2004), 174–175.
56. Leff (1957), 223.
57. On covenant, see Hamm (1977), 361–372.
58. Holcot, *Sap*. lec.146 (B1 492; B2 220rb); trans. in Oberman (1981), 149.
59. See Oberman (1962); (1981), 136–137; (2000). Hoffmann's analysis of Holcot's theological method was focused on the nature of logic and the obligational arts. He did not emphasize the covenantal nature of Holcot's thought. See Hoffmann's brief discussion of God's covenant (*Schwur Gottes*) in Hoffmann (1972), 355–358.
60. Oberman (1981), 136–137.
61. See Holcot, *Sap*. lec.146 (B1 492; B2 220rb). When discussing the covenant, Holcot distinguishes between compulsory necessity (*necessitas coactionis*) and unfailing necessity (*necessitas infallibilitatis*). God's compulsory necessity does not apply to the covenant; however, God's unfailing necessity is applicable to God by means of his promises and his covenant. Further, Holcot argues that this necessity is not an absolute necessity but a necessity of the consequences (*et haec non est necessitas absoluta, sed necessitas consequentiae*). As such, it is a necessity brought about by a previously enacted contingent act (in this case, God ordaining a particular covenant or dispensation).
62. This is even clear in the passage discussed by Oberman (1981), 149. See Holcot, *Sap*. lec.146 (B1 492; B2 220^{rb-va}): *Posset tamen Deus mutare* . . .
63. Though for two persons contradictory propositions can be true simultaneously.
64. Holcot, *Sap*. lec.146 (B1 492; B2 220va): *Dato quod foret* . . .
65. Holcot concludes the discussion of the potter and the clay with the statement that in this matter one should speak more piously than logically (*magis pie quam logice*). Holcot, *Sap*. lec.146 (B1 492; B2 220va). Here Holcot demonstrates a pastoral sensibility for his audience: that is, preachers should follow the rule of piety and not strict logic when discussing this analogy.
66. Gelber (2004), 339. On the distinction, see Courtenay (1984, 1990); Oakley (1984); and Oberman (2000). See, for example, Albert the Great, *Summa theologiae*, pt.1, tract.19, qu.78, membrum 2 (31: 832–834); Alexander of Hales, *Summa theologica* I, inq.I, tract.4, q.1, c.2, resp.2 (I, 207, col. 2); Aquinas, *ST* I, q.25, a.5 (Leonine IV, 295–296).
67. Courtenay (1984), IV, 2–7; Oakley (1984), 47–48.
68. Lombard, *Sent*. I, d.42 (Brady I, 294–298).

69. Gordon Leff argued that Holcot's distinction between the two powers meant that God "is capable of anything:" "while always paying court to God's law as ordained in this world, he is not confined by it." Leff attributed this *skepticism* to the fact that Holcot had a "lack of working faith." See Leff (1957), 222 and 227; and Kennedy (1993), 5.

70. Courtenay (1990), 16. For a historiographical overview, see 11–21.

71. See Vignaux (1948).

72. Oberman (2000), 38–50, here 37.

73. Ockham, *Quodl.* 6, q.1, a.1 (*OT* IX, Wey, 585^{14}–586^{30}) (Freddoso-Kelley, 491–492).

74. Courtenay (1974), 40–43.

75. Holcot, *Sent.* II, q.2, a.6 (L j.4va; O 152vb): *Deus potest facere quicquid* ... Holcot often employs the language of *ex privilegio speciali* interchangeably with *potentia absoluta*. This is evidence, as Courtenay argues, that Holcot understood the *potentia absoluta* in a juridical sense. See Courtenay (1984), IV, 17; and Gelber (2004), 339.

76. Holcot, *Quodlibet* 98 (B 200ra–200rb; P 220vb–221ra). It is transcribed and discussed in both Gelber (2004), 334–335; and Kennedy (1993), 180–181.

77. Gelber (2004), 334.

78. Here we follow Gelber (2004), 333–339, over and against Incandela (1994), 181–188 and Tachau (1996), 255.

79. The one caveat is that Holcot argued that God can replace one ordained order with another. The transition from one ordained system to another, Gelber argues, enabled theologians to explain the shift from one dispensation to the next without "involving God in a contradiction of His nature" (Gelber [2014], 4.2).

80. Ockham, *Quodl.* 6, q.1, a.1 (*OT* IX, Wey, 586$^{31-39}$) (Freddoso-Kelley, 492).

81. Quoted (with alterations) from Gelber (2004), 334, n50.

82. Courtenay (1990), 189.

CHAPTER 2

1. Holcot, *Sent.* I, q.1 (L a.2rb; O 121ra): *Ad oppositum quaestionis* ...

2. Holcot, *Sent.* I, q.1 (L a.2ra; O 120va): *Utrum quilibet viator existens* ...

3. The sense of divine *acceptatio* that Holcot has in mind presumes the assistance of a medicinal grace and then asks, within the context of this grace, what is required to achieve, acquire, or merit this second divinizing kind of grace. See Gillespie's (1974) 227, n1, discussion of Rondet.

4. Holcot, *Sent.* I, q.1 (L a.2ra; O 121ra): *Sexto sic ad principale* ...

5. Holcot, *Sent.* I, q.1 (L a.2ra; O 121ra): *Confirmatur ista ratio, quia* ...

6. E.g. Holcot, *Sent.* I, q.4 (L e.4^{va-vb}; O 137rb) ... *iste fruitur creatura, et tamen meritorie, quia ignorantia sua est invincibilis* ...

7. On the pastoral issue, note Laemers (2011), 125: "Perhaps it is even justifiable, especially from a pastoral viewpoint, to designate Holcot's and others'

theology, which lacks both fixed obligations and fixed rewards, as 'destructive' ..." We are arguing precisely the opposite of this claim.

8. Leff (1957), 221.

9. On Holcot's treatment of this topic in the context of his discussion with Peter Aureoli, see Gillespie (1974), 207–224, esp. 214. Cf. Aureoli, *Sent.* I, d.17, a.2 (Rome 1596), 408.

10. Clear definitions of these terms can be found in Thomas Aquinas, *Scriptum* II, d.27, q.1, a.3 (Mandonnet II, 701–703) and IV, d.15, q.1, a.3 (Moos IV, 650–658). Cf. Wawrykow (1996), 72.

11. Oberman (1981), 129.

12. See Gillespie (1974), 227–228.

13. Holcot, *Sent.* I, q.1, a.2 (L a.3[vb]; O 121[va]): *Omne meritum vel demeritum* ...

14. Holcot, *Sent.* I, q.1, a.2 (L a.3[vb]; O 121[va–vb]): *Ideo enim homo meretur* ...

15. Holcot, *Sent.* I, q.1, a.2 (L a.3[vb]; O 121[vb]): *Secundo sic: et est* ...

16. Holcot, *Sent.* I, q.1, a.2 (L a.3[vb]; O 121[vb]): *Tertio patet hoc idem de meritorio* ...

17. Holcot, *Sent.* I, q.1, a.2 (L a.3[vb]; O 121[vb]): *Tertio patet hoc idem de meritorio* ...

18. Holcot, *Sent.* I, q.4, a.3 (L d.6[vb]; O 134[va]): *Prima est affirmativa* ... Holcot's position is rather infamous, and scholastic thinkers continued to attribute it to him in the late fourteenth century. In his *Sentences* commentary, Peter Plaoul (fl. 1390s) attributed this position to both Holcot and Adam Wodeham. Plaoul, *Comm.*, lec.47 (R4 75[ra]). See Witt (2014) for lecture divisions.

19. Holcot, *Sent.* I, q.4, a.3 (L d.7[ra]; O 134[va]): *Secunda conclusio est ista* ...

20. Holcot, *Sent.* I, q.1, a.2 (L a.3[vb]; O 121[vb]): *Licet quodammodo ex pacto* ...

21. Oberman (2000), 148, 167–174, 246–247; McGrath (2005), c.2; and Hamm (1977).

22. Holcot, *Sent.* I, q.1, a.2 (L a.3[vb]; O 121[vb]): *Sit tamen Deus illud* ...

23. For a discussion of the historiography, see Oberman (2000), 30–38. For a critical presentation of Holcot, see Kennedy (1993), 29–34.

24. Holcot, *Sent.* I, q.1, a.4 (L a.4[rb]; O 121[vb]): *Ista propositio quantum ad* ...

25. Meissner (1953), 87–93; cf. Gillespie (1974), 73–76.

26. Holcot, *Sent.* I, q.1, a.4 (L a.4[rb]; O 121[vb]): *Et isto modo videtur* ...

27. On the *de lege communi*, see Holcot, *Sap.* lec.4 (B1 15; B2 7[va]), lec.16 (B1 59; B2 27[vb]). For a discussion of *lege statuata*, see Gillespie (1974), 75.

28. See chapter 1.

29. Oberman (2000), 212–213.

30. For an interpretation of Ockham along these lines, see Leff (1975), 528–560.

31. Cf. Oberman (1962), 328, and Vignaux (1948).

32. See Gillespie (1974), 96.

33. Holcot, *Sent.* I, q.1, a.5 (L a.4[va–vb]; O 122[ra]): *Ubi sciendum est quod* ...

34. Holcot, *Sent.* I, q.1, a.5 (L a.5[ra]; O 122[ra]): "Si ponatur quod aliquis assentiat et sit in gratia, dicendum est quod talis meretur non quia credit, nec quia

vult credere praecise, sed quia vult credere, et Deus acceptat actum suum credendi tamquam dignum praemio. Ideo tamquam praecipua causa concedendum est quod ipse meretur, sic ergo patet ad formam quaestionis."

35. Holcot, *Sent.* I, q.1, a.1 (L a.2va; O 121ra): *Unde non intelligo* ... This qualification is criticized by later readers, for example, Plaoul, *Comm.*, lec.4 (R4 5rb).

36. Holcot, *Sent.* I, q.1, a.1 (L a.2va; 121ra): *Sed pono aliquem* ...

37. Holcot, *Sent.* I, q.1, a.1 (L a.2va; 121ra): *Tunc quaero an iste* ...

38. Holcot, *Sent.* I, q.1, a.1 (L a.2va; O 121^{ra-rb}): "Primo sic: non est in potestate hominis opinari libere unam propositionem sibi dubiam, ergo non est in potestate hominis credere articulo fidei, vel assentire propositioni sibi dubiae."

39. For example, consider the definition of faith as "certain but non-evident assent" offered by Pierre d'Ailly, *Sent.* I, prol., q.1, a.2 (*CCCM* 258, 175$^{70-75}$).

40. Hugolino, *Sent.* I, q.4, a.2 (Eckermann I, 132).

41. The position of Hugolino should be seen as the common or moderate position. In two separate listings of possible descriptions of faith—by Peter Plaoul and John Mair—this is adopted as the best description and is situated between two extremes, one of which is, in both cases, attributed to Holcot. Cf. Plaoul, *Comm.*, lec.1 (R4 1^{ra-vb}); Mair, *Sent. I*, prol., q.1 (1510 1^{rb-va}).

42. Cf. Chisholm (1964), 11. See Scotus, *Ord.* I, prol., pars 5, q.1–2, n.231 (Vatican I, 157).

43. Chisholm (1964), 11.

44. Hugolino, *Sent.* I, q.3, a.1 (Eckermann I, 111–112).

45. See the previous discussion.

46. Hugolino, *Sent.* I, q.3, a.1 (Eckermann I, 111–112).

47. Hugolino, *Sent.* I, q.3, a.1 (Eckermann I, 111–112).

48. Holcot, *Sent.* I, q.1, a.6 (L a.6rb; O 122vb): "Unde concedo quod homo quantumcumque fuerit infidelis, si coram eo fierent miracula insolita ad ostensionem veritatis talium articulorum; puta quod mortui resuscitarentur per praedicationes talium articulorum, qui mortui similiter testarentur veritatem talium. Dico quod talis infidelis necessitaretur ad credendum. Similiter si constaret sibi evidenter unam multitudinem hominum esse veracem in verbis, et honestam in vita et peritam et circumspectam in naturalibus sive in naturaliter scibilibus; et talis multitudo assereret constanter quaedam esse credenda; ad quae ratio naturalis non attingit nec attingere potest in praesenti. Dico quod esset bene possibile necessitare talem infidelem et capacem rationis ad assensum quorumcumque credendorum, ad hoc enim deserviunt miracula et rationes quaedam probabiles, quae sufficiunt ad causandum fidem."

49. Cf. Hugolino, *Sent.* I, prol., q.3, a.3 (Eckermann I, 118–119).

50. Cf. Lang (1930), 159–164; Gillespie (1974), 63–64.

51. Aristotle, *Post. An.* I, c.2 (72^{a}25–72^{b}4).

52. Holcot, *Sent.* I, q.1, a.6 (L a.5rb; O 122rb): "Contra, [P1] omne quod contrariatur fidei, est falsum, [P2] sed conclusum per rationem naturalem contrariatur fidei, [C] ergo conclusio demonstrationis est falsa."

53. Holcot, *Sent.* I, q.1, a.6 (L a.6vb; O 123ra): *Sed tu dicis quod* ...

54. Holcot, *Sent.* I, q.1 (L a.6vb–a.7ra): *Unde omnis talis demonstratio* ...

55. Scholastic criticism of Holcot's position is present in the writings of Hugolino, *Sent.* I, prol., q.3, a.3 (Eckermann I, 118); Plaoul, *Comm.*, lec.11, n.5 (R4 16ra); and Mair, *Sent. I*, prol., q.1 (1510 3rb).

56. The possibility of a sophism being mistaken for an actual demonstration is mentioned by Aquinas in *SCG* I, 7 (Pegis I, 74–75). Aquinas believes that one reason God provided humans with revealed truths was to expose these instances of apparent natural reasoning as false.

57. Holcot, *Sent.* I, q.1, a.6 (L a.5rb; O 122rb): *Praeterea gratia non destruit* ... Cf. Aquinas, *ST* I, q.1, a.8, ad.2 (Leonine IV, 22).

58. Holcot, *Sent.* I, q.1, a.6 (L a.7ra; O 123ra): *Unde illud desiderium naturale* ...

59. Holcot, *Sent.* I, q.1, a.6 (L a.7ra; O 123ra): *Fides est instituta* ...

60. Holcot, *Sent.* I, q.1, a.6 (L a.7ra; O 123ra): *Ergo non perficit naturam* ...

61. See the previous discussion.

62. Holcot, *Sent.* I, q.1, a.6 (L a.7va; O 123^{ra-rb}): *Ad istud dico quod* ...

63. Holcot, *Sent.* I, q.1, a.6 (L a.5rb; O 122rb): *Praeterea si ratio naturalis* ...

64. Holcot, *Sent.* I, q.1, a.6 (L a.7ra; O 123ra): *Ad tertium quando arguitur* ...

65. Holcot, *Sent.* I, q.1, a.6 (L a.5rb; O 122rb): *Praeterea si sic, tota* ...

66. Holcot, *Sent.* I, q.1, a.6 (L a.5vb; O 122va): "Uno modo assentire quod sic est in re sicut per illam propositionem denotatur, et sic accipitur credere communissime."

67. Holcot, *Sent.* I, q.1, a.6 (L a.5vb; O 122va): *Unde illa propositio* ...

68. Holcot, *Sent.* I, q.1, a.6 (L a.5vb; O 122va): "Alio modo accipitur credere magis stricte, pro assentire propositionibus de quarum veritate non constat nisi per testimonium alienum ..."

69. Holcot, *Sent.* I, q.1, a.6 (L a.5vb; O 122va): "Tertio modo accipitur credere strictissime pro assentire revelato a Deo et testimonio per miracula, et velle vivere et operari secundum ea."

70. Holcot, *Sent.* I, q.1, a.6 (L a.5vb; O 122va): *Sic credere includit* ...

71. This threefold division of the meaning of belief is not unique to Holcot. See Mair, *Sent. I*, prol., q.1 (1510 1rb) and Lombard, *Sent.* III, d.23, c.3 (Brady II, 142$^{2-4}$). What is different about Mair's third and strictest definition (and, for that matter, the definition of Lombard) is that Holcot couples this assent with a *desire to believe* and a desire to live according to the apparent truths of religion. This ethical impulse is absent in the definitions offered by both Mair and Lombard.

72. Holcot, *Sent.* I, q.1, a.6 (L a.5vb; O 122va): "Similiter potest dici quod velle assentire vel acceptare assensum vel gaudere de assensu est meritorium."

73. Holcot, *Sent.* I, q.1, a.5 (L a.5ra; 122ra): "Si ponatur quod aliquis assentiat et sit in gratia, dicendum est quod talis meretur non quia credit, nec quia vult credere praecise, sed quia vult credere, et Deus acceptat actum suum credendi

tamquam dignum praemio. Ideo tamquam praecipua causa concedendum est quod ipse meretur, sic ergo patet ad formam quaestionis."
74. Holcot, *Sent.* I, q.1, a.6 (L a.5ra; O 122^{ra-rb}).
75. See Plaoul, *Comm.*, lec.82 (R4 129ra); and Mirandola, *Apologia*, 199–229.
76. Holcot, *Sent.* I, q.1, a.6 (L a.5ra; O 122rb): *Praeterea tunc nec* ... and Holcot, *Sent.* I, q.1, a.6 (L a.6vb; O 122vb): *Ad quartum argumentum* ...
77. Holcot, *Sent.* I, q.1, a.6 (L a.6vb; O 122vb): "Infidelitas est nolle credere quae ecclesia credit."
78. Holcot, *Sent.* I, q.1, a.6 (L a.6vb; O 122vb): "Vel nolle vivere secundum fidem, id est, secundum praecepta fidei."
79. Holcot, *Sent.* I, q.1, a.6 (L a.6vb; O 122vb): "Unde odire fidem mores et ritum Christianorum est peccatum infidelitatis."
80. Holcot, *Sent.* I, q.1, a.6 (L a.6vb; O 122vb): "Non omnis autem error in iis quae fidei sunt est peccatum infidelitatis vel haeresis, quia posito quod aliquis in generali velit credere omnia quae Spiritus Sanctus revelavit ecclesiae esse credenda, et sub hac fide credat errando contineri quoddam oppositum alicui articulo subtili, ad cuius fidem explicitam non omnes tenentur, et per consequens si adhaereat illi, habens tamen promptum animum credendi ea sola quae ecclesia credit, talis non est haereticus nec infidelis."

CHAPTER 3

1. Gelber (1974), 268.
2. Prantl (1855–1870), III, 328.
3. Prantl (1855–1870), IV, 6–9.
4. For the historiography, see Gelber (1974), 268–270 (who we follow here).
5. Boehner (1992), 372. The *Centiloquium theologicum* was edited (as spurious) in *OP* 7, 371–505.
6. See Gelber (1988), 255–289 and (2004), 79–83, esp. 80–81.
7. See Leff (1957), 216–227 and Smalley (1956), 82.
8. Meissner (1953), 52–57. Meissner accepts the general claim that Holcot is a skeptic but begins the process of rethinking the critical passages where Holcot discusses the two logics.
9. See Hoffmann (1972).
10. Oberman (2000), 241.
11. See chapter 2.
12. Schepers (1970, 1972).
13. Hoffmann (1972), 11.
14. Hoffmann (1972), 25–26 and 303.
15. Hoffmann (1972), 34.
16. Hoffmann (1972), 40.
17. See Kitanov (2014), 93–95.
18. Holcot, *Sent.* I, q.4 (L d.4rb–e.8va; O 133rb–139rb).
19. Holcot, *Sent.* I, q.4 (L e.1rb; O 135va): *Probatur prima sic: non potest* ...

20. Holcot, *Sent.* I, q.4 (L e.1rb; O 135va): *Prima sic: nulla propositio* . . .
21. Holcot, *Sent.* I, q.4 (L e.1^{ra-rb}; O 135va): *Secunda est, haec hypothetica* . . .
22. Gelber (*SEP*).
23. For our discussion of the reception of Anselm's argument we follow closely Logan (2009), 131–149.
24. Hoffmann used the anachronistic Kantian phrase "Ontological Argument" to describe this argument in Anselm and Holcot. See Hoffmann (1972), 118–120; (1971), 302, n24. We follow the medieval tradition, including Holcot, and simply refer to the argument as Anselm's argument (*ratio Anselmi*).
25. Anselm, *Proslogion* 2 (Schmitt I, 101^{13}–102^3) (Davies-Evans 88–89).
26. Logan (2009), 131.
27. Logan (2009), 131–137.
28. Logan (2009), 13–143.
29. Cf. Holcot, *Quodl.* 86 (Muckle 147).
30. Holcot, *Sent.* I, q.4 (L e.2^{rb-va}; O 136ra): *Anselmus Proslogion, ca. secundo* . . .
31. Holcot, *Sent.* I, q.4 (L e.3^{rb-va}; O 136^{va-vb}).
32. Holcot, *Sent.* I, q.4 (L e.3rb; O 136va): *Ad aliud potest dici* . . .
33. Holcot, *Sent.* I, q.4 (L e.3rb; O 136va): *Unde ad argumentum in sua forma* . . . Note that Hoffmann (1971), 302, n24 quotes an identical passage and mistakenly attributes it to Holcot's *Quodlibets* (R 28rb). However, in R the commentary on the *Sentences* is on folios 7–137 and the quodlibets begin on folio 141.
34. Holcot, *Sent.* I, q.4 (L e.3va; O 136^{va-vb}): *Unde per eandem formam* . . . See also Logan (2009), 147.
35. Logan (2009), 147.
36. For a review of the literature, see Oberman (1962) 319, nn14–16.
37. Oberman (1962), 318.
38. Holcot, *Sent.* I, q.4 (L e.2vb; O 136rb): *Contra Apostolus dicit* . . . Cf. Hoffmann (1971), 638.
39. Holcot, *Sent.* I, q.4 (L e.2vb; O 136rb): *Ad dictum Apostoli, invisibilia* . . .
40. This section is consistent with the arugment Holcot defends in his commentary on Wisdom. See chapter 8.
41. The objection is found at Holcot, *Sent.* I, q.4 (L e.2rb), the response at (L e.3^{ra-rb}). The text is cited by Oberaman (1962), 321, n25.
42. Holcot, *Sent.* I, q.4 (L e.3^{ra-rb}; O 136va): *Ad auctoritatem Apostoli, gentes* . . .
43. See chapter 1.
44. Holcot, *Sent.* I, q.4 (L e.3^{ra-rb}; O 136va): *Viventes secundum principia* . . .
45. Oberman (1962), 321.
46. Hoffmann (1971), 638.
47. Servetus, *De Trinitatis erroribus*, I (Alcalá II-2, 667).
48. Ockham, *SL* III-1, c.16 (*OP* I, 403$^{4-5}$).
49. Holcot, *Quodl.* 90 (Gelber, 79^{368}–80^{416}).
50. Ockham, *SL* III-1, c.16 (*OP* I, 403$^{9-12}$).

51. Ockham, *SL* III-1, c.16 (*OP* I, 403$^{24-28}$).
52. Ockham, *SL* III-1, c.16 (*OP* I, 404$^{32-37}$).
53. Gelber (1974), 223–226.
54. Ockham, *SL* III-4, c.16 (*OP* I, 822$^{120-121}$).
55. Ockham, *SL* III-1, c.16 (*OP* I, 404$^{44-45}$).
56. Holcot, *Sent.* I, q.5 (L e.8va; O 139rb). Holcot argues that it would seem that God is not three distinct persons, because three persons are three gods (*tres personae sunt tres dii*), therefore one God is not three persons (*igitur, unus Deus non est tres personae*).
57. Holcot, *Sent.* I, q.5 (L e.8va; O 139rb).
58. Holcot, *Sent.* I, q.5 (L e.8vb; O 139rb).
59. Holcot, *Sent.* I, q.5 (L f.1rb; O 139va): *Ad istam quaestionem* . . .
60. See Anselm, *Epistola de incarnatione Verbi* 1 (Schmitt II, 6^6–7^4) (Davies-Evans 235). Holcot, *Sent.* I, q.5 (L f.1rb; O 139va).
61. Holcot, *Sent.* I, q.5 (L e.8vb; O 139rb). See also Knuuttila (1993).
62. Holcot, *Sent.* I, q.5 (L f.2ra; O 139vb–140ra). A transcription of this passage is found in Gelber (1983), 26–27, n72.
63. See Hoffmann (1972), 280–281 and (1998), 640. More broadly, see Hoffmann (1972), 88–92, 104–107.
64. Gelber (1974), 266–267.
65. Holcot, *Quodl.* 90 (Gelber 80$^{398-401}$).
66. See Hoffmann (1972), 281, n89; 347–348, n161; and Gelber (2004), 183–184.
67. Kennedy (1993), 9–21.
68. Holcot, *Sent.* I, q.5 (L f.2ra; O 140ra).
69. Augustine, *De Trin.* 5.1.1–8.9 (*CCSL* 50, 206–215; *WSA* 1.5, 189–194).
70. Anselm, *De processione Spiritus Sancti* 1 (Schmitt II, 181$^{2-4}$). On the origin of the *regula Anselmi* and its reception in the fourteenth century, see Slotemaker (2012b).
71. Holcot, *Quodl.* 90 (Gelber 68$^{78-81}$; 77$^{318-319}$; and 108$^{1152-1154}$).
72. Holcot, *Sent.* I, q.5 (L e.8vb; O 139rb).
73. See the statement *Extra de summa Trinitate et fide catholica*, in *Dec. Greg.*, lib. I, tit.1, c.1 (Friedberg 2.7): "Et ideo in Deo solummodo trinitas est, non quaternitas . . ."
74. Holcot, *Sent.* I, q.5 (L f.2ra; O 140ra): *dico quod si non* . . .
75. Holcot, *Sent.* I, q.5 (L f.2ra; O 140ra): *si vis vocare logicam* . . .
76. See Gelber (1974), 267.
77. Hoffmann (1998), 637.
78. Holcot, *Quodl.* 87 (Gelber 33$^{45-48}$).
79. Holcot, *Quodl.* 87 (Gelber 33$^{51-57}$).
80. Gelber (1974), 280–281.
81. For the *rationem fidei* see Romans 12:6.
82. William, *Enigma fidei*, 41 (*PL* 180, 417) (trans. J.D. Anderson, 73–74).
83. See Ayres (2010) and Gioia (2008).

84. See quodlibetal questions 87, 90, and 91, in Gelber (1983), 29–51, 63–112 and 53–61. See also Friedman (2010), 155–158; and Friedman (2013), II, 733–742.
85. See Friedman (2013), II, 601–871; Slotemaker (2012a), 248–326 and 338–394.
86. See Cross (2005), 184–202 and 233–244.
87. On these debates see Friedman (2013), I, 1–216.
88. On Chatton and Crathorn, see Friedman (2013), II, 683–715 and 733–742.
89. Holcot, *Quodl.* 87 (Gelber $40^{198-201}$); and *Quodl.* 90 (Gelber $102^{1001-1003}$).
90. Holcot, *Quodl.* 87 (Gelber $48^{391-394}$).
91. Holcot, *Quodl.* 90 (Gelber $102^{1038-1042}$).
92. Holcot, *Quodl.* 90 (Gelber $107^{1119-1120}$).
93. Holcot, *Sap.* lec.29 (B1 103; B2 47vb): *Natura non deficit in necessariis* . . .
94. Holcot, *Sap.* lec.29 (B1 103; B2 47vb): *Nam si homo facit quod in se est* . . .
95. Holcot, *Sap.* lec.29 (B1 102; B2 47rb): *Si invincibilis, excusatur* . . .
96. Holcot, *Sap.* lec.29 (B1 102; B2 47rb): *Si est error vincibilis* . . .

CHAPTER 4

1. Holcot, *Sent.* II, q.2 (Streveler-Tachau-Courtenay-Gelber $122^{227-233}$). This is the fourth of Holcot's arguments in response to this debated proposition.
2. Holcot, *Sent.* II, q.2 (Streveler-Tachau-Courtenay-Gelber $122^{230-232}$).
3. Cf. Hintikka (1973), 148–149; Frede (1985); Gaskin (1995); and Byrd (2010).
4. Byrd (2010), 160.
5. Aristotle, *De Interpretatione* (18^a28-19^b4). Cf. Schabel (2000), 18.
6. Schabel (2000), 19.
7. Byrd (2010), 161.
8. Holcot, *Sent* II, q.2 (Streveler-Tachau-Courtenay-Gelber $122^{233-241}$).
9. Aristotle, *Post. An.*, I, c.2 (71^b9-72^b4).
10. Boethius, *Consolation of Philosophy*, IV and V.
11. Tachau (1996), 244. Cf. Gelber (2004), 205: "If the contingency of events were denied, the problem of uncertainty about propositions about the future would be resolved. However, free will, both divine and human, would be forfeit."
12. Later, in article 7, Holcot identifies the position of future indeterminacy and freedom with the philosophers and the position of the determinacy and omnipotence with the theologians. Cf. Holcot, *Sent.* II, q.2, a.7 (Streveler-Tachau-Courtenay-Gelber 145–146); and Schabel (2000), 249, n84.
13. As we will see, from one perspective this is partly what he does, though we need to be attentive to the nuances that he believes makes this concession palatable. Once again, Holcot will show his penchant for putting forward an

extreme or paradoxical position and then softening the sting of that assertion with important qualifications.

14. Holcot, *Sent.* II, q.2, a.7 (Streveler-Tachau-Courtenay-Gelber $145^{754-747}$).
15. Holcot, *Sent.* II, q.2, a.7 (Streveler-Tachau-Courtenay-Gelber 145^{750}).
16. Holcot, *Sent.* II, q.2 (Streveler-Tachau-Courtenay-Gelber $126^{318-320}$); cf. Holcot, *Sent.* II, q.2, a.7 (Streveler-Tachau-Courtenay-Gelber $146^{758-759}$).
17. Schabel (2000), 248–249.
18. Cf. Holcot, *Sent* II, q.2 (Streveler-Tachau-Courtenay-Gelber $127^{324-325}$); and Gelber (2004), 172.
19. Schabel (2000), 248.
20. Cf. Schabel (2000), 250.
21. See Schabel (2000), 249, esp. n86. Holcot, *Quodl.* 68 (Streveler-Tachau-Courtenay-Gelber [*Quodl.* 3.1] 63^{93-96}).
22. See Schabel (2000), 241.
23. The move to privileging modality and subsequently identifying distinct categories of truth is visible in some "nontraditional" interpretations of Aristotle. See for example Anscombe (1956) and a refutation of this view in Frede (1985), 46.
24. Gelber (2014).
25. Holcot, *Sent.* II, q.2, a.7 (Streveler-Tachau-Courtenay-Gelber $146^{758-760}$).
26. See Gelber (2004), 177.
27. See Holcot, *Sent.* II, q.2 (Streveler-Tachau-Courtenay-Gelber 126^{320}); see Gelber (2004), 172. Cf. Schabel (2000), 248.
28. See Gelber (2004), 172; she points to Holcot, *Sent.* II, q.2 (Streveler-Tachau-Courtenay-Gelber $127^{324-325}$).
29. See Tachau (1996), 253–254; Schabel (2000), 249.
30. Cf. Holcot, *Quodl.* 86 (Muckle, 127–153), here 129.
31. Holcot, *Sent.* II, q.2, a.8 (Streveler-Tachau-Courtenay-Gelber $151^{853-863}$).
32. Holcot, *Sent.* II, q.2, a.8 (Streveler-Tachau-Courtenay-Gelber $151^{853-855}$).
33. Holcot, *Sent.* II, q.2, a.8 (Streveler-Tachau-Courtenay-Gelber $151^{855-858}$).
34. Holcot, *Sent.* II, q.2, a.8 (Streveler-Tachau-Courtenay-Gelber $151^{858-863}$).
35. Tachau (1996), 253.
36. Holcot, *Sent.* II, q.2, a.8 (Streveler-Tachau-Courtenay-Gelber $152^{870-874}$).
37. Cf. Tachau (1996), 253.
38. As Schabel notes, this concern was in ascendency at Oxford when Holcot was lecturing there, a fact he attributes to the preoccupation of Holcot's predecessor Richard FitzRalph. See Schabel (2000), 246; cf. Tachau (1996), 249. See also Holcot, *Sent.* II, q.2, a.8 (Streveler-Tachau-Courtenay-Gelber $159^{919-924}$).
39. In this section we follow closely Incandela (1994). For a brief qualification/correction of Incandela, see Gelber (2004), 335, n51.
40. Incandela (1994), 167.
41. Cf. Gelber (2004), 200.

42. Holcot, *Quodl.* 70 (Streveler-Tachau-Courtenay-Gelber [*Quodl.* 3.3] 76^{37-46}), trans., with changes, in Incandela (1994), 171.

43. See Holcot, *Quodl.* 73 (Streveler-Tachau-Courtenay-Gelber [*Quodl.* 3.8] $88^{189-197}$).

44. See chapter 5.

45. Holcot, *Quodl.* 73 (Streveler-Tachau-Courtenay-Gelber [*Quodl.* 3.8] $108^{667-669}$), trans. in Incandela (1994), 172–173.

46. Holcot, *Sent.* II, q.2, a.8 (Streveler-Tachau-Courtenay-Gelber $156^{954-966}$), cf. Incandela (1994), 172; cf. Tachau (1996), 250: "For Holcot, however, divine deception was not only logically possible *de potentia Dei absoluta*, but *also* possible under the divine order presently constituted."

47. Gelber (2004), 202–203.

48. Richard FitzRalph, *Sent.* I, q.18, a.4, resp. ad 8 (BN1 134vb). See Leff (1963), 30. Note that Leff identifies this as q.16, but the ongoing FitzRalph edition identifies this as q.18.

49. Holcot, *Quodl.* 73 (Streveler-Tachau-Courtenay-Gelber [*Quodl.* 3.8] $99^{442-443}$), cf. Incandela (1994), 172.

50. Holcot, *Sent.* II, q.2 (Streveler-Tachau-Courtenay-Gelber $134^{490-492}$), cf. Incandela (1994), 176.

51. Holcot, *Quodl.* 70 (Streveler-Tachau-Courtenay-Gelber [*Quodl.* 3.3] $77^{71}-78^{80}$), trans. in Incandela (1994), 177.

52. See note 51.

53. Incandela (1994), 178; cf. Gelber (2004), 219.

CHAPTER 5

1. Cameron (1991), 157; see *DThC* x, 335–354; xiv, 532ff., and 579ff.

2. In the medieval context, Harran links the concept of conversion to these three sacraments (1983), 44–45. Cf. Trigg (1994), 157–158.

3. See Harran (1983), 56–85; Trigg (1994), 160–161.

4. Cameron (1991), 79–80.

5. In light of Marcia Colish's account of "baptism by desire" in Lombard and early Lombardians, Holcot's position seems fairly in step with the overall tradition. See Colish (2014), 56.

6. Holcot, *Sent.* IV, q.1, a.1 (L $n.5^{rb-va}$; O 192rb): *Ita quod si aliquod* . . .

7. Here Holcot identifies three general modes, further divided into six special modes of changing the verbal form of baptism. These are (1) change in substance, (2) change in quantity, and (3) change in order. These are divided further into (1a) whole or (1b) in part; (2a) adding or (2b) subtracting; (3a) transposing or (3b) inserting. Holcot, *Sent.* IV, q.1, a.2 (L $n.5^{vb}-n.6^{ra}$; O 192va).

8. Holcot, *Sent.* IV, q.1, a.2 (L $n.6^{ra}$; O 192va): *Si modica sicut sternutatio* . . .

9. Holcot, *Sent.* IV, q.1, a.2 (L $n.5^{vb}$; O 192va): *Sicut fecit Arius* . . . Many of these are stock examples, see Guido, *HFC* I.2 (20).

10. After providing the example of Arius, Holcot explains that a change of the form introduced out of simplicity and devotion—such as adding the name "blessed virgin, mother of God"—would not block the efficacy of the sacrament. See Holcot, *Sent.* IV, q.1, a.1 (L n.5vb; O 192va): *Si tamen addit aliquid* ... and *Si fiat transpositio* ... Cf. Guido, *HFC* I.2 (20).

11. See note 28.

12. See Spinks (2006) for some precedent for this concern about water as the most fitting element in earlier scholastics like Hugh of St. Victor, Peter Lombard, and Bonaventure.

13. Holcot, *Sent.* IV, q.1, a.3 (L n.6ra; O 192^{va-vb}).

14. Holcot, *Sent.* IV, q.1, a.6 (L n.6va; O 192vb): *Deletio peccati originalis* ...

15. Holcot, *Sent.* IV, q.1, a.6 (L n.6va; O 192vb): *Infusio gratiae de novo* ...

16. See Lombard, *Sent.* IV, dd.2–6 (Brady II, 239–276); see also Holcot, *Sent.* IV, q.1 (L n.4vb; O 192ra).

17. Holcot, *Sent.* IV, q.1, a.6 (L n.6va; O 192vb): *Remissio poenae satisfactoriae* ... Holcot is not the only one to identify the removal of the penalty and the guilt as separate effects (e.g., see the discussion of Biel in Spinks [2006], 148).

18. Holcot, *Sent.* IV, q.1 (L n.5ra; O 192rb): *Sexto ad principale* ...

19. Holcot, *Sent.* IV, q.1, a.8 (L 0.2^{ra}; O 194va): *Ad sextum quando arguitur* ...

20. Holcot, *Sent.* IV, q.1, a.6 (L n.6va; O 192vb). Cf. Colish (2014), 72.

21. Colish (2014), 72–73; see William of Auxerre, *Summa aurea* 4, tract.5, c.2, q.1 (4:72–74).

22. Colish (2014), 73.

23. Ibid.

24. Holcot, *Sent.* IV, q.1 (L n.4vb; O 192ra): *Si sic baptismus foret aliquo modo causa effectiva gratiae* ...

25. See Spinks (2006), 146–148; Cross (1999), 136; and Humber (1926), 9–38.

26. Spinks (2006), 147.

27. Contrast this view with that of Thomas Aquinas, e.g. Spinks (2006), 146.

28. Holcot, *Sent.* IV, q.1, a.8, ad.3 (L 0.1^{vb}; O 194rb): "Ad tertium principale quando arguitur quod si baptismus foret gratia effectiva gratiae, tunc posset creatura causare, potest dici quod aliquid dicitur causa effectiva dupliciter, proprie et metaphorice. Sacramenta enim non sunt efficientes causae proprie gratiae, sed solus Deus. Metaphorice dicuntur merita nostra causae tam gratiae quam augmenti gratiae, et similiter sacramenta, quia ad perfectionem sacramentorum Deus confert et causat gratiam."

29. Holcot, *Sent.* IV, q.1, a.5 (L n.6va; O 192vb): *Dicendum est quod regulariter* ...

30. Trigg (1994), 81–92, esp. 82–83; for Luther on infant baptism see Brinkel (1958).

31. See Luther's discussion in the *Larger Catechism* (*WA* 30, I, 219).

32. Holcot, *Sent.* IV, q.1, a.4 (L n.6rb; O 192vb): *Si parvulus, nihil requiritur* ...

33. Holcot, *Sent.* IV, q.1, a.4 (L n.6rb; O 192vb): *In articulo tamen necessitatis* ...

34. Holcot, *Sent.* IV, q.1, a.4 (L n.6rb; O 192vb): *Si vero manus vel pes* . . .
35. Holcot, *Sent.* IV, q.1, a.4 (L n.6rb; O 192vb): *Nihil tamen nocet si aspergatur* . . .
36. See Cross (2012).
37. Holcot, *Sent.* IV, q.1, a.4 (L n.6va; O 192vb): *Et ideo amentes et dormientes* . . .
38. Holcot, *Sent.* IV, q.1, a.4 (L n.6va; O 192vb): *Si vero adultus baptizandus* . . .
39. Holcot, *Sent.* IV, q.1, a.4 (L n.6va; O 192vb): *Si tamen voluntarium est mixtum* . . .
40. See Colish (2014), 55–71, *passim*.
41. One mention of a case where the *sacramentum* is received without the *res* can be found in Colish (2104), 68, in her discussion of Radulphus Ardens.
42. Cf. Wodeham, *Ord.* IV, q.3 (S 165va–166vb).
43. Holcot, *Sent.* IV, q.1, a.7 (L n.6vb; O 193ra): *Credo quod salvaretur* . . .
44. This scenario is recognized and mocked by Peter of Poitiers, *Sententiarum libri quinque* V, c.5 (*PL* 211, 132). Guido, *HFC* I.4 (25–26). This case is also discussed in Wodeham, *Ord.* IV, q.3, dub.4 (S 166^{ra-rb}).
45. Holcot, *Sent.* IV, q.1, a.7 (L n.7va; O 193rb): *Quia sacramenta ecclesiastica sunt sacramenta unitatis* . . . (cf. Wodeham, *Ord.* IV, q.3, dub.4 [S 166rb]).
46. See Gratian's *Decretum* in *Dec. Greg*, p.2, ca.7, q.1, cn.16 (Friedberg 1.573–574); p.1, d.23, cn.14 (Friedberg 1.84).
47. Wodeham uses the same example to make the same point regarding the indivisibility of essential parts. See *Ord.* IV, q.3, dub.4 (S 166rb).
48. See Goering (2008), 221.
49. Goering (2008) provides a helpful picture of the scholastic positions on confession and penance that Holcot inherited.
50. See Goering (2008), 222, n9.
51. Goering (2008), 224.
52. See Goering (2008), 224.
53. Frantzen (1983), 202–203, quoted in Goering (2008), 225.
54. Lombard, *Sent.* IV, d.17 (Brady II, 342–355).
55. Goering (2008), 229.
56. Cf. Goering (2008), 228.
57. Kelly (2008), 241.
58. Canon 21 of Lateran IV can be found in, *Dec. Greg.*, V, tit.38, cap.12 (Friedberg 2.887–888), cf. Goering (2008), 227.
59. Goering (2008), 227.
60. Holcot, *Sent.* IV, q.4, resp. (L p.1vb; O 199ra): "Ad quaestionem dico quod aliquid est necessarium ad salutem dupliciter. Vel quia sine illo impossibile est habere salutem vel quia sic ordinatum quod non est in libera potestate voluntatis illud contemnere et salutem habere. Primo modo nullum sacramentum est necessarium ad salutem . . . Secundo modo confessio est necessaria ad salutem hoc est confessio est medium ordinatum ad salutem, ita quod non est in potestate hominis isto contempto obtinere salutem."

61. Holcot, *Sent*. IV, q.4, resp. (L p.1vb–2ra; O 198vb): *Quod non quia ex sola contritione peccatum remittitur* ...
62. Holcot, *Sent*. IV, q.4 (L p.1vb; O 199ra): *Ad primam rationem dico* ...
63. Holcot, *Sent*. IV, q.4 (L p.1vb; O 199ra): *Argumentum tamen bene concludit* ...
64. Holcot, *Sent*. IV, q.4 (L p.1va; O 199ra): *Praeterea confessio facienda* ...
65. Lombard, *Sent*. IV, d.17, c.4 (Brady II, 351$^{12-13}$).
66. Holcot, *Sent*. IV, q.4 (L p.1vb; O 199ra): *Ad tertium dicitur quod scientia adquisita* ...
67. Holcot, *Sent*. IV, q.5 (L p.2ra; O 200vb): "Utrum poenitenti et confesso non proprio sacerdoti, habenti tamen commissionem generalem audiendi confessiones, necesse sit eadem peccata iterum confiteri proprio sacerdoti."
68. Holcot, *Sent*. IV, q.5 (L p.2ra; O 200vb): *quia sic, quia Extra* ...
69. See Pantin (2010), 155.
70. The three assertions, condemned and subsequently targeted by Holcot, were advanced by John of Pouilly in his quodlibetal questions. On John of Pouilly, see Sikes (1934) and Thijssen (1998), 17–26.
71. For more on the controversy, see Szittya (1986); Sikes (1934); and Koch (1933).
72. Hingeston-Randolph (1894–1899), I: 557–558, II: 953, 1128–29, 1135, 1143–1147, 1208; found in Szittya (1986), 63.
73. Hingeston-Randolph (1894–1899), II: 1197–98; found in Szittya (1986), 62.
74. Szittya (1986), 63.
75. Holcot, *Sent*. IV, q.5 (L p.2rb; O 201ra) (L reads 1326).
76. Holcot, *Sent*. IV, q.5 (L p.2rb; O 201ra): *Primo quod confessi* ... *Secundo quod stante* ... *Tertio dicit quod papa* ...
77. Holcot, *Sent*. IV, q.6 (L p.5rb; O 200va): "Ad quaestionem dicendum quod quia sacerdos qui nec est ab episcopo licentiatus, nec a curato, nec ullam materiam habet sibi subiectam, nec per consequens in quam possit iurisdictionem exercere."
78. Holcot, *Sent*. IV, q.5 (L p.2va; O 201ra): *Ex istis patet* ...
79. Holcot, *Sent*. IV, q.5 (L p.2va; O 201ra): *Ad horum maiorem intellectum* ...
80. Holcot, *Sent*. IV, q.5 (L p.2vb; O 201ra): *Et arguo primo sic* ...
81. Holcot, *Sent*. IV, q.5 (L p.2vb; O 201rb): *Si subditus velit* ...
82. Holcot, *Sent*. IV, q.5 (L p.2vb; O 201rb): *Tertio sic: in eadem constitutione dicitur* ...
83. Holcot, *Sent*. IV, q.5 (L p.2vb–p.3ra; O 201rb): *Quarto, in propositione istius statuti quando* ...
84. Holcot, *Sent*. IV, q.3 (L 0.5^{vb}; O 196rb): "Deus potest facere plus quam possumus intelligere et potest facere cuius modum et causam non possumus investigare, ergo ista consequentia non valet homo non potest declarare

sufficienter quomodo sub speciebus panis et vini existat realiter corpus christi ergo non potest sic esse in re vel non debet sic credi."

85. Holcot, *Sent.* IV, q.3 (L 0.2^{vb}; O 194vb): *Si non manet panis, nec est aliquod de pane generatum, igitur panis est annihilatus* . . .

86. Holcot, *Sent.* IV, q.3 (L 0.2^{vb}; O 194vb): *Si talis conversio unius rei in aliam foret possibilis* . . .

87. Holcot, *Sent.* IV, q.3 (L 0.7^{va}; O 197vb): *et ideo convenientius exprimitur miraculum* . . .

88. Holcot, *Sent.* IV, q.3 (L 0.5^{vb}–6ra; O 196rb): "Nam ex quo indubitanter credimus Deum plus posset facere quam nos possumus ex naturalibus investigare, consequens est quod in iis quae dicit nobis esse credenda captivemus intellectum et hoc est mirabile quod Deus velit nos in quibusdam singularibus ab eo institutis captivare intellectum nostrum."

89. See Lahey (2009), 113; Denery (2005), 137.

90. Holcot, *Sent.* IV, q.3 (L 0.6^{ra}; O 196rb): ". . . quod non est sic intelligendum quod homo non debeat circa illa quae sunt fidei arguere, sed quod non debet affirmare se posse rationem perfectam assignare."

91. Holcot, *Sent.* IV, q.3 (L 0.6^{rb}; O 196va): *Similiter nec requiritur Latinum* . . .

92. Holcot, *Sent.* IV, q.3 (L 0.6^{va}; O 196va): "Durum inquam esset dicere quod tales non absoluerent nec consecrarent quia sic peccatores essent defraudati et multa inconvenientia possent sequi."

93. Holcot, *Sent.* IV, q.3 (L 0.6^{va}; O 196va): *Quod istorum sit verius* . . .

94. Holcot, *Sent.* IV, q.3 (L 0.8^{va}; O 198rb): *Unde proprie loquendo non debet concedi* . . .

95. Debates over whether the eucharist requires the right intention of the consecrating priest has a significant historical precedent. See, e.g., Macy (2014), 18.

96. Holcot, *Sent.* IV, q.3 (L p.1ra; O 198vb): *Dico quod non debet dubitare* . . .

97. Gelber (2004), 358.

98. Holcot, *Sent.* II, q.2, a.3 (L h.5vb; O 149rb): *Primo sic quilibet experitur* . . .

CHAPTER 6

1. Courtenay (1985a), 184.
2. Courtenay (1985a), 183.
3. Schepers provides evidence that the work was probably written while Holcot was a *baccalaureus biblicus*. (Schepers [1970], 342–343, 353–354). See also Courtenay (1980), 103–105.
4. See R 136ra–137ra and O 120ra–120va.
5. Schepers (1970), 353–354.
6. Ibid.
7. Courtenay (1980), 109–110.
8. Courtenay (1980), 112.
9. Anstey (1868), 391–392: "ac aliquem librum de canone bibliae legisse . . ."

10. Kaeppeli (1959), 95. For a discussion of the difference between an academic *introitus* and a *principium*, see Wenzel (1995a), 320.
11. T2 178^v. See Kaeppeli (1959), 95.
12. The commentary on the Twelve Prophets is extant in four manuscripts and was never published in an early modern edition. See GI 1ra–72ra; SC 1^r–140^r; B3 1^r–176^v; V 125ra–169rb. For a discussion of the manuscripts, see Rivers (1993), 27–28.
13. Smalley (1960), 142.
14. The edition is found in Rivers (1993).
15. See R1 90^r–159^v. Sharpe (2001), no. 1475, also lists BR, LP, and MD as containing a copy (though Sharpe is to be used with caution). More reliably, see VD 132^r–136^r and VO1 97^r–109^r (as noted in Frank [1966], 364). Thanks to Ueli Zahnd for bringing Frank (1966) to our attention.
16. Smalley (1960), 142.
17. This is perhaps due to Smalley's judgment that "the script is so rough [in R1] as to be barely legible in places." Smalley (1960), 142, n1.
18. The name *Ecclesiasticus* or *liber Ecclesiasticus* was adopted by the Latin Fathers; e.g., Cyprian refers to the book as *In Ecclesiastico* or other variants. Stegmüller records that the work is preserved in 11 manuscripts, and Thomas Kaeppeli expands the list to 18. Stegmüller (1950–1980), no. 7421; Kaeppeli (1980), n. 3496.
19. Holcot, *Sup. Eccl.* (V1 62vb): *Clarissimi Sacrae theologiae* . . . Cf. Smalley (1956), 16.
20. Holcot, *Sup. Eccl.*, lect.88 (V1 62ra–62vb; BA3 97ra–98rb).
21. Stegmüller (1950–1980), no. 7426.
22. Cited in Smalley (1956), 30, n6; 58, n107; 60, n115.
23. Quétif-Échard (1719–1721), I, 629–632. See Smalley (1956), 9, n19.
24. The omission by Kaeppeli is more difficult to explain, although it is possible he was relying here on Quétif-Échard and Smalley.
25. E.g., Smalley (1960), 142, n2.
26. VC 106rb. The text occupies 92 folios (1^r–92^v) and includes a substantial index (93^r–106^r).
27. VC (front flyleaf): "Non est impressa, immo nec inter opera manuscripta eius recensetur Baleo, sed stilus ipsissimus eius est." The reference to Bale here is likely a reference to John Bale's handwritten notebook of British authors (Cod. Sedl. supra 64 [No. 3452 in Bernard's Catalogue]). However, it could also refer to one of Bale's two printed catalogues. The first catalogue was published in 1548 and the second catalogue was published in 1557–1559. It is presumed that Bale worked on the notebook throughout his life, which expired in 1563 (Bale 1902, vii). Thus 1563 is the most likely *terminus a quo* the colophon could have been added, but certainly it was not added before 1548.
28. Quétif-Échard (1719–1721), I, 631.
29. See Darling (1859), 579.

30. Petrarch records an account of their meeting. See Petrarch, *Ep. Fam.* iii. I.
31. Bury, *Philobiblon*, prol. (7, 159) (n.b.: all citations include the page number for both the Latin and English text).
32. Bury, *Philobiblon*, c.10 (90, 217).
33. Bury, *Philobiblon*, c.14 (113, 226).
34. Bury, *Philobiblon*, c.4 (24, 171–172).
35. Bury, *Philobiblon*, c.4 (29, 175).
36. Bury, *Philobiblon*, c.5 (43, 184).
37. Bury, *Philobiblon*, c.5 (43, 183).
38. Bury, *Philobiblon*, c.6 (46–47, 186).
39. Bury, *Philobiblon*, c.6 (53, 190).
40. Bury, *Philobiblon*, c.6 (53–54, 190). Cf. II Tim. 4:13.
41. Bury, *Philobiblon*, c.6 (54, 190).
42. Smalley (1960), 1.
43. On early Italian humanists, see Smalley (1960), 280–298.
44. Smalley (1960), 282.
45. Smalley (1960), 300–301.
46. Smalley (1960), 301.
47. Smalley (1960), 306 (Smalley's point holds, even if we perhaps disagree with her strict gender assumptions).
48. For information on Waleys, Ridevall, Lathbury, D'Eyncourt, Hopeman, and Ringstead, see Smalley (1960), 75–108, 109–132, 221–239, 204–208, 209–211, and 211–220.
49. See B2 317[ra]–383[vb]. The text is labeled as *Lectura Willelmi Dencourt super Ecclesiasten* on folio 317[ra]. Cf. Smalley (1960), 204, n3.
50. See R2 1[v].
51. Smalley (1960), 2.
52. Smalley (1960), 110.
53. Smalley (1960), 204.
54. Smalley (1956), 65.
55. Yates (2001) and Carruthers (2008).
56. See Courtenay (1985a), 178–181.
57. Rouse-Rouse (1979).
58. Rouse-Rouse (1979), 4, see also 3–42.
59. The "Vatican Mythographers" is a term used to refer to an anonymous collection of mythographies in which a Greek or Roman myth is interpreted in an allegorical way.
60. While Welter does catalogue Holcot's use of sources in the *Convertimini* and the *Moralitates*, we limit our discussion to the Wisdom commentary for the sake of brevity. See Welter (1927), 364–365.
61. Smalley (1960), 154.

62. On Waleys see Smalley (1960), 79–108, esp. 102–108; for the quotation regarding Holcot, see 156.
63. Smalley (1960), 156 (text transcribed at 321–322). Smalley's transcription follows B2 (268vb–269rb). N.b.: B1 (599) does not include Calyce, but reads "Sulpitia Lentuli, Alcmena, et de aliis infinitis . . ."
64. Smalley (1956), 33.
65. See Welter (1927), 364–365, n62.
66. See B1 24, 28, 30, 24, and 25.
67. See Tachau (1991), 337–345.
68. Wey (1949), 222.
69. Wey (1949), 223.
70. For a discussion of self-references, see Trapp (1965), 146–274.
71. It is also possible that Holcot intends to mean *hol* as in hole, and *cot* as in small house or cottage (as early as the eleventh century, *cot* meant a cottage or hut).
72. Holcot, *Sap*. lec.1 (B1 4; B2 3^{rb-va}): *De qua Cant. 2* . . .
73. Holcot, *Sap*. lec.1 (B1 4; B2 3va): *Igitur Sacrae scripturae foramen* . . .

CHAPTER 7

1. The commentaries of Cyril and Theodore have been translated into English. For Cyril, see *FOC* 115, 116, 124; for Theodore, see *FOC* 108.
2. See *Enarratio in duodecim prophetas minores* (*PL* 117, 9–294). It is attributed to Haimo of Auxerre (†c. 878).
3. The work is unedited and preserved in R3. Cited in Minnis (2010), 246 (n.b.: referenced incorrectly as Rawlinson G 427).
4. Smalley (1978), 227.
5. See LM.
6. See William of Luxi, *Postilla super Baruch* and *Postilla super Ionam*.
7. Smalley (1956), 29–30 (see also ON). Cf. Stegmüller (1950–1980), nn. 7651–7684 and Kaeppeli (1980), nn. 3595–3602, esp. 3597. See also Smalley (1946), 57–85 and (1948), 97–108.
8. Smalley (1956), 30. See Peter Aureoli, *Compendium sensus litteralis totius divinae Scripturae*.
9. Smalley (1956), 30.
10. This dating is still generally accepted. For more on Lyra see Krey-Smith (2000).
11. Smalley (1956), 31.
12. See Rivers (2010), 222; Smalley (1960), 138–141; and Courtenay (1985a), 178–181.
13. Smalley (1956), 28.
14. Smalley (1956), 28.
15. See Appendix C.

16. See Smalley (1978), 66–82, here 74.
17. Smalley (1956), 29.
18. See de Lubac (1998), I.
19. Quoted in de Lubac (1998), I, 1.
20. On the picture technique see Allen (1971), 29–53; Smalley (1960), 165–183; Rivers (1993) and (2010), 212–250. On the use of sermonic rhymes, see Wenzel (1986), 61–100.
21. Wenzel (2005a), 294.
22. E.g., BA1 275^r–279^v lists: *pictura orationis*, *pictura peccati mortalis*, *pictura luxuriae*, *imago amoris*, *pictura amoris pro nativitate et passione Christi*, *imago poenitentiae*, *pictura superbiae*, and *pictura fortunae* (*Moralizations* 2, 3, 4, 6, 7, 9, 10, and 11). Cf. BA4 1^r–6^r.
23. See sermons 69^g (108^v), 92^h (147^r), and 105^b (169^r) in P1. See Rivers (2010), 212, n14.
24. For references to the remaining pictures, see Smalley (1960), 165–183.
25. Smalley (1960), 166.
26. Smalley (1960), 172–178, transcribes all 26 pictures (based on SC).
27. Cf. with Holcot's *dubitatio* on God's justice and mercy, *Sap.* lec.53 (B1 188–190; B2 87rb–88ra).
28. Holcot, *Nahum* (Rivers$^{7-9}$), B3 104^v. (We provide only line numbers for the edition of Rivers because the pagination in our copy of the text was altered from the original.)
29. See also Holcot's discussion of patience in Holcot, *Sup. Eccl.*, lec.18 (V1 15rb–16ra; BA3 22rb–23rb).
30. Holcot, *Nahum* (Rivers$^{27-32}$), B3 104^v: *Unde Seneca* . . . As Rivers (1993), 61, notes, this passage is found in Martin of Braga's *Formula vitae honestae*.
31. See Rivers (1993), 61.
32. Holcot, *Nahum* (Rivers$^{49-56}$), B3 105^r.
33. Rivers (2010), 223–224 (Rivers's translation with modifications); Holcot, *Nahum* (Rivers$^{60-63}$), B3 105^r.
34. Holcot, *Nahum* (Rivers$^{64-71}$), B3 105^r.
35. Holcot, *Nahum* (Rivers$^{72-82}$), B3 105^r.
36. Holcot, *Nahum* (Rivers$^{83-101}$), B3 105^{r-v}.
37. Holcot, *Nahum* (Rivers$^{102-117}$), B3 105^v.
38. Holcot, *Nahum* (Rivers$^{118-128}$), B3 105^v.
39. Holcot, *Nahum* (Rivers$^{127-128}$), B3 105^v: *Omnes religiosi et clerici* . . .
40. Holcot, *Nahum* (Rivers$^{129-170}$), B3 105^v–106^r.
41. Holcot, *Nahum* (Rivers$^{135-137}$), B3 105^v.
42. Rivers (1993), 62.
43. Holcot, *Nahum* (Rivers$^{171-193}$), B3 106^{r-v} (here Rivers$^{171-172}$; B3 106^r): *Septimo pingitur patientia* . . .
44. Cf. I Kings 10:18–19.
45. Holcot, *Nahum* (Rivers$^{194-199}$), B3 106^v.

46. Holcot, *Nahum* (Rivers[200–231]), B3 106^v.
47. Holcot, *Nahum* (Rivers[223–225]), B3 106^v.
48. Holcot, *Nahum* (Rivers[232–271]), B3 106^v–107^r.
49. Holcot, *Nahum* (Rivers[239–240]), B3 106^v.
50. Holcot, *Nahum* (Rivers[241–243]), B3 106^v: "Magni animi est injurias despicere; ultionis contumeliosissimum genus est non esse visum dignum ex quo peteretur ultio." See Seneca, *De ira* 2.32.3.
51. Holcot, *Nahum* (Rivers[245–250]), B3 106^v–107^r. Seneca, *De ira* 2.33.2.
52. For further references, see Rivers (1993), 62.
53. Rivers (2010), 224; Cf. Holcot, *Nahum* (Rivers[272–275]), B3 107^r.
54. Holcot, *Nahum* (Rivers[276–277]), B3 107^r.
55. Smalley (1960), 172.
56. Holcot, *Sap.* lec.9 (B1 34–35; B2 16rb): *Certe sic dicit ille frater gratissimus* ...
57. Smalley (1960), 172.
58. The Franciscan John Ridevall writes that his images (*poeticae picturae*) are painted according to the poet (*pingitur a poetis*). Smalley (1960), 112. Cf. e.g., Holcot, *Moralitas* 19 (B1 725): *Unde oratio depingebatur* ...
59. Saxl (1942), 82–134, 102, and (1927), 104–121. See Smalley (1960), 134; Rivers (2010), 242.
60. Saxl (1942), 82–83. See BC.
61. Saxl (1942), 102–103.
62. Smalley (1960), 118.
63. On the use of *picturae* as homiletic aids in the period following Holcot, see Rivers (2010), chs. 7 and 8.
64. Carruthers (2008), 292.
65. Rivers (2010), 222–240.
66. Rivers (2010), 240–246.
67. Rivers (2010), 240–241.
68. Smalley (1960), 171.
69. Holcot, *Sap.* 21 (B1 77; B2 36ra). Here we reject Smalley's suggestion to read *vitro* and *vitream* as a corruption of *viteo* and *viteam* (thus referring to leaves of a vine, not glass). Smalley (1960), 171.
70. Rivers (2010), 241.
71. Rivers (2010), 240–246; Wenzel (1978), 118.
72. Holcot, *Sap.* 21 (B1 76; B2 36ra).
73. Holcot, *Moralitas* 33 (B1 737).
74. Holcot, *Moralitas* 33 (B1 737): *Ut habetur II Machabaeorum.* ... Cf. II Maccabees 9:8.
75. Holcot, *Moralitas* 33 (B1 737): *Exemplum de hoc habetur* ...
76. Holcot, *Moralitas* 33 (B1 737): *Et tandem ad tantam* ...
77. Holcot, *Moralitas* 33 (B1 737): *Secunda conditio, quod omni* ...

78. Holcot, *Moralitas* 33 (B1 737): *Exemplum de hoc habetur* ... Cf. I Kings 12:10–11, 14.
79. Holcot, *Moralitas* 33 (B1 737): *Tertia condition est* ...
80. Holcot, *Moralitas* 33 (B1 737–738): *Heliodoro, qui tantum* ... Cf. II Maccabees 3:25–26.
81. This is not the only pictorial hybrid between Type I and Type II. See also the pictures of *humilitas* (humility), Holcot, *Moralitas* 21 (B1 727–728), and *luxuria* (luxury), Holcot, *Moralitas* 38 (B1 740–741).
82. Holcot, *Moralitas* 21 (B1 727).

CHAPTER 8

1. Holcot's commentary on Wisdom is his most famous work and, as noted in the introduction, exists in at least 175 manuscripts and 12 incunabula and early modern printings (Kaeppeli [1980], 315–318). We have prioritized the Basel 1586 edition of the work (B1) and Balliol 27 (B2).

After comparing B1 with B2 (and B6), Smalley observed that the results were both "reassuring and disappointing": disappointing in that the manuscripts shed little light on Holcot's obscure sources and references and reassuring in that the comparisons prove that "the edition was based on a good text." We have followed Smalley given that B1 does provide a good reading of the text. We have read B1 against B2 in all instances. Smalley writes that in the margins of B2 there are four references to the *liber magistri* (book of the master) written in a hand that is contemporary with the text itself, indicating that B2 was copied from a book belonging to Holcot, the *magister*. We have confirmed this finding and also noted that there is an additional marginal notation in the same hand (overlooked by Smalley) that also mentions the book of the master. See B2 119ʳ: "Hoc erat scriptum cum plumbo in libro magistri in margine in inferiori in fine istius lectionis. Et idem inseras in divisione sequentis, si vis" (the *in* prior to *inferiori* is a mistake by dittography). Smalley argues that B2 belongs to the period before 1350 and that it is "quite close to an autograph" (Smalley [1956], 11).

2. Note the contrast with the *glossa ordinaria* and Meister Eckhart's focus on a christological understanding of Wisdom (see notes 32 and 33); likewise contrast with Clarke's insistence on the universal "everyman": "the theme of the book is wisdom's importance for everyman" (Clarke [1973], 1).

3. Ps.-Bonaventure, *Commentarius in librum Sapientiae*.

4. Lorin, *Sap*. In the Lyon edition of the text there are no clear lecture divisions. Rather, it is primarily divided by verse, though occasionally a leading header will alert the reader to what will follow.

5. Bellamah (2011), 16: "Among the postill's most conspicuous characteristics is a high level of organization or structuring. Its basic component is the individual lesson (or *lectio*), which itself comprises a few distinct components."

6. These lecture divisions do coincide with chapter divisions so that no chapter break happens within a lecture. Nevertheless, the lecture divisions decidedly and fundamentally divide the text.

7. Lecture 124 considers four verses; lecture 162 and lecture 168 consider five verses. Again, this is notably different from the way Ps.-Bonaventure or Lorin approaches the text.

8. Smalley (1956), 13, notes that some manuscripts have 212 lectures while others have 211.

9. Cf. Bellamah (2011), 15–16, introduces the prologue first, before turning to the lecture division, making it appear as though the prologue precedes the lecture division, however in Holcot's commentary they are combined.

10. For example, B2 (like B) counts the opening prologue as lecture 1.

11. Bellamah (2011), 15–16.

12. See Bellamah (2011), 16.

13. Holcot, *Sap*. lec.2 (B1 6; B2 4ra): *Circa librum istum* . . .

14. For further evidence one might look to the prologues of the sixteenth and seventeenth centuries, where questions of authorship, subject matter, and intention are routinely seen as part of the prologue, preceding the formal commentary. See Lorin, *Sap*. 1–8, and Lapide, *Sap*. 1–7.

15. This fact alone may suggest that B1 made an error by printing verse 1 at the beginning of lecture 2 (cf. B2).

16. Bellamah (2011), 16.

17. Smalley (1956), 33.

18. Holcot's preference for the moral interpretation stands in line with Mulchahey's assessment of some of the earliest scholastic commentators and their preference for the moral or tropological interpretation. This, she notes, stands in contrast to later thirteenth-century tendencies to "ignore tropology" in favor of "theological speculation." (See Mulchahey [1998], 484–485.)

19. The kind of discussions introduced by *notandum est* in Holcot's commentary are scarce in the commentaries of Ps.-Bonaventure and Jean de Lorin.

20. Holcot, *Sap*. lec.64 (B1 224; B2 103va).

21. See, e.g., the discussion of the name of "Jesus" in Holcot, *Sap*. lec.135 (B1 445; B2 203rb): *Est igitur notandum quod istud nomen* . . .

22. Holcot, *Sap*. lec.163 (B1 538; B2 240va). In B1 such clauses are introduced by a phrase such as *circa illam clausulam*, while in the manuscript tradition (e.g., B2), the biblical quotation is simply underlined.

23. Holcot, *Sap*. lec.4 (B1 15; B2 7va) includes a *dubium* that begins "Primo potest esse dubium hic . . ." followed by "Et videtur quod non." The *dubia* are generally noted in the manuscript tradition as *dubitatio* in the margin (e.g., B2 7va).

24. Compare with Bellamah, who reports questions beginning simply with *contra*. Bellamah (2011), 22.

25. See, e.g., lectures 3, 14, 15, 17, 40, 46, 66, 71, 79, 104, 105, 120, 160, and 201. For a comparison to other commentaries, see Bellamah (2011), 22.

26. For a complete list of these formal questions, see Appendix C.

27. See Smalley (1956), 33.

28. See Smalley (1956), 34, 44–50; Cf. Welter (1927) 95–101, 360–361 for a discussion of the use of medieval *exempla* and their presence in Holcot's commentary.

29. The following story is retold by the late-fourteenth-century chronicler Joannis de Fordun, *Scotichronicon*, vol.2, c.15 (Bower 238).

30. Holcot, *Sap*. lec.91 (B1 310; B2 138^{rb-va}): *Narratur de quodam histrione* . . .

31. Mulchahey (1998), 489.

32. *Glossa ordinaria*, III 1886 (*PL* 113, 1167): "Qui proinde Sapientiae nominatur, quia in eo Christi adventus qui est sapientia patris, et passio ejus, evidenter exprimitur."

33. Duclow (1987), 219.

34. Lapide, *Sap.* 5a: "Porro sapientia hic non tam speculativa, quam practica accipitur." Cf. Lorin, *Sap*. 7, which offers a list of various historical interpretations of the work's subject matter, including the "doctrine of justice," "the prophecy of Christ," "all the virtues," and "moral philosophy," among others.

35. Winston (1979), 42. Winston points specifically to chapter 7, which is similar to the interpretation provided by Clarke (1973). See our later discussion, where Holcot works hard to give these references, to what seem like speculative knowledge, a very practical interpretation.

36. Aristotle, *NE* VI, c.7 (1141^{a}8–^{b}8); id., *Metaph*. I, c.1 (982^{a}1–2).

37. Holcot, *Sap*. lec.2 (B1 6; B2 4ra): *Sapiens est qui scit omnia* . . .

38. Holcot, *Sap*. lec.2 (B1 6; B2 4^{ra-rb}): *Secundo apud theologos* . . .

39. Holcot, *Sap*. lec.2 (B1 6; B2 4rb): *Tertio modo accipitur sapientia* . . .

40. Today it is believed that the book of Wisdom was written by a "thoroughly hellenized Jew of Alexandria" (Winston [1979], 3).

41. See Clarke (1973), 1.

42. For Jerome see *Praefatio in libros Salomonis* (*PL* 28, 1242): "apud Hebraeos nusquam est, quia est ipse stylus Graecam eloquentiam redolet; et nonnulli scriptorum veterum hunc esse Judei Philonis affirmant."

43. In post-reformation commentaries, these discussions notably happen within a larger discussion of the overall canonicity of the text. (See Lorin, *Sap*.; Lapide, *Sap*., among others.)

44. Hugh of St. Victor, *Didascalicon* 4.8 (*PL* 176, 783–784).

45. Ps.-Bonaventure, *Commentarius in librum Sapientiae*, prologue (Quaracchi VI, 108b).

46. Holcot, *Sap*. lec.2 (B1 7; B2 4va): *Videtur enim Hieronymum dicere quod* . . .

47. Holcot, *Sap*. lec.2 (B1 7; B2 4vb): *Possibile est autem quod Iudaeus* . . .

48. Holcot, *Sap.* lec.2 (B1 8; B2 4vb): *Ex istis patet quod iste liber* . . . (Note the divergences between B1 and B2, cf. reading of B1 with T1 2vb).

49. Holcot, *Sap.* lec.2 (B1 8; B2 4vb–5ra): *Ubi sciendum quod finis Sapientiae* . . .

50. Ps.-Bonaventure, *Commentarius in librum Sapientiae*, prologue (Quaracchi VI, 109b).

51. Holcot, *Sap.* lec.74 (B1 261; B2 119ra): *Quia vero finis et perfectio sapientiae* . . . (See the marginal note on B2 119ra regarding lecture 74).

52. R. Cornely, *Commentarius in Librum Sapientiae* (Paris, 1910), p. 11, qtd. in Reese (1965).

53. Consider for instance the difference between Winston (1979), 9–12, who divides the book into three large divisions, and Clarke (1973), 3, who identifies four main subdivisions. Likewise, see the list of 16 different organizing schemas provided by Pfeiffer (1949), 321–233, as well as the many articles on the topic, e.g., Skehan (1945), Reese (1965), Wright (1965, 1967), and Alviero (2008).

54. Holcot, *Sap.* lec.3 (B1 9; B2 5va): *Primo enim determinat* . . .

55. Holcot, *Sap.* lec.125 (B1 420; B2 187va): *Hic designatur decimum capitulum* . . . Cf. Smalley (1956), 32.

56. Holcot, *Sap.* lec.125 (B1 420; B2 187va): *In ista parte prosequitur sapientiae utilitatem* . . .

57. Modern commentators are even less clear. As far as we can tell, Jean de Lorin, in his 1607 commentary, offers no grand division but instead divides the text into 15 main sections. Subsequently, Cornelius de Lapide opts for a threefold division, which, like Ps.-Bonaventure, wants to see a division between chapters 6 and 7, but he also argues for a third part of the book beginning where Holcot places his second division at chapter 10 (Lapide, *Sap.* 6a).

58. This discrepancy is visible not only in modern commentaries (see the disagreement in Clarke [1973] and Winston [1979]) but also in the choice of Ps.-Bonaventure and Cornelius de Lapide to make a decisive break between 6 and 7, while Holcot, like the modern commentary by Clarke (1973), sees the break coming between 5 and 6.

59. Winston (1979) titles this entire section "Wisdom's gift of immortality" and Clarke (1973) titles it "The promise of immortality."

60. For instance, Clarke (1973), 14, writes: "In these verses [1:1–1:15], man is exhorted to love justice because wisdom will not enter a perverse soul, because the spirit of God fills the whole earth, and because in the last analysis God intended man to live, not die." The implication seems to be that one ought to love justice in order to be truly wise and therefore to achieve true immortality. One should be attentive to the reoccurring themes in this opening section of the unjust believing that the just and godly person is actually a fool (see 1:21–2:20), while the argument of much of the remainder of this passage seems

to be an effort to show that the worldly wise, clinging to their material things, is the actual sign of the fool.

61. Winston (1979), 10.
62. Clarke (1973), 44.
63. Ps.-Bonaventure, *Commentarius in librum Sapientiae* (Quaracchi VI, 235, schema II).
64. Holcot, *Sap.* lec.3 (B1 9; B2 5va): *Secundo quomodo adquisita* ... and again in lecture 74 (B1 261; B2 119ra): *Hic consequenter declarat* ...
65. Holcot, *Sap.* lec.74 (B1 261; B2 119ra): "Est tamen notandum quod ista divisio libri vel processus non est ita praecise facta, quin in utraque parte utrumque fiat; nam in praecedentibus aliquando dictum est quomodo sapientia possit in hominem perficere. Et in sequentibus docebitur aliquando quomodo homo possit sapientiam adquirere."
66. Holcot, *Sap.* lec.3 (B1 9; B2 5va): "Notandum autem quod in generatione animalis natura non incipit a digito vel a pede, sed a corde, pulmone, et capite, et membris principalibus, sic huius libri autor, volens informare corpus Ecclesiae in virtutibus moralibus incipit a dominis et praelatis, quibus incumbit ordinare et iudicare: Extendit enim se haec doctrina moralis generaliter ad omnes." (Here we follow B1, but note the divergences in this text between B1 9, B2 5va, and T1 3^{ra-rb}.)
67. See note 50.
68. Clarke (1973), 14–15.
69. Holcot, *Sap.* lec.3 (B1 10; B2 5vb): "Videmus enim quod illud quod est preciosum, charum vel amatum a principe, in ornatu, gestu vel victu illud trahitur ad consequentiam a subditis, et sive sit utile sive inutile ... Unde si iudices, domini et praelati vellent amare iusticiam, non est dubium, quin eam subdit amarent."
70. Holcot, *Sap.* lec.3 (B1 12; B2 6va): *Est autem hic primo dubium* ...
71. Holcot, *Sap.* lec.3 (B1 12; B2 6vb): *Secunda causa est, quia sine iustitia* ...
72. Consider especially 2:1–2:9.
73. Holcot, *Sap.* lec.74 (B1 261; B2 119ra): "Postquam a Spiritu Sancto ostensum est a principio libri, usque huc, quomodo per iusticiam et bonos mores potest homo sapientiam adquirere: Hic consequenter declarat quomodo sapientia adquisita possit hominem perficere" (again, note divergences between B1 and B2 and the marginal note at B2 119ra. Here T2 72rb agrees with B2 and even omits the first six lines of B1.)
74. See note 65.
75. Holcot, *Sap.* lec.74 (B1 261; B2 119ra): *Unde intentio huius capituli est informare reges* ...
76. Holcot, *Sap.* lec.74 (B1 261; B2 119ra): *Quomodo homo possit sapientiam impetrare* ...
77. See Lewis-Short (1879): *impetro* "to accomplish, effect, bring to pass; to get, obtain, procure, esp. by exertion, request, entreaty."

78. Holcot, *Sap.* lec.88 (B1 299; B2 133ra): *Postquam declaratum est doctrinaliter* ...
79. See note 51.
80. Clarke (1973), 44.
81. Clarke (1973), 47.
82. Winston (1979), 156.
83. For instance, Clarke (1973), 49, writes: "In these chapters (7–9) the pursuit of wisdom is discussed in the first person as if the king were speaking."
84. Holcot, *Sap.* lec.105 (B1 355; B2 159va): *Intentio sapientis Salomon* ...
85. Holcot, *Sap.* lec.105 (B1 355; B2 159va): *Primo ostendit quantum* ...
86. Regarding to the reference to praying for wisdom in 7:7, Clarke (1973), 51, writes: *"prayed:* which introduces the prayer recorded in c. 9." See also Winston (1979), 158 and 200.
87. Holcot, *Sap.* lec.118 (B1 394; B2 176vb–177ra): "Postquam Salomon declaravit quod sapientiam, quae est verus Dei cultus, acquirere non potuit, nisi illam a Deo petendo per instantiam summae devotionis, in isto capitulo consequenter explanat formam et seriem suae supplicationis."
88. See the following discussion of chapter 13:1.
89. Holcot, *Sap.* lec.88 (B1 299; B2 133ra): "quarum aliquae praecedunt sapientiam acquirendam, aliquae sequuntur sapientiam adquisitam."
90. Holcot, *Sap.* lec.88 (B1 299; B2 133ra): *Primo ergo ponit humiliationem* ... (note the omission by homeoteleuton in B2 133ra).
91. Holcot, *Sap.* lec.99 (B1 335; B2 150va): *Primo enumerat quorum* ... (note lecture 99 is labeled incorrectly as CIX in B1).
92. Clarke (1973), 52.
93. See the earlier discussion of Holcot's understanding of the subject matter of the book of Wisdom.
94. Clarke (1973), 52.
95. Holcot, *Sap.* lec.99 (B1 335; B2 150va): *Ut sciam dispositionem orbis terrarum* ...
96. Holcot, *Sap.* lec.99 (B1 336; B2 150vb): *Id est, diversas consuetudines* ...
97. Holcot, *Sap.* lec.99 (B1 336; B2 150vb): *Id est, affectiones* ...
98. Holcot, *Sap.* lec.3 (B1 9; B2 5va): *Secundo eius utilitatem et operationem* ...
99. Holcot, *Sap.* lec.133 (B1 447; B2 199va): *Postquam declarati sunt multiplices effectus sapientiae* ...
100. Holcot, *Sap.* lec.133 (B1 447; B2 199va): *Nam primo tangit breviter* ...
101. Holcot, *Sap.* lec.135 (B1 454; B2 203ra): *Et ideo tam in philosophia* ...
102. We borrow this phrase from the title of section 6 of Smalley's article. Some, including Smalley, have attempted to explain Holcot's use (and approval) of classical sources by pointing out that he is receptive to the Augustinian idea of an "aboriginal revelation" (see Augustine, *City of God*, 18.28 [*WSA* 1.7; 306–307]) to Adam that made its way both to the Hebrews and the philosophers. See lecture 157 (B1 522) for Holcot's approval, and see Smalley (1956), 83, for her

discussion. However, both Oberman and our following discussion show that Holcot's interest in pagan wisdom comes from a higher valuation of the use of natural reason than Smalley, Leff, and others are willing to admit. Oberman writes: "We are, however, forewarned that Holcot's position cannot simply be identified with that of Augustine by the fact that this gift of knowledge of God is not bestowed on the elect but on those who live according to the principles of natural law. Unlike Augustine and Bradwardine, Holcot is not interested in an aboriginal revelation to explain the great insights of Hermes and Aristotle. He is more interested in the general ethical corollary that such knowledge of God is available to all who live according to the principles of natural law" (Oberman [1962], 321–322). See our discussion at the end of this chapter.

103. Note here the Dominican Order's historical, albeit slow and controversial, recognition of the importance of the study of arts (the development of the *studia artium* and *studium naturalium*) in the formation of a sound preacher. See Mulchahey (1998), 219–350.

104. Holcot, *Sap.* lec.136 (B1 457; B2 204rb): *In hac parte consequenter sapientiam* ...

105. Holcot, *Sap.* lec.136 (B1 457; B2 204rb): *Primo ergo ostenditur* ...

106. Holcot, *Sap.* lec.136 (B1 457; B2 204rb): *Secundo quanta fuerit eorum culpa* ...

107. Holcot, *Sap.* lec.155 (B1 515; B2 230va): *Consequenter insistit autor huius libri* ...

108. Holcot, *Sap.* lec.176 (B1 579; B2 260ra): *Modo consequenter in ista parte, ut cultum unius Dei complete suadeat* ...

109. Holcot, *Sap.* lec.176 (B1 579–580; B2 260ra): *Ostendens quod illi erant iuste puniti* ...

110. In ch.13, lec.155 (B1 515, B2 230va), Holcot is less than clear about identifying 13–15 as a distinct unit. Rather he seems to be first dividing 13–19 into units. Subsequently he divides the material into subsections 13–15 and 16–19.

111. Clarke (1973), 4.

112. Cf. Winston (1979), 249; Clarke, (1973), 88.

113. Holcot, *Sap.* lec.155 (B1 516; B2 230vb): *Haec scientia est timor et reverentia* ...

114. Holcot, *Sap.* lec.155 (B1 516; B2 230vb): *Et ideo infideles nihil boni superaedificant* ...

115. Holcot, *Sap.* lec.155 (B1 516; B2 231ra): *Sed posset quaeri, qualiter est quod philosophi* ... Cf. Smalley (1956), 83.

116. Holcot, *Sap.* lec.155 (B1 516; B2 231ra): *Ad hoc dicendum ut aestimo* ...

117. See Smalley (1956), 82–83.

118. Holcot, *Sap.* lec.155 (B1 516; B2 230vb): *Hoc est ergo primum de quo reprehenduntur* ...

119. Holcot, *Sap.* lec.155 (B1 516; B2 231^{ra-rb}): "Sed quicunque se innocenter habent ad Deum, et rationem naturalem exercent studendo, nec divinae gratiae

obicem praebent, Deus eis sufficienter sui communicat notitiam, sic quod eis sufficiat ad salutem."

120. This was the definition of faith singled out in book 1; see chapter 2.

121. See the earlier consideration of Holcot's analysis of Wisdom 6–9.

122. Smalley (1956), 85.

123. Here we are in agreement with Oberman's analysis of Holcot's exposition of Wisdom 7. Oberman concludes with an exhortation to the same kind of caution with respect to the label "skeptic" that we are advocating here. He writes: "The main reason however why one should be sceptical about such charges as agnosticism, fideism and scepticism is that whereas Holcot consistently enough emphasizes that all these semi-arguments as such are insufficient without revelation on the part of God, this revelation is granted only to those who use their rational capacities to the utmost to seek and understand God" (Oberman [2000], 243).

CHAPTER 9

1. Cf. Minnis (2010), 182.

2. Holcot, *Sap*. lec.47 (B1 167; B2 77rb): "Consummatio et completio hominis est uniri Deo per cognitionem et amorem."

3. Holcot, *Sap*. lec.47 (B1 167; B2 77rb): "Unde omnis homo a Deo divisus, est imperfectus, et inconsummatus. Et quasi mali filii et indisciplinati sunt a Deo divisi, ideo merito vocantur rami inconsummati et isti confringentur."

4. Holcot, *Sap*. lec.47 (B1 167; B2 77rb): *Unde quia isti peccatores* ...

5. Holcot, *Sap*. lec.47 (B1 167; B2 77rb): *Sed beati et sancti suaviter* ...

6. Holcot, *Sap*. lec.47 (B1 168; B2 77vb): *Video homines sicut arbores* ...

7. Holcot, *Sap*. lec.47 (B1 168; B2 77vb): *Arbor enim non vivit nisi* ...

8. Holcot, *Sap*. lec.47 (B1 168; B2 77vb): *Humilitas oritur de terra* ...

9. See chapter 8 and the following discussion of authority.

10. Holcot, *Sap*. lec.47 (B1 168; B2 77vb): *Ita personae humiles refugientes dignitates* ... This concern to be content with the simplicity of one's office is consistent with Holcot's later distinction between the prince and the tyrant. The prince is identified as one who labors on behalf of the people and for whom the simple honor of obedience is sufficient. The tyrant, on the other hand, is precisely the one for whom this is not sufficient and who labors on behalf of an external good such as public honor, wealth, and the like. Cf. Holcot, *Sap*. lec.165 (B1 547; B2 245ra): "Sed princeps laborat pro tota multitudine. Haec autem merces est honor et gloria. Et cui ista non sufficiunt, tyrannus est et non princeps."

11. Holcot, *Sap*. lec.47 (B1 168; B2 77vb): *vivunt diutius et stant stabilius*.

12. Holcot, *Sap*. lec.47 (B1 168; B2 77vb): *vivunt multo quietius in suis conscientiis* ...

13. Holcot, *Sap*. lec.47 (B1 168; B2 77vb): *Ita illi homines qui se diligentius* ...

14. Holcot, *Sap*. lec.47 (B1 168; B2 77vb): *Quia quamvis inferior pars terrae* ...

15. This position is consistent with Holcot's adoption of Cicero's definition of a true commonwealth as a people united by a common sense of what is right or just, over and against a peaceful existence wherein individuals maintain their own sense of what is right. (See the following discussion of Holcot's consideration of Cicero's and Augustine's definitions of the republic.). This is consistent with Holcot's disdain for false notions of peace: e.g., the kind of peace found among a band of thieves or in a society that turns its back on vice in the name of peace (see Holcot, *Sap.* lec.167 [B1 551–554; B2 246vb– 248vb]).

16. Holcot, *Sap.* lec.47 (B1 168; B2 78ra): *Sicut enim arbores primo germinant* ...

17. See also the discussion of the three kinds of bad fruits. Holcot, *Sap.* lec.47 (B1 168; B2 78ra).

18. Holcot, *Sap.* lec.47 (B1 168; B2 78ra): *Quarto assimilatur homo arbori in cadendo* ...

19. Holcot, *Sap.* lec.30 (B1 106–108; B2 48vb–50ra), lec.125 (B1 421–422; B2 187va–188va).

20. Cf. Holcot, *Sap.* lec.199 (B1 656; B2 294va): *Triplex enim fuit antiquorum sententia de eo* ...

21. Holcot, *Sap.* lec.125 (B1 422; B2 188ra): *Utrum Adam in statu innocentiae* ...

22. While Anselm is not mentioned here, Holcot's response clearly follows the generally Anselmian position.

23. Holcot, *Sap.* lec.125 (B1 422; B2 188rb): *Dicendum quod licet Deus hoc potuisset* ...

24. Holcot, *Sap.* lec.30 (B1 106; B2 49^{ra-rb}): *Quaeritur tamen utrum corpus primi hominis* ...

25. Holcot, *Sap.* lec.30 (B1 107; B2 49vb): *Ad primum dicendum, quod concludit* ...

26. Holcot, *Sap.* lec.30 (B1 107; B2 49^{rb-va}): *Secundum est quod homini fuisset* ...

27. Holcot, *Sap.* lec.12 (B1 45; B2 21^{ra-rb}): "Tertio propter consimilem aspectum: quantumcunque enim fuerit homo amabilis et pulcher et delicatus, statim post mortem est horribilis, turpis et abominabilis, et a communione hominum sequestrabilis et separandus. Sic anima ante peccatum pulcherrima et famosa videtur ... Per peccatum vero spoliatur gratuitis et vulneratur in naturalibus, fit foeda et abominabilis coram Deo ... Et tunc per peccatum anima misera separatur a communione fidelium et amicitia Dei et angelorum bonorum ..."

28. Holcot, *Sap.* lec.199 (B1 656; B2 294va): "Sed cum virtutes morales sint in appetitu, non sufficit cum naturali dispositione doctrina, sed ulterius requiritur consuetudo, per quam ipse appetitus inclinetur ad bonum."

29. Holcot, *Sap.* lec.199 (B1 656; B2 294va): *Tertio conclusio videlicet quod ad bonam consuetudinem*. This idea connects to what we have already seen as the central message of the book of Wisdom, which is that rulers must not simply

become personally wise, but must also acquire the wisdom, skill, and moral probity required to lead others to wisdom.

30. Holcot, *Sap.* lec.199 (B1 656; B2 294va): *Secundo requirunt leges utilitatem* ...

31. Holcot, *Sap.* lec.199 (B1 657; B2 294vb–295ra): *Tertio requirunt leges in republica* ...

32. Cf. Holcot's discussion of a bad peace (*pax mala*) in *Sap.* lec.167 (B1 553–554; B2 247va–248ra).

33. Holcot, *Sap.* lec.46 (B1 164; B2 75vb): *Primo quod sint concorditer ordinatae* ... Note that this mandate is in agreement with Lon Fuller's fifth criteria for a successful rule of law. See Fuller (1977), 33–35.

34. See Hart (2012), 82.

35. Holcot, *Sap.* lec.199 (B1 655; B2 294ra): *Requiruntur namque leges ad hoc* ... Note numbers 1–3 correspond fairly well with the list in lecture 46.

36. Holcot, *Sap.* lec.199 (B1 655; B2 294ra): *Sunt enim leges, quae ordinantur* ...

37. It is precisely at this point that Holcot introduces the account about how men become good, discussed earlier. Cf. lec.199 (B1 655–656; B2 294^{ra-va}).

38. Holcot, *Sap.* lec.199 (B1 656; B2 294va): *Haec est causa finalis legis* ...

39. Aristotle, *NE*, VIII, c.1 (1155^{a}21–22; trans. Ross); cf. Holcot, *Sap.* lec.199 (B1 656; B2 294vb).

40. Holcot, *Sap.* lec.199 (B1 656; B2 294vb): *Secundo tamen De civitate capitulo 21* ... Augustine, *City of God*, 19.21 (*WSA* 1.7; 378).

41. Holcot, *Sap.* lec.199 (B1 656; B2 294vb): *Aliam adhuc replicat definitionem populi* ... Augustine, *City of God*, 19.24 (*WSA* 1.7; 385).

42. See the following discussion of a "false peace" in our explication of Holcot's treatment of authority.

43. Holcot, *Sap.* lec.199 (B1 657; B2 294vb): *Sed in omnibus istis definitionibus* ...

44. Holcot, *Sap.* lec.199 (B1 657; B2 295ra): "Et videtur quod sic, quadrupliciter. Tum quia sic est in aliis artibus quibuscunque, sicut in medicinali, et in musica, quod aliqua approbata ab antiquis doctoribus [auctoribus B2] sunt mutata: tum quia multae de legibus talibus sunt valde barbaricae et irrationabiles, sicut quod cives poterant vendere uxores suas proferro; tum quia homines antiqui fuerunt quasi brutales, et insensati; tum quia leges sunt Scripturae universaliter, actus autem hominum particulares sunt et varii, nec possunt per unam legem regi."

45. Austin (1995), 158; see Finnis (2011), 355.

46. Cf. Finnis (2011), 359.

47. Finnis (2011), 359–360.

48. Finnis (2011), 361.

49. Cf. Finnis (2011), 269, for a discussion of predictability as one of the main features of the legal order.

50. Holcot, *Sap.* lec.199 (B1 657; B2 295^(ra-rb)): "Unde faciliter condere leges novas, et mutare antiquas, est multipliciter nociuum, quia hoc nihil aliud est quam assuefacere homines ad solvendum leges, et ad parvipendendum obligationem legis, et ideo melius est sinere modicos et leves errores, quam solvere leges antiquas. Quia qui frequenter leges mutant, plus nocent quam prosunt; quia assuefaciunt cives ad non observanda statuta principum, et praecepta. Unde tenet Aristoteles quod qui faciliter legem mutat, legis virtutem debilitat."

51. Holcot, *Sap.* lec.199 (B1 657; B2 295^(rb)): "Leges autem positivae in multis non habent obligationem, nisi ex consuetudine, et observantia, et vetustate, et ideo debilitare consuetudinem est debilitare legem."

52. Holcot,*Sap.* lec.199 (B1 657; 295^(rb)): "Si vero essent aliquae leges antiquae, quae manifeste continerent perniciem civitatis, de maturuo consilio abrogari deberent, sed quod nullo consensu, nec hoc communiter frequentaretur."

53. See Brett (1997), 23, n45.
54. Mair, *Sent. IV*, d.15, q.17 (1509).
55. Tierney (1997), 80–81.
56. Tierney (1997), 86–87.
57. Tierney (1997), 84.
58. Holcot, *Sent.* IV, q.7 (L p.7^(ra); O 191^(vb)): *cum nullus teneatur occidere seipsum* ...
59. Holcot, *Sent.* IV, q.7 (L p.6^(vb); O 199^(va)): "Non magis obligatur talis ad aliquam mortem propter iudicium datum quam aliquis obligatur ad aliquid per votum licitum vel per iuramentum licitum, sed possibile est quod aliquis iuste faciens post obligationem per votum vel per iuramentum licitum illud minus bonum commutet in maius bonum ..."
60. Holcot, *Sent.* IV, q.7 (L p.6^(vb); O 199^(va)): *sicut qui vovit ire in terram sanctam* ...
61. Holcot, *Sent.* IV, q.7 (L p.7^(ra); O 199^(va)): *Praeterea ponatur quod sit talis homo pro cuius morte fiat schisma in ecclesia* ...
62. See Appendix A on the ordering of books 3 and 4.
63. MacIntyre (2007), 52–53.
64. See MacIntyre's discussion of Hume (2007), 232.
65. Holcot, *Sent.* III, q.1, a.4 (L m.7^(rb); O 175^(ra)): *Cuius ratio est quia cum poenae debeant esse medicinae* ...
66. Holcot, *Sent.* III, q.1, a.4 (L m.7^(va); O 175^(ra)): *Lex enim numquam praecipit hominem occidi* ...
67. Holcot, *Sent.* III, q.1, a.4 (L m.7^(rb); O 175^(ra)): *Si talis damnatus habeat dictamen conscientiae* ...
68. Cf. Kaminsky (1983), 164–165.
69. Holcot, *Sent.* IV, q.7 (L p.7^(ra); O 199^(va)): *non licet sic sibi fugere* ...
70. Holcot, *Sent.* III, q.1, a.4 (L m.7^(vb); O 175^(rb)): *Dico quod licite potest mortem declinare* ...

71. Holcot, *Sap.* lec.75 (B1 264; B2 120^(rb)): *Concludit hic Spiritus Sanctus ex omnibus praecedentibus* ...
72. Holcot, *Sap.* lec.75 (B1 264; B2 120^(rb)): "Persuadet ergo Spiritus Sanctus in hoc textu quatuor, scilicet humilitatem addiscendi, *Audite reges*: Subtilitatem advertendi, *intelligite*: Aviditatem inquirendi, *Discite*: Severitatem exequendi, *Iudices finium terrae*."
73. See chapter 8.
74. Holcot, *Sap.* lec.75 (B1 264–265; B2 120^(ra–vb)). Cf. Smalley (1956), 49–50.
75. Holcot, *Sap.* lec.75 (B1 265; B2 121^(ra)): *Non solum autem isti in Sacra Scriptura reges dicuntur* ...
76. Holcot, *Sap.* lec.75 (B1 265; B2 121^(ra)): *Intelligere est quasi intus legere* ...
77. Holcot, *Sap.* lec.75 (B1 265–266; B2 121^(ra)): *Et sequitur: 'omnes declinaverunt, simul inutiles facti sunt.'*
78. Holcot, *Sap.* lec.75 (B1 266; B2 121^(ra–rb)).
79. Holcot, *Sap.* lec.75 (B1 265; B2 121^(ra)): *qui se et alios bene regunt* ...
80. Holcot, *Sap.* lec.120 (B1 403; B2 180^(va)): *Dicitur optimo rege, quia impossibile est* ...
81. Holcot, *Sap.* lec.75 (B1 266; B2 121^(rb–va)): *Ultimo persuadet gubernatoribus* ...
82. Holcot, *Sap.* lec.75 (B1 266; B2 121^(va)): *Quia munera excaecant oculos iudicum* ...
83. Holcot, *Sap.* lec.167 (B1 554; B2 248^(ra)): *Tertia est pax curialium praelatorum* ...
84. Holcot, *Sap.* lec.120 (B1 403; B2 180^(va)): *Quia contingit frequenter filium boni regis* ... [frequenter *om.* B2].
85. Holcot, *Sap.* lec.120 (B1 403; B2 180^(va)): *Dicit Aristoteles quod non est credibile* ...
86. Holcot, *Sap.* lec.120 (B1 403; B2 180^(va)): *immo difficile esset et quasi supra naturam humanam* ...
87. Holcot, *Sap.* lec.120 (B1 403; B2 180^(va)): *Sed dicunt expositores, quod melius* ...
88. Holcot, *Sap.* lec.120 (B1 403; B2 180^(va)): "Primo propter discordiam et dissensionem eligentium, secundo propter consuetudinem dominandi in una domo; tertio quod aequali sibi nullus vult subiici de facili; et ideo mutatio regni est periculosa per electionem paci communitatis, sed hoc est per accidens."
89. Holcot, *Sap.* lec.120 (B1 403; B2 180^(va)): *Si enim essent omnes rationabiles* ...
90. Holcot, *Sap.* lec.44 (B1 155; B2 72^(ra)): *Et correspondent istis tribus* ... The Augustinian assertion that three goods flow from marriage (i.e., *fides, proles,* and *sacramentum*) appears to be a common fourteenth-century apology for the value of marriage alongside virginity. See the discussion of Dorothy of Montau (†1394) as described by her confessor John of Marienwerder, "Revera inter eos erat castum et venerabile conjugium, et thorus immaculatus, triplici bono

matrimonii, scilicet *fide, prole, sacramento* praediti et dotati" (Marienwerder, *Vita Dorotheae* 512).

91. Holcot, *Sap.* lec.44 (B1 155–155; B2 72^(rb)): *Sed est quaedam virtus moralis* . . .

92. Holcot, *Sap.* lec.44 (B1 156; B2 72^(rb–va)): *Unde qui habet multos et male educatos* . . .

93. Holcot, *Sap.* lec.44 (B1 156; B2 72^(va)): *Similiter istud intentione sufficienter excusat matrimonium* . . .

94. Holcot, *Sap.* lec.44 (B1 156; B2 72^(va)): *Vir autem et mulier* . . .

95. Holcot, *Sap.* lec.44 (B1 156; B2 72^(va)): *Casta generatio est quando* . . .

96. Holcot, *Sap.* lec.45 (B1 160; B2 74^(rb)): *Non ad divitias, non ad parentęs* . . .

97. Holcot, *Sap.* lec.45 (B1 160; B2 74^(va)): *Cum ergo viri ad uxorem* . . .

98. Holcot, *Sap.* lec.45 (B1 160; B2 74^(va)): *Sed tertia amicitia quae est propter bonum honestum* . . .

99. Holcot, *Sap.* lec.45 (B1 161; B2 74^(vb)): *Secundo est uxor regenda mansuete, non cum tyrannica* . . .

100. Holcot, *Sap.* lec.46 (B1 163; B2 75^(vb)): "Modo prius ostensum est, quod ut communiter personae de fornicatione [de fornicatio concubitu B2] generatae non sunt morigeratae, nec bonae personaliter, propter defectum educationis personalis. Ideo Spiritus Sanctus hic consequenter ostendit, quod non sunt apti ad communitatem civilem, unde continuatio talis est. Postquam ostendit, quod generatio coniugalis summe valet ad continuandum terreni regni perpetuitatem, quia sicut dictum est in *perpetuum coronata triumphat*. Hic ostendit quod generatio adulterina summe dispergit terreni regni civilitatem."

101. Holcot, *Sap.* lec.46 (B1 163; B2 75^(vb)): "Est tamen hic notandum quod omnis humana persona duplicem habere potest bonitatem: unam sibi propriam vivendo virtuose in sua persona; aliam civilem vivendo civiliter reipublicae."

102. Holcot, *Sap.* lec.46 (B1 163; B2 75^(vb)): "Unde non est idem esse bonum virum et bonum civem. Cuius ratio est, quia bona persona dicitur quae vivit conformiter legi datae communiter pro omnibus, sed civis bonus non est nisi qui vivit utiliter civitati, cuius pars est."

103. Holcot, *Sap.* lec.46 (B1 163; B2 75^(vb)): *Primo ostendit quod talis* . . .

104. Holcot, *Sap.* lec.46 (B1 163; B2 75^(vb)): *Secundo ostendit, quod dato, quod leges rationabiles* . . .

105. See the discussion of these three critieria in the beginning of the section on laws in this chapter.

106. Holcot, *Sap.* lec.46 (B1 164; B2 76^(ra)): "Leges civiles per tales gentes nunquam poterunt bene ordinari, probatur sic: Nulla lex potest statui ex concordi voluntate gentis alicuius, sed talis gens quae ex una parte est impia in se ipsa, et ex alia parte multigena: id est, ex distinctis et diversis generibus

educata: nunquam bene concordabit in lege statuenda. Ergo talis gens non est utilis ad constituendum leges civiles."

107. Holcot, *Sap.* lec.46 (B1 164; B2 76[ra]): *Ista ratio exprimitur sub hac forma* . . .

108. Holcot, *Sap.* lec.46 (B1 164; B2 76[ra]): "Secundo necessarium est, quod leges bene excogitatae sint per approbationem longam et consuetudinem radicatae; sed hoc non potest fieri in humano genere, dato indifferenter fornicario concubitu et adulterino."

109. Holcot, *Sap.* lec.46 (B1 164; B2 76[ra]): *Et ratio est, quia talis* . . .

110. Holcot, *Sap.* lec.46 (B1 163; B2 76[ra–rb]): *Tertio necessarium est quod leges* . . .

111. Holcot, *Sap.* lec.46 (B1 164; B2 76[rb]): "Quia nulla lex durabit hoc stante, etiam si per seniores ordinetur. Cuius ratio est quia filii tales non recipiunt monita patrum. Sicut enim rami debile nutrimentum recipientes a radicibus germinare vel florere possunt, sed non fructificare, ita nec isti, licet possint incipere virtuose agere, non tamen possunt continuare."

CHAPTER 10

1. Tugwell (1982), 14.
2. Tugwell (1982), 11.
3. Tugwell (1982), 14.
4. See Mulchahey (1998), 130–218.
5. For a list of the manuscripts, early printed editions, and modern editions of Humbert's works, see Mulchahey (1998), 563–564; Tugwell (1982), 477–479.
6. Humbert, *OFP*, 190.
7. On Simon, see Gelber (2004), 75–76; Forte (1952), 321–345.
8. See B5 1[r]–152[v]; SA 2[ra]–244[va].
9. Gelber (2004), 85.
10. Our general discussion of late medieval preaching has benefitted greatly from: d'Avray (1985); Spencer (1993); O'Carroll (1997); and Wenzel (2005a), 227–394. For a useful historiographical essay, see Muessig (2002).
11. See Humbert, *OFP*, 326–370.
12. See Spencer (1993) and Wenzel (2005a). Cf. Humbert, *OFP*, 326–363.
13. We use the term "lectionary" in its strict sense (as distinct from a missal) because our focus is on the scriptural texts and not the accompanying prayers (which are included in the missal but not the lectionary).
14. On the Sarum Use, see Pfaff (2009), 350–387 and 412–444; on the York Use, see 445–462.
15. See O'Carroll, (1979); Pfaff (2009), 311–349.
16. Holcot's sermon collection in P1 follows the Sarum Use.
17. See Pierce (1997).

18. For a fuller account of the Proper, see Spencer (1993), 24–33. Our description benefits from Spencer's account.
19. Wenzel (2005a), 7.
20. Wenzel (2005a), 9.
21. Wenzel (2005a), 10. Recent scholarship on fourteenth-century vernacular sermons has demonstrated the reliance of the vernacular sermons on the Latin sermon tradition. See Fletcher (2004).
22. Spencer (1993), 16. Spencer also notes that this is perhaps true for other Latin preachers, such as John Waldeby (†c. 1372), Thomas Brinton (†1389), and Robert Rypon (†c. 1420). See also Wenzel (2005a) 40–44, 45–49, and 66–73. For a discussion of FitzRalph, see Walsh (1981), 182–238.
23. Wenzel (2005a), 10.
24. Holcot, *Sermon* 1 (P1 1ra–2vb).
25. Wenzel (2005a), 9.
26. Holcot, *Sermons* 109 and 111 (P1 176^r *in marg.* and 177^r *in marg.*). Smalley (1960), 145, also notes *Sermon* 72 (P1 113ra–115vb).
27. Wenzel (2005a), 9.
28. Holcot, *Sermon* 111 (P1 177ra).
29. For extensive examples of the latter, see Owst (1926).
30. Walsh (1981), 214. On FitzRalph, see Wenzel (2005a), 271–275.
31. Holcot, *Sermon* 42 (P1 51vb): "Ista verba possunt applicari praedicari."
32. Courtenay (1987), 41–48.
33. On fourteenth-century *principia*, see Brown (1976, 1991, and 1997); Courtenay (2011).
34. See also Wenzel (1995a).
35. Holcot, *Sermon* 47 (P1 60va). See Smalley (1960), 144, n5.
36. See Wey (1949). It is also probable that sermon 59 of the Toulouse manuscript originated from a similar context, as it is preserved as an *academic introitus* (an inaugural lecture). See T2 176^v–179^r.
37. Holcot, *Sap.* lec.97 (B1 330; B2 148rb).
38. Holcot, *Sap.* lec.97 (B1 330; B2 148rb): *Ista verba sunt* ...
39. As Wenzel argues, Holcot here puns on the term *universitatis* (meaning both universality and the university). See Wenzel (1986), 70.
40. On the development of thirteenth-century sermons, see Rouse-Rouse (1979), 65–90; Spencer (1993), 235–247; and Wenzel (1986).
41. Spencer (1993), 235–242.
42. On Waleys see Smalley (1954), 50–107. The text is edited in Charland (1936), 328–403, and translated by Grosser (1949).
43. In sermon 107 (P1 172ra) Holcot makes a distinction between ancient and modern preachers. Here he notes a difference between ancient and modern preachers with respect to doing miracles.
44. See also Mulchahey (1998), 401–419, here 402.

NOTES 321

45. The structure of a scholastic sermon was sometimes depicted visually in an *arbor de arte praedicandi* (a tree of the art of preaching). See Charland (1936), 1–2 and Dieter (1965).
46. See Charland (1936), 109–226; Spencer (1993), 247–251 and 335–358; and Wenzel (2005a), 11–16.
47. Throughout we use the Latin term *thema*, as there is no suitable English equivalent.
48. Holcot, *Sermon* 50 (P1 64vb–68vb). We use this sermon as an exemplar because, as Wenzel has argued, it was quite popular. He notes that it is found in W 106ra–107vb and A 136^{r}–140^{v}. See Wenzel (2005b).
49. See Wenzel's useful discussion and examples (2005), 12–14; also Wenzel (1986), 66–100.
50. Holcot, *Sermon* 50 (P1 65^{va-vb}).
51. Holcot, *Sermon* 50 (P1 65vb).
52. Mulchahey (1998), 407 (see also her description of *dilatatio* on 409–419).
53. Some have argued that this structure is rather devoid of inspiration and somewhat formulaic. For example, see Coleman (1981a), 193ff. *Pace* Coleman, see Wenzel (1986), 61–100.
54. Wenzel (2005a), 16.
55. See the *Dec. Greg.*, pars.1, tit.31, cap.15 (Friedberg 2.192).
56. The present discussion follows that of Wenzel (2005a), 230–235. See also Spencer (1993).
57. See *Councils and Synods* I, 268.
58. *Councils and Synods* I, 900–905, here 900.
59. Wenzel (2005a), 232. *Councils and Synods* I, 900–901.
60. See Boyle (1955).
61. See Charland (1936) and Briscoe-Barbara (1992).
62. Mulchahey (1998), 419–447.
63. *Florilegia* is a term used to designate collections or gatherings of sayings by authorities such as Ambrose of Milan, John Chrysostom, Jerome, and Augustine of Hippo. Mulchahey (1998), 448–458.
64. See also the *Fasciculus Morum* (edited by Wenzel). Wenzel argues that the *Fasciculus Morum* deserves closer analysis alongside Holcot's sermons (1986), 233; id. (1978), 31, 33, 59, 89, and 118.
65. Humbert's *De eruditione praedicatorum* consists of two works: the *De eruditione praedicatorum* and the later *De modo prompte cudendi sermones*. See Brett (1984), 153.
66. Wenzel (2008) makes a compelling case that sermon 60 (A 120^{v}–123^{v}) was written by Robert Holcot. Holcot's now lost *De praedicationis officio opusculum* was probably a work on the art of preaching.
67. See Mulchahey (1998), 476, n228; and Brett (1984), 151–166.
68. On the seven parts see Humbert, *OFP*, 184–325.

69. See Mulchahey (1998), 477. Mulchahey (1998), 476, argues that while Humbert's text is often placed in the *artes praedicandi* literature, it is a unique work.
70. Humbert, *OFP*, 186, 187, and 190.
71. Waleys, *DMCS*, 328.
72. Waleys, *DMCS*, 329–341.
73. Waleys, *DMCS*, 338. See Murphy (1974), 333.
74. For a discussion of the distinction between the two types of sermons, see Waleys, *DMCS*, 341–349, esp. 344.
75. For a discussion of attribution, see Wenzel (2008), 55 and 59. The sermon is preserved in sermon 60 (A 120^v–123^v). We follow the analysis of Wenzel.
76. Wenzel (2008), 56 and 62.
77. Wenzel (2008), 56 and 65.
78. Wenzel (2008), 56 and 66–73.
79. Wenzel (2008), 57 and 73–75.
80. Wenzel (2008), 60.
81. Robert Holcot is linked to a *distinctiones* collection, and Richard Sharpe references it as authentic in his catalogue. Sharpe (2001), no. 1475. Cf. Bloomfield (1979), no. 0063 and no. 0066. Sharpe observes that the work is found in five manuscripts (incipit *Abominabitur autem Deus tales*) and should be distinguished from the work by Eustasius de Portu (incipit *Abicere debemus*). However, the situation is somewhat more complicated. An example of Eustasius de Portu's *Distinctiones* can found in the Lambeth Palace Library (incipit, *Abicere debemus*; LA 58va–154rb). Cf. Kaeppeli (1980), no. 1063. Here the work attributed to Eustasius by Sharpe and others begins with the incipit *Abicere debemus* and occupies about 77 folios (58va–145vb). This is followed by a short unidentified work (146ra–148vb) and a table (149ra–154rb) attributed to Holcot on the header of every recto leaf and in the colophon (*Explicit tabula super distinctiones Holkote*).

While it is possible that there is an authentic collection of *distinctiones* written by Robert Holcot, we have not discovered such a collection. The Lambeth manuscript that we consulted contains a *distinctiones* collection by Eustasius de Portu and a table that was attributed to Holcot. The Basel manuscript contains the text of Eustasius but not the table attributed to Holcot (see BA 230ra–255vb). Further, the incipit usually given for Holcot's *distinctiones* collection (*Abominabitur autem Deus tales*) is in fact the incipit of the table that corresponds to Eustasius' text and is attributed to Holcot. This fact does not inspire confidence that there is an authentic collection yet to be discovered. On *distinctiones* literature, see Pfander (1934); Rouse-Rouse (1974); Smalley (1978), 246–249; Bataillon (1982, 1994); and Ohly (2005).
82. Mulchahey (1998), 474.
83. Holcot, *Sermon* 106 (P1 171ra): *Dici potest, 'Multi ambulant'* . . .

CHAPTER 11

1. Welter (1927), 1. We have used the Latin *exemplum/exempla* throughout as it is a technical term with no strict English equivalent.
2. Palmer (1996), 584.
3. Palmer (1996), 585.
4. Holcot, *Moralitas* 30 (B1 734); 31 (B1 734–736), and 35 (B1 738–739). We use the Basel edition (B1), see Smalley (1956), 25.
5. Aquinas, *ST* I, q.1, a.10 (Leonine IV, 25). For a discussion of the four senses of interpreting Scripture, see de Lubac (1998, 2000, 2009).
6. This phrase is from Allen (1971), 4.
7. Allen (1971), 6. Allen's work builds on Smalley (1960) and seeks to define precisely the notion of a "spiritual sense of fiction."
8. Justin Martyr, *First Apology* 59.1 and 59.5–59.6.
9. Origen, *The Song of Songs*, 60–61.
10. Origen, *A Letter from Origen to Gregory*, 393–394.
11. Augustine, *Confessions* 7.9.15 (*WSA* 1.1; 133–134). On the relationship between Christian thought and Classical culture, see Pelikan (1993).
12. Alan, *Summa de arte praedicatoria*, c.1 (*PL* 210, 114): *In fine vero* . . .
13. Waleys, *De modo componendi sermones*, c.8 (Charland 386): *Quantum ad modum dilatandi* . . .
14. Holcot, *Sap.* lec.96 (B1 325; B2 146ra): *Ita doctrinae gentilium* . . .
15. See Oberman (1962), 320–322.
16. Fulgentius wrote a work called the *Mythologiae* in three books. See Hays (2003), 163–252 and Zink (1867).
17. See Ridevall, *Fulgentius metaforalis*.
18. On *exemplum* literature, see also Kemmler (1984).
19. Welter (1927), 366, n63.
20. Slotemaker (2016).
21. Smalley (1960), 146.
22. Welter (1927), 363.
23. Smalley (1981), 376.
24. S1 135: *Explicit tractatus, qui* . . .
25. See Ward-Herbert (1883–1910), III, 116–117; Smalley (1960), 147; Welter (1927), 362–366; and Wenzel (1978), 118.
26. A1 244^r–266^v
27. See H-C 202^r–217^r.
28. Smalley (1956), 27–28. For further information see the introduction to Hans Liebeschütz's edition of John Ridevall's *Fulgentius metaforalis*.
29. In late fourteenth- and fifteenth-century manuscripts there are numerous works misattributed to Holcot. To give just two examples, a Paris manuscript (BN) explicitly attributes three works to Holcot: the *Moralitates* (73^r–99^v), the *Imagines Fulgentii moralisatae* (99^v–115^r), and the *Aenigmata Aristotelis moralisata* (115^r–119^r). While the first is by Holcot, the *Imagines* is by John Ridevall and

the *Aenigmata* is anonymous. A similar instance is found in a Heidelberg manuscript (H) which attributes five works to Holcot: the *Moralitates* (1^r–30^v); the *Imagines Fulgentii moralisatae sive Fulgentius Metaforalis* (30^v–48^r); the *Imagines Fulgentii, sive de imaginibus virtutum* (48^r–65^r); the *Aenigmata Aristotelis moralisata* (65^r–70^r), and the *Declamationes Senecae moralisatae* (70^r–93^v) (by Nicholas of Trevet). As with the Paris manuscript, only the *Moralitates* was written by Holcot. Cf. BA4 1^r–42va which includes: *Moralitates* (1^r–16^v), *Aenig. Arist.* (16v–18v), *Imag. Fulg. moral.* (19^r–29^v), and *Decl. Senec. moral.* (29^v–39^r).
30. See Krug (2009).
31. See Smalley (1960), 183; Rivers (2010), 213, n17; Palmer (1991), 137–172; and Welter (1927), 369–375, esp. 371.
32. Hermann Oesterley lists 138 manuscripts in his introduction to the *Gesta Romanorum* and another 27 in an appendix (1872), 750–751.
33. Wright, *Gesta*, ix.
34. Holcot, *Moralitas* 11 (B1 720–721).
35. Of course lust, pride, and greed are counted among the seven deadly sins. On this, see Newhauser-Ridyard (2012).
36. Holcot, *Moralitas* 11 (B1 720): *Quia lex naturae fuit* . . .
37. Holcot, *Moralitas* 11 (B1 720): *Lex Mosaica, quae* . . .
38. Holcot, *Moralitas* 11 (B1 720–721): *Sed tertius miles Dei* . . .
39. Holcot, *Moralitas* 11 (B1 721): *Nam ipsa lex Evangelica* . . .
40. Holcot, *Moralitas* 11 (B1 721): *Et quicunquae istos* . . .
41. See Holcot, *Moralitas* 2 (B1 710).
42. *Fasciculus morum* I.i–I.vii (Wenzel 65–93) and I.viii–I.xi (Wenzel 65–93).
43. *Fasciculus morum* VII.i–VII.xvi (Wenzel 648–701) and VII.xvii–VII.xx (Wenzel 703–727).
44. *Fasciculus morum* IV.i–IV.ix (Wenzel 312–371) and IV.xi–xii (Wenzel 383–395).
45. Holcot, *Moralitas* 12 (B1 721).
46. Holcot, *Moralitas* 12 (B1 721): *In circuitu vero* . . .
47. Holcot, *Moralitas* 12 (B1 721): *In circuitu scriptum erat* . . .
48. Holcot, *Moralitas* 35 (B1 738–739).
49. Holcot, *Moralitas* 35 (B1 739): . . . *per longas aures eius.*
50. Holcot, *Moralitas* 35 (B1 739): *Quae induit vel vestit* . . .
51. Holcot, *Moralitas* 35 (B1 739): *Quia despicit superbos* . . .
52. The 1586 edition of the *Moralitates* includes biblical citations in the margins of the text for the majority of the entries.
53. Holcot, *Moralitas* 8 (B1 716): *Versus amor fortis* . . .
54. Holcot, *Moralitas* 8 (B1 716): *Pro primo versu habemus* . . .
55. Holcot, *Moralitas* 8 (B1 716): *Nota quadruplex est signum* . . .
56. Holcot, *Moralitas* 8 (B1 716): *Pro secundo versu* . . .
57. Holcot, *Moralitas* 8 (B1 716): *Secundo quittavit* . . .

58. Holcot, *Moralitas* 8 (B1 716): *Pro tertio versu* . . .
59. Holcot, *Moralitas* 8 (B1 716): *Quia habemus advocatum* . . .
60. Holcot, *Moralitas* 8 (B1 716): *Pro quarto versu* . . .
61. Cf. *De septem clamoribus Christi* in ST 202^v.
62. Liturgically the order has traditionally been: Luke 23:34, Luke 23:43, John 19:26–27, Matthew 27:46/Mark 15:34, John 19:28, John 19:29–30, and Luke 23:46.
63. See Alan of Lille, *Sermones Octo, Sermon* 8 (*PL* 210, 218). Alan lists seven heptads (although Holcot's list is not limited to Alan's).
64. Wenzel (2005b), 146.
65. Holcot repeats this phrase "Is this not great humility" (*nonne magna humilitas*) for each of the seven cries.
66. Holcot, *Moralitas* 8 (B1 717): *Bernhardus 'Super Cantica'* . . .
67. For a discussion of love as the boy with four wings, see the analysis of Holcot, Dirc van Delf, and the *Gesta Romanorum* in Lievens (2012), 167–194, here 186.

CHAPTER 12

1. Quoted in Ozment (1981), 238.
2. The Toulouse manuscript (T2) is of Dominican origin and contains 90 sermons by six English preachers who flourished during the fourteenth century. This work has been studied extensively in Kaeppeli (1959), 89–110. See also Wenzel (2005a), 132–135; Kaeppeli (1980), n3494 and n3502.
3. Thomas Kaeppeli noted that the Padua manuscript (A) contains sermons by Holcot. Kaeppeli (1980), n3502 (Kaeppeli referenced A 81^r–117^v and 119^r–123^v). Here Kaeppeli followed the catalog of Giuseppe Abate and Giovanni Luisetto (Abate and Luisetto (1975), II, 529–530). Katherine Tachau subsequently debated the attribution by Abate and Luisetto of the entire section (i.e., A 81^r–117^v) to Holcot. Tachau notes that there is marginal attribution for three specific sermons (on folios 78^v, 81^r, and 119^r) and that scholars must withhold judgment until further comparative work on Holcot's sermon manuscripts is completed. See Tachau (1991), 337–345 (see A 78^v–79^r, 81^r–81^v, and 119^r–120^v). Siegfried Wenzel further complicated the picture by arguing that a sermon on the *ars praedicandi* on folios 120^v–123^v is probably of Dominican origin and perhaps by Robert Holcot. See Wenzel (2008). We concur with Tachau's judgment that until a comparative study between the Cambridge, Toulouse, and Padua manuscripts is complete, it is difficult to determine with certainty what other sermons in A are by Holcot.
4. See Slotemaker (2015).
5. Fletcher (2004), 27–98, here 31, n13. See Holcot, *Sermon* 24 (P1 32ra): "In quibus verbis tria includuntur, quae curatuum quaelibet fructuo suum commendant, scilicet ligamen obedientiae [oportet], conamen diligentiae et sedulitatis, me esse; solamen reverentiae et magnae dignitatis, quia in hiis que patris

mei sunt. In hiis, inquam, etc. Anglice: *bond of buxumnesse, lif of bysynesse, stat of worthynesse*." See also Wenzel (1994) and (1978).

6. See *The Sarum Missal*. Smalley (1960), 143, n3.
7. P1, flyleaf: "Rob. Holcoth, Mr. Oxon. multiplicis eruditionis vir obiit 1349: sermones per annum."
8. P1 1^r: "Holkot in sermonibus tam dominicis quam feriis."
9. Wenzel (2005a), 2.
10. Wenzel (2005a), 3.
11. On this issue, see Wenzel (2005a), 2–4, in particular his discussion of d'Avray (1985), 78–90.
12. For the foliation, *thema*, Scripture passage, and incipit for each sermon, see Slotemaker (2015), 91–115.
13. I.e., the 1st (99, 100), 2nd (101); 3rd (102, 103), 5th (104); 6th (105); 7th (106), 13th/18th (108), 15th (110), 20th (112–114), 21st (115), 22nd (116), and 23rd (117, 118).
14. Holcot, *Sermon* 76 (P1 121rb–124ra). Our discussion in the remainder of this chapter borrows from that in Slotemaker-Witt (in press).
15. See Wright (2000).
16. P 121^r.
17. In this sermon Holcot's focus is not on the implications of Christ's suffering for trinitarian theology or divine impassibility. Cf. e.g., Johnson (2012), 45.
18. Holcot, *Sermon* 76 (P 121va): *Secundum quod dicit beatus Augustinus* ...
19. Holcot, *Sermon* 76 (P 121va): *Dolor proprie est tristitia animae* ...
20. Holcot, *Sermon* 76 (P 121va): *Primo do quod* ...
21. Holcot, *Sermon* 76 (P 121va): *Satan autem dedit* ...
22. Holcot, *Sermon* 76 (P 121^{va-vb}). Holcot continues to build on this arugment by observing that God created man in his own image and likeness.
23. Holcot, *Sermon* 76 (P 121vb): *Cum ergo Deus tantum dilexit* ...
24. Holcot, *Sermon* 76 (P 121vb): *Dixi secundo quod* ...
25. Holcot, *Sermon* 76 (P 121vb): *Sed Christus cum* ...
26. Holcot, *Sermon* 76 (P 121vb): *Et certe Christus* ...
27. Holcot, *Sermon* 76 (P 122ra): *Tertio dixi quod* ...
28. Holcot, *Sermon* 76 (P 122rb): *Dicit enim Cassiodorus* ...
29. Holcot, *Sermon* 76 (P 122rb): *Et istius opinionis* ...
30. Holcot, *Sermon* 76 (P 122vb): *Nec mirum quia* ...
31. Cf. Jonah 4:3 and Job 10:18–19.
32. Holcot, *Sermon* 76 (P 123ra): *Ubi virtutes animae* ...
33. Holcot, *Sermon* 76 (P 123ra): *Sed quamvis quilibet regna* ...
34. Holcot, *Sermon* 76 (P 123ra): *Ex quibus omnibus* ...
35. Holcot, *Sermon* 76 (P 123rb): *Sic peccatores, quando* ...
36. Holcot, *Sermon* 76 (P 123^{rb-va}): *Primi sunt cupidi mercatores* ...
37. Holcot, *Sermon* 76 (P 123va): *Sic plures moderni* ...
38. Holcot, *Sermon* 76 (P 123^{va-vb}): *Sunt etiam alii peccatores* ...

39. Holcot, *Sermon* 76 (P 123vb): *Sed modicum post pascha* . . .
40. Holcot, *Sermon* 76 (P 123vb): *Tertio sunt alii peccatores* . . .
41. Judges 9:17.
42. Holcot, *Sermon* 76 (P 123vb): *Non sit, carissimi* . . .
43. Holcot, *Sermon* 76 (P 124ra): *Si autem animam tuam* . . .

APPENDICES

1. The difficulty with the manuscripts was evident to the Augustinian Hermit Augustinus de Ratispona (who edited L1). Augustinus writes in the preface: "Subtilissimas dico Magister Roberti de Holkot *Super libros Sententiarum* disquisitiones . . . Incredibili siquidem labore fere ab interitu redemptae sunt." Further, at several points Augustinus notes textual problems. See *Sent.* I, q.1, a.4 (L1 a.4ra): "Nota quod iste articulus est diminutus et incompletus. . . .". Streveler-Tachau-Courtenay-Gelber (1995), 36–38, list 48 manuscripts of Holcot's *Sentences* commentary, to which BA2 must be added (we have been able to consult BA2, BA4, CC, M, O, and T).
2. Tachau (1995), 197–199.
3. Streveler and Tachau also skipped number 2 when ordering the questions in book 4, such that their list reads, Q1, Q3, Q4, etc. Tachau (1995), 199.
4. See Gelber (2004), 294–306; Tachau (1994); and Schepers (1970).
5. Gelber notes that book 3 is primarily a response to a *socius* and relies on some of the discussion of the *Six Articles*—therefore, she positions the *Six Articles* in the summer after lecturing on books 1 and 2 and before lecturing on 3 and 4. However, she still seems to follow Streveler-Tachau-Courtenay-Gelber by seeing book 3 as preceding book 4. She writes: "The debate betweeen Chitterne and Holcot did not end with the *Sex articuli*. Chitterne continued to object to Holcot's views, and during the fall of 1332, in his *Sentences* commentary, book 3, q.1 Holcot again addressed the objections of his *socius*" (Gelber [2004], 303). By locating this response in the fall, Gelber suggests that his lectures on book 3 were delivered prior to book 4.
6. Note that in the Mazarine (M) 55vb, this position is recorded as "dixi sic: sit aequalis deliberatio et aequalis consensus et circumstantiae . . ." The perfect tense of *dixi* once again confirms that Holcot is jumping into an ongoing conversation.
7. Holcot, *Sent.* III, q.1 (L m.1rb; O 172ra): *Sicut nitebar persuadere per quatuor rationes. . . Sed contra istam conclusionem* . . .
8. The third argument introduced in book 4 does not seem to have a parallel, while book 3 adds a fourth and fifth argument that were not present in book 4. This is corroborated by the fact that arguments 1 through 3 in book 3 begin in the imperfect tense while arguments 4 and 5 do not. Likewise, after finishing the third argument, Holcot writes: "ad hoc nihil dictum est" (O m.3ra;

L 172vb) suggesting that he is reintroducing three of the original arguments that his *socius* ignored.

9. arguebam O, arguo L.
10. For a further discussion of these passages see chapter 9.
11. Courtenay (1994), 325–350; Schabel (2009), 150.
12. Farago-Bermon (2013), 176.
13. Note that Streveler-Tachau-Courtenay-Gelber do not list Q2 and move directly to Q3.
14. Gelber, following Schepers, explains that the *Six Articles* were written during the summer between lecturing on books 1 and 2 and books 3 and 4. See Gelber (2004), 296–297. Thus they should probably be placed betweeen Streveler and Tachau's 12 and 13.
15. This question is also found in B4 101ra–110rb and R 89vb–98vb (note that the question lists in B4 and R are identical for all four books, as is the inclusion of four of the *Six Articles*).
16. This question is also found in B4 110rb–120ra and R 98vb–108vb.
17. For information regarding the manuscripts, see Glorieux (1935), 258–261; Molteni (1967), 155–165; Hoffmann (1972), 414–430; Gillespie (1971), 480–490, and (1974), 99–152; and Gelber (1983), 113–117. The table here benefits from those of Molteni (1967), 159–165 and Gelber (1983), 113–116.
18. Courtenay (1980), 109–110.
19. Keele (2007), 681–682, esp. n72.
20. This question is also found in B4 91ra–100va and R 85va–89rb.
21. This question is also found in B4 100va–101ra and R 89^{rb-vb}.
22. Kennedy (1993), 156–157.
23. Kennedy (1993), 158–159.
24. This question title is identical to question 77 (although the content is distinct).
25. Kennedy (1993), 160–163.
26. Kennedy (1993), 164–170.
27. Kennedy (1993), 171–175.
28. Kennedy (1993), 176–179.
29. Streveler-Tachau-Courtenay-Gelber (1995), 59–72.
30. Streveler-Tachau-Courtenay-Gelber (1995), 73–74.
31. Streveler-Tachau-Courtenay-Gelber (1995), 75–79.
32. Molteni (1967), 174–204; Gillespie (1974), 167–206.
33. Streveler-Tachau-Courtenay-Gelber (1995), 80–111.
34. Muckle (1958).
35. Gelber (1983), 29–51.
36. Gelber (1983), 63–112.
37. Gelber (1983), 53–61.
38. Moody (1964) (from R); Courtenay (1971) (imbibed from P, B, and R).

39. Kennedy (1993), 180–183.
40. Molteni (1967), 166–173; Gillespie (1974), 207–224.
41. Smalley (1956), 11.
42. potentiam] violentiam VP-list.
43. persecutores] Iudaei VP-list.
44. sancti] beati VP-list.
45. filiis debeant aliquod damnum propter defectum natalium] filii adulterini debeant aliquod incommodum T-list, VP-list.
46. vim] violentiam VP-list.
47. The phrasing here is taken from the tables in VP and T, since B1 simply states: "an ipse peccaverit hoc faciendo."
48. Lecture 71 is shorter in B2 and breaks off after the first question.
49. In B2 a quire is missing between 125^v and 126^r of the modern foliation. As a result, part of lecture 79 (including part of the *quaestio*) is missing.
50. stellarum] *om.* B2.
51. adorandus] *in marg.* B2.
52. prophetiae] sapientiae B2.
53. Note that the VP-list suggests that this appears in lecture 188 (or lecture 189 in B1) and the wording of the question is slightly different: "Utrum divinae ordinationi omnia dantur". Nevertheless, we think it is the same question as it appears here in lecture 105.
54. praelatorum] *om.* B2.
55. VP-list and T-list read: "Utrum liceat imagines facere planetis existentibus in ceteris locis."
56. This phrasing comes from the VP-list. The text itself phrases the *dubitatio* as "Ecce, inquit, ancilla Domini fiat mihi secundum, etc. De dictis hic dubitatio oritur. Impossibile videtur apud grammaticos, quod nomen reddat suppositum verbo, et tamen non regatur a verbo" (B1 670).

BIBLIOGRAPHY

PRIMARY SOURCES

A. Manuscripts: Robert Holcot

Basel, Universitätsbibliothek
   A.II.26 (*Dist.*)
   A.V.33 (*Moral.*)
   A.XI.36 (*Sent.*)
   B.V.11 (*Sup. Eccli.*)
   B.VIII.10 (*Moral.*)
Braunschweig, Stadtbibliothek
   136 (*Sup. Eccle.*)
Cambridge, Pembroke College Library
   236 (*Quodl.*)
Cambridge, Peterhouse
   210 (*Serm.*)
Düsseldorf, Universitäts-und Landesbibliothek
   F.5 (*Quodl.*)
Heidelberg, Universitätsbibliothek
   Cod. Sal. VII, 104 (*Moral.*)
Leipzig, Universitätsbibliothek
   344 (*Sup. Eccle.*)

London, British Library
    Royal 2.D.IV (*Sup. Eccli.*)
    Royal 2.F.VII (*Sap.*)
    Royal 10.C.VI (*Quodl.*)
London, British Museum
    Add. 21,429 (*Tractatus de septem vitiis*)
    Sloane 1616 (*Convertimini*)
London, Gray's Inn
    2 (*Sup. XII*)
London, Lambeth Palace
    221 (*Distinctiones*)
Madrid, Biblioteca Nacional
    507 (*Sup. Eccle.*)
Oxford, Balliol College Library
    26 (*Sup. XII*)
    27 (*Sap.*)
    71 (*Sent.*)
    246 (*Quodl.*)
Oxford, Bodleian Library
    SC 2648 (Bodl. 722) (*Sup. XII*)
Oxford, Corpus Christi
    138 (*Sent.*)
Oxford, Oriel College
    15 (*Sent.*)
Padua, Biblioteca Antoniana
    515 (*Serm.*)
Paris, Bibliothèque Nationale
    lat. 590 (*Moral.*)
Paris, Mazarine
    905 (*Sent.*)
Toulouse, Bibliothèque Municipale
    342 (*Introitus serm.*)
Troyes, Médiathèques de l'agglomération Troyenne
    634 (*Sent.*)
    907 (*Sap.*)
Valencia, Cathedral
    191 (*Sup. XII*)
Vatican, Biblioteca Apostolica Vaticana
    Chigiani A.IV.84 (*Apoc.*)
    Ottoboniani Latini 215 (*Sap.*)
    Palatini Latini 118 (*Sap.*)
Vienna
    Dominikanerbibliothek 14/14 (*Sup. Eccle.*)
    Österreichische Nationalbibliothek 4149 (*Sup. Eccle.*)

Worcester, Cathedral Library
F.126 (*Serm.*)

B. *Manuscripts: Other Authors*

Halle, Universitäts- und Landesbibliothek Sachsen-Anhalt
Yc 2° 1 (S. Boraston, *Distinctiones*)
Oxford, Bodleian Library
216 (S. Boraston, *Distinctiones*)
Laud Misc. 160 (W. Middleton, *Super XII Prophetas*)
Rawlinson C 427 (S. Langton, *Super XII Prophetas*)
Oxford, New College
53 (S. Hinton, *Super XII Prophetas*)
Paris, Bibliothèque de la Sorbonne
193 (A. Wodeham, *Ord. Ox.*)
Paris, Bibliothèque Nationale
Lat. 15853 (R. FitzRalph, *Sent.*)
Reims, Bibliothèque Municipale
506 (P. Plaoul, *Comm.*)
Rome, Biblioteca Casanatense
cod. Basil A.V.23 (Fifteenth-Century Picture Book)
Strasbourg, Bibliothèque nationale et universitaire
0.074 (*De septem clamoribus Christi*)

C. *Incunabula and Early Printed Editions*

Cornelius de Lapide. *Commentarius in librum Sapientiae.* Antwerp, 1725.
Jacques Almain. *Dictata ... super Sententias magistri Roberti Holcot.* Paris, 1526.
Jean de Lorin. *Commentarius in librum Sapientiae.* Lyon, 1607.
Johannes Trithemius. *Liber de scriptoribus ecclesiasticis.* Basel, 1494.
Johannes von Werden. *Sermones dormi secure de tempore.* Nürnberg, 1498.
John Mair. *Joannes Major in primum Sententiarum.* Paris, 1510.
John Mair. *Quartus Sententiarum Johannis Majoris.* Paris, 1509.
Robert Holcot (spurious). *Heptalogus ... de origine diffinitione et remediis peccatorum.* Basel, 1517.
Robert Holcot. *In librum Sapientiae regis Salomonis praelectiones.* Basel, 1586.
Robert Holcot. *In quatuor libros Sententiarum quaestiones.* Lyon, 1518; reprinted Frankfurt, 1967.
Robert Holcot. *Moralitates.* Venice, 1514.
Robert Holcot. *Super librum Ecclesiastici.* Venice, 1509.
Robert Holcot. *Super libros Sapientiae.* Hagenau, 1494; reprinted Frankfurt, 1974.
Robert Holcot. *Super quatuor libros Sententiarum quaestiones.* Lyon, 1497.

Robert Holcot. *Super quatuor libros Sententiarum quaestiones.* Lyon, 1505 and 1510.

Thomas Buckingham. *Quaestiones . . . in quattuor libros Sententiarum.* Paris, 1505.

D. Works by Robert Holcot: Edited Texts

Robert Holcot. *Commentary on the Twelve Prophets.* The book of Nahum is edited in Kimberly A. Rivers, "Pictures, Preaching and Memory in Robert Holcot's Commentary on the Twelve Prophets." MSL Thesis, University of Toronto, 1993.

Robert Holcot. *Quaestiones quodlibetales.* In *Exploring the Boundaries of Reason: Three Questions on the Nature of God by Robert Holcot, OP.* H. Gelber (ed.). Toronto, 1983.

Robert Holcot. *Quaestiones quodlibetales.* In *Roberto Holcot O.P.: Dottrina della grazia e della giustificazione con due questioni quodlibetali inedite.* Paolo Molteni (ed.). Pinerolo, 1967.

Robert Holcot. *Quaestiones quodlibetales.* In *Seeing the Future Clearly: Questions on Future Contingents.* P. Streveler, K. Tachau, W.J. Courtenay, and H. Gelber (eds.). Toronto, 1995.

Robert Holcot. *Quaestiones quodlibetales.* In Ernest A. Moody, "A Quodlibetal Question of Robert Holcot, O.P. on the Problem of the Objects of Knowledge and of Belief." *Speculum*, 39 (1964), 53–74, 142–150.

Robert Holcot. *Quaestiones quodlibetales.* In J.T. Muckle, "*Utrum Theologia sit scientia.* A Quodlibetal Question of Robert Holcot, O.P." *Mediaeval Studies*, 20 (1958), 127–153.

Robert Holcot. *Quaestiones quodlibetales.* In Kurt Villads Jensen, "Robert Holkot's *Questio* on Killing Infidels: A Reevaluation and an Edition." *Archivum Fratrum Praedicatorum*, 63 (1993), 207–228.

Robert Holcot. *Quaestiones quodlibetales.* In William J. Courtenay, "A Revised Text of Robert Holcot's Quodlibetal Dispute on Whether God is Able to Know More Than He Knows." *Archiv für Geschichte der Philosophie*, 53 (1971), 1–21.

Robert Holcot. *Sermo finalis.* In J.C. Wey, "The *Sermo finalis* of Robert Holcot." *Mediaeval Studies*, 11 (1949), 219–224.

Robert Holcot. *Sex articuli.* In *Die "Conferentiae" des Robert Holcot O.P. und die akademischen Auseinandersetzungen an der Universität Oxford 1330–1332.* Fritz Hoffmann (ed.). (BGPTM 36). Münster, 1993, 65–127.

Robert Holcot. *Tractatus de stellis.* See Thorndike (1957).

E. Works by Holcot: Translations

Robert Holcot. *Quodl.* I, q.6. In *The Cambridge Translations of Medieval Philosophical Texts, vol. 3: Mind and Knowledge.* Robert Pasnau (ed.). Cambridge, 2002, 302–317.

Robert Holcot. *Sent.* III, q.1, a.8. In *Philosophie et théologie au Moyen Âge, Anthologie tome II.* Olivier Boulnois (ed.). Paris, 2009, 451–454.
Robert Holcot. *Super libros Sapientiae,* chap. 3, lects. 35 and 52; chap. 12, lect. 145, in Oberman (1981), 142–150.

F. Other Primary Sources

Adam Wodeham. *Lectura secunda in librum primum Sententiarum.* Rega Wood and Gedeon Gàl (eds.). St. Bonaventure, NY, 1990.
Alan of Lille. *Sermones Octo.* In *PL* 210, 197–222.
Alan of Lille. *Summa de arte praedicatoria.* In *PL* 210, 111–198.
Anonymous. *Fasciculus Morum: A Fourteenth-Century Preacher's Handbook.* Siegfried Wenzel (ed. and trans.). University Park, PN, 1989.
Anselm. *Proslogion.* In *Anslem of Canterbury: The Major Works.* Brian Davies and G.R. Evans (eds.). Oxford, 2008.
Augustine. *Answer to Faustus, a Manichean.* Boniface Ramsey (trans.). *WSA* 1.20. New York, NY, 2007.
Augustine. *City of God.* William Babcock (trans.). *WSA* 1.6, 1.7. London, 2003.
Augustine. *Confessions.* Maria Boulding (trans.). *WSA* 1.1. New York, NY, 1997.
Augustine. *Propositionum ex epistolae ad Romanos.* In *Augustine on Romans: Propositions from the Epistle to the Romans, Unfinished Commentary on the Epistle to the Romans.* Paula Fredriksen (trans.). Atlanta, 1982 [also cited as Fredriksen, (1982)].
Augustine. *De Trinitate,* 2 vols. W. J. Mountain and Fr. Glorie (ed.). In *CCSL* 50 and 50A. Turnhout, 1968.
Augustine. *The Trinity.* Edmund Hill (trans.). *WSA* 1.5. New York, NY, 1991.
Benedict of Nursia. *The Rule of Saint Benedict.* (Dumbarton Oaks Medieval Library). Cambridge, MA, 2011.
Ps.-Bonaventure. *Commentarius in librum Sapientiae.* In *Opera Omnia* 6. Ad Claras Aquas (Quaracchi), 1893, 107–233.
Councils and Synods, with Other Documents Relating to the English Church, 2 vols. F.M. Powicke and C.R. Cheney (eds.). Oxford, 1964.
Decretales Gregorii IX. In *Corpus iuris canonici,* 2 vols. Aemilius Friedberg (ed.). Leipzig 1879; reprinted Graz, 1959.
Gesta Romanorum. Hermann Oesterley (ed.). Berlin, 1872; reprinted Hildesheim, 1963.
Gesta Romanorum, or, Entertaining Stories Invented by the Monks as a Fire-Side Recreation . . . Thomas Wright (ed. and trans.). New York, NY, 1871.
Giovanni Pico della Mirandola. *Apologia.* Basel, 1557.
Guido de Monte Rochen. *Handbook for Curates: A Late Medieval Manual on Pastoral Ministry.* Anne T. Thayer (trans.). Washington, DC, 2011.
Henry Harclay. *Ordinary Questions,* 2 vols. Mark G. Henninger (ed.); Raymond Edwards and Mark G. Henninger (trans.). Oxford, 2008.

Hugh of St. Victor. *De Sacramentis legis naturalis et scriptae*. In *PL* 176, 17–42.
Humbert of Romans. *Treatise on the Formation of Preachers*. In Tugwell (1982).
Isidore of Seville. *The Etymologies of Isidore of Seville*. S.A. Barney, W.J. Lewis, J.A. Beach, and O. Berghof (trans.). Cambridge, 2010.
Joannis de Fordun. *Scotichronicon: cum supplementis et continuatione Walteri Boweri . . . E codicibus mss. editum. cum notis et variantibus lectionibus. Præfixa est ad historiam Scotorum introductio brevis*. Walter Bower (ed.). Edinburgh, 1759.
Johannes Marienwerder. *Vita Dorotheae*. In *Acta Sanctorum*, 68 Vols. Socii Bolandiani (ed.). Paris, 1863–1940, vol. 13.
John Ridevall. *Fulgentius Metaforalis*. Hans Liebeschütz (ed.). (Ein Beitrag zur Geschichte der antiken Mythologie im Mittelalter). Leipzig, 1926.
Meister Eckhart. *Expositio libri Sapientiae*. In *Die deutschen und lateinischen Werke*. Latin Works, vol. 2. Stuttgart 1992, 301–643.
Michael Servetus. *De Trinitatis erroribus libri semptem*. In *Obras Completas II-2: Primeros Escritos Theológicos*. Ángel Alcalá (ed.). Zaragoza, 2004.
Origen of Alexandria. *A Letter from Origen to Gregory*. A. Cleveland Coxe (trans.). *ANF* 4. New York, NY, 1885, 393–394.
Origen of Alexandria. *The Song of Songs, Commentary and Homilies*. R.P. Lawson (trans.). *ACW* 26. New York, NY, 1957.
Peter Aureoli. *Compendium sensus litteralis totius divinae Scripturae*. Philibert Seeböck (ed.). Quaracchi, 1896.
Peter Lombard. *Sententiae in IV libros distinctae*. Grottaferrata, Rome, 1971–1981.
Peter Lombard. *The Sentences: Books I–IV*, 4 vols. Giulio Silano (trans.). Toronto, 2007–10.
Rabanus Maurus. *Commentariorum in librum Sapientiae*. In *PL* 109, 671–762.
Richard de Bury. *Philobiblon*. E.C. Thomas (ed. and trans.). Oxford, 1960.
Robert Grosseteste. *De cessatione legalium*. Richard C. Dales and Edward B. King (eds.) (Auctores Britannici Medii Aevi 7). London, 1986.
The Sarum Missal: Edited from Three Early Manuscripts. J. Wickham Legg (ed.). Oxford, 1916; reprinted 1969.
Thomas Aquinas. *Opera omnia iussu impensaque Leonis XIII P. M. edita, t. 4-5: Pars prima Summae theologiae*. Rome, 1888–1889.
Thomas Aquinas. *Scriptum super libros Sententiarum*, 4 vols. P. Mandonnet and F.M. Moos (eds.). Paris, 1929–1956.
Thomas Aquinas. *Summa contra gentiles. Book One: God*. Anton C. Pegis (ed. and trans.). Notre Dame, 1975.
Thomas Bradwardine. *Insolubilia*. Stephen Read (ed. and trans.). Leuven, 2010.
Thomas Waleys. *De modo componendi sermones*. In Charland (1936), 328–403.
Walter Chatton. *Lectura super Sententias*, 3 vols. Joseph Wey and Girard Etzkorn (eds.). Toronto, 2007–2009.
Walter Chatton. *Reportatio super Sententias*, 4 vols. Joseph Wey and Girard Etzkorn (eds.). Toronto, 2002–2005.

Walter Hilton. *The Scale of Perfection*. Thomas H. Bestul (ed.). Kalamazoo, 2000.
Walter Hilton. *The Scale of Perfection*. John P.H. Clark and Rosemary Dorward (trans.). New York, NY, 1991.
William Crathorn. *Quaestiones super librum Sententiarum*. In *Quästionen Zum ersten Sentenzenbuch*. F. Hoffmann (ed.). Münster, 1988.
William de Chambre. *Continuatio historiae Dunelmensis*. J. Raine (ed.). New Castle, 1839.
William of Luxi. *Postilla super Baruch, Postilla super Ionam*. A.T. Sulavik (ed.). CCCM 219. Turnhout, 2006.
William of Ockham. *Opera philosophica et theologica*, 17 vols. Philotheus Boehner, Gedeon Gàl, et al. (eds.). St. Bonaventure, NY, 1967–1988.
William of Ockham. *Predestination, God's Foreknowledge, and Future Contingents*. Marilyn McCord Adams and Norman Kretzman (eds. and trans.). Indianapolis, IN, 1983.
William of Ockham. *Quodlibetal Questions, Volumes 1 and 2, Quodlibets 1–7*. Alfred J. Freddoso and Francis E. Kelley (trans.). New Haven, CT, 1991.

SECONDARY SOURCES

Abate, Giuseppe and Giovanni Luisetto (1975). *Codici e Manoscritti della Biblioteca Antoniana*. Vicenza.
Adams, Robert (1983). "Piers' Pardon and Langland's Semi-Pelagianism." *Traditio* 39, 367–418.
Allen, Judson B. (1969). "The Library of a Classiciser: The Sources of Robert Holkot's Mythographic Learning." In *Arts libéraux et philosophie au moyen âge*. Paris, 721–729.
Allen, Judson B. (1971). *The Friar as Critic: Literary Attitudes in the Later Middle Ages*. Nashville, TN.
Alviero, Niccacci (2008). "The Structure of the Book of Wisdom: Two Instructions (Cs. 1–5, 6–9) in Line with Old Testament Wisdom Tradition." *Liber Annuus* 58, 31–72.
Anscombe, G.E.M. (1956). "Aristotle and the Sea Battle." *Mind* 65.257, 1–15.
Anstey, Henry (1868). *Munimenta Academica, or Documents Illustrative of Academical Life and Studies at Oxford* (Rerum Britannicarum Medii Aevi Scriptores, Rolls series 50). London.
Armitage, J. Mark (2008). "Aquinas on the Divisions of the Ages: Salvation History in the *Summa*." *Nova et Vetera* 6, 253–270.
Aurélien, Robert (2011). "William Crathorn." *SEP*. Available at http://plato.stanford.edu/entries/crathorn/.
Austin, John (1995). *The Province of Jurisprudence Determined*. Cambridge.
Ayres, Lewis (2010). *Augustine and the Trinity*. Cambridge.
Bainton, Roland H. (1938). "New Documents on Early Protestant Rationalism." *Church History* 7, 179–187.

Baker, Denise (1980). "From Plowing to Penitence: Piers Plowman and Fourteenth-Century Theology." *Speculum* 55, 715–725.
Bale, John (1902). *Index Britanniae scriptorum quos ex variis bibliothecis non parvo labore collegit Ioannes Baleus, cum aliis*. Reginald Poole and Mary Bateson (eds.). Oxford.
Bataillon, L.-J. (1982). "Intermédiaires entre les traités de morale pratique et les sermons: les *Distinctiones* bibliques alphabétiques." In *Les genres littéraires dans les sources théologiques et philosophiques médiévales. Définition, critique et exploitation*. Louvain-la-Neuve, 213–226.
Bataillon, L.-J. (1994). "The Tradition of Nicholas of Biard's *Distinctiones*." *Viator* 25, 245–288.
Bejczy, István P. (2011). *The Cardinal Virtues in the Middle Ages: A Study in Moral Thought From the Fourth to the Fourteenth Century*. Leiden.
Bellamah, Timothy F. (2011). *The Biblical Interpretation of William of Alton*. Oxford.
Beumer, J.S.J. (1962). "Zwang und Freiheit in der Glaubenszustimmung nach Robert Holkot." *Scholastik* 37, 514–529.
Bloomfield, M.W., et al. (1979). *Incipits of Latin Works on the Virtues and Vices, 1000–1500* AD. Cambridge, MA.
Boehner, Philotheus (1992). *Collected Articles on Ockham*. St. Bonaventure, NY.
Boguslawski, Steven C. (2008). *Thomas Aquinas and the Jews: Insights into His Commentary on Romans 9–11*. New York, NY.
Bolyard, Charles (2013). "Medieval Skepticism." *SEP*. Available at http://plato.stanford.edu/entries/skepticism-medieval/.
Bougerol, Jacques Guy (2014). "Bonaventure as Exegete." In *A Companion to Bonaventure*. Jay M. Hammond, Wayne Hellman, and Jared Goff (eds.). Leiden, 167–187.
Boyle, Leonard E. (1955). "The *Oculus sacerdotis* and Some Other Works of William of Pagula." *Transactions of the Royal Historical Society* 5, 81–110.
Brady, Ignatius (1965). "The Distinctions of Lombard's Book of *Sentences* and Alexander of Hales." *Franciscan Studies* 25, 90–116.
Brett, Annabel S. (1997). *Liberty, Right and Nature: Individual Rights in Later Scholastic Thought*. Cambridge.
Brett, Edward Tracy (1984). *Humbert of Romans: His Life and Views of Thirteenth-Century Society*. Toronto.
Brinkel, Karl (1958). *Die Lehre Luthers Von der Fides Infantium bei der Kindertaufe*. Berlin.
Brinkley, Ann Wegner (1972). "Toward an Empirical Theory of Knowledge." PhD dissertation, Harvard University.
Briscoe, Marianne, and Barbara H. Jaye (1992). *Artes praedicandi; Artes orandi*. Turnhout.

Brown, Stephen F. (1976). "Peter of Candia's Sermons in Praise of Peter Lombard." In *Studies Honoring Ignatius Charles Brady, Friar Minor*. R.S. Almagno and C.L. Harkins (eds.). St. Bonaventure, NY, 141–176.
Brown, Stephen F. (1991). "Peter of Candia's Hundred Year History of the Theologian's Role." *Medieval Philosophy and Theology* 1, 156–190.
Brown, Stephen F. (1997). "Peter of Candia on Believing and Knowing." *Franciscan Studies* 54, 251–276.
Byrd, Jeremy (2010). "The Necessity of Tomorrow's Sea Battle." *The Southern Jounral of Philosophy* 48.2, 160–176.
Cameron, Euan (1991). *The European Reformation*, 2nd ed. Oxford.
Caplan, Harry (1934). *Medieval Artes Praedicandi. A Hand List* (Cornell Studies in Classical Philology 24). Ithaca, NY.
Caplan, Harry (1936). *Medieval Artes Praedicandi. A Supplementary Hand-list* (Cornell Studies in Classical Philology 25). Ithaca, NY.
Carruthers, Mary (2008). *The Book of Memory: A Study of Memory in Medieval Culture*, 2nd ed. Cambridge.
Charland, Thomas Marie (1936). *Artes praedicandi: Contribution à l'histoire de la rhétorique au moyen âge*. Paris.
Chenu, Marie-Dominique (2005). *St. Thomas d'Aquin et la théologie*. Paris.
Chisholm, Roderick M. (1964). *Human Freedom and the Self* (The Lindley Lecture, University of Kansas). Lawrence, KS.
Clarke, Ernest G. (1973). *The Wisdom of Solomon*. Cambridge.
Cohen, Jeremy (1984). *The Friars and the Jews: The Evolution of Medieval Anti-Judaism*. Ithaca, NY.
Cohen, Jeremy (1999). *Living Letters of the Law: Ideas of the Jew in Medieval Christianity*. Berkeley, CA.
Coleman, Janet (1981a). *English Literature in History, 1350-1400: Medieval Readers and Writers*. London.
Coleman, Janet (1981b). *Piers Plowman and the moderni*. Rome.
Colish, Marcia L. (1994). *Peter Lombard*, 2 vols. Leiden.
Colish, Marcia L. (2014). *Faith, Fiction & Force in Medieval Baptismal Debates*. Washington, DC.
Courtenay, William J. (1971). "A Revised Text of Robert Holcot's Quodlibetal Dispute on Whether God is Able to Know More Than He Knows." *Archiv für Geschichte der Philosophie* 53.1, 1–21.
Courtenay, William J. (1974). "Nominalism and Late Medieval Religion." In *The Pursuit of Holiness in Late Medieval Renaissance Religion*. Charles Trinkaus and Heiko A. Oberman (eds.). Leiden, 26–59.
Courtenay, William J. (1978). *Adam Wodeham: An Introduction to His Life and Writings*. Leiden.
Courtenay, William J. (1980). "The Lost Matthew Commentary of Robert Holcot, O.P." *Archivum Fratrum Praedicatorum* 50, 103–112.

Courtenay, William J. (1984). *Covenant and Causality in Medieval Thought: Studies in Philosophy, Theology, and Economic Practice*. London.
Courtenay, William J. (1985a). "The Bible in the Fourteenth Century: Some Observations." *Church History* 52.2, 176–187.
Courtenay, William J. (1985b). "The Dialectic of Omnipotence in the High and Late Middle Ages." In *Divine Omniscience and Omnipotence in Medieval Philosophy*. Tamar Rudavsky (ed.). Dordrecht, 243–269.
Courtenay, William J. (1987). *Schools and Scholars in Fourteenth-Century England*. Princeton, NJ.
Courtenay, William J. (1990). *Capacity and Volition: A History of the Distinction of Absolute and Ordained Power*. Bergamo.
Courtenay, William J. (1994). "Programs of Study and Genres of Scholastic Theological Production in the Fourteenth Century." In *Manuels, programmes de cours et techniques d'enseignement dans les universités médiévales*. J. Hamesse (ed.). Louvain-la-Neuve, 325–350.
Courtenay, William J. (2007). "Postscript: The Demise of the Quodlibetal Literature." In *Theological Quodlibeta in the Middle Ages: The Fourteenth Century*. Christopher Schabel (ed.). Leiden, 693–699.
Courtenay, William J. (2011). "Theological Bachelors at Paris on the Eve of the Papal Schism. The Academic Environment of Peter of Candia." In *Philosophy and Theology in the Long Middle Ages: A Tribute to Stephen F. Brown*. K. Emery Jr., R.L. Friedman, and A. Speer (eds.). Leiden, 921–952.
Cross, Richard (1999). *Duns Scotus*. Oxford.
Cross, Richard (2005). *Duns Scotus on God*. Burlington, VT.
Cross, Richard (2012). "Baptism, Faith and Severe Cognitive Impairment in Some Medieval Theologies." *International Journal of Systematic Theology* 14.4, 420–438.
Dahan, Gilbert (1990). *Les intellectuels Chrétiens et les Juifs au Moyen Âge*. Paris.
Dahan, Gilbert (1999). *L'Exégèse chrétienne de la Bible en Occident médiéval: XIIe-XIVe siècle*. Paris.
Darling, James (1859). *Cyclopaedia Bibliographica: A Library Manual of Theological and General Literature*. London.
d'Avray, David (1985). *Preaching of the Friars*. Oxford.
de Ghellinck, Joseph (1922). "Un Évêque bibliophile au XIVe siècle: Richard Aungerville de Bury (1345)." *Revue d'histoire ecclésiastique* 18, 491–500.
Delany, Sheila (1972). *Chaucer's House of Fame: The Poetics of Skeptical Fideism*. Chicago, IL.
Del Pra, Mario (1956). "Linguaggio e conoscenza assertiva nel pensiero di Roberto Holcot." *Rivista critica di storia della filosofia* 11, 15–40.
Del Pra, Mario (1974). "La proposizione come oggetto della conoscenza scientifica nel pensiero di Roberto Holcot." In *Logica e realtà: momenti del pensiero medievale*. Rome, 83–119.

de Lubac, Henri (1998, 2000, 2009). *Medieval Exegesis, The Fourfold Sense of Scripture*, 3 vols. Mark Sebanc and M. Macierowski (trans.). Grand Rapids, MI.
Denery II, Dallas G. (2005). "From Sacred Mystery to Divine Deception: Robert Holcot, John Wyclif and the Transformation of Fourteenth-Century Eucharistic Discourse." *Journal of Religious History* 29.2, 129–144.
Dieter, Otto (1965). "*Arbor picta*: The Medieval Tree of Preaching." *Quarterly Journal of Speech* 51, 123–144.
Duclow, Donald F. (1987). "Meister Eckhart on the Book of Wisdom: Commentary and Sermons." *Traditio* 43, 215–235.
Dunne, Michael (2010). "Richard FitzRalph's *Lectura* on the *Sentences*." In Rosemann (2010), 405–437.
Emden, A.B. (1962). "Dominican Confessors and Preachers Licensed by Medieval English Bishops." *Archivum Fratrum Praedicatorum* 32, 180–210.
Emden, A.B. (1967). *Survey of Domincans in England: Based on the Ordination Lists in Episcopal Registers (1268 to 1538)*. (Dissertationes Historicae, no. 18). Rome.
Emile, Amann, Eugène Mangenot, and Alfred Vacant (eds.) (1899–1950). *Dictionnaire de théologie catholique*. Paris.
Evans, G.R. (ed.) (2002). *Mediaeval Commentaries on the* Sentences *of Peter Lombard: Volume I, Current Research*. Leiden.
Farago-Bermon, Pascale (2013). "Les manuscrits conservés à Paris des *Quaestiones super libros Sententiarum* de Robert Holkot." *Przegląd Tomistyczny* 19, 143–176.
Finnis, John (2011). *Natural Law & Natural Rights*, 2nd ed. Oxford.
Fletcher, Alan John (1998). *Preaching, Politics and Poetry in Late-Medieval England*. Dublin.
Fletcher, Alan John (2004). "Variations on a Theme Attributed to Robert Holcot: Lessons for Late-Medieval English Preaching from the Castle of Prudence." *Mediaeval Studies* 66, 27–98.
Fletcher, Alan John (2009). *Late Medieval Popular Preaching in Britain and Ireland: Texts, Studies, and Interpretations*. Turnhout.
Forte, Stephen L. (1952). "Simon of Boraston, His Life and Writings." *Archivum Fratrum Praedicatorum* 22, 321–345.
Frank, Isnard W. (1966). "Leonhard Huntpichler O. P. (+ 1478), Theologieprofessor und Ordensreformer in Wien." *Archivum Fratrum Praedicatorum* 36, 313–388.
Frede, Dorthea (1985). "The Sea-Battle Reconsidered: A Defence of the Traditional Interpretation." *Oxford Studies in Ancient Philosophy* 3, 31–87.
Fredriksen, Paula (1982). See Primary Sources (I, F), Augustine, *Propositionum ex epistolae ad Romanos*.
Fredriksen, Paula (1991). "Apocalypse and Redemption in Early Christianity: From John of Patmos to Augustine of Hippo." *Vigiliae Christianae* 45, 151–183.
Fredriksen, Paula (2010). *Augustine and the Jews: A Christian Defense of Jews and Judaism*. New Haven, CT.

Friedman, Russell L. (2010). *Medieval Trinitarian Thought from Aquinas to Ockham*. Cambridge.

Friedman, Russell L. (2013). *Intellectual Traditions at the Medieval University: The Use of Philosophical Psychology in Trinitarian Theology Among the Franciscans and Dominicans, 1250–1350*. Leiden.

Fuller, Lon (1977). *The Morality of Law*. New Haven, CT.

Gaskin, Richard (1995). *The Sea Battle and the Master Argument: Aristotle and Diodorus Cronus on the Metaphysics of the Future*. New York, NY.

Gelber, Hester Goodenough (1974). "Logic and the Trinity: A Clash of Values in Scholastic Thought, 1300–1335." PhD dissertation, University of Wisconsin-Madison.

Gelber, Hester Goodenough (1983). "Introduction." In *Exploring the Boundaries of Reason: Three Questions on the Nature of God by Robert Holcot, OP*. Toronto, 1–28.

Gelber, Hester Goodenough (1988). "Ockham's Early Influence: A Question about Predestination and Foreknoweldge by Arnold Strelley, O.P." *Archives d'histoire doctrinale et littéraire du moyen âge* 55, 255–289.

Gelber, Hester Goodenough (2004). *It Could Have Been Otherwise: Contingency and Necessity in Dominican Theology at Oxford, 1300–1350*. Leiden.

Gelber, Hester Goodenough (2014). "Robert Holcot." *SEP*. Available at http://plato.stanford.edu/entries/holkot/.

Gelber, Hester Goodenough (in press). "Robert Holcot, Obligational Theology, and the Incarnation."

Gilbert, Neal (1976). "Richard de Bury and the 'Quires of Yesterday's Sophisms.'" In *Philosophy and Humanism. Renaissance Essays in Honor of P.O. Kristellar*. E. Mahoney (ed.). New York, NY, 229–257.

Gillespie, Richard E. (1971). "Robert Holcot's Quodlibeta." *Traditio* 27, 480–490.

Gillespie, Richard E. (1974). "*Gratia creata* and *Acceptatio divina* in the Theology of Robert Holcot O.P.: A Study of Two Unedited quodlibetal questions." PhD dissertation, Graduate Theological Union.

Gioia, Luigi (2008). *The Theological Epistemology of Augustine's De Trinitate*. Oxford.

Glorieux, Palémon (1925, 1935). *La littérature quodlibétique de 1260 à 1320*, 2 vols. Paris.

Goering, Joseph (2008). "The Scholastic Turn (1100–1500): Penitential Theology and Law in the Schools." In *A New History of Penance*. Abigail Firey (ed.). Leiden, 219–237.

Gracia, Jorge J.E. and Timothy B. Noone (eds.) (2003). *A Companion to Philosophy in the Middle Ages*. Oxford.

Grassi, Onorato (1979). "Le tesi di Robert Holcot sul valore non scientifico della conoscenza teologica." *Rivista di filosofia neo-scolastica* 71, 49–79.

Grassi, Onorato (1994). "Il 'De obiecto actus credendi' di Robert Holcot. Introduzione e edizione." *Documenti e studi sulla tradizione filosofica medievale* 5, 487–521.

Grosser, Dorothy E. (1949). "Thomas Waleys' *De modo componendi sermones* Rendered into English." MA thesis, Cornell University.

Hallamaa, Olli (2010). "On the Limits of the Genre: Roger Roseth as a Reader of the *Sentences*." In Rosemann (2010), 369–404.

Halverson, James L. (1998). *Peter Aureol on Predestination: A Challenge to Late Medieval Thought*. Leiden.

Hamm, Berndt (1977). *Promissio, Pactum, Ordinatio: Freiheit und Selbstbindung Gottes in Der Scholastischen Gnadenlehre* (Beiträge zur historischen Theologie 54). Tübingen.

Harran, Marilyn J. (1983). *Luther on Conversion: The Early Years*. Ithaca, NY.

Hart, H.L.A. (2012). *The Concept of Law*. 3rd ed. Oxford.

Hays, Gregory (2003). "The Date and Identity of the Mythographer Fulgentius." *Journal of Medieval Latin* 13, 163–252.

Hingeston-Randolph, F.C. (ed.) (1894–1899). *The Register of John de Grandisson, Bishop of Exeter, (A.D. 1327–69)*. London.

Hintikka, Jaakko (1973). *Time and Necessity: Studies in Aristotle's Theory of Modality*. Oxford.

Hoffmann, Fritz (1963). "Robert Holcot—Die Logik in der Theologie." In *Die Metaphysik im Mittelalter: Ihr Ursprung und Ihre Bedeutung*. Paul Wilpert, et al. (eds.). (Miscellanea Mediaevalia 2). Berlin, 624–639.

Hoffmann, Fritz (1971). "Der Satz als Zeichen der theologischen Aussage bei Holcot, Crathorn und Gregor von Rimini." In *Der Begriff der Repraesentatio im Mittelalter: Stellvertretung, Symbol, Zeichen, Bild*. Albert Zimmermann (ed.) (Miscellanea Mediaevalia 8). Berlin, 296–313.

Hoffmann, Fritz (1972). *Die theologische Methode des Oxforder Dominikanerlehrers Robert Holcot*. Münster.

Hoffmann, Fritz (1974). "Thomas-Rezeption bei Robert Holcot?" *Theologie und Philosophie* 49, 236–251.

Hoffmann, Fritz (1993). See Primary Sources (I, D), Robert Holcot, *Sex articuli*.

Hoffmann, Fritz (1995). "Der Wandel in der scholastischen Argumentation vom 13. zum 14. Jahrhundert, aufgeseigt an zwei Beispielen: Robert Holcot und William (Johannes?) Crathorn (1330–1332 in Oxford)." In *Die Bibliotheca Amploniana: Ihre Bedeutung im Spannungsfeld von Aristotelismus, Nominalismus und Humanismus*, Andreas Speer (ed.). (Miscellanea Mediaevalia 23). Berlin, 301–322.

Hoffmann, Fritz (1998). "Robert Holcot—Philosophische Implikationen seiner Theologie." In *Qu'est-ce que la philosophie au Moyen Âge?* Jan Aertsen and Andreas Speer (eds.). (Miscellanea Mediaevalia 26). Berlin, 637–641.

Humber, Raphael M. (1926). "The Doctrine of Ven. John Duns Scotus. Concerning the Causality of the Sacraments." *Franciscan Studies* 4, 9–38.

Incandela, Joseph M. (1994). "Robert Holcot, O.P., on Prophecy, the Contingency of Revelation, and the Freedom of God." *Medieval Philosophy and Theology* 4, 165–188.

Kaeppeli, Thomas (1959). "Un sermonnaire anglais contenu dans le MS. Toulouse 342." *Archivum Fratrum Praedicatorum* 29, 89–110.

Kaeppeli, Thomas (1970–1993). *Scriptores Ordinis Praedicatorum medii Aevi*, 4 vols. Rome.

Kaeppeli, Thomas (1980). *Scriptores Ordinis Praedicatorum Medii Aevi: Volume III, I-S*. Rome.

Kaminsky, Howard (1983). *Simon de Cramaud and the Great Schism*. New Brunswick, NJ.

Keele, Rondo (2007). "Oxford *Quodlibeta* from Ockham to Holcot." In *Theological Quodlibeta in the Middle Ages: The Fourteenth Century*. Christopher Schabel (ed.). Leiden, 651–692.

Keele, Rondo (2014). "Walter Chatton." *SEP*. Available at http://plato.stanford.edu/entries/walter-chatton/.

Kelly, Henry Ansgar (2008). "Penitential Theology and Law at the Turn of the Fifteenth Century." In *A New History of Penance*. Abigail Firey (ed.). Leiden, 239–318.

Kemmler, Fritz (1984). *'Exempla' in Context: A Historical and Critical Study of Robert Mannyng of Brunne's 'Handlyng Synne.'* Tübingen.

Kennedy, Leonard A. (1993). *The Philosophy of Robert Holcot, Fourteenth-Century Skeptic*. Lewiston, NY.

King, Peter (1991). "Mediaeval Thought-Experiments: The Metamethodology of Mediaeval Science." In *Thought Experiments in Science and Philosophy*. Tamara Horowitz and Gerald J. Massey (eds.). Savage, MD, 43–64.

Kirjavainen, Heikki (1986). *Onko Teologia Tiedettä? Robert Holkotin quodlibet disputaatio 1, kvestio 1. Kääntänyt ja johdannolla varustanut*. Helsinki.

Kirjavainen, Heikki (1990). "Existential Presuppositions in Semantics According to Ockham and Holcot." In *Knowledge and the Sciences in Medieval Philosophy*, vol. 2. Simo Knuuttila, Reijo Työrinoija, and Sten Ebbesen (eds.). Helsinki, 196–209.

Kitanov, Severin Valentinov (2014). *Beatific Enjoyment in Medieval Scholastic Debate: The Complex Legacy of Saint Augustine and Peter Lombard*. Lanham, MD.

Knapp, Ethan (2001). *The Bureaucratic Muse: Thomas Hoccleve and the Literature of Late Medieval England*. University Park, PA.

Knuuttila, Simo (1993). "Trinitarian Sophisms in Robert Holcot's Theology." In *Sophisms in Medieval Logic and Grammar*. Stephen Read (ed.). Dordrecht, 348–356.

Koch, J. (1933). "Der Prozess gegen den Magister Iohannes de Polliaco und seine Vorgeschichte (1312–21)." *Recherches de Théologie ancienne et médiévale* 5, 391–422.

Kretzmann, Norman (1970). "Medieval Logicians on the Meaning of the Propositio." *The Journal of Philosophy* 67, 767–787.

Krey, Philip D.W. and Lesley Smith (eds.) (2000). *Nicholas of Lyra: The Senses of Scripture*. Leiden.
Krug, Rebecca (2009). "Shakespeare's Medieval Morality: *The Merchant of Venice* and the *Gesta Romanorum*." In *Shakespeare and the Middle Ages*. Curtis Perry and John Watkins (eds.). Oxford, 241–262.
Laemers, Jeroen Willem Joseph (2011). "Invincible Ignorance and the Discovery of the Americas: The History of an Idea from Scotus to Suárez." PhD dissertation, University of Iowa.
Lahey, Stephen E. (2009). *John Wyclif*. Oxford.
Lang, Albert (1930). *Die Wege der Glaubensbegründung bei den Scholastikern des 14. Jahrhunderts*. Münster.
Leff, Gordon (1957). *Bradwardine and the Pelagians: A Study of his "De causa Dei" and its Opponents*. Cambridge.
Leff, Gordon (1963). *Richard FitzRalph: Commentator of the Sentences*. Manchester.
Leff, Gordon (1975). *William of Ockham: The Metamorphosis of Scholastic Discourse*. Chatham.
Lewis, Charlton T., and Charles Short (1879). *A Latin Dictionary*. Oxford.
Lievens, Robrecht (2012). "The 'pagan' Dirc van Delft." In *Paganism in the Middle Ages: Threat and Fascination*. Carlos Steele, John Marenbon, and Werner Verbeke (eds.). Leuven, 167–194.
Logan, Ian (2009). *Reading Anselm's Proslogion: The History of Anselm's Argument and its Significance Today*. Burlington, VT.
Macy, Gary (2014). "The Medieval Inheritance," in *A Companion to the Eucharist in the Reformation*. Lee Palmer Wandel (ed.). Leiden, 15–37.
MacIntyre, Alasdair (2007). *After Virtue: A Study in Moral Theory*, 3rd ed. South Bend, IN.
Marenbon, John (ed.) (2012). *The Oxford Handbook to Medieval Philosophy*. Oxford.
Martin, Conor. (1964). "Walter Burleigh." In *Oxford Studies Presented to Daniel Callus*. W.H. Hinnebush (ed.). Oxford, 194–230.
McGrade, Arthur Stephen (1987). "Enjoyment at Oxford after Ockham: Philosophy, Psychology, and the Love of God." In *From Ockham to Wyclif*. Anne Hudson and Michael Wilks (eds.). Oxford, 63–88.
McGrath, Alister E. (2005). *"Iustitia Dei": A History of the Christian Doctrine of Justification*. Cambridge.
Meissner, Alois (1953). *Gotteserkenntnis und Gotteslehre: Nach dem Englischen Dominikanertheologen Robert Holcot*. Limburg.
Minnis, Alastair (2009). *Translations of Authority in Medieval English Literature: Valuing the Vernacular*. Cambridge.
Minnis, Alastair (2010). *Medieval Theory of Authorship: Scholastic Literary Attitudes in the Later Middle Ages*. 2nd ed. Philadelphia, PA.

Molteni, Paolo (1967). *Roberto Holcot O.P.: Dottrina della grazia e della giustificazione con due questioni quodlibetali inedite*. Pinerolo.

Muessig, Carolyn (2002). "Sermon, Preacher and Society in the Middle Ages (Historiographical Essay)." *Journal of Medieval History* 28, 73–91.

Mulchahey, M. Michèle (1998). *"First the Bow is Bent in Study": Dominican Education before 1350*. Toronto.

Murphy, James J. (1974). *Rhetoric in the Middle Ages: A History of Rhetorical Theory from St. Augustine to the Renaissance*. Berkeley, CA.

Newhauser, Richard G. and Susan J. Ridyard (eds.) (2012). *Sin in Medieval and Early Modern Culture: The Tradition of the Seven Deadly Sins*. Suffolk.

Nolan, Maura (2005). *John Lydgate and the Making of Public Culture*. Cambridge.

Novaes, Catarina Dutilh (2007). *Formalizing Medieval Logical Theories: Suppositio, Consequentia and Obligationes*. Berlin.

Oakley, Francis (1984). *Omnipotence, Covenant, & Order: An Excursion in the History of Ideas from Abelard to Leibniz*. Ithaca, NY.

Oberman, Heiko A. (1962). "*Facientibus quod in se est Deus non denegat gratiam*: Robert Holcot, OP and the Beginnings of Luther's Theology." *Harvard Theological Review* 55, 317–342.

Oberman, Heiko A. (ed.) (1981). *Forerunners of the Reformation: The Shape of Late Medieval Thought Illustrated by Key Documents*. Philadelphia, 1981.

Oberman, Heiko A. (2000). *The Harvest of Medieval Theology: Gabriel Biel and Late Medieval Nominalism*. Grand Rapids, MI.

O'Carroll, Mary E. (1997). *A Thirteenth-Century Preacher's Handbook: Studies in MS Laud Misc. 511*. Toronto.

O'Carroll, Maura (1979). "The Lectionary for the Proper of the Year in the Dominican and Franciscan Rites of the Thirteenth Century." *Archivum Fratrum Praedicatorum* 49, 79–103.

Ohly, Friedrich (2005). "The Spiritual Sense of Words in the Middle Ages." In *Sensus Spiritualis: Studies in Medieval Significs and the Philology of Culture*. Samuel P. Jaffe (ed.) and Kenneth J. Northcott (trans.). Chicago, 1–30.

O'Mara, Philip (1992). "Holcot and the 'Pearl'-Poet: Part II." *The Chaucer Review* 27.1, 97–106.

Owst, G. R. (1926). *Preaching in Medieval England: An Introduction to Sermon Manuscripts of the Period c. 1350–1450*. Cambridge.

Ozment, Steven (1981). *The Age of Reform, 1250–1550. An Intellectual and Religious History of Late Medieval and Reformation Europe*. New Haven, CT.

Palmer, Nigel (1991). "Das 'Exempelwerk' der englischen Bettelmönche: Ein Gegenstück zu den '*Gesta Romanorum*.'" In *Exempel und Exempelsammlungen*. Walter Haug and Burghart Wachinger (eds.). Tübingen, 137–172.

Palmer, Nigel (1996). "Exempla." In *Medieval Latin: An Introduction and Bibliographical Guide*. F.A.C. Mantello and A.G. Rigg (eds.). Washington, DC, 582–588.

Pantin, William Abel (2010). *The English Church in the Fourteenth Century: Based on the Birkbeck Lectures, 1948.* Cambridge.

Pasnau, Robert (ed.) (2010). *The Cambridge History of Medieval Philosophy*, 2 vols. Cambridge.

Pelikan, Jarolsav (1959). *Luther the Expositor: Introduction to the Reformer's Exegetical Writings.* St. Louis, MO.

Pelikan, Jaroslav (1993). *Christianity and Classical Culture: The Metamorphosis of Natural Theology in the Christian Encounter with Hellenism.* New Haven, CT.

Pfaff, Richard W. (2009). *The Liturgy in Medieval England: A History.* Cambridge.

Pfander, H. (1934). "The Medieval Friars and Some Alphabetical Source Books for Sermons." *Medium Aevum* 3.1, 19–29.

Pfeiffer, R.H. (1949). *History of New Testament Times.* London.

Pierce, Johanne M. (1997). "The Evolution of the *Ordo Missae* in the Early Middle Ages." In *Medieval Liturgy: A Book of Essays.* Lizette Larson-Miller (ed.). New York, NY.

Prantl, Carl (1855–1870). *Geschichte der Logik im Abendlande*, 4 vols. Leipzig.

Quétif, Jacobus and Jacobus Échard (1719–1721). *Scriptores ordinis Praedicatorum*, 2 vols. Paris.

Randall, Lilian M.C. (1957). "*Exempla* as a Source of Gothic Marginal Illumination." *Art Bulletin* 39.1, 97–107.

Renedo, Xavier (1990–1991). "Una imatge de la memòria entre les *Moralitates* de Robert Holcot i el *Dotzè* de Francesc Eiximenis." *Annals de l'Institut d'Estudis Gironins* 31, 53–61.

Reese, J.M. (1965). "Plan and Structure in the Book of Wisdom." *Catholic Biblical Quarterly* 27, 391–399.

Rigg, A.G. (1992). *A History of Anglo-Latin Literature, 1066–1422.* Cambridge, 1992.

Rivers, Kimberly A. (1993). "Pictures, Preaching and Memory in Robert Holcot's Commenary on the Twelve Prophets." MSL thesis, University of Toronto.

Rivers, Kimberly A. (2002). "The Fear of Divine Vengeance: Mnemonic Images as a Guide to Conscience in the Late Middle Ages." In *Fear and its Representations in the Middle Ages and Renaissance.* Turnhout, 66–91.

Rivers, Kimberly A. (2010). *Preaching the Memory of Virtue and Vice: Memory, Images, and Preaching in the Late Middle Ages.* Turnhout.

Rorem, Paul (2009). *Hugh of St. Victor.* Oxford.

Rosemann, Philipp W. (2004). *Peter Lombard.* Oxford.

Rosemann, Philipp W. (2007). *The Story of a Great Medieval Book: Peter Lombard's Sentences.* Peterborough, Ont.

Rosemann, Philipp W. (ed.) (2010). *Mediaeval Commentaries on the Sentences of Peter Lombard: Volume II, Current Research.* Leiden.

Rosemann, Philipp W. (ed.) (2015). *Mediaeval Commentaries on the Sentences of Peter Lombard: Volume III, Current Research*. Leiden.
Rouse, Richard H. and Mary A. Rouse (1974). "Biblical *Distinctiones* in the 13th century." In *Archives d'histoire doctrinale et littéraire du moyen âge* 41, 27–37.
Rouse, Richard H. and Mary A. Rouse (1979). *Preachers, Florilegia, and Sermons: Studies on the* Manipulus florum *of Thomas of Ireland*. Toronto.
Rubin, Miri (1992). *Corpus Christi: Eucharist in Late Medieval Culture*. Cambridge.
Saxl, Fritz (1927). "Aller Tugenden und Laster Abbildung." In *Festschrift für Julius Schlosser zum 60 Geburtstage*. Arpad Weixlgärtner and Leo Planiscig (eds.). Zurich, 104–121.
Saxl, Fritz (1942). "A Spiritual Encylopaedia of the Later Middle Ages." *Journal of the Warburg and Courtauld Institutes* 5, 82–134.
Schabel, Christopher D. (2000). *Theology at Paris, 1316–1345: Peter Auriol and the Problem of Divine Foreknowledge and Future Contingents*. Aldershot.
Schabel, Christopher D. (ed.) (2006). *Theological Quodlibeta in the Middle Ages: The Thirteenth Century*. Leiden.
Schabel, Christopher D. (ed.) (2007). *Theological* Quodlibeta *in the Middle Ages: The Fourteenth Century*. Leiden.
Schabel, Christopher D. (2009). "The Commentary on the *Sentences* by Landulphus Caracciolus, OFM." *Bulletin de Philosophie Médiévale*, 145–219.
Shank, Michael H. (1988). *"Unless You Believe, You Shall Not Understand": Logic, University, and Society in Late Medieval Vienna*. Princeton, NJ.
Schepers, Heinrich (1970). "Holkot contra dicta Crathorn I. Quellenkritik und biographische Auswertung der Bakkalareatsschriften zweier Oxforder Dominikaner des XIV. Jahrhunderts." *Philosophisches Jahrbuch* 77, 320–354.
Schepers, Heinrich (1972). "Holkot contra dicta Crathorn II. Das 'significatum per propositionem.' Aufbau und Kritik einer nominalistischen Theorie über den Gegenstand des Wissens." *Philosophisches Jahrbuch* 79, 106–136.
Schneyer, Johannes Baptist (1969–1990). *Repertorium der lateinischen Sermones des Mittelalters, für die Zeit von 1150–1350*, 11 vols. (*BGPTM* 43.1–11). Münster.
Sharpe, Richard (2001). *A Handlist of Latin Writers of Great Britain and Ireland before 1540, with Additions and Corrections*. Belgium.
Sikes, J.G. (1934). "John de Pouilli and Peter de la Palu." *English Historical Review* 49, 219–240.
Skehan, Patrick W. (1945). "The Text and Structure of the Book of Wisdom." *Traditio* 3, 1–12.
Slotemaker, John T. (2012a). "Pierre d'Ailly and the Development of Late Medieval Trinitarian Theology: (With an Edition of *Quaestiones super primum Sententiarum*, qq. 4–8, 10)." PhD dissertation, Boston College.

Slotemaker, John T. (2012b). "The Development of Anselm's Trinitarian Theology: The Theological Origins of a Late Medieval Debate." In *Anselm of Canterbury and His Legacy*. Giles E.M. Gasper and Ian Logan (eds.). Toronto, 203–219.
Slotemaker, John T. (2014). "Robert Holcot the Homilist: A Sermon Index for Cambridge, Peterhouse 210." *Archa Verbi* 11, 73–123.
Slotemaker, John T. (2016). "*Mediaevalia*: Studies in Medieval and Reformation Theology." Available at https://slotemaker.wordpress.com/.
Slotemaker, John T. and Jeffrey C. Witt (2012). "Adam de Wodeham." *SEP*. Available at http://plato.stanford.edu/entries/wodeham/.
Slotemaker, John T. and Jeffrey C. Witt (in press). "*Tristis est anima mea*: The Suffering of Christ and Humanity in Robert Holcot's Sermon 76." *Archa Verbi*.
Smalley, Beryl (1946). "Two Biblical Commentaries of Simon of Hinton." *Recherches de théologie ancienne et médiévale* 13, 57–85.
Smalley, Beryl (1948). "Some more Exegetical Works of Simon of Hinton." *Recherches de théologie ancienne et médiévale* 15, 97–108.
Smalley, Beryl (1949). "Some Thirteenth-Century Commentaries on the Sapiential Books." *Dominican Studies* 2, 318–355.
Smalley, Beryl (1950). "Some Thirteenth-Century Commentaries on the Sapiential Books." *Dominican Studies* 3, 41–77, 236–274.
Smalley, Beryl (1950–1951). "Some Latin Commentaries on the Sapiential Books in the Late Thirteenth and Early Fourteenth Centuries." *Archives d'histoire doctrinale et littéraire du moyen âge* 25–26, 103–128.
Smalley, Beryl (1954). "Thomas Waleys." *Archivum Fratrum Praedicatorum* 24, 50–107.
Smalley, Beryl (1956). "Robert Holcot, OP." *Archivum Fratrum Praedicatorum* 26, 5–97.
Smalley, Beryl (1960). *English Friars and Antiquity in the Early Fourteenth Century*. Oxford.
Smalley, Beryl (1961). "Jean de Hesdin O. Hosp. S. Ioh." *Recherches de théologie ancienne et médiévale* 28, 283–330.
Smalley, Beryl (1978). *The Study of the Bible in the Middle Ages*. Notre Dame, IN.
Smalley, Beryl (1981). *Studies in Medieval Thought and Learning from Abelard to Wyclif*. London.
Spade, Paul Vincent (1992). "If *Obligationes* Were Counterfactuals." *Philosophical Topics* 20, 171–188.
Spade, Paul Vincent (2014). "Medieval Thories of *Obligationes*." *SEP*. Available at http://plato.stanford.edu/entries/obligationes/.
Spencer, H. Leith (1993). *English Preaching in the Late Middle Ages*. Oxford.
Spinks, Bryan D. (2006). *Early and Medieval Rituals and Theologies of Baptism: From the New Testament to the Council of Trent*. Aldershot.

Stegmüller, Friedrich (1950–1980). *Repertorium Biblicum Medii Aevi*, 11 vols. Madrid.
Sylla, Edith (1982). "The Oxford Calculators," in *CHLMP*. Norman Kretzmann, Anthony Kenny, and Jan Pinborg (eds.). Cambridge, 540–563.
Sypherd, Wilbur O. (1907). *Studies in Chaucer's "House of Fame."* London.
Szittya, Penn (1986). *The Antifraternal Tradition in Medieval Literature*. Princeton, NJ.
Szittya, Penn (1992). "The Apocalypse in Medieval English Literary Culture." In *The Apocalypse in the Middle Ages*. Richard Kenneth Emmerson and Bernard McGinn (eds.). Ithaca, NY, 374–397.
Tachau, Katherine (1987). "Wodeham, Crathorn, and Holcot: The Development of the *complexe significabile*." In *Logos and Pragma: Essays on the Philosophy of Language in Honor of Professor Gabriel Nuchelmans*. L.M. de Riijk and H.A.G. Braakhuis (eds.). Nijmegen, 161–187.
Tachau, Katherine (1988). *Vision and Certitude in the Age of Ockham: Optics, Epistemology, and the Foundations of Semantics (1250–1345)*. Leiden.
Tachau, Katherine (1991). "Looking Gravely at Dominican Puns: The 'Sermons' of Robert Holcot and Ralph Friseby." *Traditio* 46, 337–345.
Tachau, Katherine (1994). "Robert Holcot on Contingency and Divine Deception." In *Filosofia e teologia nel trecento: Studi in ricordo di Eugenio Randi*. Luca Bianchi (ed.). Louvain-la-neuve, 157–196.
Tachau, Katherine (1995). "Introduction" and "Appendices." In *Seeing the Future Clearly: Questions on Future Contingents*. P. Streveler, K. Tachau, W. Courtenay, H. Gelber (eds.). Toronto, 1–56 and 196–199.
Tachau, Katherine (1996). "Logic's God and the Natural Order in Late Medieval Oxford: The Teaching of Robert Holcot." *Annals of Science* 53, 235–267.
Thayer, Anne (1995). "Sermon Collections in Print, 1450–1520." *Medieval Sermon Studies Newsletter* 36, 50–63.
Thijssen, J.M.M.H. (1998). *Censure and Heresy at the University of Paris, 1200–1400*. Philadelphia, PA.
Thorndike, Lynn (1957). "A New Work by Robert Holcot (Corpus Christi College, Oxford, MS 138)." *Archives internationales d'histoire des sciences* 10, 227–235.
Tierney, Brian (1997). *The Idea of Natural Rights: Studies on Natural Rights, Natural Law, and Church Law 1150–1625*. Grand Rapids, MI.
Tranvik, Mark D. (1999). "Luther on Baptism." *Lutheran Quarterly* 13, 75–90.
Trapp, Damasus (1965). "Augustinian Theology of the 14th Century: Notes on Editions, Marginalia, Opinions and Booklore." *Augustiniana* 6, 146–274.
Trigg, Jonathan D. (1994). *Baptism in the Theology of Martin Luther*. Leiden.
Tugwell, Simon (ed.) (1982). *Early Dominicans, Selected Writings*. Mahwah, NJ.

Turner, Nancy L. (2002). "Robert Holcot on the Jews." In *Chaucer and the Jews: Sources, Contexts, Writings*. Sheila Delany (ed.). New York, NY, 133–144.
Työrinoja, Reijo (2001). "Faith and the Will to Believe. Thomas Aquinas and Robert Holkot on the Voluntary Nature of Religious Belief." *Documenti E Studi Sulla Tradizione Filosofica Medievale* 12, 467–492.
Vignaux, Paul (1948). *Nominalisme au XIVe siècle*. Paris.
Walsh, Katherine (1981). *A Fourteenth-Century Scholar and Primate: Richard FitzRalph in Oxford, Avignon and Armagh*. Oxford.
Ward, H.L.D. and J.A. Herbert (1883–1910). *Catalogue of Romances in the Department of Manuscripts in the British Museum*, 3 vols. London.
Wawrykow, Joseph P. (1997). *God's Grace and Human Action: 'Merit' in the Theology of Thomas Aquinas*. South Bend, IN.
Welter, J.-Th. (1927). *L'exemplum dans la littérature religieuse et didactique du Moyen Âge*. Paris-Toulouse.
Wenzel, Siegfried (1978). *Verses in Sermons: "Fasciculus Morum" and Its Middle English Poems*. Cambridge, MA.
Wenzel, Siegfried (1986). *Preachers, Poets, and the Early English Lyric*. Princeton, NJ.
Wenzel, Siegfried (1994). *Macaronic Sermons: Bilingualism and Preaching in Late-Medieval England*. Ann Arbor, MI.
Wenzel, Siegfried (1995a). "Academic Sermons at Oxford in the Early Fifteenth Century," *Speculum* 70, 302–329.
Wenzel, Siegfried (1995b). "The Classics in Late-Medieval Preaching." In *Medieval Antiquity*. Andries Welkenhuysen, Herman Braet, and Werner Verbeke (eds.). Leuven, 127–143.
Wenzel, Siegfried (1998). "The Dominican Presence in Middle English Literature." In *Christ Among the Medieval Dominicans*. Kent Emery Jr. and Joseph P. Wawrykow (eds.). Notre Dame, IN, 315–331.
Wenzel, Siegfried (2005a). *Latin Sermon Collections from Later Medieval England: Orthodox Preaching in the Age of Wyclif*. Cambridge.
Wenzel, Siegfried (2005b). "Preaching the Seven Deadly Sins." In *In the Garden of Evil: The Vices and Culture in the Middle Ages*. Richard Newhauser (ed.). Toronto, 145–169.
Wenzel, Siegfried (2005c). "The Arts of Preaching." In *The Cambridge History of Literary Criticism, Vol. 2: The Middle Ages*. Cambridge, 84–96.
Wenzel, Siegfried (2008). "A Dominican (?) Ars Praedicandi in Sermon Form." *Archivum Fratrum Praedicatorum* 78, 51–78.
Winston, David (1979). *The Wisdom of Solomon: A New Translation with Introduction and Commentary*. Garden City, NY.
Witt, Jeffrey C. (2015). "Petrus Plaoul: *Editio Critica Electronica Commentarii in Libros Sententiarum*." Available at http://petrusplaoul.org.

Wood, Susan K. (2009). *One Baptism: Ecumenical Dimensions of the Doctrine of Baptism*. Collegeville, MN.
Wright, Addison G. (1965). "The Structure of Wisdom 11–19." *Catholic Biblical Quarterly* 27, 28–34.
Wright, Addison G. (1967). "The Structure of the Book of Wisdom." *Biblica* 48.2, 165–184.
Wright, Craig (2000). "The Palm Sunday Procession in Medieval Chartres." In *The Divine Office in the Latin Middle Ages*. Margot E. Fassler and Rebecca A. Baltzer (eds.). Oxford, 344–371.
Yates, Frances A. (2001). *The Art of Memory*. London.
Young, Noël Denholm (1937). "Richard de Bury (1287–1345)." *Transactions of the Royal Historical Society* 4.20, 135–163.
Zink, Michael (1867). *Der Mytholog Fulgentius*. Würzburg.

INDEX

Abelard, Peter, 111, 143
Abraham, 17–19, 38, 172, 180, 236, 240
Acton, John, 3
Acts, book of, 17, 22, 219
Albert the Great, 137, 286n66
Alcyone, 137
Alexander IV, 141
Alexander of Hales, 5, 69, 141
Allan of Lille, 137
Allen, Judson Boyce, 234
Ambrose, 137, 235, 321n63
Amos, book of, 138, 142
Anselm of Canterbury, 68–71, 79–81, 96, 137, 183, 263, 271, 292n23–24, 314n22
Anselm of Havelberg, 18
Anselm of Laon, 143
Aquinas, Thomas, 5, 11, 13, 15, 25, 35, 69, 84, 106, 138, 161, 234, 285n33, 288n10, 290n56, 297n27
Aristotle, 25, 55, 71, 74, 76, 81, 88, 89–94, 98, 104, 137, 164, 168, 174, 179, 183, 196, 200, 205–208, 210, 295n23, 311n102
Arnold of Strelley, 5, 6, 65, 91, 94, 282n28, 285n39
Augustine, 18, 20–22, 25–26, 30, 37, 79, 81, 83, 120, 132, 136–138, 148, 175, 181, 196–197, 209, 235–236, 241, 254, 311n102, 314n15
Augustine of Dacia, 144
Augustine of Ireland, 137
Augustinian Order (OESA), 25, 133, 138
Aureoli, Peter, 142, 288n9, 303n8
Austin, John, 198–199
Averroes, 78

Bale, John, 129, 301n27
baptism, 22–24, 37–38, 43, 96, 101–110, 120, 123, 227, 265, 285n39, 296n5, 296n7, 297n30
Beaver, Lord John, 135

354 INDEX

Benedict of Nursia, 215
Benedictine Order, 69, 130, 215, 218
Bentworth, Richard, 3
Bernard of Clairvaux, 111, 146
Bernard Silvestris, 137
Biel, Gabriel, 34, 250, 297n17
Boehner, Philotheus, 65
Boethius, 89, 93, 137, 169
Boguslawski, Steven C., 285n33
Bologna, University of, 134
Bonaventure, 5, 10–11, 69, 106, 163, 297n12
Ps-Bonaventure, 163, 165–166, 170–171, 173–174, 283n51, 307n7, 307n19, 309n57–58
Boniface VIII, 115
Bradwardine, Thomas, 3, 12, 27, 311n102
Bromyard, John, 235
Bruno of Chartreux, 143
Burley, Walter, 3, 27, 137, 285n39, 286n52

Calyce, 137
Cambridge University, 1, 3–4, 12, 15, 130, 135, 221, 282n19
Carmelite Order, 133, 138, 218
Carruthers, Mary, 136, 153
Cassiodorus, 10, 137, 256
Chatton, Walter, 11, 84, 126, 250, 294n88
Chenu, Marie-Dominique, 13
Chisholm, Roderick, 51
Chitterne, William, 2, 6, 203, 262, 282n33
Christ, 5, 8–9, 18–21, 24–26, 28, 105, 112, 118–119, 121–122, 138, 149–150, 152, 185, 190, 209, 228–232, 234–236, 239–249, 252–257, 260, 265–266, 268–269, 271, 274, 276–279, 326n17
Cicero, 137, 196–197, 234, 236, 314n15

circumcision, 17, 23–24, 37–38, 105, 252, 285n33
Clarke, Ernest, 174, 176, 179, 182, 306n2, 308n35, 309n53, 309n58–60, 311n83, 311n86
classicizing friars, 12, 128, 130, 133–135, 234, 236
Claudius, 137
Cohen, Jeremy, 285n33
Colish, Marcia, 23, 106, 296n5
Colossians, epistle, 148, 246
Comestor, Peter, 137
confession, 4, 102, 111–117, 120, 123, 134, 216, 220, 265, 298n49
contrition, 111–113, 256–257
I Corinthians, epistle, 244
II Corinthians, epistle, 149
Courtenay, William, 3, 7, 33, 125, 127, 264, 267, 282n37, 287n75
covenant, 17–19, 26, 30–32, 37, 87, 106–107, 240, 286n59, 286n61
Crathorn, William, 2, 5, 65, 84, 216, 282n28, 294n88
Cyril of Alexandria, 141

Damascene, John, 137
Daniel, book of, 150
David, King, 23, 161, 249, 270
De Ghellinck, Joseph, 13
Dencourt, William, 135
Deuteronomy, 19, 35, 146
Dominican Order, 14, 115, 125, 130, 132–133, 138, 167, 215–218, 222–223, 228–229, 231–232, 281n1, 312n103
Dorothy of Montau, 317n90
Durand of St. Pourçain, 126

Eadmer of Canterbury, 138
Ecclesiastes, 128
Ecclesiasticus, 4, 128, 142, 301n18
Échard, Jacques, 128–129, 282n19, 301n24

INDEX 355

Edward III, 130
envy, 150, 194, 213
eucharist, 101–102, 110, 114, 118–123, 265, 300n95
Exodus, book of, 19, 96, 140
Ezekiel, book of, 113

faith, 14, 20, 25, 32, 38, 40–44, 47–63, 64–68, 70–74, 76–82, 86, 98–100, 104–105, 107–109, 118, 120, 122–123, 134, 150, 154, 163, 169, 184–185, 188, 206, 209–210, 227, 287n69, 289n39, 289n41, 313n120
family, 208–214
Farago-Bermon, Pascale, 264
Fasciculus morum, 157, 241, 321n64
fideism (fideist), 33, 64–65, 71, 119, 120, 313n123
Finnis, John, 197–200
FitzRalph, Richard, 3, 5–6, 97, 221–222, 282n28, 295n38, 320n22
Fletcher, Alan, 250
fomes peccati, 104–105
Fourth Lateran Council, 81, 102, 112, 216, 227–229, 232, 298n58
Franciscan Order, 115, 130, 133, 218, 227, 238
Frantzen, Allen, 111
Fredriksen, Paula, 21
Fulgentius the Mythographer, 137, 237, 245, 323n16
Fuller, Lon, 315n33

Galatians, epistle, 17, 20
Gaunilo, 70
Gelber, Hester Goodenough, 3, 7, 26–27, 64–65, 68, 75, 91–93, 98, 124, 267, 282n19, 287n79, 327n5, 328n14
Gellius, Aulus, 137
Genesis, book of, 17, 19, 37, 127, 150, 157, 159, 235–236, 244–245

Gentiles, 19, 20, 24, 72–73, 183–185, 236
Geoffrey Monmouth, 137
Gerald of Frachet, 137
Gerald of Wales, 137
Gesta Romanorum, 153, 234, 238, 324n32, 325n67
Gilbert of Tournai, 137
Giovanni Pico della Mirandola, 291n75
Glorieux, Palémon, 267
Goering, Joseph, 111–112, 298n49
Gosford, Roger, 139, 216
grace, 18–24, 26, 38, 40, 42–45, 48, 56–57, 60, 62, 72, 101–107, 109–110, 112–113, 118, 121, 123, 185–186, 191, 193–194, 240–241, 244–245, 285n33, 287n3
Grafton, John, 216
Grandisson, John, 115–116
Gratian, 110–112, 136
Gregory the Great, 137, 256
Gregory of Rimini, 126
Gregory of Thaumaturgus, 235
Grosseteste, Robert, 18, 227–228
guilt, 96, 102, 105, 113, 182, 191, 285n33

Haimo of Auxerre, 303n2
Halifax, Robert, 126
Harclay, Henry, 250, 285n42
Hart, H. L. A., 195
Hebrews, epistle, 40, 48
Hélinand of Froidmont, 137
Henry of Ghent, 201–202
heresy, 58, 61, 86, 98
Hermes Trismegistus, 71, 136, 137
Hilton, Walter, 25–26
Hoffmann, Fritz, 26–27, 65–66, 71–72, 78, 267, 282n32, 286n59, 292n24, 292n33

356 INDEX

Holy Spirit, 8, 21, 23, 37, 61, 75–76, 80–84, 101, 104, 175, 206, 210–211, 236, 247
Homer, 137
Hopeman, Thomas, 135
Horace, 137
Hugh of Lawton, 216
Hugh of St. Cher, 166
Hugh of St. Victor, 11, 18, 21, 137, 170, 297n12
Hugolino of Orvieto, 43, 50–54, 126, 289n41
Humbert of Romans, 216–217, 228–231, 319n5, 321n65
humility, 120, 148, 154, 161, 178, 183, 185, 190, 206, 240–241, 245, 248–249, 306n81, 325n65

Incandela, Joseph, 95, 98–100, 295n39
Isaac, 18, 236
Isaiah, book of, 248
Isho'dad of Merv, 141
Isidore of Seville, 18–20, 245

Jacob, 18, 172, 180, 249
James, epistle, 62, 114, 149–150
Jerome, 9, 137, 141, 149, 151, 170, 308n42, 321n63
Jews (Jewish People), 19–22, 24–26, 38, 97, 182, 240, 256
Joannis de Fordun, 308n29
Job, 20, 24–25, 38, 149, 254–255, 257
Job, book of, 20, 147, 149, 150, 254
Joel, book of, 142
I John, epistle, 247
John XXII, 115–116, 130, 285n39
John, Gospel of, 23, 37, 190, 245, 247–248
John of Marienwerder, 317n90
John of Pouilly, 115, 117, 299n70
John of Reading, 126
John of Ripa, 126
John of Rodington, 126

John of Varzy, 283n51
Jonah, 97, 257
Joseph, 172, 180
Josephus, 137–138
Joshua, book of, 248
Judges, book of, 148, 258
Juvenal, 137

Kaeppeli, Thomas, 127–128, 301n18, 301n24, 325n2, 325n3
Keele, Rondo, 7, 267
Kennedy, Leonard, 267
Kilvington, Richard, 3
king, 176, 206–207, 311n83
I Kings, book of, 138, 158, 159, 256
II Kings, book of, 164
Kirjavainen, Heikki, 267
knowledge, 50, 52–54, 60, 66–73, 82–87, 89, 90–96, 123, 168, 171, 178–180, 183–185, 188, 196, 206–207, 230, 244, 308n35, 311n102

Lactantius, 137
Lahey, Stephen, 119–120
Lang, Albert, 58
Langton, Stephen, 141
Lathbury, John, 135, 302n48
law, 18–26, 30–31, 34–38, 43–47, 72, 102, 110, 134, 175–176, 179, 185, 192, 194–209, 211–214, 227, 234–236, 239–241, 256, 285n33, 287n69, 312n102, 315n33
Lector, Theodorus, 137
Leff, Gordon, 30, 42, 287n69, 296n48, 312n102
Leviticus, book of, 19, 23
Logan, Ian, 70, 292n23
logic, 65–66, 74, 76–81, 90–93, 286n59, 286n65
Lombard, Peter, 5, 23–26, 33, 66, 105, 112, 114, 120, 138, 143, 222, 282n25, 290n71, 296n5, 297n12

INDEX 357

London, 1–3, 239, 278
Luke, Gospel of, 46, 147, 149, 155,
    191, 219, 244–248, 325n62
Luther, Martin, 108, 250,
    297n30, 297n31
Lyndwood, William, 221
II Maccabees, book of, 158–159

MacIntyre, Alasdair, 203
Macrobius, 137
Mair, John, 289n41, 290n71
malice, 85–86, 96, 104
Marbodius of Rennes, 137
Martial, 137
Martin of Braga, 137, 304n30
Martin, Conor, 3
Martin of Opava, 137
Matthew, Gospel of, 104, 138, 191,
    224, 228, 230, 247, 249, 253–254,
    269, 274
Maudith, John, 3
Maurus, Rabanus, 10, 137, 166
Maximus, Valerius, 11, 137
Meissner, Alois, 46, 65, 291n8
Meister Eckhart, 10, 168,
    283n51, 306n2
Melchizedek, 20
merit, 14, 16, 22–23, 40–48, 58–64, 73,
    98–99, 104, 107, 203, 260, 266,
    269–273, 277, 287n3
Meyronnes, Francis, 126
Michalski, Konstantyn, 65
Minnis, Alastair, 25
Molteni, Paolo, 267
Montpellier, University of, 134
Moses, 18–21, 23, 38, 72, 140, 235,
    240–241
Mulchahey, M. Michèle, 167, 224,
    229, 307n18, 321n52, 322n69

Nahum, book of, 145–146, 148, 160
Nequam, Alexander, 69, 137
Nicholas of Lee, 216

Nicholas of Lyra, 10, 142, 303n10
Noah, 17, 20, 157, 172, 180
nominalism, 33, 65, 67
Numbers, book of, 19, 132

Oberman, Heiko, 31–32, 34, 42–43,
    47, 65, 71–72, 312n102, 313n123
obligational art, 26–30, 37, 79
obligational theology, 18, 26–30,
    31–33, 38–39, 124
On the Formation of Preachers (by
    Humbert of Romans), 216–217,
    228–229
On the Method of Composing Sermons
    (by Thomas Waleys), 228, 230
Origen of Alexandria, 235–236
Ovid, 11, 137, 149
Owst, G. R., 13
Oxford University, 1–3, 5–7, 10, 12,
    15, 65, 83, 89–91, 126–127, 130,
    134–136, 139, 142–143, 216,
    222–223, 282n25, 295n38

pact, 18, 45, 106. *See also* covenant
paralogism, 76, 78
Paul, Apostle, 20, 72, 132, 143, 193,
    241, 273
Paul of Venice, 27
Pelikan, Jaroslav, 15–16, 283n61
penance, 43, 101–102, 111–114, 222,
    298n49. *See also* confession
Peter, Apostle, 17, 22, 253
Peter of Ravenna, 137
Petrarch, 13, 130, 134, 302n30
Philippians, epistle, 232
Philo of Alexandria, 9–10, 170
Philobiblon, 3, 13, 130–133
pictures (*picturae*), 144–145, 153, 156,
    305n58, 305n63
Plaoul, Peter, 288n18, 289n35,
    289n41, 290n55
Plato, 25, 71, 75, 97, 196, 235
Pliny, 11, 137

Plutarch, 137
power
  divine, 18, 32–39, 47, 72, 87, 95, 111, 118, 287n69
  ecclesiastical, 114–117
  human, 44–45, 48–54, 57–62, 64, 73, 85, 113
  political, 170, 174, 187, 192, 196, 206, 208
Prantl, Carl von, 64–65
prayer, 159, 177–178, 225–226, 248, 258, 311n86, 319n13
Proverbs, book of, 147–148, 155, 158
Psalms, book of, 142, 147, 183, 245, 257
Pseudo-Dionysius, 82, 83, 169

Quétif, Jacques, 128–129, 282n19, 301n24

reason, 14, 24, 33, 48, 53, 54–58, 65, 66–68, 70–74, 77, 79, 81–82, 84, 94, 97, 118–119, 123, 163, 181, 183–186, 188, 195, 199, 206, 211–212, 231, 235–236, 244, 256, 290n56, 312n102
Remigius of Auxerre, 141
Revelation, book of, 129, 248
Richard de Bury, 2–4, 10, 12–13, 15, 125, 130–131
Richard Fishacre, 5, 69
Ridevall, John, 134–135, 153, 235, 237, 302n48, 305n58, 323n29
Ringstead, Thomas, 135, 235, 302n48
Rivers, Kimberly, 10, 127, 145, 154, 156–157, 159–160, 304n30
Robert of Melun, 143
Romans, Ancient, 131, 212, 239
Romans, epistle, 20, 23, 32, 71–72, 143, 146, 183, 193, 204, 247
Rorem, Paul, 21
Rosetus, Roger, 6, 283n42
Rouse, Richard and Mary, 136

Rupert of Deutz, 18
Ruth, 20, 249

I Samuel, book of, 161
II Samuel, book of, 139
Sanctorale, 218–219
Saxl, Fritz, 153
Scale of Perfection (by Walter Hilton), 25–26
Schabel, Christopher, 91, 264, 295n38
Schepers, Heinrich, 7, 65, 126, 127, 282n37, 300n3, 328n14
Scotus, John Duns, 5, 11, 15, 83, 84, 106–107, 161
Second Council of Lyons, 133
Segrave, Walter, 3
Seneca, 11, 136–137, 146, 148, 150–152, 169, 236
sermons
  Peterhouse, ms. 210 (Holcot's sermon collection), 221, 250–253
  sermo finalis, 138, 223
  structure, 224–226
  thema, 220, 222, 224–226, 230–232, 321n47
  types of, 219–223
Servetus, Michael, 74
Simon of Hinton, 142
sin, 21, 23, 43, 58, 61, 86, 93, 96, 102, 104–105, 111, 113–114, 146, 193–194, 202, 226, 247, 254, 256, 258
Six Articles, 2, 5–6, 262–263, 265, 327n5, 328n14, 328n15
skepticism (skeptic), 12, 33, 64–66, 71, 74, 79, 81, 184–186, 195, 241, 291n8, 313n123
Smalley, Beryl, 3, 9–10, 12–13, 127, 128–130, 133–137, 141–143, 145, 152–154, 156–157, 165–166, 185, 237–238, 251, 275, 301n17, 301n24, 303n63, 305n69, 306n1, 311n102

Socrates, 25, 27–28, 75, 169, 201
Solon, 137
Song of Songs, 139–140
Spencer, Leith, 221, 320n18, 320n22
Spinks, Brian, 106
Stegmüller, Friedrich, 128–129, 301n18
Suetonius, 137
Szittya, Penn, 115–116

Tachau, Katherine, 7, 89, 261–262, 282n37, 325n3, 328n14
Temporale, 218–219, 251
Theodore of Mopsuestia, 141
Theodoret of Cyrus, 141
Thomas of Ireland, 136
Thomas of Strasbourg, 126
Tierney, Brian, 201
II Timothy, epistle, 132
Titus Livius, 137
Tobit, book of, 139
Trevet, Nicholas, 235, 324n29
Trinity, 7, 8, 14, 74–83
truth, 27, 30, 51, 53, 59, 61, 68, 73, 79, 86, 88, 90–93, 98, 134, 181, 235, 295n23

Varro, 137
Vignaux, Paul, 34, 47
Virgil, 137

Waleys, Thomas, 134–135, 137, 224, 230–231, 235–236, 302n48, 303n62, 320n42

Walsh, Katherine, 222
Welter, Jean-Thiébaut, 13, 136–137, 233, 237–238, 302n60
Wenzel, Siegfried, 144, 157, 220–221, 226, 228, 230, 241, 251, 320n39, 321n48–49, 321n56, 321n64, 321n66, 325n3
will, 48, 50–53, 58–59, 60, 64, 98, 113, 185
William of Alnwick, 126
William of Alton, 283n51
William of Auvergne, 285n42
William of Auxerre, 69, 106
William of Evange, 137
William of Lavicea, 238
William of Luxi, 142
William of Middleton, 141
William of Ockham, 5–6, 11, 15, 27, 33–38, 65, 74–78, 84, 91, 96–97, 161, 250, 288n30
William of Pagula, 228
William of Peraldus, 238
William of St. Thierry, 82–83
Winston, David, 177, 182, 308n25, 309n53, 309n58, 309n59
Wisdom, book of, 9, 85, 137, 148, 154, 162–188, 195, 206, 209, 308n40, 313n121, 313n123, 314n29
Wodeham, Adam, 6, 11, 109, 205, 288n18, 298n47
Wright, Thomas, 238

Yates, Francis, 136